The Fiction of
Walker Percy

John Edward Hardy

The Fiction of
Walker Percy

UNIVERSITY OF ILLINOIS PRESS
Urbana and Chicago

© 1987 by the Board of Trustees of the University of Illinois
Manufactured in the United States of America
C   5   4   3   2   1

This book is printed on acid-free paper.

Library of Congress Cataloging-in-Publication Data

Hardy, John Edward.
   The fiction of Walker Percy.

   Bibliography: p.
   Includes index.
   1. Percy, Walker, 1916–   —Criticism and
interpretation. I. Title.
PS3566.E6912Z7   1987   813'.54   86-19345
ISBN 0-252-01387-5 (alk. paper)

To my mother
Mary McCoy Hardy
and in memory of my father
Roger Barlow Hardy, 1890–1974

Contents

Acknowledgments

I am grateful to innumerable present and former colleagues, students and learned friends for talking to me about Percy
and related matters. Among these good people are: Lina Mainiero,
who first suggested that I write a book on Percy; Jay Levine, who
approved; Cleanth Brooks, who encouraged it from near the beginning; William Slavick, of the University of Southern Maine, and
W. Guyon Pendleton, of Randolph-Macon College, who invited me
to their campuses to read papers on Percy; Dean Frank Fennell of
Loyola University, and Louise and Howard Kerr, who made it possible for me to meet Percy; James Degnan, Michael Anania, James
Park Sloan, Leslie Sullivan, Eugene Wildman, Mary Thale, Samuel
Weiss, Christian Messenger, John Huntington and Virginia Wex-
man, Gloria and Harold Fromm, Clark Hulse, Martin Wine, Chad-
wick Hansen, Mary Carruthers, Lore Segal, LaVonne and Gene
Ruoff, Katherine and George Herbert Johnson, Paul Carroll, Preston
Browning, Moreen and Don Jordan, Bernard Kogan, Frederick
Stern, Burke Shipley, Roslyn and Michael Lieb, Gerald Sorensen,
Alan Friedman, Ned Lukacher, Ralph Mills, Bonnie and John Nims,
Hillis Miller, Arthur Morris, Kevin O'Donoghue, George Dunea,
Richard Giannone, William V. Davis, Robert and Mahin Maines
Mayer, Ellen and Robert Steinberg, John Mellon, Lawrence Poston,
Judith Gardiner, David Jolliffe, David Spurr, Catherine and Richard
Macksey, Patrick F. Quinn, Martin Steinmann, Merton Paddleford,
Peggy and Ted Farris, Charles Pastors, LaVerne Seranko, Douglas
Clark, my brother Donald McCoy Hardy and his wife Effie, Leroy

Shaw, Claude Jay Summers and Ted-Larry Pebworth, who offered a vast variety of ideas, opinions, arguments, on the fictive art in general, Percy and that art, Percy and religion, Percy and medicine, Percy and law, Percy and morality, Percy and language, Percy and politics, Percy and golf, Percy and fishing, Percy and Louisiana. I am especially indebted to Robert Brinkmeyer and Louis Rubin, who read the book in manuscript for the University of Illinois Press and suggested ways that I might improve it.

Longer ago than I like to believe it was, in 1978, the University of Illinois at Chicago kindly gave me a three-month sabbatical leave to begin work on a Percy book. The grant was a great help in getting me started on the project, and I trust I may still be forgiven for having so badly underestimated the time it would take me to complete it.

In keeping with the principles of my critical method in this book, I have resisted any temptation to try out my ideas on Percy himself. The one time I met him, in February, 1984, on the Loyola campus in Chicago, we spent a pleasant hour or so at lunch talking mostly of people and places we both had known back in Mississippi and Louisiana. It struck me he was rather relieved to discover I did not want to talk about his work. But I am grateful to him for his cheerful and prompt responses to my notes since then, about such practical matters as anticipated publication dates of his books.

It is quite impossible for me to express adequate thanks to my wife, Willene Schaefer Hardy, for the generous investment of love, patience, learning, and critical intelligence she has seen fit to make in this risky and arduous enterprise.

1

Introduction

My primary purpose in this book is to study the art of Walker Percy's fiction, an art which in many of its affective and formal properties has not been examined at length by other critics. I am concerned here with Percy's life and education, with his non-fictional writings, and with remarks attributed to him in various published interviews, only to the extent that reference to such matters may help to illuminate the fiction.

First, the hero in Percy's fiction is a man much given to brooding upon his personal and family history. It seems safe to assume that Percy himself has been from time to time so preoccupied, and the case is inevitably attractive to practitioners of biographical criticism. I shall not pursue that line of inquiry much beyond a few introductory observations on the generally accepted biographical facts as they suggest possible sources for characters, situations, and recurrent themes in the fiction.[1] Each of the principal chapters to follow is devoted all but exclusively to a single novel as work of art, essentially intelligible, if at all, without final regard to biographical sources and analogues. But a brief preliminary look at the evidence can be worthwhile simply to ensure our seeing at last how different the fiction is from the "real life" story, if not to explain or account for the one in terms of the other.

Born May 28, 1916, in Birmingham, Alabama, Walker Percy is descended of a long-established and rather prominent Southern family whose American genealogy is fairly clearly traceable back to the year 1776, when an Englishman named Charles Percy, with a

Spanish land grant and a cargo of slaves picked up in the Bahamas, settled in the Spanish territory south of Natchez, took an American wife, and started a plantation. The house was known as Northumberland Place.[2]

It appears that Charles had abandoned at least one other wife, in England. Perhaps there was another in the Bahamas. In any event, the Englishwoman later showed up in America, with a son she said Charles had fathered. The ensuing dispute, over property rights and the duties of rival affections, might have been partly responsible for Charles's deciding to kill himself.[3]

Following the ancestral example, Walker's father, LeRoy Pratt Percy, a Birmingham lawyer, committed suicide in 1929.[4] Some two years later, Walker's mother died in an automobile accident, and Walker and two younger brothers were adopted by their father's bachelor first cousin William Alexander Percy, of Greenville, Mississippi.[5] Also a lawyer, and owner of a plantation, William Alexander took himself most seriously as a poet, but is best remembered today for the prose work *Lanterns on the Levee: Confessions of a Planter's Son.*

After graduating from the public high school in Greenville, Walker took his B.S. at the University of North Carolina and, in 1941, his M.D. at Columbia. He had thought of a career in psychiatry. But, twice hospitalized with tuberculosis which he contracted while serving a residency in pathology at Bellevue hospital in New York, he abandoned the practice of medicine almost before he had begun it. Because of his illness, he did not enter military service during World War II.

Following his second bout with tuberculosis, Percy returned briefly to Greenville at about the same time many friends his age were coming home from war. With one of these, the aspiring writer Shelby Foote, he traveled in the Southwest and soon took up residence on a ranch near Santa Fe. Foote left after a few weeks, but Percy stayed on two or three months longer, rejoicing in the healthful air and the spectacular scenery, studying Indian customs, and continuing the extensive readings in modern philosophy and fiction which he had begun while he was hospitalized in New York and Connecticut.[6]

Back in Mississippi once more, he underwent what Robert Coles "think[s] it fair to say . . . [was] an especially intense religious crisis,"[7] and at about the same time seriously renewed his acquaintance with Mary Bernice ("Bunt") Townsend, whom he had first met some years before, either just before he entered medical school, or just after he received his M.D., when he was briefly employed at a Greenville clinic where she worked as a technician.[8] According to Coles, the couple were married on November 7, 1946, at a Baptist church in New Orleans,[9] but the next year both became Roman Catholics and have continued in that communion ever since. Their two daughters, Ann and Mary, are now married and have children of their own. The Percys live on a quiet riverfront property near the small town of Covington, Louisiana, just across Lake Pontchartrain from New Orleans.[10]

Like a number of real-life Percys for many generations, characters in Walker's fiction risk, attempt, and sometimes accomplish self-destruction by various means. They go into military combat as over-age volunteers, drink themselves into lunacy and disabling physical illness, slash their wrists and take overdoses of sleeping pills, put guns to their heads, fill the house with gas and blow it up. Charles Percy, the eighteenth-century ancestor, quietly drowned himself. Walker's father, the most likely model in this respect for the character of old "Lawyer Ed" Barrett in *The Last Gentleman* and *The Second Coming*, shot himself. Neither within nor outside the fiction have the self-killers the power to quit the stage of their descendants' imagination.

The burden of family consciousness weighed heavy upon William Alexander Percy even before he assumed the difficult role of bachelor foster father to the orphaned Walker and his brothers. William Alexander's own father, LeRoy Percy (1860–1929), had been widely known and much respected, if not universally loved, for his varied exploits as gentleman planter, sportsman, lawyer, patriot, and political activist.[11] In everything except marriage and the sporting life, Will worked dutifully and with some success at following the paternal example. In one respect, indeed, he might be said to have improved upon it, with his experience of authentic, front-line soldiering in World War I. But in all his striving there was a fatal strain of anxiety and misgiving, a morbid sense of personal inadequacy for the task of living up to his father's ideals.

He could bring himself neither to renounce nor wholeheartedly to pursue his literary ambitions. He taught for a time at Sewanee. He was editor of the Yale Series of Younger Poets. His *Sappho in Levkas*, the first of several volumes of verse, was published by Yale University Press in 1915. A *Collected Poems*, planned before his death, was brought out by Knopf in 1943, and Hodding Carter's Levee Press printed a little volume entitled *Of Silence and Stars* in 1953.

His talents were modest at best; it would not appear that anything he wrote served Walker directly as a literary model. But the environment of his household was, in general, certainly favorable for development of the foster son's native intellectual and artistic tendencies. And *Lanterns on the Levee*—in part social history and apologetics, in part autobiography, intensely personal at the same time that it is curiously stylized—clearly reveals an important life-source not only of many central thematic concerns in Walker's essays and novels, but of fictional events and characters as well.

For example, *Lanterns* is among other things the fascinating record of a son's failed rebellion against the father: a record that is often revealing in ways we may suspect are not a part of the author's fully conscious design. Various aspects of the father-son relationship are of considerable interest in all Walker's novels. In at least two—*The Last Gentleman* and its "sequel," *The Second Coming*—the pattern of the so-called "father search," with its characteristic alternating episodes of flight and return, clearly dominates much of the central action. In *Lancelot*, the hero is obsessed with shameful memories of his father as bribe-taker and probable cuckold.

When *Lanterns* was first published in the spring of 1941, less than a year before the author's death, many reviewers focused their attention—some deploringly, some more or less approvingly, some merely tolerantly—upon Will Percy's treatment of black-white relations in the South, particularly his defense of the sharecropping system which he and his father used in managing their Mississippi plantations. Both LeRoy and Will were well-known as effective local champions of black civil rights against the blatantly racist policies of KKK-influenced "populist" politicians in Mississippi such as J. K. Vardaman. As a patron of new literary talent, Will was especially interested in helping black writers. But neither of the aristocratic

Percys could pass muster as a true liberal even by pre–World War II standards.[12]

At the risk of oversimplification, we may characterize LeRoy's motives for defending the blacks as a matter of "enlightened self-interest"; he wanted to keep them happy, so that they would stay and provide cheap labor for the big Mississippi farms, instead of all running off to Chicago and Detroit. For high-minded William Alexander, the principle of *noblesse oblige* was more important. It was simply beneath the hereditary dignity of a Percy to be anything but magnanimously concerned for both the economic and the moral welfare of the Negroes. Will also indulged himself in vague romantic notions of the blacks as a mysteriously happy, god-favored race of incorrigible innocents, somehow charming even in their violence.[13]

In any event, the racial issues too, often in intimate connection with problems of family relationships, figure prominently in the psychological and moral experience of Percy's heroes. Lance Lamar's dealings with his wife and children, in *Lancelot*, involve reliance in various ways upon the services of a family of black retainers, the Buells. In *Love in the Ruins*, Dr. Thomas More is repeatedly involved in negotiations of great moral and emotional complexity with black neighbors, black colleagues, and black revolutionaries. In the bewilderment and disabling anguish of Will Barrett's memories (*The Last Gentleman* and *The Second Coming*) his father is revealed, not only as a suicide, but as a man who at least once tried to kill the son too, and further, despite his much-publicized championship of civil rights, as essentially a racist. Will Barrett himself, in *The Last Gentleman*, is briefly caught up in the grotesquely comic and morally dubious adventures of a white Yankee journalist who disguises himself as a Negro to investigate life in Mississippi, "behind the cotton curtain."

There can be little doubt that elements of both William Alexander and his father, as well as of Walker's father, LeRoy Pratt Percy, are combined in the characterization of "Lawyer Ed" Barrett. And something of Will Percy is discernible in Will Barrett too. In *The Moviegoer*, even a woman character, Binx Bolling's great-aunt Emily, who serves Binx as foster mother, has not only ideas but personality traits that strongly resemble Will Percy's.

Characters whose personalities and experiences to a greater or lesser extent resemble Walker Percy's own include the male protagonists in all the novels, and, in at least two of them, other men as well—Sutter Vaught of *The Last Gentleman* and "Percival" of *Lancelot*. Sutter the derelict physician and reluctant guru and Percival the priest/psychiatrist, with Will Barrett and Lance Lamar respectively, may be thought of as engaged in a kind of "dialogue of selves" which never quite yields a single, consistent authorial voice.[14]

In marriage and fatherhood, Percy seems to have been more successful than any of the heroes of his novels. Binx Bolling, of *The Moviegoer*, divides his time between two women, with no very passionate interest in either. In the epilogue, he is married to one of them; but, in part because of his wife's mental illness, the outlook for the union is unpromising. Will Barrett, in *The Last Gentleman*, pursues the same girl throughout, trying to convince her, and himself, that they are destined for each other. But the project is little if at all advanced at the end. In three later novels, the male protagonists are all middle-aged widowers. Only Thomas More of *Love in the Ruins*, after briefly testing himself in the rake's role as an escape from grief and remorse over the death of his first wife and their only child, appears in an epilogue chapter—dated five years following the main action—reasonably assured of continuing happiness in a second marriage. Lance Lamar, of *Lancelot*, is twice a widower. His first wife died of natural causes. He murdered the second. In various ways, he is estranged from all his children. At the end of the novel, he talks of marrying again. But, all things considered, the future looks highly doubtful. Will Barrett, recently widowed in his mid-forties at the beginning of *The Second Coming*, is still on speaking terms—but not really in communication—with his only child, a grown daughter. After much suffering and many misadventures, he falls in love with, and makes love and proposes marriage to, a woman who is literally "young enough to be his daughter." She agrees; and they seem, to say the least, emotionally and intellectually compatible. But, once again, many uncertainties cloud the final outlook.

Yet, if not in many particulars of character and situation readily identifiable with his personal experience, Percy's depictions of married life are always superbly convincing. Certainly it would be difficult to imagine as author of these books a man who had no firsthand experience of living with a wife and children.[15]

Percy is very much an intellectual novelist. His fiction is replete with literary and learned allusions. His characters, sometimes consciously on their own parts and sometimes not, often imitate the roles of other fictional and historical personages. They carry on passionate philosophical arguments—sometimes with one another, more often with themselves. Their actions are frequently patterned in accordance with what the reader may recognize as the dialectic of the *author's* dispute with himself; or, in accordance with a quasi-allegorical design, of Percy's satiric commentary on the modern world.

As a teenager, Walker probably got at least as much of his education at home—where he had the benefits not only of his Uncle Will's tutelage but of an extensive private library—as he got at the public high school in Greenville.[16] There is evidence, in *Lanterns on the Levee* and elsewhere, that William Alexander was fairly well acquainted with modern literature. But his dominant tastes in poetry and fiction remained decidedly old-fashioned. And for guidance in questions of the foundation of ethical judgments, the meaning of death, the limits of human intelligence, the decline of civilization, and other such weighty matters with which it appears Walker and his younger brothers were wont to trouble the poor man, he had recourse to an essentially faithless but curiously "traditional" doctrine built mainly out of elements of the Christian Gospels and the *Meditations* of Marcus Aurelius.

Such quaint philosophical equipment was obviously inadequate for a vigorous intellectual career in William Alexander's own generation, not to speak of the next. Inevitably, despite his continuing respect for his "uncle," Walker was beginning to explore distinctly different ways of thinking at least by the time he entered the university if not before.

In high school he had rather casually tried his hand at writing poetry and fiction. During his undergraduate years at the University of North Carolina, where he majored in chemistry and took courses in biology and physics, the only clear evidence of his continuing interest in literature and related arts was two essays he published in *Carolina Magazine* in 1934 and 1935: one a study in author psychology, on the identity of the detective-story writer known as S. S. Van Dine, and the other an analytic, lightly satiric commentary on movie magazines and their readers.

Despite the exhausting concurrent demands of his regular medical studies at Columbia, according to Robert Coles he underwent psychoanalysis for three years, five days each week, in the East Side office of Dr. Janet Rioche.[17] He received his M.D. in 1941, spent that summer working in a Greenville clinic, and returned to New York in September to begin a residency in pathology at Bellevue Hospital. Many of his "patients" were victims of tuberculosis; and, early in 1942, probably because he had failed to take the standard precautions against infection required in such work (wearing of mask and rubber gloves, etc.), Percy himself contracted the disease.

He was first hospitalized at a sanatarium in the Adirondacks near Lake Saranac. There, under the pressure of enforced idleness and isolation, as well as the anxieties inevitably attendant upon his life- and career-threatening illness, he began an intensive, self-directed course of readings in modern European fiction and philosophy which in the long run was probably more important for his development as artist and thinker than anything he had studied in school.

After two years at Saranac he was enough improved that he could try going back to the city, where he was appointed to an instructorship in pathology at Columbia. But he soon suffered a relapse, and again entered a sanatarium, this time in Connecticut. Another year, and he seemed once more recovered, except that somewhere along the way he had given up the idea of a career in medicine.

Some of his comments in later years suggest that he was, in fact, never very enthusiastic about pursuing any kind of medical *practice*. Perhaps he had, in the first place, entered medical school mainly to please his Uncle Will.[18] (Compare Binx Bolling's deference to Aunt Emily's wishes, in *The Moviegoer*.) There can be little doubt that Percy keenly enjoyed many of his courses at Columbia. It is quite possible to enjoy *studying* medicine, I should think, both as a science and as an art, without much wanting to practice it.

In any event, the effects of Percy's medical education are everywhere apparent in his fiction: in character and situation; in language (dictional habits, recurrent patterns of metaphor, a persistent impulse to "anatomize" the world, and to "diagnose" its troubles); in a certain bland self-assurance, a benignly authoritarian turn of mind, which is generally characteristic of the American medical profession and shared by the "implied authors"[19] of all these novels. At one time, as we have noted, he had thought of becoming a psychiatrist. Recollections of that ambition, and of his sessions with Dr. Rioche, one must assume, are involved in many different episodes of the fiction. Among the protagonists, Dr. Thomas More of *Love in the Ruins* is a psychiatrist; and Binx Bolling, in the epilogue of *The Moviegoer*, appears to be testing his aptitude for the trade.

But the true philosophical center of Percy's art—the central source of the great creative urge that finally overcame him in middle age, of the impulse to fictionalize as a way of truth-seeking—is not to be found anywhere within the area either of his medical training or of the purely scientific studies he so delighted in as an undergraduate. Over and over again, while asserting his great admiration for the scientific mind and scientific method, his appreciation of the many benefits that modern empirical science, in its practical applications, has brought to mankind, Percy has put the final emphasis upon questions which such science *cannot* answer.

Robert Coles quotes Percy's remarks (presumably in conversation) on his experience at Saranac: "I was in bed so much, alone so much, that I had nothing to do but read and think. I began to question everything I had once believed. . . . I had found [the scientific] method a rather impressive and beautiful thing. . . . But I gradually began to realize that as a scientist—a doctor, a pathologist—I knew so very much *about* man, but had little idea what man *is*."[20]

Coles goes on to comment on the obvious existentialist implications of the word "is" in this context, and to mention some of the authors Percy might have been reading at the time: Mann, Kafka, Tolstoi, Dostoevsky, and Kierkegaard. There are, for our purposes in studying the fiction, several matters of great interest here.

Existentialism is one of them. Along that line, if Percy started with Kierkegaard, he soon went on to others such as Heidegger, Jaspers, Marcel, Sartre.[21] But it seems clear that all the while, along with formal philosophical works, he was eagerly reading *novels*, with no necessary regard for doctrinal content. One must take into account the commonplace existentialist notion that fiction is, or can be, in and of itself as truly "philosophical" a form of literature as the essay can be.[22] Still, there are important differences between an essay and a novel or a short story. And even in the case of an author like Sartre who wrote both fiction and formal philosophy, it would appear that Percy was always capable of properly differentiating the two activities, capable of reading (and critically evaluating) a novel as a novel.[23]

A good many critics, in *their* enthusiasm for discovering and classifying doctrinal content, have sadly neglected the formal properties of Percy's fiction: his competence, and shortcomings, in a task that the would-be novelist can learn (to the extent that human aid of any kind will avail) only by reading other people's novels, not their essays. Percy, clearly, has read a great many novels. And that is a matter of *first* importance. In having done so, he has set the best possible example for any would-be critic of his novels. Before we start trying to interpret Percy's or anyone else's work as "existentialist fiction"—or Marxist fiction, or behaviorist fiction, or logical-positivist fiction (I suppose such a thing might be)—we had better see what can be made of it as fictivist fiction.

In sorting out the bio-bibliographical facts, then, with a view to reading the fiction as fiction, it is important to know that Percy read a lot of existentialist philosophy after he got sick and began to face the possibility that he must give up the profession for which he had been trained—more important, perhaps, than the fact that the profession in question was medicine. When the matter is fiction, philosophers take us nearer the heart of it than doctors of science and physic can take us. But fictionists—novelists and short-story writers, dramatists and poets—take us closer still.

In this perspective, those two essays Percy wrote as an undergraduate for the *Carolina Magazine* might begin to seem more importantly predictive of his ultimate vocation, not only than the chemistry and biology courses he was taking at the time, and the whole medical education that was to follow, but even than the still later readings in the existentialist philosophers. The essay on "S. S. Van Dine," with its theory that the invention of the pseudonymous author was for the real-life Willard Huntington Wright an act of psychological suicide, is clearly concerned with themes and artistic stratagems which are of central importance in all Percy's novels. And much the same can be said for the piece on movie magazines.

Percy is hardly the first modern novelist to appreciate the profound influence of the films on the development of all other forms of fiction in our time. But, beginning with the title of his first published novel, it is impossible to overlook the sheer persistence of his concern with the subject. And it is no casual measure of the relative competence of his critics to note which have detected some of the particular ways in which he is *different* from, if not necessarily superior to, other novelists who are preoccupied with the cinema.

But, among those who have strongly influenced Percy's *literary* imagination, there are a good many writers who are not in any obvious way associated either with the movies or with existentialism. More and less conscious echoes of Virgil, Dante, Chaucer, Malory, Marlowe, Shakespeare, Milton, Fielding, Keats, Tennyson, Hopkins —to name just a few—are at least as important as the studied allusions to Kierkegaard and Camus. And it could be plausibly argued that in any adequate account of Percy's aesthetic his experience of music and painting deserves almost as much attention as all his literary interests combined.

There have been many Catholics among the American Percys, one of them William Alexander Percy's mother, who was before her marriage Camille Bourges, of New Orleans. William Alexander himself, as a boy, was ardent in his mother's faith, but later rejected it.[24] Ellen Douglas, in an introductory essay on *The Last Gentleman*, says that one set of Walker Percy's great-grandparents were French Catholics, and that "Catholicism has been toyed with or embraced by various members of the family."[25] For Walker it is clearly a matter of embracing rather than toying with.[26] Ellen Douglas paraphrases William Alexander to describe the dominant faith of the Percys as "the Stoicism of Marcus Aurelius with a leavening of Episcopal frivolity and a ballast of Presbyterian Calvinism."[27] If such mishmash as this is hardly anything that a man of Walker's intense intellectuality could make do with for long, neither is it anything to inspire rebellion. The motives of the quest for religious conviction are seldom if ever easy to define. In Walker Percy's case, the complex family history of religious practice and non-practice offers at best only obscure precedent for his own affirmation of faith.

It is reasonable to assume that his attraction to Catholicism— with its strong, formidably systematized and comprehensive body of theological teachings, at once insistently rational and dedicated to the defense of mystery, at once grounded in extra-personal truth and insistent upon the supreme sovereignty of self—was influenced at least as much by the reading he had been doing, and by anxieties attendant upon the two great decisions he was faced with at that time, about career and marriage, as by any impulse he might have had to pick and choose among the offerings of family heritage.

Percy's Catholicism, regardless of how he came to it, is enormously important in his art. But neither marriage and the declaration of faith nor his decision not to return to active medical practice launched him immediately upon a successful career as novelist. According to both Luschei and Coles,[28] he had enough money, presumably from inheritances, to support himself and his wife in reasonable comfort without regular employment. Luschei says that Percy was working on fiction "through most of the early 1950's,"[29] and that he wrote two unsuccessful novels (neither of them ever published) before achieving a "breakthrough" with *The Moviegoer*. In any case, it was first with a number of philosophical essays, not with fiction, that he began to build his reputation as a writer.

His essay "Symbol as Need," an admiring but finally dissatisfied response to Suzanne Langer's *Feeling and Form* which goes back to her earlier book *Philosophy in a New Key* to examine the epistemological foundations of Langer's aesthetic doctrine, appeared in the journal *Thought* in 1954.[30] The brief essay credits Langer with an especially convincing statement of the "general thesis that the peculiarly human response is that of symbolic transformation," and with making clear, "for once and for all" it might be hoped, "the generic difference between sign and symbol." But Percy goes on then, in the context of references to St. Thomas Aquinas, Jacques Maritain, and others, to express his regret that Langer has not been willing, or able, to accept the full implications of "the thorough wrecking job [she has] done on behaviorist theories of meaning." Langer's insights, he suggests, properly lead to a theory of "symbolic transformation . . . [as] a means of *knowing*, . . . not in the sense of possessing facts but in the Thomist and existential sense of identification of the knower with the object known."

"Symbol as Need," the first thing Percy had published since his undergraduate days at North Carolina, was followed over the next few years by numerous articles in literary and philosophical journals. Of the pieces collected in *The Message in the Bottle*[31] (1975), ten (including the title essay) had appeared in periodicals between 1954 and 1961, the year *The Moviegoer* was published. Some of the collected essays—such as "Metaphor as Mistake," "The Man on the Train," and "Notes for a Novel About the End of the World" —deal more or less directly and centrally with poetry and fiction. But Percy's dominant, continuing concern as essayist is with the kind of problems raised in "Symbol as Need." The genially provocative, unwieldy "subtitle" of the volume *The Message in the Bottle* reads as follows: *How Queer Man Is, How Queer Language Is, and What One Has to Do with the Other.*

Percy is an impressively learned student of language and language theory, an *amateur*, in the root and best sense of the word, who is able to maintain an intellectual attitude that is in some respects more disinterested than the attitudes of professional specialists in any of the fields concerned. Still, even in his most abstrusely and soberly philosophical essays, inquiry is subordinate to persuasion. The mode of his polemic discourse is often satiric, seldom if ever hortatory. But an essential purpose not primarily to investigate observable phenomena but to demonstrate a conviction, not merely to inform but to enlighten his readers, is always apparent.

Fundamental to all the rest is Percy's idea of man as *homo loquens*, or *homo symbolificus*. Although Percy's scientific training will not permit him to deny the remote *possibility* that evidence will one day be found to invalidate his position, he is so far convinced, from "Symbol as Need" in 1954 to *Lost in the Cosmos* in 1983,[32] that the power of language is uniquely human. Employing a terminology borrowed from Charles Sanders Peirce,[33] Percy holds that the transactions of human language—i.e., the uses of symbols—are essentially "triadic" events, not reducible to components which fit the "dyadic" model of stimulus-response behavior. The refusal of many influential thinkers, including a number of language specialists as well as physicists, biologists, and assorted social-engineering types, to accept the fact of man's uniqueness as "the creature who talks," their persistence in trying to account for human behavior on the dyadic model, is in Percy's view a source of much mischief and silliness in the modern world. Such thinking, if not directly causative, is at the least symptomatic of our ultimate perversity, the impulse to destroy all life on earth.

A long footnote in *Lost in the Cosmos* presents a valuable summary of the development of Percy's thinking about semiotics and the creaturely status of man (pp. 85–87). Here, man is referred to as being "preeminently the sign-using creature." Percy goes on to explain that whereas "in earlier writings" he had used Peirce's (and Suzanne Langer's) terminology in distinguishing between *sign* and *symbol*—e.g., the word *ball* as you use it when calling to your dog to fetch the object in question and the same word as you use it when speaking to a human friend, who might respond "Ball? What about it"—more recently he has found it less confusing to refer to the former as a *signal* and (following Ferdinand de Saussure) to the latter as a *sign*, "and to avoid *symbol* as much as possible." But between *The Message in the Bottle* and *Lost in the Cosmos* little of substance has changed in Percy's views on man and his language, man and his spiritual *predicament* to which language is the essential key. From the implicit contextual metaphor of seafaring in the title of the earlier volume to that of spacefaring in the later there is, by Percy's standards, no giant leap to be made. The only matter of fundamental importance is the faring. It is man's fate to be always and ceaselessly traveling, and by necessity of, and perhaps as the principal object of, such traveling, to be always seeking others with whom he can talk: hold converse, exchange and share information and ideas, stories of adventure. Sometimes it is hard to distinguish the talking, the telling and the listening, from the adventure itself. As throughout the long heroic tradition that begins with Homer's treatment of Odysseus, so in Percy's fiction and in his philosophical writings *homo viator* and *homo loquens* coalesce.[34]

Lost in the Cosmos: The Last Self-Help Book is a curiously, deliberately amorphous not-so-little work (262 pages) which mingles chatty, gossipy satire, take-offs on TV "talk shows" and the writings of various populist intellectuals, with sober disquisition and prophecy, in a manner that is if anything more familiar from Percy's novels than from the earlier volume of essays. The subtitle cues us to an elaborate spoofing, complete with numbing statistics and exhaustively irrelevant questionnaires, of the kind of guides to self-help, in everything from dieting and investing to sex, parenting, and dying, which make up so large a part of currently popular non-fiction. But the parody masks a serious and finally straightforward concern with the definition of self, and self-knowledge, which is essentially inseparable from the concern with language.

In a footnote to an essay entitled "Toward a Triadic Theory of Meaning"—first published in 1972, and reprinted as chapter 8 of *The Message in the Bottle*—Percy remarks that in any "utterance of a . . . sentence . . . there is not only an utterer and a coupling of sentence elements, but also a listener or receiver of the sentence." He then goes on to quote the following passage from a still earlier essay, "The Symbolic Structure of Interpersonal Process" (1961):

> The second person is required as an element not merely in the genetic event of learning language but as the *indispensable and enduring condition of all symbolic behavior.* The very act of symbolic formulation, whether it be language, logic, art, or even thinking, is of its very nature a formulation for a *someone else.* Even Robinson Crusoe, writing in his journal after twenty years on the island, is nevertheless performing a through-and-through social and intersubjective act[35] (emphasis Percy's).

Percy's intention is, most immediately, to explain certain refinements and elaborations of his thinking over the years. But my own point here is, again, that nothing essential has changed from one stage to another, up to and including *Lost in the Cosmos.* To say that an act of symbolic formulation—the fundamental act of language—is a triadic event is essentially the same thing as to say that it is an intersubjective act. It is only in such acts that we are, not "a higher organism, standing in direct continuity with rocks, soil, fungi, protozoa, and [other?] mammals," but a unique being, "in Heidegger's words, that being in the world whose calling it is to find a name for Being. . . ."[36] According to Percy in *Lost in the Cosmos* (e.g., p. 91ff. and p. 168ff.), chimpanzees, dolphins, humpback whales, pigeons, and parrots—despite all the time, effort, and money spent by scientists and government agencies in the evident hope of proving otherwise—simply cannot speak. The animal "communications" observed in certain well-known experiments—involving as they do merely "using signs and responses in order to obtain rewards . . . [without] the basic elements of language [such as]

15

symbols, sentences, productivity, [and] cultural transmissions"—
Percy sees as "dyadic events" which "bear little if any resemblance
to human language." [37] Only humans can talk. It is only through
language, properly understood in *its* triadic nature, that they can
possibly hope to understand, and to help, *themselves*. And that,
again and inevitably, means that they must in the process help, or
fail to help, other selves.

Thus the study of semiotics—"A Semiotic Primer of the Self"
is Percy's title for what he calls an "intermezzo" section of *Lost in
the Cosmos*—leads in the end to mystery, precisely the *Christian*
mystery, irreducible paradox, of mankind's self-sovereignty which is
somehow identical with its radical dependence. Percy sets up in *Lost
in the Cosmos* a kind of satiric shooting-gallery. Prominent among
the revolving targets are Phil Donahue, a troop of Skinnerians, various bemused primatologists and zoo-semioticists, and Carl Sagan.
In an age in which, while the technical media are every day more
and more astoundingly improved, it daily becomes more and more
difficult for thoughtful people to communicate with one another, no
wonder we yearn as never before to converse with the birds and
beasts—or, failing that, are eager to sign on with Sagan in the hope
of talking to ETs. But the voyage described in the two-part final
section, "A Space Odyssey"—which, as Percy explains in a none
too kindly footnote (p. 201), "owes a good deal to Carl Sagan's
splendid picture book, *Cosmos*"—brings us back to earth with a
vengeance.

Having failed in an initial attempt to find a home on another
planet, the original travelers and their space-born progeny land according to plan on the Utah desert (p. 240), "eighteen years after
launch in starship time, 457 years in earth time." [38] They are greeted
by an odd little company of rescuers—a young blond astronomer
named Aristarchus Jones, originally from California, and three Bene-
dictine monks, of whom two are Negroes and the third, their abbot,
is a converted Jew—and taken to a shabby but comfortable cinder-
block monastery, where they can rest, get their earthlegs back, and
decide what to do next. The monks and Jones, besides "a dozen or
so . . . genetically malformed and misbegotten" children who also
live at the monastery, are descendants of the few people who survived a nuclear holocaust late in the twenty-first century. No one

knows for sure, but it may be that the entire earth's population can now be numbered in the thousands, and that most of those are threatened with sterility.

The star-trekkers' plausible choices for the future are finally reduced to two. Either they are to go with Aristarchus Jones, who is a kind of latter-day Saganite, and try to colonize Europa, one of the satellites of Jupiter which is known to be potentially habitable, or they can follow Abbot Liebowitz, an ex-physicist who knows a thing or two about residual radiation levels and the like as well as about race and religion, to a probably still habitable valley in the Smoky Mountains.

All remains more or less hypothetical. We are never told which plan is actually chosen. But it is plain which of the two scenarios, so to speak, Walker Percy considers more probable, even if he does not necessarily in all senses "prefer" it. World population statistics and technological considerations aside, the situation envisaged for the aging star-trek captain and his family and friends in Lost Cove, Tennessee, some five hundred years hence, is essentially not much different from the human situation at any time and place since A.D. 33.

Lost Cove people of the twenty-fifth century are still brutish in their appetites, selfish, ignorant (especially of themselves), suspicious, clannish, parochial, racist. Still, they are capable of love and of faith. Still, they are able at least to imagine a world superior to their own, and to remain alert for news from such a world. Perhaps they have somewhat the advantage of us, at least in being less inclined to imagine that they have already found the better world. Above all, their language has not changed, is still what it always was, the clearest sign at once of their fallen nature and of their hope for redemption through Christ the incarnate Word.

I shall not attempt here an evaluation of either the originality or the theoretical adequacy of Percy's thinking about language. It seems to me that a number of well-known experts, especially those of behaviorist and structuralist persuasions, if they have read his essays with any care, must have been forced at least to re-examine if not to revise their central tenets. On the other hand, a number of critics even among those who are initially sympathetic with Percy's position have pointed out shortcomings and inconsistencies in his writings on such crucial subjects as the relationship between language acts and the physiological structure of the human brain.[39] And he is at times so preoccupied with the distinction between human language and animal communication that he tends to neglect the creaturely attributes man and beast do have in common: i.e., like the most benighted of behaviorists, to ignore the essential distinction between organism and mechanism, and to talk of a dog or a pigeon as if it were wholly and simply the latter.[40] But I am primarily concerned with Percy's novels, in which the aims of argument are necessarily subordinate to those of dramatic excitement and probability, and he manages for the most part to transcend the flawed rigor of the theoretical and polemic writings.[41] The novels and the essays have a good many thematic interests in common, notably including language. The fiction not only *is* language; frequently, it is fiction *about* language. But Percy seldom if ever gives the impression of having created the fiction to serve his theoretical purposes. In the fictional context, the real-life complexities of communication—whether of human beings with each other, or of human beings with other animals—are never oversimplified. And the kind of uncertainties and ambiguities, the hedgings, which may damage the essays, blunting their polemic purpose, are often a warrant of authenticity in the fiction.

Not that the implied authors in the fiction do not at all resemble the polemicist. They do, frequently. But the point is that one does not have to be persuaded, on any theoretical point, in order to feel all necessary sympathy with such authors, yield to their fascination with what the *characters* are doing, saying, and feeling, regardless also of whether one finds the latter altogether persuasive, or even likable.

I am not, for example, singularly fond of Binx Bolling. And the fact that the author appears to think rather well of him does not persuade me to alter my sympathies. I do like Tom More, on the other hand, and it does not in the least disturb me that the author here, who seems to share my fondness for the hero, is not conspicuously different from the one who also takes to Binx.

In an interview with Jo Gulledge, Percy spoke of the "intermezzo" section of *Lost in the Cosmos*, on the semiotics of the self, as the crowning achievement of his writing career. "I have never," he said, "and will never do anything as important. If I am remembered for

anything a hundred years from now, it will probably be for that."[42]
I cannot agree.

I imagine Percy would have had difficulty in finding a publisher
even for an essay collection like *The Message in the Bottle*, not to
speak of *Lost in the Cosmos*, if he had not established a reputation
as a novelist. Nor is it simply a matter of the novels' having secured
him a *larger* audience for the non-fiction. His greater talent is for
fiction. The most promising parts of *Lost in the Cosmos* are the
quasi-fictional sections, culminating in the account of the space voyage and its aftermath. Not even the account of life in Lost Cove,
Tennessee, complete with a character named Jason McBee who is
surely a remote descendant of a "covite" family mentioned in *The
Second Coming*,[43] achieves anything like the richness of Percy's
whole fictions. But that episode was, as I hoped at the time it might
be, a sign that his next project would be another novel—this one
(*The Thanatos Syndrome*) about the further adventures of Tom
More.

It is chiefly as novelist that Percy will be remembered, not as language theorist and pundit-observer of contemporary culture, nor yet
certainly as theorist of fiction. He has offered a number of shrewd,
random observations about the making and the reading of fiction
and its place in contemporary intellectual life. (A fair sampling of
such observations, nothing startlingly new, is offered in an essay
published in 1986, "The Diagnostic Novel: On the Uses of Modern
Fiction.")[44] But his comments do not form a coherent system for
critical interpretation and evaluation of any works of fiction, his
own notably included.

Especially in a number of interviews which he has been, perhaps,
all too willing to grant, he has had difficulty in recalling even the
basic narrative facts of his novels. Such laxity would be less dis-
tressing, perhaps, if it were not accompanied by a tendency to
dogmatize in the enunciation of critical principles, and a certain
impatience with readers whom he sees as misinterpreting specific
passages of the novels—the very passages, as often as not, which he
has trouble in recalling with much precision.

Among his favorite critical dicta is the notion that "nothing is
worse than a novel which seeks to edify the reader."[45] No doubt
there is something to this. All great art, including the art of novels,

probably *is* edifying in its final effect on the competent reader—or viewer, or listener. But I would agree that, at least in our age, it is unwise for the artist to *seek*—or, at any rate, to let it show that he is seeking—to edify. I would only insist, further, that it is not enough for the novelist merely to avoid any effect, whether that effect be edification or titillation or a vain display of learning. It is, shrewdly, as Catholic novelist that Percy is most anxious to avoid the look of edifier. Actually, he does want to persuade his reader that the Catholic view of the human predicament, and of human history, is the only view that makes whole and consistent sense of our experience.[46] But he has common sense enough to know that fictional hagiography will not serve the purpose. So far so good, as a matter of practical strategy. But Percy is so busy with trying to elevate strategem to the status of philosophical principle, with his appeals to Kierkegaard on the difference between genius and apostle and what not—again, so busy with trying *not* to look like an edifier —that he tends at times to neglect his positive responsibilities, as novelist if not as Catholic thinker, in such basically important matters as narrative probability. In spite of Percy's best efforts, Binx Bolling has far too much the look of candidate saint for my taste; and the fact that the chronology of his life story is at some points hopelessly confused makes him no more attractive.[47]

Most of the time, the strength and order of Percy's art exceeds his intention, at least to the extent that he has been able to state the principles of that intention. But now and again it is the art that falls short.

The hero of *Love in the Ruins*, Dr. More, repeatedly asserts that he really cannot see much difference between the liberal and con- servative factions among his neighbors and colleagues, that he has no great liking for either, and that he suffers the physical and psy- chological complaints characteristic of both. Nonetheless, on the climactic occasion of a debate before the medical faculty and stu- dents, he is aware of being favored by the conservatives. Questions of personal health aside, the case is somewhat the same with Percy and his readers and reviewers.

Percy has solid liberal credentials on the issues of black-white rela- tions. "I don't march in picket lines," he said to Carlton Cremeens in 1968, "but I am completely convinced of the rightness of the

Negro struggle for civil rights."[48] That conviction is not essentially compromised in anything he has said or written since, including not only the satiric treatment of civil-rights activists in the novels, but admissions that he gets along well enough with individual "klan-type," lower-class whites in everyday personal encounters.[49] One may seriously question the validity of his insights into social history when he talks of the "rise of the black middle class" in Mississippi during the seventies and early eighties, but not the passionate sincerity of his belief that blacks have an inalienable *right*, not only to "the ordinary means of life . . . what everybody else has," but to being in "as much trouble as affluent whites" of our age are in.[50]

But while it is true that super-patriots, Nixonites, Birchers, rich optimist clergymen, rich creationist clergymen, racial purists, latter-day Babbitts, and assorted other fools and knaves of reactionary persuasion are frequently made sport of in Percy's fiction, the satire at their expense is overshadowed by that directed at the scientistic salvationists of the left, myth-mongers, sexual liberationists, activists in population control, "qualitarians," all manner of false "humanists" whose common purpose is to deny the unique creaturely status of human beings. Since the groups who provide Percy's favorite targets of satire are likely also to include most *readers* of any kind of serious fiction—most readers of serious non-fiction, for that matter—it is not difficult to understand the critical antagonism his work has provoked.

Even if one discounts the protests of some of the more naive reviewers in the feminist and gay-activist press who are wont to confuse the identities of author and character in fiction, supposing that even Lance Lamar in his wildest ravings, not to speak of Will Barrett and Tom More in their troubled musings, must be voicing the settled convictions of Walker Percy on the morality and psychology of sex, still it is clear that the total "world" of Percy's fiction is one that offers little comfort to anybody who is at all sympathetic with the intellectual, ethical, and political concerns of feminists and avowed homosexuals. Percy's rather testy reaction to Jo Gulledge's questions about the treatment of women and homosexuals in *Lost in the Cosmos* was surely disingenuous. There is, to be sure, "such a thing, after all, as a promiscuous homosexual"[51] in real life. And it is true, as Percy pointed out to Gulledge, that his book also treats promiscuous heterosexuals with scant courtesy. But the trouble is that promiscuous ones are the only kind of homosexuals mentioned in *Lost in the Cosmos*, while heterosexual males may be, if not consistently chaste, at least selectively lascivious. It is also hard to credit the innocence of Percy's "what do women want?" in response to Gulledge's reference to feminist criticism of the one man/three women setup in the crew of the spaceship. In 1976, Percy admitted in an interview with Marcus Smith that "it may be" he is a male chauvinist, or at any rate that he "do[esn't] know anything about women."[52] But ignorance is no excuse, of course, for any novelist of ideas who hopes to have his views of the modern world taken seriously, and merely to confess the fault is not to correct it. The presentation of Allison Huger, in *The Second Coming*, is the best evidence that Percy has at least tried to improve his understanding of women. Still, in his conversation with Jan Nordby Gretlund in 1981 he fell back again on the old plea of ignorance, and only made matters worse with a comparison of himself to Hemingway, and the suggestion that male novelists in general have a hard time creating women characters.[53]

In talking about his work, Percy has given only limited assent to critics' classification of him as a Southern novelist. And it is probably true, and rather more fortunately than unfortunately so, that he does, as he said to John Carr,[54] deliberately "stay away from the Southern novel in several ways." Those are, however, only the more patently *imitative* ways. He does not write, and does not try to write, Faulkner's kind of Southern novel, or Eudora Welty's kind, or even Flannery O'Connor's kind, although there are important dimensions of awareness of these and other Southern writers in his creative outlook. But the new kind of novel he writes is, and all the more startlingly so for its freshness, still very Southern. The Southernness is more than the "Southern scenery," the "backdrop" Percy admitted to "mak[ing] use of."

Clearly, as he went on to say to Carr, if he "were in Colorado or New York, [he'd] be writing something different." And he is undoubtedly right in suggesting that the difference has a good deal to do with religion and Negroes. But there is also the deep fascination with language, the stuff and substance of story itself as well as subject of philosophical discourse. The concern with language escapes, of course, any narrowly regional definition, either dialectal or attitudinal, just as Percy's concern with all other aspects of human behavior—with everything from dress, manners, architecture, and modes of transportation to the forms of medical, legal, and political practice—escapes such definition. Yet, if Percy's preoccupation with language obviously amounts to a great deal more than having "a good ear" for Southern idiom and accent, even a great deal more than anything identifiable as a peculiarly Southern love of rhetoric and storytelling[55]—if, in fact, it is that preoccupation more than anything else that keeps him in touch with the larger intellectual community of Europe and America—at the same time, all the rest is somehow grounded in the regional awareness. Not even his Catholicism is more important than his Southernism in defining the kind of novelist Percy is. As Robert Brinkmeyer has shown in his book *Three Catholic Writers of the Modern South*,[56] the Catholicism in Percy's fiction cannot be adequately understood except with reference to the Southernism.

Very much like Dr. Sutter Vaught in *The Last Gentleman*, Walker Percy tries hard but with little success to convince himself and others that he is not a guru. The cultist fervor has diminished somewhat in recent years, perhaps, even as the size of both his popular and his critical audience has steadily increased.[57] But a good many readers, including some who publish their interpretations, continue primarily to react, either with enthusiasm or with suspicion and hostility, not to the artist but to the prophet/teacher.

I am, to say the very least, uncomfortable with Percy in the latter role. But the impulse to undertake this study of his art was in considerable part expressive of the need I felt to resolve the tensions of my long-sustained, as often offended and resentful as gratefully sympathetic, fascination with Percy's vision of man and his fate. There is, in the end, no separating the art and the vision, although it is the critic's crucial business first to distinguish between them, before attempting to discover precisely how they are related.

I am, of course, greatly indebted to many other critics for insights and definitions as well as simply for information about Percy and his writings. Wherever possible, I have tried to identify and acknowledge specific influences on my thinking. A number of the published interviews with Percy are even more interesting to me for his interpretations of his own work that run counter to my views than for the positive guidance they provide.

William Allen's *Walker Percy: A Southern Wayfarer* (see Bibliography) is a special case in the chronology of my readings in the critical literature. Copyediting of the first version of my book, with only six chapters, was well under way at the University of Illinois Press when I learned from Percy in June, 1986, that a manuscript of *The Thanatos Syndrome* was in the hands of his publishers. After much discussion, while copyediting of my first manuscript continued to completion, my editors and I decided that publication of my book should be delayed until I could add a chapter on the new novel; and, having reached agreement with Percy and his publishers that I might have access to a copy of the uncorrected bound proofs of *The Thanatos Syndrome* as soon as possible, I sat down to wait. Meanwhile, however, Allen's study appeared, and I was faced with the further question of how I should acknowledge his insights in the final version of the parts of my book that pertain to Percy's earlier novels.

In general, I find Allen's work on the *intellectual* biography, notably the parts concerning Percy's indebtedness to American writers, especially original and convincing. I am also inclined, with exceptions in some particulars, to agree with Allen's assessment of the importance of the "father/son theme" in Percy's fiction.[58] Beyond these remarks, I have decided not to attempt inserting references to Allen in the main text of the first six chapters of my book, but to make essential acknowledgments in the notes. The decision does not affect the design of my seventh chapter, since Allen's book, perforce, does not include a study of *The Thanatos Syndrome*.

Indeed, since through the courtesy of Percy and his publishers I was granted the peculiar opportunity to write my chapter on *The Thanatos Syndrome* well before the date of the novel's release for review, absolutely no critical commentary on the novel was in print by the time I had to submit my final chapter and its notes to the copyeditor in February, 1987. Whether that will in the long run put me at advantage or disadvantage I shall not venture to predict.

My acquaintance with Percy's work began about 1972 with a reading of *The Last Gentleman*, after which I went "back" to *The Moviegoer* and then to the other novels in the chronological order of their publication. First and last, for purposes both of lecturing and of writing on his fiction, I have had recourse to the texts of the novels themselves, trying so far as possible to rid my mind of all presuppositions and of all concern with what I might find to agree or disagree about with other critics of his work, including Percy himself. It is no doubt fortunate that such a program, except in rare cases like that of my "preview" of *The Thanatos Syndrome*, is difficult to follow very rigorously. For methodic rigor is the ultimate undoing of all good sense in literary studies. Still, my greatest hope for this book is simply that the patient readers of it, once they are done here, will go back to the fiction with renewed curiosity and free and open mind.

2

The Moviegoer

I. Exile in Gentilly

John Bickerson Bolling—"Binx," as he is familiarly called, or sometimes "Jack"—is surely an original. Just as surely, in order to appreciate his originality, we must recognize his affinities with a number of alienated anti-heroes in earlier modern fiction. European influences, chiefly the obvious model of Meursault in Camus's *The Stranger*, have been much discussed. But it is highly unlikely that Percy could have created Binx without giving some thought to American literature.

A diffidently witty, well-mannered university graduate and man of good family, modestly bearing the concealed scars of war, decently skeptical and yet obsessively tempted to faith and the search for a ritual order in the ruins of history, living in self-imposed, elaborately contrived obscurity as a branch manager for his uncle's brokerage firm while he waits to discover his true vocation, Binx has at least as much in common with a number of American first-person narrator/protagonists as he has with the poor, intellectually deprived, rather dispirited Meursault. Fitzgerald's buttoned-down bond salesman, Nick Carraway, and Hemingway's Christ-haunted but always gentlemanly Jake Barnes could well have served as models for Binx in some aspects of his character and situation. Among celebrated Southern cousins in disaffection, Faulkner's Quentin Compson and Robert Penn Warren's Jack Burden come readily to mind.[1]

Like Warren as well as Camus, Percy does not have to remove his hero to foreign parts in order to enforce the sense of alienation. The famous Southern "sense of place,"[2] which Bolling like all Percy's heroes has in full measure, works in reverse to make Binx feel most poignantly estranged when he is right at home. His taking up residence in what Percy has called the "desert" of Gentilly—a lower-middle-class section of New Orleans where Binx occupies, on the street named Elysian Fields, a basement apartment in the modest home of a fireman's widow, Mrs. Schexnaydre[3]—is, on the protagonist's own part, a kind of deliberately farcical "dramatization" of his state of mind. The ever so tentative physical retreat, underground but not out of touch with the world of workaday reality, enables him simply and literally to live with the otherwise intolerably tentative state of mind, to get a workable aesthetic perspective on it, until he can transcend it with an act of faith.

It is notable that the opening paragraph of Binx's narrative fails to indicate the time and place of the action. The names of two days of the week are mentioned, but there is no reference to a month, a season, or a year. The speaker is nameless, and so is the aunt who sent him the note. The reference to "her stepdaughter Kate" is no help; a name less readily identifiable with any particular place or period is hard to imagine. Probably most readers would agree off-hand that the speaker's idiom is modern American. But there is nothing even distinctively Southern about it, let alone anything characteristic of New Orleans.

Our first impression, then, is of a man so intensely preoccupied with his personal situation that he is all but totally indifferent to his environment. The "action" recorded in the first paragraph is entirely cerebral; we do not even know whether the narrator is indoors or outdoors as he starts to think about the note. Like the references to days of the week, those to family relationships—"a note from my aunt . . . her stepdaughter Kate"—serve with their very casualness ironically to reinforce the sense of the speaker's alienation. And his use of the present tense, instead of the more common fictive past, as the time-base of his narrative—a narrative that is addressed to no one in particular, no one clearly conceived as listener or reader— operates to the same effect of keeping us, and him and his story, all somehow peculiarly suspended in time and space. The "now" of the narrative is not, of course, now, and never could be; the "present" is timeless, neither now nor then, here nor there.

In the second paragraph, we are told of the death of his older brother Scott when Binx was eight years old, and of his Aunt Emily's taking him for a walk on the street back of the hospital to break the sad news to him and to exhort him to "act like a soldier." In striking contrast to the opening account of his present situation, the reminiscence is presented in vivid sensory detail. And, on the evidence of the aunt's idiom and bearing, of Binx's reference to the "Negro shacks" across the street and to their "watching" occupants, whose presence the white woman acknowledges with an absent smile while she pursues her solemn conversation with the boy, the experienced reader will recognize the setting as a *Southern* city—presumably the same one in which Binx is still living as an adult. In the next paragraph, when Binx recalls an episode of the more recent past, again in vivid physical detail, a reference to Lake Pontchartrain finally tells us that the city is New Orleans. But if our initial impression of Binx's mental detachment from his environment is quickly altered, still it is important to observe that his acute sensitivity to his surroundings is first exercised in the context of *memory*.

Binx was later obliged to become all too literally the soldier his aunt wanted him to play as a child, but in a version of the role that was hardly what she could have had in mind. The story of the fighting man who returns from the wars as a stranger to his people is as old as war itself. But the war literature of America and western Europe in the twentieth century is almost exclusively preoccupied with the theme of the soldier's alienation. The undeclared wars in Asia are notorious for having produced generations of American veterans who were radically and often permanently estranged, not only from the parent society as a whole, but in many instances from each other. The Korean War never so severely threatened the United States itself with another civil war as did the public uproar over our later involvement in Vietnam; but the two conflicts, both entered upon with no clear definition of our national purpose, no chance of victory, and in dubious alliance with factions of populations with whom our soldiers had no cultural affinity, were essentially alike in their psychic effects upon the American participants. It is enough, then, simply to be informed that Binx fought in Korea for us to understand immediately a good many aspects of his inner conflict, of the estrangement he feels from great-aunt Emily's world and the structure of values implicit in her use of the word "soldier."

Besides his war experience, Binx's personal history reveals a number of other probable causes for his difficulty in deciding where he "belongs." First, he is the product of a doubtful marriage. Binx's Roman Catholic and distinctly folksy if charming mother, nee Anna Castagna, was the aristocratic, nominally Protestant Dr. Bolling's employee, his office nurse, before she became his wife. While Binx was still a child, his older brother Scott died—furnishing occasion even then, as we have seen, for his Aunt Emily to start taking control of Binx's destiny. Then, in the crucial years of his adolescence, his father too departed, romantically enlisting as a flight surgeon in the World War II Canadian air force and dying in action off the coast of Crete. Finally, when his widowed mother returned to her job in the hospital in Biloxi where she had worked before her marriage, Binx was more or less "adopted" by Emily. Sent away to prep school at his aunt's expense, he then came back to live in her house during his college years at Tulane.

As if all this were not enough, Aunt Emily too, while plainly if discreetly deploring Binx's father's choice of a wife, has herself "married beneath her." Jules Cutrer, Binx's stepuncle-father-surrogate, despite his wealth and personal charm and Emily's best efforts to romanticize him as a modern-day "Cato," remains serenely and unapologetically what Binx has tagged him (p. 49), the "canny Cajun straight from Bayou Lafourche." And Aunt Emily, despite her eternal youthfulness, is as we have noted Binx's *great*-aunt, sister to his grandfather, not to his father. The distinctions among the generations, as well as the ethnic strains and social classes, are hopelessly blurred.

But if the causes of Binx's alienation are fairly easy to define, his behavior during the Gentilly years follows no familiar pattern of nonconformity. It was not always so. He lived in the Quarter for two years (p. 6), until he "got tired of Birmingham businessmen smirking around Bourbon Street and the homosexuals and patio connoisseurs on Royal Street." Shortly after returning from the war, he took off with two fellow veterans on a hiking and hoboing trip up the Appalachian Trail, intending at first to go all the way from

Tennessee to Maine—picking up girls along the way, drinking and talking around the campfires, "spiel[ing] about women and poetry and Eastern religion . . . sleeping in shelters or under the stars in the cool evergreens . . ." (p. 41). But the charm of such vagabondage was exhausted for him even more quickly than was the enchantment of the Vieux Carré. In Gentilly, it appears, he neither talks nor drinks very much. Unless one is to count television and movies, he is addicted to nothing. Zen is no longer his bag, if it ever was. He chases girls, but with thoroughly "normal" intent. There is no hint of deviate sexual interests, nor of subversive political activity. He has never, so it would seem, had the slightest inclination to join either a motorcycle gang or the Trappist order. He is not a practicing artist of any description. He has committed no crimes, either bizarre or commonplace.

No doubt we are meant to see it as evidence of the extreme depth of his alienation that, while he has abandoned the values of both his paternal and his maternal heritage, he is unable to articulate any alternative faith which would require him to form alliances, or commit him to any definite program of action either alone or in company. None of his relatives has a lifestyle that suits him. He is in some measure out of place both at Emily's house in the Garden District and at the fishing camp on Bayou des Allemands where his mother, now Mrs. Smith, is at last thoroughly in her element with her earthy second husband and their numerous offspring. His uptown-successful-young-businessman cousin Eddie Lovell, and wife Nell, give him the willies with their earnestly modish enthusiasms —for Mardi Gras organizations, and Khalil Gibran, and spurious "restorations" of old shotgun cottages in rundown neighborhoods. And he is no more comfortable with his friends of the beard-and-bicycle set who occasionally stop off to see him in Gentilly on their way to the Quarter for music and whores (p. 42). Once upon a time, it seems, the way of the globe-trotting journalist and third-rate intellectual novelist Sam Yerger had strongly appealed to him. Sam's stories had aroused in him "an appreciation so keen and pleasurable that it bordered on the irritable" (p. 180). But that time, clearly, is long past. Now, it is hardly less difficult to imagine his wanting to emulate Sam than it is to conceive of his sharing the grotesquely comical, back-country Southern fanaticisms of his Uncle Oscar (p.

177). Within narrow limits, Binx has a sustained sympathy of mind with his teenage half-brother, Lonnie Smith, whose keen intelligence and comic wit are not wholly obscured either by his deep piety or by the wrenching pathos of his situation as an incurable paraplegic. Occasionally, and very briefly, a responsive chord is struck in Binx's conversations with Emily. His early-morning colloquy with his mother on the porch overlooking the water at Bayou des Allemands (p. 149ff.), where she muses upon her memories of her first husband, touches for a moment long-buried springs of yearning in the fatherless Binx. But with neither of the older women is his rapport consistent and dependable. He has not turned his back on either of his families; he is still, in the everyday sense of the phrase, communicating with them. But it might often seem that he has kept in touch mainly for lack of any strong commitment to ideas and people, causes, a way of life, beyond the circle of their interests.

Life *chez* Schexnaydre is tolerable precisely because it requires next to no effort, either intellectual or emotional. Binx has entered the brokerage business because, through Uncle Jules, it is readily available as a way of making a living, and because, having nothing directly to do with the production, handling, or consumption of real goods, nor with the basic rights or needs of man or beast, it is a morally neutral occupation. His effort to convince the reader, or himself, of his admiration for the neo-technic architecture of the new schoolhouse in Gentilly (p. 10) is as obviously tongue-in-cheek as his solemn avowal of the joy he takes in credit cards and deodorants and questionnaires (pp. 6, 7, 14). He approaches the exercise of making love to his Marcia or Linda, two in a succession of pretty secretaries he has pursued beyond business hours, with all the moral seriousness of a child petting a puppy. (His attempt to convince himself that his passion for Sharon goes deeper is the surest sign that the Gentilly retreat cannot continue.) He has his particular tastes, of course, his mild prejudices, his affinities both innate and cultivated for certain people and places and spectacles; in his pains as well as his pleasures, in art and manners, in the play of voice and gesture wherever people meet, he is acutely discriminating, quick to distinguish the spurious from the genuine, and quick to assert, at least to himself if not to others, his preference for the latter. At least in others, neither false reasoning nor false pretense of motive is likely long to deceive him. And yet he is the most tolerant man imaginable, ready to see almost anyone's "point of view" on virtually any subject: to understand, and not simply to forgive, but to *sympathize*. He is tolerant—if ever the phrase was applicable, "tolerant to a fault"—of everything because he is convinced of nothing. To understand is one thing; to believe, or believe *in*, is quite another. And not infrequently, as in Binx's case, the capacity for one negates the other.

II. Binx and the Movies

Binx's moviegoing is a complex passion.[4] The influence of film techniques is pervasive in this novel as it is in all Percy's fiction. Witness, for example, the sudden scene-shifts and the action "sequences," the rapid alteration of visual perspectives, with the camera eye of Binx's imagination frequently creating optical effects beyond the power of normal vision, as when he looks at Canal Street (pp. 17–18) under a sky filling with thunderheads and sees the people of the noonday crowd suddenly diminished, ". . . tiny and archaic, dwarfed by the great sky and the windy clouds like pedestrians in old prints." (The blending of the cinematic effect with that of the allusion to the technique of the "old prints" typifies Percy's aesthetic subtlety and sophistication, his awareness that the art of one historical era can and often does anticipate effects that the unknowledgeable might suppose to belong exclusively to a later age and a different medium.) But it is important to note that Binx has very little to say about the art of filmmaking.

There is no trace of the jargon of "serious" film criticism in his observations. He has no highbrow enthusiasm for arty foreign films, no purist preference for classics of the silent era. The films and actors he talks about are the standard popular favorites of his time. When he speaks of going to the "movies," that is just what he means, with respect both to the mood of his attendance and to the kind of thing he is seeing.

Beyond its value to him simply as pastime, Binx's moviegoing is an essential ritual in what may be called the cult of the ordinary he has taken up in the Gentilly years. It is of a piece with his collection of credit and identification cards, his pursuit of Marcia and Linda

and Sharon, his dutiful responses to questionnaires, his quiet efficiency in business matters. But, normality of taste and disavowal
of intellectual pretensions notwithstanding, no *ordinary* full-grown
man goes to the movies four or five times a week.

An ordinary fan might occasionally go to a remote suburban
theater to see a film in which he has some special interest. For Binx
(p. 10) such excursions are routine. Most Americans approximately
of Binx's generation will recognize something of themselves, no
doubt, in his observation that his recollections of certain scenes in
movies are keener, more to be cherished, than his memories of dramatic occurrences in his own life (p. 7). And the phrases "so I have
read" and "as they say in books" clearly suggest that he is skeptical
of the authenticity of those "memorable moments" which "other
people" are said to treasure. The examples he gives of such experiences—"climbing the Parthenon at sunrise," meeting "a lonely girl
in Central Park"—look very much like those "intimate revelations
of young men" which Nick Carraway described in *The Great Gatsby*
(p. 1), typically "plagiaristic and marred by obvious suppressions." If
they could but recognize it, or admit it, Binx suggests, the "personal"
experiences that other people cherish are no more truly personal
than the movie scenes which he remembers. For most people, the
memorable events of "real life" are actually derivative, modeled on
popular fiction or, indeed, on the movies. Most of us, no doubt,
will feel a pang of melancholy recognition when we read of that
process of "certification," as Binx calls it (p. 63), whereby a person's
neighborhood becomes for the first time real to him only when he
sees it in a movie. But except for those in some way professionally
connected with the film industry, it seems unlikely that many people
share Binx's inability to do or observe much of anything without
thinking either of something he has already seen in a movie or of
how the real-life situation might be adapted to the screen.

It is not "for the usual reasons" (p. 17) that Binx is attracted to
movie stars. When he sees William Holden in the French Quarter,
he has "no desire to speak to [him] or get his autograph." It is,
rather, "an aura of heightened reality" (p. 16) that he feels in the
actor's presence which so excites his imagination. And while it may
be true that "all who fall within it" in some way sense that emana-
tion, one must assume that neither the Northern college boy nor any

of the others along the street who observe the wonder of Holden's passage would describe their experiences as anything much like Binx's.

In every way, Binx is far too self-consciously ironic, too subtly analytical in his concern both with his own responses and with the general significance of the films as cultural institution, to qualify as an ordinary movie fan. Ultimately, of course, what distinguishes Binx among his fellow citizens—not only of Gentilly, but of that whole community of unwitting despair,[5] the whole community of the modern world as underworld, world of the dead, which is epitomized in the street called Elysian Fields—is his dedication to "the search." And, besides other benefits, the moviegoing provides what might be called a kind of "sensibility training" which prepares him for the ultimate search.

Binx's search has many dimensions, of course, rather obviously including that of the inevitable "father search." But in so far as it may be regarded as a version of the so-called "quest for identity" so familiar in modern literature, the plot of the movie Binx first describes (p. 4)—about an amnesiac, who "found himself a stranger in a strange city . . . [where] he had to make a fresh start, find a new place to live, a new job, a new girl"—furnishes a clear, if subtly ironic, analogy to Binx's own situation. Moviegoing is not *identical* with the search, as Binx carefully explains (p. 13): "The movies are onto the search, but they screw it up. The search always ends in despair. They like to show a fellow coming to himself in a strange place—but what does he do? He takes up with the local librarian, sets about proving to the local children what a nice fellow he is, and settles down with a vengeance. In two weeks time he is so sunk in everydayness that he might just as well be dead." But simply their being "onto it" in the first place, no matter how tentatively and clumsily, justifies Binx's appreciation of the movies as an aid to understanding of the search. And, finally, the fact that moviegoing is involved in many of Binx's exercises in Kierkegaardian "rotation" and "repetition"—terms whose source Percy unquestionably expects his reader to recognize, although Binx's first direct reference to "the great Danish philosopher" appears in the epilogue (p. 237)—clearly indicates the importance of the movies in the hero's preparations for the quest.

III. The Search, and Binx as Unreliable Narrator

Following the passage I have quoted, on the movies and the search (p. 13), a hypothetical reader intervenes to put a question to Binx: "What do you seek—God? you ask with a smile." Binx is characteristically whimsical and evasive in his response. He hesitates to answer directly, "since all other Americans have settled the matter for themselves and to give such an answer would amount to setting myself a goal which everyone else has reached. . . . For, as everyone knows, the polls report that 98% of Americans believe in God and the remaining 2% are atheists and agnostics—which leaves not a single percentage point for a seeker."

"Truthfully," he asserts, "it is the fear of exposing my own ignorance which constrains me from mentioning the object of my search." He ends the colloquy with a question of his own (p. 14): "Have 98% of Americans already found what I seek or are they so sunk in everydayness that not even the possibility of a search has occurred to them? Upon my honor, I do not know the answer."

But the rhetoric of the final question is clearly tendentious. All the protestations of honor and candor and the disarming avowals of honest ignorance notwithstanding, we can be fairly sure that Binx does consider his own case extremely rare: so rare, precisely, that it is not statistically measurable. Not only is he not one of the 98% of Americans who profess belief in God, but neither is he classifiable with the small minority of committed atheists and agnostics. He is, simply, a seeker. And, if this should seem at first glance merely to take us back where we started—to the question "what do you seek?"—the frustration is purposeful.

Binx speaks of his reluctance to "mention" the object of his search. But the implication is clear, in the context of the reference to the polls, that what he cannot do is *define* that object. It might be, in a sense, what the *hypocrite lecteur* has suggested—God. But, if so, it is probably not the same God with whom the pollsters are concerned. For such a God, Binx seems to suggest—a God about whom it is possible to make up one's mind after the definite fashion of the believers, deniers, and unknowers whose opinions the pollsters can record, a God the definition of whose essential nature all respondents are assumed to be agreed upon—obviously cannot be the goal of a *search*. One does not "search" for God as one does for a mislaid earring or credit card, or even for a suitable birthday gift or the causes of earthquakes. The effect of Binx's "response" to the inquiring reader is to ask the questioner to *join* him in the search— with the understanding that if one has to know in advance even approximately what he is looking for, there is no point in beginning.

Perhaps it would be best, putting the word "God" out of mind for the moment, to go back to Binx's first mention of the search (pp. 10–11) to see whether some important clue has not been over-looked. Is it not, perhaps, significant that Binx recalls having first felt the "immense curiosity" that distinguishes this quest from all others, the overwhelming sense of being "onto something," while he watched the dung beetle that scratched about under the leaves, six inches from his nose, as he lay gravely wounded in the Korean forest? Is there not some fundamental question about the nature of *man* implicit here: the question, say, of how or whether the man is essentially different from the beetle he watches, or, for that matter, different from the bit of filth for which the insect is searching?

In any event, all this is so excitingly problematical that it is easy to understand how some readers might feel a bit let down by the rather conventional affirmation of faith, in the epilogue scene at the hospital, with which Binx concludes his narrative. The thematic connection is clear. It is entirely fitting that the story which began with Binx's recollection of his first, temporary deliverance from dunghood, on the floor of the Korean forest, should end with his specific avowal of faith in the Resurrection. But such clarity of thematic design, in so complex an art form as the novel, is not always either emotionally or intellectually satisfying.

What I find it almost impossible to understand is anyone's reading *The Moviegoer* the way John Carr says he read it the first time, without anticipating Binx's reconversion at the end, or anyone's taking it so "lightheartedly" as Martin Luschei says he took it, that it came as a "shock" to him to recognize Binx's deadly seriousness in the passage describing his despair following the Ash Wednesday interview with Aunt Emily.[6] It seems to me the book offers few real surprises, with regard to Binx's career, or his love affairs, or his spiritual journey. It is apparent from the very first paragraph that the two topics of the "serious talk" he anticipates having with his aunt—Kate's troubles and his future—will probably turn out to be one topic. Only a few pages further on, "the search" is mentioned for the first time, in a tone that is, for all the surface brightness and levity, the lightly ironic self-mockery, unmistakably earnest at bottom. In our age, Percy could hardly expect a hero who did *not* wear some such mask to be taken seriously on such a topic. By the time we have seen him at Bayou des Allemands discussing the niceties of Christian conscience with Lonnie Smith (p. 162ff.), if not considerably earlier, we have good cause to suspect that Binx is not, after all, merely the "nominal Catholic" he has pretended to be.

And yet, again, to say that the outcome of the novel is "not surprising," that it is somehow inevitable, is not necessarily to say that it is convincing. To say that one is, or ought to be, able all along to take Binx *seriously* is not necessarily to say that he is altogether persuasive.

Among Percy's more or less "normal" heroes—all, that is, except Lance Lamar—I find Binx Bolling the least attractive. He is amusing enough much of the time, at the expense of the follies and false pieties of our age. The producers of the "This I Believe" program, and the guileless contributors, are easy pickings, to be sure. So are people like Eddie and Nell Lovell. But at its mordant best, as in the half-waking dream about sexologists Dr. and Mrs. Bob Dean (pp. 188–89) which precedes his effort to make love to Kate on the train, Binx's satiric "wit" is a good deal more than amusing, something uniquely hair-raising at the same time that it is irrepressibly funny.

The delicate balance of humors—of affectionate caricature and the embarrassed memory of admiration in his account of Sam Yerger, of caricature and something beyond affection, something touching awe, in the portrait of Lonnie Smith—is profound comedy. In still another mode, his play-acting with Emily, as Falstaff to her Hal, recalling as it does the plays-within-the-play put on by the Shakespearean originals with elaborate role-reversals, is as engaging as it is extravagantly witty.

But he is a snob,[7] too, and something of a moral impostor. There is more than a bit of the effete aristocratic in the ennui of his Gentilly sojourn, his daily play-acting in the role of "ordinary fellow," which is all the worse for the fact that he is by birthright only half an aristocrat. It is surely an occasion for applause that on their way back to New Orleans from Bayou des Allemands—where Binx had meant to take honest workinggirl Sharon to bed, but was frustrated by the unexpected presence of the Smiths at the camp—the saucy wench gives him a genial but firm come-uppance (p. 166), telling him she has "got his number" now, and that he is not to "mess" with her.

Aside from the untimely loss of a father and two brothers, as the fortunes of this world go Binx is not intolerably deprived. He is, after all, *not* Jake Barnes; his war wound has in no way permanently disabled him. He got his appointment as brokerage branch manager, in a firm controlled by Jules Cutrer, simply for the asking, and can give it up any time he likes on the same terms. His inheritance, the "defunct duck club" (p. 6), notwithstanding the all too obvious wordplay, has not left him entirely defenseless against fate. Twenty-five thousand dollars, Mr. Sartalamaccia's final cash offer for the property (p. 236), is not quite the patrimony a physician's only surviving son might have hoped for. But, then, it is a sight better than nothing. And besides, there is the prospect of his having a go at doctoring on his own—thanks lastly to Aunt Emily. Perhaps entering the profession is not what he would have chosen without Emily's prompting—the fact that she can get him into medical school, at the age of thirty and with a mediocre undergraduate record to boot (p. 51), firmly attests both her wealth and her social prestige—but we do know (pp. 94, 196) that he has his own real respect for money. And in modern America, as everybody knows, nothing is more difficult for the physician to avoid than making money. Binx suffers much, no doubt, in mind and soul. But the metaphysical anguish is surely no harder to bear with a good income than without. In short, he deserves no particular moral credit for bearing his lot without complaint.

Regardless of the provocation, people who kick dogs on the sly are not to be trusted. Old "Rosebud," it is true, is a hard dog to like. But if Binx can so easily forgive the beast his reputed racism (p. 76), one might reasonably expect him to overlook other defects of character and breeding.

Nor is our hero a menace only to dogs. The none too charming doctrine of edification by asskicking, none too humorously enunciated in the course of his epilogue reflections on Kierkegaard (p. 237), is distressingly recognizable as a holdover from the "smart aleck" thinking of his adolescence (p. 109) which we might have thought he had permanently repudiated. What makes the reversion so alarming is that the Binx of the epilogue is the newly re-Christianized Binx. Your sanctified asskicker is always the most dangerous kind.

Binx's cute "Gregorish Peckerish" sexual humor in the episodes with Sharon wears thin pretty quickly. And neither the tone of faint self-mockery nor the by-play of allusions to *Tillie the Toiler* and *The Waste Land* can disguise the quite appallingly vulgar sentimentality of his invocation of Rory Calhoun as witness to his impotence with Kate on the train (pp. 199–201).

Particular disaffinities aside, however, I find it difficult to define Binx's "status" as narrator. The case is not altogether unprecedented. Again, in earlier modern American fiction, Jake Barnes or Nick Carraway comes to mind as a first-person narrator who, like Binx, appears to be created out of some obscure quarrel the author is carrying on with himself. But Hemingway and Fitzgerald provide, in the characters Robert Cohn and Jay Gatsby, a constant reminder to the reader that there *is* a quarrel: that the narrators are themselves but characters, necessarily fallible, to one extent or another necessarily "unreliable," [8] and at no time exclusively and unqualifiedly authorized to speak for the authors. In *The Moviegoer* Percy has left his narrator much less vulnerable, on crucial points much less readily distinguishable from the "implied author," than either Carraway or Barnes is.

But Binx's direct acknowledgment of the reader's presence (p. 13) is at least an implicit reminder of the author's presence as well. Perhaps we would be justified in seeing here a cue—unobtrusive, but notable for the fact that it comes so near the outset of the action—a subtle signal from the author, not only that that we as readers are invited to join Binx in "the search" on fully equal terms, without having to accept a predetermined definition of its goal, but that we are, by the same token, licensed to maintain a constant scrutiny of the narrator's intentions and motives in everything he says and does, whether it is directly concerned with the search or not. Moreover, although there is in this novel no character like a Robert Cohn or a Jay Gatsby—no one person with whom the narrator is so preoccupied that it necessarily and obviously colors his perceptions and judgments in dealing with all the others—Binx's behavior and thinking are not infrequently criticized by a number of people. Aunt Emily heads the list; but the opinions of Sharon, Binx's mother, and most certainly Kate, are not to be ignored.

At least "for the sake of the argument," then, we may assume that we are free not only, if such is our disposition, to dislike Binx in certain respects, but also to take exception both to his philosophical notions and to his personal judgments, free to question his analysis of his experience. That is, we may at least provisionally assume that we are free to disagree with the narrator, without necessarily falling out of sympathy with the implied author.

Binx is not omniscient. After due diversionary display of intellectual candor and humility, charming admissions of ignorance— how anxious he is to assure us, "upon his honor," that he "does not know the answer," that "actually" he is "not very smart"—he often *assumes* omniscience, telling us exactly what is going on in the head of the Northern college boy in the presence of William Holden, or in the old black servant Mercer's (p. 21ff.) or Walter Wade's head (p. 33ff.), even in Aunt Emily's or Kate's. But the reader who has taken his cue at the beginning will not be deceived.

Perhaps Binx's tendency to attribute certain thoughts and feelings to other people tells us more about him than it does about the others. Probably he is right to question his aunt's simplistic view of Mercer as the "faithful retainer"; on the face of it, the fact that the old man steals from his employer would seem to compromise his faithfulness. But is Binx correct in attributing the inconsistencies of Mercer's behavior, his evident confusions and frustration, to his inability simply to choose between the stereotype that Emily sees—the "retainer," the "living connection with a bygone age" (p. 23)—and the other that Binx describes, the character of self-taught "expert in current events" (p. 24) which is supposed to typify the "aspirations" of the American black in the mid-twentieth century? Perhaps Binx is correct; it is a melancholy truth that most Americans, white and black, do seem to spend more effort in trying to type themselves than in seeking true self-knowledge. But then again, we cannot be very sure of anything about Mercer, except that he makes Binx uncomfortable.

As high-grade slapstick Binx's routine with Mercer is very good; but there is no reason for trying to make anything more of it. Binx's insight into Mercer, whom he has known for many years, no more compels our assent than does his speculation on the thoughts and motives of the black man he sees outside the church in Gentilly (pp. 233–35). Binx, suddenly overwhelmed with the belated realization of what day it is, both the momentous thirtieth anniversary of his birth *and* Ash Wednesday, savoring the dark ironies of that coincidence, covering himself with the bitter ashes of the humiliation he has suffered at Emily's hands, is understandably disposed to see portents on every side. But the black man in the Mercury[9] might well be thinking of *none* of the things with which Binx is preoccupied, might well be visiting the church for reasons having nothing whatever to do with either religion or social-climbing. Perhaps he is only trying to sell an insurance policy to the janitor.[10] It is, even as Binx says (p. 235), but beyond the conscious intent of his observation, "impossible to say" what the black man is thinking, just as "it is impossible to be sure [by looking at his dusky forehead] that he received ashes." Except physically, Binx does not necessarily get any closer to either Mercer or the Negro at the church than he does to the purely allegorical *ramoneur* (p. 226), whose chant eerily reinforces the dark prophetic mood into which Emily has fallen as she berates her grandnephew. (It is interesting that the blacks—Mercer with his coal scuttle, the *ramoneur* whose cry promises a thorough cleaning of the chimneys "from top to bottom," the man outside the church in Gentilly—all are associated in one way and another with fire and ashes, serving to remind the white man of his own mortality and of the impending demise of his civilization.)

The chronology of Binx's account of his actions after Korea is hopelessly confused. First he tells us (p. 6) that he has been living in Gentilly only *four* years—which, on the tightest of reckonings relative to his present age, the date of his father's death, and the dates of the Korean War, makes sense. But, a few lines further on, he informs us that he lived for two years in the French Quarter, presumably just prior to the move to Gentilly. Since at this point the reader does not yet have the other relevant information, on Binx's age and on his and his father's military service, no discrepancy is immediately apparent. By the time we get to the tale of the Appalachian adventure, however, an event which we are told (pp. 41–42) occurred *eight* years earlier, following Binx's recovery from his war wound and immediately preceding his settling in Gentilly, we have heard enough that this latest yarn must seem wildly improbable. It would appear that Binx and his fellow veterans were back from the war in Korea four years or so before it started.[11]

Now, if we met such a fellow as Binx in real life, on a long train ride, say, we would know very well what to think of his spiel. He is amusing; certainly very interesting in a lot of ways. We might go on listening indefinitely; but, beyond the first thirty minutes at the outside, we would not be inclined to *believe* a word he said.

But we have not met him in real life. We have met him in a novel. He is, to repeat, a fictional character, created by Walker Percy. The discrepancies in the fictive calendar are, in all likelihood, the result of simple carelessness on Percy's part.[12] While they tend, unfortunately, to raise general doubts about the adequacy of Percy's artistic control in the novel, they are not immediately relevant to the critical problem we have been examining: the question of Binx's "reliability" as narrator.

With due allowance for Percy's carelessness, assuming no more than that Binx is meant to be reasonably accurate in his account of events and the order in which they occur, of what he and other people say to each other—assuming, that is, from internal evidence, that the author has not meant to represent him either as an outright liar or as a totally irresponsible fantasist—what we are obliged to consider is the question whether his perceptions and judgments in any given situation are necessarily to be preferred to contrary or divergent notions expressed by other characters. The Northern college boy and the man outside the church in Gentilly are not given the opportunity to speak for themselves. But, as we have noted, Aunt Emily and Mrs. Smith, and Sharon and Kate, frequently get in their licks. When we first see them together at Emily's house, Kate is at moments openly hostile to him. Binx sees Kate as caught in a "dialectic of hatreds" between her father and stepmother, and would like to think that she is simply taking out on him her current resentment of Emily. But, in fact, he is not entirely innocent of the condescending attitude toward Walter Wade of which Kate accuses him (p. 47).

Indeed, Binx makes a habit of condescension. Except Lonnie, and perhaps Uncle Jules, he patronizes virtually everyone at one time or another—Mercer, Eddie and Nell, Sharon, even in a measure his mother, even, finally, both Emily and Kate herself. Kate is too preoccupied with her own troubles, and her need for Binx, to see the full truth of her own observations, but there are good grounds for her characterizing him as "a cold one . . . cold as the grave" (p. 83) and as "the most self-centered person alive" (p. 197). No doubt she exaggerates a bit, as it is her style to do. But in virtually everything he does, there is certainly something aloof and disingenuous about Binx, a cool, detached, quietly observant air that is only the more irritating for the mannered diffidence of his self-assessments and the subdued attitudes he strikes in the presence of other people. Perhaps his canny maneuverings in pursuit of Sharon, such as the calculating advantage he takes of the automobile accident (p. 124ff.) and the chance to let her see his war scars, are merely amusing. At least he has an honest and healthy desire to justify him here; all's fair, in love and war. But when in the course of his betrothal to Kate he is able to take note of her "not-quite-pure . . . slightly reflected Sarah Lawrence solemnity" (p. 234), there is nothing to relieve the chill intellectuality of his attitude. Here is a man who is unable, even for a moment, to let himself go. He is not loving Kate; to the extent that he is conscious of her at all, he is studying her.

On the other hand, there is a further question whether Binx is not finally the dupe of his own self-regard. To go back for a moment to chapter 1 and his encounter with Kate after lunch at the Cutrers' house, it is worth noting more precisely what it was in his treatment of Walter Wade that she found so offensive. During lunch, Binx has observed Walter's own naive inclination to patronize Emily. "I have to grin," Binx says to the reader. "What is funny is that Walter always starts out in the best brilliant-young-lawyer style of humoring an old lady by letting her get the better of him, whereas she really does get the better of him" (p. 33). Unquestionably, Kate has noticed that sly grin, and has that among other things in mind when she says to Binx later (p. 47): "Don't you dare patronize Walter. . . . Do you think I didn't see the two of you [Binx and Emily] upstaging him at lunch. What a lovely pair you are."

Whether Kate has or has not quite accurately surmised what Binx was thinking when he smiled over the exchange between Walter and Emily at lunch is not clear. But, in the light of the final events of the novel, Binx's marrying Kate and entering medical school, we might well recall this episode and question whether Walter is not entitled to the last laugh. Is it not Binx, finally, who sees himself as "humoring an old lady by letting her get the better of him, whereas she really does get the better of him"?

A plausible case could be made for Emily's having engineered the whole thing, marriage and medical school both. She never openly urges the marriage, of course. Binx's mother does that, along with getting in, independently, her own plug for a career for him in "research" (p. 159). But Emily is in every way a much more cagey character than Mrs. Smith. Binx is indulgently amused (p. 49) at Emily's way of idealizing the men in her family. But Binx idealizes Emily, as idealist. Simply her willingness to scheme in the matter of Kate's illness, her capacity to adjust her tactics when circumstances require, ought to tell Binx that she is not altogether guileless. Has she not already, somewhat surprisingly to Binx (p. 52), compromised on the matter of his career, proposing now that he become a mere practitioner rather than the heroic researcher she once envisaged? She never suggests to Binx that he marry Kate. But she certainly does her best to put him in her way.

It is, no doubt, very annoying to Emily that Binx and Kate traipse off to Chicago without warning, thwarting the plans Yerger has made for getting Kate into the care of the New York psychiatrist. No doubt, the old lady is fundamentally sincere in her adherence to the "broadsword virtues"[13] in the tongue-lashing she gives Binx after he returns from Chicago. Still, the grandeur of her sorrowful indignation seems not only a bit contrived, consciously "stagey," but contrived to a purpose, calculating.

When she demands to know whether he and Kate have been "intimate" during the trip, no one but the hopelessly self-involved Binx could suppose that this is the first time the possibility of such intimacy has occurred to her. Actually, it is never quite clear how closely she has worked with Yerger; but, in the absence of any evidence to the contrary, we are free to assume that she was a party to the plot to send Binx and Kate off together to New York. What *moral* difference could it make, if they were likely to sleep together anyway, whether they chose to do it in Chicago or New York, or en route to either? None, of course; and we may further suppose that Emily knows quite well that Kate had at least as much to do with it as Binx had if they were "intimate." Although she goes at Binx with a fine show of moral outrage at his dastardly conduct in taking the "poor child" Kate off on such a trip in her "suicidal" state, we would do well to remember Binx's own observation shortly before he and Kate left for Chicago—an observation (p. 173) which he seems to have forgotten—that Emily did not appear to be quite as deeply disturbed about Kate's condition as she should have been if Sam's story of the suicide attempt were not exaggerated.

None of this is to say that Emily is without moral purpose in her handling of Binx, her staging of the Grand Remonstrance. She is genuinely concerned about both Binx and Kate. She thinks she knows what is best for both of them. Whether she is right in that assessment or not has nothing whatever to do with the legitimacy of her moral *purpose*; she acts according to her lights, and one can only admire the shrewdness of her psychological insight. She does indeed "know" (p. 224) that Binx is "not a bad boy" in spite of everything. All the while she is "despairing" of Binx in the matter of his sexual morality, his alleged blindness to the alleged wrong he has done Kate, she knows very well that she can count on his fundamental decency—fundamental conventionality, or whatever it is— count on him finally to do-the-right-thing-by-the-girl. Moreover, she probably knows equally well that she can count on Kate to cooperate.

When Kate informs Binx later in Gentilly that she has told Emily they are to be married, and that the old lady did not respond, we may well suppose that at least one reason she did not is that she was not surprised. If Binx is disingenuous, his aunt is past master at the game. Nor does it seem likely that Kate herself is altogether guile-less; it would appear that she is not very much surprised by her aunt's lack of surprise.

Only poor Binx might seem to be quite in the dark about what has happened to him. I have argued for a certain inevitability of the match he makes. As his mother has seen from the first, Sharon is "not the one" for him. And whether Binx's contention that his mother does not really know Kate is justified or not, the truth of

Mrs. Smith's "proverb" that he should marry his cousin (p. 155) is clearly borne out by what we learn of Kate's personality. Certainly, however, no marriage is made without someone's taking action to bring it about. The question is simply that of who has the primary responsibility in this case.

Martin Luschei is at pains to assert the importance of the existential "choices" Binx makes. But the existential hero is almost by definition one who must appear lackadaisical when it comes to decisions; and Binx's behavior exceeds the type. The velleity of his inclination at crucial junctures is so delicate as to be hardly discernible to the unprejudiced observer. Binx certainly does not choose between Sharon and Kate. By the time he gets back to Gentilly on Ash Wednesday, Sharon is no longer available to him. Again, it is evidence only of his remarkable fatuity that he could have supposed she might be available, in the light of what she told him after the trip to Bayou des Allemands. And if either he or Kate truly *proposes* marriage, it is she.

From the very first, Binx never makes more than a guarded suggestion—often in the form of a question—about what he and Kate might do. In chapter 1, he does not actually invite her even to go out on the town with him, but only asks: "Why don't you come with me?"[14] (p. 60). Going to Chicago with him is her idea. Although on the telephone to Sharon's roommate (p. 231)—in part, at least, as a transparent face-saving device after learning that Sharon is now engaged to Stan Shamoun, and getting the further message that the roommate does not want to see him alone—Binx speaks of Kate as his "fiancée," he never gets around to directly asking her to marry him. In effect, Kate simply announces the engagement, first to Emily and then to him, and he goes along with it. She says that he will have to be with her a great deal, because of her illness. He promises that he will. She asks: "Do you want to?" He answers: "Yes" (p. 234). And that is that. His "yes" is unequivocal. He does not hedge, exactly. He is, no doubt, "sincere" in his commitment. But it is difficult to imagine a less enthusiastic avowal. She has to prompt him to every word.

Percy spoke to Carr of Binx's "accommodating" way with Kate concerning her illness.[15] The word accurately describes his attitude toward the engagement as well.

About his "decision" to go to medical school there is, of course, no question whose idea that was in the first place. And he makes it plain (p. 233) that he will do it merely to please Emily—that his true "vocation" is spiritual, one that might be, perhaps, just as well pursued in the occupation of service-station manager as in that of physician. But this, too, must be scanned.

It is difficult to take the sentimental, "urban pastoral" dream of service-station ownership at all seriously. Binx has hardly as realistic a hope of making a go of that as he had for a successful marriage with Sharon. If he is to get out of the brokerage business, there is no reasonable, immediately available alternative to his becoming a physician. In the absence of any evidence to the contrary, we may assume that his aunt is probably right in thinking that medicine is what he is best cut out for. The idea of the spiritual "vocation" looks very much like the notion of claiming Kate as his fiancée, a face-saving device, with the difference only that in this instance he saves face merely with himself—finding a way of avoiding the humiliating admission that Emily has, after all, simply "got the better of him."

Luschei accepts Binx's claim to the vocation at face value. Binx is his own man regardless of his bowing to Emily's wishes. "He will put on the outward forms, which are trivial. The inner content will be his own." [16]

But, in practical terms, it is difficult to see much difference between the "long useful life serving [his] fellowman" which Binx sees his aunt as urging upon him—or, in her own words, the duty to "live by his lights and do what little he can and do it as best he can" (p. 54)—and the kind of career in spiritual spelunking he envisions for himself on the occasion of his betrothal to Kate, wherein he will "listen to people, see how they stick themselves into the world, hand them along a ways in their dark journey and be handed along . . ." (p. 233). The two philosophical outlooks are widely at variance, no doubt. Although both Emily and Binx feel that the world is falling apart, "the fabric is dissolving," Binx rightly observes that "for her even the dissolving makes sense." Emily's use of the phrase "the going under of the evening land" (an awkwardly literal translation of *Der Untergang des Abendlandes*, the original title of Oswald Spengler's book published in English as *The Decline of the West*) would suggest that she sees the coming age of chaos only as the end of a major historic cycle. From Binx's radical absurdist point of view, the notion of such cycles is as irrelevant as any other rational theory to his experience of the fundamental inscrutability of human actions. Binx would also reject her notion of altruistic virtue. The mutual "handing along" in which he will engage is to be undertaken (p. 233) "for good and selfish reasons." But, again, the question I raise is whether there are likely to be any significant differences between the way he will conduct himself toward other people, in or out of his professional role as Dr. Bolling, and the way she has envisaged for him.

Or, if there are to be real differences, are they such as to certify his reconversion to Christianity?

Luschei is eloquent in his conviction that Binx has freely chosen Kate as his "princess," that there is something truly sacramental in his kissing of her much-abused and bloodied thumb as they plight their troth (p. 234), that in his commitment to her he has already made the "leap of faith," is already in the process of becoming the Kierkegaardian "knight of faith"—thereafter " 'to live joyfully and happily every instant by virtue of the absurd, every instant to see the sword hanging over the head of the beloved, and yet not to find repose in the pain of resignation, but joy by virtue of the absurd.' " [17] But a good many facts of Binx's behavior are not accommodated in Luschei's interpretation.

If it were only momentarily that Binx falls into the mood of odd, almost clinical detachment I have mentioned before, which permits him to observe Kate's "not-quite-pure solemnity" at the same time he is supposed to be declaring his lifelong fidelity to her, he might be all the more convincing in the role of true lover. Such lapses of ardor are not uncommon in love's experience. It is only the false and deceitful lover who is not prepared to see, and to acknowledge to himself that he sees—even, or especially, on the most solemn occasions of intimacy, on the instant preceding "the awful daring of a moment's surrender" [18]—the imperfections of his beloved, imperfections of mind and manner, even of character, as well as of body. But with Binx the detachment is not momentary, not a lapse; it is his settled and customary manner. There simply is no ardor in his acceptance of Kate. No daring. The surrender never comes. If in any sense he loves Kate, it would seem to be finally because of her imperfections, not in spite of them.

Binx is strangely distracted, diffident, almost absent-minded, throughout the betrothal scene. And he is not at all improved in the epilogue.

Despite marriage and school and the relaxation of tensions in his relationship with Emily, he seems inwardly more isolated than ever. Whether intentionally on Percy's part or not, the sense of deepening alienation is enforced by the curiously varied narrative technique of the epilogue.

IV. Of Time, Love, and God

Binx never makes it clear precisely how much time has elapsed between the conclusion of the novel's main action and his resumption of his account. It is clear only that all the principal events mentioned in the epilogue, including Lonnie's death, are already in the past. And Binx's first rapid summary of those events (p. 236ff.) is a conventional past-tense narration. Then, midway in his recollection of the visit he and Kate made to the hospital the day before Lonnie died, he shifts unobtrusively back to the present-tense technique of the novel proper (p. 239), and proceeds in that mode to the end.

In any event, the instability of Binx's time-consciousness as narrator is appropriate to his general state of moral and psychological detachment. Not that he is confused or bumbling in his conduct of his daily affairs. Far from it. He is very busy and dependable and competent, the moral mainstay of both his unwieldy families, looking after Emily's eccentric business affairs, his wife's precarious mental health, and the spiritual welfare of the Smith children, all with the same gravely good-humored efficiency and almost executive élan, the while we know without being told that he is also doing a fine job in his medical studies. With the Smith children, it is Kate who seems the more aloof. She "stands a ways off" (p. 239), smiling somewhat abstractedly at them while Binx gets into the car to talk, he suffering the children's closest scrutiny ("their eyes search out mine," p. 240) as he answers their questions. But if by contrast to Kate, whose mortal terror at the sight of the dying Lonnie has rendered her incapable of consoling the others, Binx seems to have achieved complete and unaffected rapport with the children, his relations with adults are quite another matter.

If the evidence of Emily's concern about her bonds is to be considered, wanting to get them out of the brokerage vault and keep them at home in case war should come (p. 241)—a war this time, with atomic weapons, whose finality she obviously has not envisioned—the old lady has fallen into her dotage. Binx's indulgence of her whim is purest patronizing. And his enlistment of Kate as messenger to Mr. Klostermann (whose name is suited to the vaguely melodramatic comedy of the whole scene) has much the same quality of benign condescension.

Percy commented to Carr on the nature of the therapeutic technique Binx is employing in his treatment of Kate here. But whatever justification Binx's behavior may have from his point of view as the future Dr. Bolling, getting in a little preliminary field training with his wife as patient, it is surely questionable as husbandly deportment.

Luschei takes a generally upbeat view of Binx's situation in the epilogue. He is, I think, quite correct in his reading of the final reference Binx makes to his "brothers and sisters." The former half brothers and sisters are now Binx's full-fledged spiritual siblings, brothers and sisters in Christ, as well, perhaps, as in a new condition of mundane affection. But, pursuing an architectural metaphor developed earlier with reference to Binx's status as "underground man" in Mrs. Schexnaydre's basement, Luschei interprets his change of residence after marriage in a way that does not, it seems to me, quite square with the facts. In keeping with his new spiritual state after the move, according to Luschei, Binx "inhabits the full house now and it is his."[19] But if the *metaphor* is to work, we must be permitted to keep in mind the actual circumstances. And, in fact, it is not even clear whether Binx and Kate have purchased the renovated shotgun cottage in which they live while he goes to medical school. Perhaps they are renting it. If they have bought it, there is nothing to indicate whether he or Kate, or both, put up the money. The only definite information we are given (pp. 236–37) is that the *taste* satisfied in the selection of the house is Kate's, not his. We have already learned, much earlier in the novel, what Binx thinks of Nell Lovell and her pseudotraditionalism in the "renovation" of the cottages. Binx's attitude as spiritual "wayfarer," I think, is much better defined if we see him as totally indifferent to the kind of quarters he occupies, except to the extent that living in the cottage provides him another occasion for "humoring" Kate, this time in the infirmity of her aesthetic sense, to the further enhancement of his spiritual superiority. The spiritually renovated Binx, as Luschei would have it, lives "in the infinite passion." Poor old Kate does not, of course; and that is why she does not understand the nature of the consolation Binx offers the Smith children when he assures them that Lonnie will be made whole on the day of the Resurrection.[20]

Talk of "the infinite passion" makes me profoundly uneasy in contemplation of Binx's behavior at the end. If he experiences any such passion, Kate is certainly excluded from it. But the trouble is that Binx seems all too content to have her excluded—her, and Emily, and everybody else for that matter, except the children.

Some plausible excuse can be made for Binx's having funked it when he had the chance to explain himself to Aunt Emily. For nearly a week, after all, he had slept very little. The trip to Chicago had been both physically and emotionally exhausting. Perhaps he was simply too tired to talk then. And when he and Kate got together later the same day in Gentilly, he was still unrested. But weariness alone will not account for it; he is consistently reluctant to talk, consistently disposed to plead the *impossibility* of communication, on one pretext or another, whenever a topic of any complexity and seriousness is up for discussion. By the time we see them in the epilogue, he and Kate have certainly had time for a good long rest, ample opportunity for a good long talk, if only they were mutually disposed to have it. The epilogue tells us nothing of whether they have managed any better sexually after marriage than they did on the way to Chicago before. Neither are we told whether they were married in the Church. But all the available evidence points to the possibility that they do not share the "infinite passion" at least partly because they have never shared any finite passion, either sexual or intellectual.

Some of Percy's own comments on the novel, in the interview with Carr, tend to support Luschei's Kierkegaardian argument on the "leap of faith" Binx is supposed to have made at the end. From the "aesthetic mode" of his Gentilly sojourn, according to Percy, Binx "jumps . . . clear across the ethical to the religious. He has no ethical sphere at all. That's what Emily can't understand about him." And, in Kate's observations on Binx's encounter with the Smith children in the epilogue, Percy asserted that she "missed it, missed the whole thing"—the "it," presumably, being the fact of Binx's religious faith.[21]

But, aside from the fact that in that interview Percy's memory of his own novel was woefully hazy—he could not even recall whether Lonnie has already died when Binx talks to the other children—I am no more persuaded by the "ex-author's" view of Binx's general condition than I am by Luschei's comments. Percy simply does not convince me, the *story* he has told through Binx does not convince me, that Binx could not have communicated with Kate, not to speak of Emily, more effectively than he has.

Binx mutters darkly of its being "too late" (p. 237), presumably in the history of Christendom or of the world as a whole, for him to speak "edifyingly" of religion. Perhaps it is, for him or anyone— although I am habitually suspicious of the motives of such eschatologists. But, "edification" aside, if it is too late in the history of Binx's relationship with Kate, by the time they leave Lonnie's bedside, for him to explain to her a good deal more than he does about the general nature of his communication with the Smith children, he has done much to hasten the darkness.

Kate may be crazy, and variously perverse, and have very bad taste in houses and what not, but she is not stupid—not nearly as intelligent as Binx, perhaps, but not stupid. If Binx finds it hard to talk to her, then he could at least have suggested some readings in Kierkegaard which might help her to understand his state of mind. She is not so sick, surely, that she cannot read; and even Kierkegaard could hardly throw her any deeper into depression than she has already fallen. Binx could have put Kate onto Kierkegaard; he might even have tried it with Emily. But Binx does not want to communicate. That is the long and short of it.

At times during their "courtship" it appears that Binx actually has tried at least to acquaint Kate with some of the Kierkegaardian terminology. Once he has tried to talk to her even of the search (pp. 80–83), has been on the point of getting at, with Kate, the crucial issue of his inarticulate conflict with Emily—the distinction between "search" and "research." But the moment Kate starts to close in he backs off into male attitudinizing, an irritable intellectual vanity provoked by the threat of being classified with BoBo the iron-deer hunter of Westchester County, and terminates the discussion with a surly "never mind" (p. 83). Rebuffed, Kate turns mysterious, saying to him: "It is possible, you know, that you are overlooking something, the most obvious thing of all. And you would not know it if you fell over it." Belatedly, he presses her to speak her mind plainly. "What?" he asks. But she will not tell him. For she knows, of course, that he really does not want to know, has already convinced himself that she really has nothing to disclose. The moment is lost, and she retreats into the conventional woman's role he has assigned her, becoming "gay and affectionate" with him on the streetcar, watching him "with brown eyes gone to discs."

Whatever she had in mind to tell him he had "overlooked," it is clear from this and other exchanges that Kate once had the capacity to render Binx a service no one else he knows can provide: to penetrate the mask of his false tolerance and diffidence and confront him with the unpleasant truth of his patronizing egotism. But she is soon so enfeebled by her emotional dependence upon him, a habit in which he clearly encourages her, that she loses the essential focus of her moral vision, and with it the essential dignity and virtue of married love.

In the scene following their visit to the hospital room there is nothing left of her former sensitivity but a cringing hysteria. Still unnerved by the sight of Lonnie's wasted body, she reproaches Binx for the callousness of his medical student's jargon, winces morbidly at his touch when he attempts to soothe her with a kiss and an ill-timed compliment on her good looks, and, plucking at her shredded thumb the while, feebly protests that there is "something grisly" about him. But all the old proud fire is gone, the scalding candor of her earlier attacks. And it is all too easy for the unfortunate Binx to go on untouched in his customary moral complacency, his smug male conceit—now newly confirmed, perhaps beyond hope, as Christian forbearance. It is hard to imagine that he and Kate will ever be able to talk seriously again about anything, in the category either of search or of research. He has got her in the portable pumpkinshell of his holy solicitude, and intends to keep her there.

On the evidence of the interview with Carr, it seems that Walker

Percy himself might have "missed it" on several points. In the novel proper, as we have noted, there is much that might well be taken as evidence of a deliberate "distancing" of narrator and implied author. Then, in the epilogue, suddenly we are confronted with Binx's reflections on what is or is not appropriate in "a document of this kind" (p. 237). The word "document," in everyday usage, most often refers to a *written* record. Has Binx, then, been composing a written account of his thoughts and experiences? Although this is the first we have heard of it, there is nothing to suggest that he has anything else in mind. But what is the "kind" of written composition he refers to, in which "reticence . . . hardly [has] a place"? Does he mean a diary, perhaps, or other form of personal chronicle? Or does he mean a work of literary art, work of fiction? Is the "document" he refers to, the thing *he* has been writing and is about to complete, identical with the novel we have been reading all this time? (Novel, or whatever else our principles of genre definition might dictate that we call it.)

In the context of a dialogue with Carr on the subject of religion and the art of the novel, Percy's compressed and rather obscure paraphrase of Binx's comments might suggest that we were meant to see Binx himself as novelist. "Nothing is worse than a novel which seeks to edify the reader. As Binx Bolling said, 'It's not my business to edify anybody.' " [22]

In his habits of morally and emotionally detached observation, of "mind-reading," of seeing everything in the world about him as charged with symbolic meaning, of ritualizing and "dramatizing" his everyday experience, Binx certainly could be regarded as a man of authorial sensibility. And novels in which the narrator-hero presents himself as also the *writer* of the book, in whole or in part, are common enough. Nor is there anything in the inherent design of such a novel that would prevent the reader's being kept consistently aware of a distinction between the narrator-hero-author and the "implied author." The distinction is easily maintained if, as is ordinarily the case, we are definitely informed somewhere near the beginning that the narrator is writing. But we cannot be expected simply to *assume*, unless we are told otherwise, that the narrator is writing. And the samples of Binx's compositions we see—the business letters he dictates to Sharon Kincaid (pp. 105–6), his scribblings in a notebook (p. 146)—are plainly distinguishable from the main text of the narrative. If the narrative proper was conceived as Binx's written record of his experiences, Percy's failure even to hint at such a design until very near the end makes it very difficult to determine the limits of the implied author's sympathy with Binx: a situation that I find profoundly disturbing.

The trouble with the Binx of the epilogue is not that he has changed too much, or too abruptly or unaccountably, but that he has not changed enough. I do not mean that I am discontent with his remaining some kind of crypto- or closet-Catholic. The principal point, perhaps, of the coordination of the novel's main action with the liturgical calendar—the point of Binx's being for the most part indifferent not only to the secular festival of the Mardi Gras but, until the last minute, to the coincidence of Ash Wednesday with his birthday and the event of his humiliation by Emily—is to suggest the peculiar obscurity of the relationship between the operations of the visible church and the needs of the spiritual "seeker" in the modern world, the man whose consciousness is so overtaxed in its dual subjection to myth and history that he has little or no strength left for pure believing, and little or no dependable sense of a ritual *community* of belief. If such is the point, it is a point well worth making. And it would be difficult to credit a Binx in the epilogue who had settled in even as a regular communicant, let alone a maker of First Fridays and member in good standing of the Knights of Columbus. Rather, it is Binx in his immediate personal relationships who is insufficiently changed, or if changed, changed for the worse.

He remains, as I have suggested, much the same old egotist, the same sly old condescender he always was. The only notable difference, alas, now he has got religion, is that he is not nearly as funny as he used to be. That is a great pity. He reports that "both women," Emily and Kate, "find [him] comical" (p. 237). It is hard to see what amuses them so.

He has lost his humor, with nothing to make up for it. Again, he seems indisposed to give enough of himself, to Kate and Emily, indisposed to pay them the essential courtesy, even to try to explain what has happened to him. It is not his responsibility to *convert* them, certainly. Explanation does not convert. Conversion is by faith, and faith is a divine gift. But the trouble with Binx's Christianity, finally, is that it is deficient in charity. One appreciates the exclusion of cymbals and brass. But the score for the other and necessary instruments, in this strange coda, lacks some essential depth.

V. A Tentative Conclusion

The novel I read, bearing the title of *The Moviegoer*, has little in common with the one described by Percy's more devotedly enthusiastic interpreters. Further, on the basis not merely of external evidence such as the interview with Carr—in which Percy was, after all, only another (and rather forgetful) reader/discussant of a text he composed some time before—but also, and more tellingly, of internal evidence such as Binx's reference to the "document" he is composing, I am inclined to think that my version of *The Moviegoer* is in many important respects not the novel Walker Percy meant to write. As I have said before, I find this situation critically disturbing. It is not that I am distressed to discover what Wolfgang Iser calls "gaps" in the text.[23] All novels (and short stories, and poems and plays) have them; it is the reader's necessary and proper collaborative task to fill in the gaps. But we most admire, and delight in, those works in which we feel that the gap-filling *is*, precisely, a collaboration, a task in which the author has invited us to engage. In *The Moviegoer*, the reader is very often left to labor over gaps that he cannot be confident the author has recognized as such.

But the book I read is still a very fine book. The lavish sensuous artistry of the thing—with its pervasive musicality, its marvelously evocative urban and rural landscapes, its exquisitely detailed portraits of living creatures in their form and posture and motion, its acute and meticulously discriminate renderings of idiom and accent, of the sounds too of machinery and of wind and water, of all manner even of tastes and smells, of the infinitely various touches of things—is joy unending.[24] The opening paragraph, with its supremely casual economy, its subtle revelation within nine lines of the speaker's mind and temper and all the essential shape of his story to come, is as quietly arresting a beginning as any modern novelist has achieved, unmistakably original at the same time that it is altogether free of stylistic sensationalism.[25] In the episode of Binx's early-morning conversation with his mother on the porch of the fishing camp at Bayou des Allemands, the landscape-painting and the intimate human portraiture, the acutely sensitive representation of the white heron and the swimming snake in their mysterious and vital, unspeaking presence before the talkative humans, the woman interrupting her dialogue with her son to address an admonitory summons to the unseen fish for which she is angling, all are brought together with the continuing development of the plot, the story of Binx's continuing searches, in a complex artistic unity, a realization of the indissoluble union of body and soul in the human state, which tests our methods of critical analysis as they are rarely tested by the novel. Reminiscences of *The Waste Land* are inevitably commonplace in novels written anytime within the past half-century. But in very few of them are the poetic allusions so successfully adapted as they are here to distinctly novelistic formal purposes. Finally, I can think of no other novelist who has managed anything quite comparable to Percy's rendering of marginal states of consciousness, like those Binx experiences in his awakening at Bayou des Allemands, and during the train ride to Chicago.

Such, beyond the ones I have earlier tried to define, are the great and undeniable strengths of the book. And with my adverse criticism of Percy's handling of characterization and point of view, my attempt to define my dissatisfaction with his dramatization of Binx's conversion, I have not meant to suggest that any of the characters lacks the basic human *plausibility* which it is the chief task of the novelist to produce. Binx, and Kate, and Emily, all have the *mysterious* quality of real human beings which is the main source of plausibility in fiction. They are all inexplicable, finally, somehow unaccountable, in and for their actions, in the way that real human beings actually are, whatever anyone, including the self-observer, might be tempted from time to time to think they ought to be. As for Percy's undeniable further purposes—his purposes, shall we say, as *visionary* novelist, since he has disavowed the role of "apostle"[26] —he has shown us here, if nothing else, just how difficult it is for anyone to be at once a Christian and a competent critic of the age. How difficult and how necessary, perhaps, but difficult, of necessity.

3

The Last Gentleman

I. Strange Birds in Central Park

The narrative technique of *The Last Gentleman* is in several ways radically different from that of *The Moviegoer*. To be sure, the third-person-past-tense narrator's "omniscience" is strictly limited. Nothing of the thoughts, words, or actions of other characters is revealed except what Will Barrett is in a position either to observe or to have reported to him. But the narrator's point of view is almost always readily distinguishable from the hero's.[1] Further, while the opening paragraph of Binx Bolling's first-person-present narration is exclusively concerned with his thoughts and feelings, telling us nothing about the physical setting, the situation is exactly reversed in the first four sentences of *The Last Gentleman*.

> One fine day in early summer a young man lay thinking in Central Park.
> His head was propped on his jacket, which had been folded twice so that the lining was outermost, and wedged into a seam of rock. The rock jutted out of the ground in a section of the park known as the Great Meadow. Beside him and canted up at mortar angle squatted a telescope of unusual design.

We are told that the young man is thinking. But the subject of his thoughts is not revealed. Rather, the narrator is first concerned very precisely to locate the scene—not simply in Central Park, but in the particular section called the Great Meadow—and to provide a sharply detailed "still" impression of the young man, with his meticulously folded coat wedged into the rock, and his formidable telescope, before directly disclosing anything of the nature of his mental processes, or presenting him in a series of physical movements which might suggest his purposes in the park.

The effect of the new emphasis on place is, in large part, clearly ironic. As we are soon informed, Will is an alien, a "displaced person," in the simple sense that he is a Southerner living in New York. Moreover, the particular setting in which we first see him has no cultural identity. Within the city of New York, there are a number of definable human communities; but Central Park is not a part of any one of them, although countless thousands of people go there every day, for a countless variety of public and private purposes. Combining aspects of wilderness and pastoral landscape with virtually every other facility that the term "park" might conceivably cover, abstract center of the still larger abstraction of the city, the great *Weltstadt*, this place is no place at all. On one hand, the names of some of its topographical features—the Great Meadow, the Pond—might as well be the names of places on the surface of the moon. On the other, "the tough old hide of the earth" (p. 4) endlessly trodden over by the lonely crowd, the bark of the trees holding bits of hair where the great beast of the populace has rubbed against them, the park is our whole worn and weary, used old planet itself:[2] an anywhere and nowhere.

The sense of alienation is further heightened when we learn why Barrett has come to the park. This information is briefly withheld, of course, as a simple device for sustaining the curiosity the reader will have felt at the first mention of the telescope. And—here as always Percy clearly perceives his reader as one avid of novelty—it is gratifying just to discover that the pensive young man is not the professional photographer, say, or the ordinary voyeur we might at first have supposed him to be.

Everybody even mildly interested in the preservation of endangered species of wildlife has by now read an article or seen a Public Television program about experiments for encouraging the peregrine falcon's adaptation to urban environments.[3] But at the time Percy's novel was first published the reader would have been a rare one indeed who could have anticipated the revelation of Barrett's purposes with the telescope. And even now that the novelty is gone, the passage describing his earlier observations of the great falcon retains all the essential excitement of the young man's experience, the sense he had of something approaching epiphany when he first caught sight of the bird perched atop the hotel. It is, inevitably, rather a letdown when we are informed that the hawk does not reappear (p. 5), and Barrett's expedition with the telescope is transformed, after all, into an exercise in mere girl-watching.

But, before that happens, the image of the falcon has been firmly fixed in the reader's mind: the more firmly, if anything, for the fact that Will is not able, as he had hoped, to photograph it. The "chance event" anticipated at the beginning of the narrative, "as a consequence of [which] the rest of his life was to be changed," is his telescopic encounter with Rita and Kitty. But if the latter "bird" of his own biological species is to become the immediate and ostensible object of his continuing quest—and if at one level that airborne "pair of ragged claws," the hawk in its forays among the fat city pigeons, is plainly an embodiment of the uninhibited, predatory male spirit that poor Barrett, frustrated by self-doubt and the un-informed but stubborn promptings of conscience, has tried vainly to cultivate in himself—at another level the falcon is emblem of a transcendent kinship, of which Barrett has at this point only the vaguest intimation, but in which it is his ultimate quest to discover or re-establish himself as heir, all the while that he consciously con-ceives of no higher purpose than the pursuit of Kitty.

The peregrine, or "pilgrim" hawk, from any but a sophisticated conservationist point of view so obviously out of place in the urban park, is in its confident adaptability inevitably appealing, and inspir-ing, to Southern-gentleman-manqué Barrett as exile in New York. But by virtue of a complex of associations embracing scriptural tradition and the works of a number of Percy's literary ancestors besides other writings of his own,[4] the brief appearance (or non-appearance) of the falcon at the beginning of the novel foreshadows the development of the theme of explicitly spiritual quest which dominates the ending, in the account of Jamie's final suffering and death. At first glance, Will's conscious purpose in going to the park, to try to photograph the falcon, might seem to be an elaborately casual hobbyist exercise which is important only as it provides occasion for the lucky "accident" of his falling in love with Kitty.

Actually, however, if we read the book in its aspect of spiritual romance rather than in that of the traditional novel, it can be argued that the entire lengthy narrative of the love affair and attendant misadventures, if not merely an entertaining distraction, is important in the final analysis only as a record of the *trials* the hero must undergo in preparation for his ordeal in the desert.

II. More Signs and Wonders

Percy loves the movies. The episode of Will's falling in love with Kitty "at first sight and at a distance of two thousand feet" (p. 7) is quite uncynically designed to satisfy the taste of readers who are devoted to the kind of Hollywood films in which it is obligatory, as Percy put it in his essay "The Man on the Train," that the lovers "meet cute." But, however affectionately, Percy is deliberately parodying the cinematic technique at the same time that he so expertly imitates it.[5] The novelist, through his quasi-omniscient narrator, can tell us directly what it would be difficult for the filmmaker even to suggest at the instant of Kitty's first appearance in the "brilliant theater" of the telescope's lenses: what Will is thinking and feeling as he watches. "His heart gave a leap. He fell in love. . . . It was not so much her good looks, her smooth brushed brow and firm round neck bowed so that two or three vertebrae surfaced in the soft flesh, as a certain bemused and dry-eyed expression in which he seemed to recognize—himself!" (p. 7). The exclamation mark, following the dash, is about as obvious a cue, indeed, as the sophisticated reader could be expected to tolerate.

If with anybody, Will is "in love" with himself, not with Kitty. Or, he is in love with the idea of love. Kitty simply happens to be the one who comes to the park bench, to pick up the verse missive left for her by the Handsome Woman, at the moment that Will's complex *need* for love—stimulated in part by the words of the poem, of course, and in part by the subtly erotic excitement of the spying game itself—is briefly and sharply, but still distortedly, focused in and through the telescope. His new "love," like his acquisition of the instrument through which he "discovers" its object, can be explained as merely symptomatic of a continuing emotional disturbance that has developed over many years.

Will has, as the narrator is soon to reveal at considerable length, ample reason to believe that something is badly wrong—either with him, or with the world, or both—and, having abandoned hopes of getting an adequate diagnosis and therapy from his psychiatrist, Dr. Gamow, he buys the telescope and sets out looking for signs and wonders. He would not, of course, conceive of what he searches for as belonging to the order of divine mystery. "Being of both a scientific and a superstitious turn of mind" (p. 5)—the mentality which is typical of our befuddled post-Christian era—he is, rather, "always on the lookout for chance happenings which lead to great discoveries." But, regardless of whether one's intellectual predisposition is theological or scientific, the main point is that when one *wants* strongly enough to see a sign, to wander into the momentous chance happening, one is sure to find something that will satisfy the need—and, finding it, inevitably defeat oneself. For that which we are "on the lookout for," and which, when we see it, we are confident will "lead to great discoveries," cannot in any very strict sense be said to occur by *chance.*

There is, to be sure, an element of chance in Will's letting the barrel of the telescope drop into the position that points it directly at the bench where Rita is sitting. But in a place like Central Park the odds against such an accident are not terribly high. And beyond the initial coincidence Will is for some time about as much in control of the situation as any of us ever is in real-life encounters. Not only is there nothing especially remarkable about a woman's leaving a note concealed in a park bench, or, although some observers might find it mildly disquieting, about the fact that the recipient of the note is another woman, young and beautiful, but Will's spying on the pair is a matter entirely of his own free choice and conscious planning.

The narrator records in meticulous detail (p. 5ff.) the alert engineer's calculations of angle and distance as he locates the bench, packs up his gear, goes to find the note and read it and replace it in its hiding place, and returns to his original vantage point to set up the telescope again and wait. Beyond the hero's limited and notably faulty design, there is the author's, the design of the novel. By a variety of means, Percy frequently reminds his reader that this is a work of fiction. After a lengthy digression to fill in the background of Barrett's personal history, when the narrator comes back to the events following the opening episode, we are teased with what may seem, depending upon our accustomed tastes and attitudes, either a wondrous or an outrageously contrived series of coincidences.

Although Barrett is able to observe the hawk several times more, and Rita appears once again at the bench, four days after the initial encounter, Kitty does not come back. After several weeks, Will abandons his daily vigil in the park. But then he happens to see a feature story in the Sunday *Times* about a hypothetical enemy's nerve-gas bombing attack on New York, and discovers that "ground zero" on the accompanying map is precisely at the location of the bench in Central Park where he first saw Rita and Kitty. And the next day, when he catches sight of Rita in Pennsylvania Station and follows her to the hospital in Washington Heights (p. 48), he learns that the Vaught family and his own were once fairly well acquainted back home in the South.

Again, however, it is highly questionable what if anything is to be made of the coincidences. Barrett interprets the map in the newspaper as a "sign" (p. 48) that he is sure to see the two women again, and decides to renew his neglected vigil in the park. But there is no proof that ground zero of the hypothetical nerve-gas attack is *exactly* at the location of the park bench. And, even if the engineer had taken the trouble to check his first calculations and found them to be entirely accurate, the significance of the data would still be open to question. We may safely assume that any number of people would have sat on that same bench within a few days or weeks preceding the appearance of the newspaper article, and have been observed at whatever they were doing, for an incalculable variety of motives, by any number of other people: all of them, observed and observers, then and thereafter, complete strangers to Will and Kitty, and yet having as good a right as he has, should they too have happened to see the newspaper story, to interpret it as uncannily relevant to *their* personal affairs. And besides, as the narrator goes on immediately to tell us after Barrett has read the "sign" and made up his mind to resume his vigil, "he needn't have bothered" — for it is the very next day that he sees Rita in Pennsylvania Station. If in some way this episode might seem to confirm Will's interpretation of his having seen the map in the newspaper, that he was destined to see the two women again, still there is no suggestion of cause and effect in the sequence of events. Indeed, so far as the advancement of plot is concerned, the second incident simply renders the former superfluous. For plot purposes, *Percy* "needn't have bothered" about the map.

To sum up: to the extent that we are ever encouraged to forget the whole thing is fiction, about all we can be "realistically" sure of is that poor Will has a great need to believe in signs—i.e., in any surprising event which cannot be explained as a consequence of his own deliberate actions but which seems at the same time to provide him a clue to his destiny—and that he will believe, whenever the occurrence in question, while inexplicable, somehow smacks of the "scientific." The first appearance of Kitty, his "better half," qualifies simply because he observed her through the remarkable telescope, an instrument which perfectly combines (as the narrator explains, p. 29) the magical and the scientific. And nothing, surely, could be better than the *Times* story with its accompanying map—all that deliciously arcane medical-military jargon (the talk of "zones" of "fatty degeneration of the proximal nephrone" and "reversible cortical edema"), all those dizzyingly precise concentric circles. All, above all, so elegantly hypothetical. To the incomparably modern sensibilities of our "sentient engineer," of course, anything like a simple old UFO, say, would be as unacceptably vulgar, atavistic, as a fiery cross, not worth a moment's notice no matter how precisely in an actual sky it might be positioned over the sacred bench on which his love had chosen to seat herself. Only the totally invisible, totally cerebral, gas will serve.

The narrator, albeit indulgently affectionate, maintains an attitude of amused and impartial skepticism. It *may* be that Will Barrett is right to suppose that some extrapersonal power is at work in arranging the series of coincidences for his personal benefit. It may be that he is wrong to reject (p. 47) the notion he briefly entertains that some manner of nerve-gas attack on the city has already actually occurred. There are, after all, the strange phenomena he has observed of late (pp. 46–47) not only in his own states of consciousness but, to the extent that the two are distinguishable, in the world about him—with its uninhabitable museums and self-canceling concerts, the people on the subways who obviously share his disposition

64

to "feel bad in the best of environments . . . so bad, in fact, that it took the worst of news to cheer them up." Why should he *not* suppose such things to be attributable to invisible gas? But the narrator will not presume to direct our final judgment in such matters. He offers us assistance in formulating questions of general philosophical import which might be raised by the experiences he describes, and here and there he may drop some small hint of his own evaluation of the soundness of Barrett's opinions. But his primary responsibility, he tells us in effect, is simply to record what Barrett does and thinks and feels.

Barrett has a need to believe in signs, and, such was the continuing hold of the secularized romantic tradition upon the mind of youth in his generation of our post–Puritan-Christian era, a need to believe in salvation by Love: the love of a pure and beautiful woman. It somehow hardly matters whether Kitty is or is not actually "sent" by some extrapersonal agency to satisfy his need. The day after coming across the story in the *Times* he happens to see Rita in Pennsylvania Station. But what of that? There is never any telling whom one will see in a New York railroad station, or when. And Will has been, after all, for some time *looking* for Rita and Kitty. Mr. Vaught, in the corridor of the hospital, having marveled at Will's acute discriminations among Alabama accents, *claims* to have known the engineer's father, "lawyer Barrett." But there is considerable uncertainty here too. Old Vaught knows *something* about the Barretts; but it is hard to tell how much is actually the product of earlier acquaintance, and how much he is simply picking up from the cues Will gives him. It is hard to tell; and it hardly matters. When it is apparent that Vaught has confused Will's father with his Uncle Fannin (p. 51), Will corrects him; but neither on this nor on any other particular point is Will disposed to question the old man's essential veracity. The whole exchange follows a more or less set pattern—burlesque "routine" with undertones of ritual seriousness —which it is customary for Southerners like Barretts and Vaughts (acutely conscious of both the similarities and the differences of their heritages) to fall into wherever they meet, especially in "foreign" territory such as New York.

I mean, of course, Southerners in "real life," as well as Southerners in novels. It is not only that they routinely *want* to claim family acquaintance, if not, indeed, remote kinship; the chances are that the claim, more often than not, will have some basis in actuality. Will Barrett and the Vaughts, beginning with the old man, are not very much surprised to discover their common background; and neither should the reader be surprised. Granting Percy his right to decide in the first place that the Vaughts should be Southerners, it would have been, if anything, more surprising to discover that they had never heard of the Barretts.

But I mention Percy because it is also important to remember that Will and the Vaughts *are* characters in a novel, the product of Percy's artistic invention. This is a novel which is very much and very deliberately "about," among other things, truth and illusion. At least as much as Will's conversation with the old man in the hospital corridor reflects Percy's keen awareness of social ritual, it reflects his awareness of literary convention.

What readers whose expectations have been trained in the conventions of the earlier modern "realistic" novel will find it most difficult to concede to Percy is just that initial right: to decide that Barrett's fair lady of the park should belong to a family of sojourning fellow Southerners. That, no doubt, is the sticking point, no matter how plausible everything that follows may be. But if this, or any of the other preceding coincidences which are crucial to the plot, does strike us as rather too obviously contrived, our credulity is strained *only* because it happens in fiction. We have known all along that everyday life is full of such wonders, amazing events that occur not only in isolation but now and again in strange sequence. But we got used to demanding of well-made fiction that it seem, in the order of situation and events as well as in other respects, rather less wonderful than life. Rather less fictional, one might say. Percy, however, while eschewing the radicalism of various metafictionists, and the paralyzing self-consciousness of the writing-is-writing-and-nothing-but-writing school, is clearly dissatisfied also with an art of fiction that would exclude all but the inconsequential humdrum of existence. Such fiction, he would suggest, is in the final analysis not realistic at all, but profoundly unrealistic, no less a falsification of human experience, of the human condition, than are the wildest extravagances of romance.

III. Will in Love

In any event, the matter of central interest in all Will's adventures is
not so much the question of how or why certain "accidental" things
happen to him, but of how he reacts to their happening. "At first
sight and at a distance of two thousand feet," before he knows
anything about her except what she looks like and that she has
received a cryptic love-note-poem from another woman, Will falls
in love with Kitty. He is sure, no matter how, that he and she are
meant for each other, that she is his "better half," and so on; and
some subsequent events would seem to confirm his first intuitions.
But the curious thing is that as soon as they have met face to face at
the hospital, and exchanged a few words of conversation, he is not
so sure.

With Jamie and the senior Vaughts he gets on swimmingly.
Nothing that he has learned about Kitty from Mr. Vaught on his
second visit to the hospital, when she is absent, would seem likely to
diminish his ardor. He feels a trifle embarrassed at having talked too
much about himself and his medical history during the first encounter. And, after learning that the two women are living together, he is
a bit uneasy at the prospect of having to deal with Rita in order to
arrange a rendezvous with Kitty. The truth is that he really cannot
explain to himself why he hesitates: "Without quite knowing why
he did so—for now he had the Handsome Woman's name and had
looked her up in the telephone book and now knew where Kitty
lived—he kept up his vigil in the park" (p. 60). But the very fact of
his going back to the telescope should be enough to suggest to the
reader the true nature of the problem. It is, in a sense, just the
opposite of what Will himself makes it out to be.

At last Rita and Kitty appear again at the bench, this time together,
and "it was not until he saw them through the telescope that he
knew why he had kept up his vigil: it was because he did not know
enough about Kitty" (p. 61). On the contrary, he already knows too
much about her. The one meeting in the hospital has already blurred
the ideal image he first beheld in the park; and no effort to restore
it, with or without the aid of the telescope, can now avail. The more
he learns about Kitty, first eavesdropping on her and Rita at closer

quarters in the Tavern-on-the-Green (pp. 61–64), then botching an attempt at lovemaking another night in the park (pp. 107–13) before they begin the long and arduous journey "home" to the South, the harder it gets for Will to recover his faith in his original vision: until, at the end of the novel, they are not two thousand feet apart, but more than a thousand miles, too far even for the magical powers of the German telescope.

If at any point it is true that Will does not know enough about Kitty, a good part of the reason is that he does not want to know. Almost from the beginning, he is distressed by elements of her personality and manner which do not fit his preconception of the woman he wants to marry. Attempting to explain to him the nature of her relationship to Rita, she alludes to her brother Sutter's alleged mistreatment of his wife, and, when Will presses her for details, puts him off with odiously pretentious jargon: " 'Oh,' she shrugged. 'It's a long story. But what a horrible mess. Let's just say that he developed abnormal psychosexual requirements' " (p. 73).

Regardless of what might be the truth about Sutter's and Rita's relationship, such talk is not what Will has fondly expected of Kitty: "He frowned. He didn't much like her using the word psychosexual. It reminded him of the tough little babes of his old therapy group, who used expressions like 'mental masturbation' and 'getting your jollies.' It had the echo of someone else. She was his sweetheart and ought to know better. None of your smart-ass Fifty-seventh Street talk, he felt like telling her" (p. 73).

It is highly questionable, of course, as Will suspects but cannot bring himself consciously to admit, whether "his Kitty" exists outside his own wishful imagination. If she is, in fact, speaking out of character here—affecting a voice which the reader will soon recognize as borrowed from Rita—still, one must wonder how the true Kitty is to be discovered, and whether, once she is revealed, Will will find her any more answerable to his heart's desire than he has found the "tough little babes" of the therapy group or the "people-liker" from Ohio (pp. 21–22). From the scene of their conversation in the New York automat (p. 71), when "he wanted to go into a proper house and shower her with kisses in the old style," it is a long road for him yet, following the dream, to their meeting at "Cap'n Andy's" the day of the Tennessee game (p. 283). But if the "fond and ferocious and indulgent" one who shows him around the place she envisages as their future home, already adopting a manner of easy intimacy "as if they had been married five years" (p. 286), is something approaching the real Kitty, and the suburban house with its prospect of "the doleful foothills and the snowfield of G.E. Medallion homes" (p. 285) something approximating *her* notion of a "proper house" for being "showered with kisses" in, then it is clear that Will has as good reason for misgiving on the eve of his departure for Santa Fe as he had at the outset.

Rita's influence on Kitty requires considerable complication of Will's amorous strategy. Despite the activity at the park bench, the plans for weekends at Fire Island, all the fascinating ambiguities of Kitty's "confession" to Will (pp. 113–17), there is no reason not to take her word for it that "there was [never] anything really wrong" between the sisters-in-law, that "nothing has ever happened" (p. 114). There is no compelling evidence even of sublimated Lesbianism in the relationship, not to speak of physical intimacy. The two women would appear to be all too pathetically "normal," if ineffectual, in their sexual preferences. If Rita is in love with anyone, physically and otherwise, it is still with Sutter. And Kitty exhibits all the symptoms merely of prolonged virginity, desperately compensating for her fear and anxiety, in the face of Will's importunities, with the fantasy of her having cruelly and selfishly exercised her "power" over Rita—to alienate the latter's affections not only from Carlos, her Zuni Indian protégé, but even, so Kitty would like to believe, fondly savoring her guilt, from Sutter himself.

At the time of Kitty's conversation with Will in the automat, it is hard to tell; but from what we can learn later on about Rita and Sutter, it seems unlikely that Kitty had to "seduce" Rita, or that their relationship in any essential way contributed to the breakup of the marriage. Rita, obviously, is inclined to like practically anybody whose life she can contrive to manage. Within that general class, Kitty would have the advantage over Carlos simply by virtue of her being a Vaught.

In her lifelong career as secular salvationist, Rita's failed conquest of Sutter, the perversely brilliant, self-destructive physician, has provided the most severe test of her faith. His rejecting her, and reverting to the old habits of pornographic and suicidal preoccupation from which she thought she had rescued him, is more than a personal affront to Rita. She sees it as a repudiation of her most sacred belief, in the self-perfectibility of man, by the one man above all others who had seemed equipped to share her apostolate. Perhaps she neither hopes nor wants to have him again as a husband; she has despaired of saving him from professional and personal ruin, even from suicide sooner or later. Still she cannot free herself from the maddening fact of her failure to redeem him. Clearly, she feels that she cannot simply accept defeat, and turn away from it, without admitting the falsity of her faith itself. Rita has a most desperate *need* to take charge of the affairs of both Jamie and Kitty, Sutter's brother and sister, in effect to "convert" them to her faith, as the only means left to her to assuage the grief and terror she has suffered in losing Sutter. Old Mr. Vaught, talking to Will, marvels at his sometime daughter-in-law's "unselfishness" in Kitty's and Jamie's behalf. But if poor Rita is in a sense selfless — in that she has no self apart from her ideas, would be destroyed if deprived of her convictions — she is surely not, in the ordinary sense of the word, *unselfish*. Her concern for Jamie and Kitty is purest self-interest.

In any event, Will's sudden arrival on the scene is a decided nuisance for her. Under different circumstances, she might have seen him as a highly likely client for her life-management services. But she has her hands full at the moment with Jamie and Kitty, and their none too predictable father, here in New York — not to speak of the continuing threat, geographically remote for the time being but never out of mind for her, of interference from Sister Val and Sutter himself. She tries for a time relatively inconspicuous means of discouraging Kitty's interest in Will — pretending to take little notice of him during his first visit to the hospital, in the course of the conversation at the Tavern-on-the-Green warning Kitty only rather casually and impersonally that "there is nothing romantic about mental illness" (p. 63), going ahead with plans for a weekend at Fire Island, and so on. When at length it becomes apparent that Will is not to be put off — that, whatever his real motives are with regard either to Kitty or to Jamie, he is ready to follow the family back to the South — Rita attempts as a last resort a divisive tactic, offering to employ Will as *her* agent, rather than old Vaught's, in charge of Jamie. According to her scheme, Will and Jamie are to stay in New York until another and radically new course of treatment for Jamie's illness is completed, and then take off together in the Trav-L-Aire on a trip to the Canadian wilderness, while Rita herself and Kitty depart for an extended sojourn in Europe.

It is hard to tell whether Rita ever imagines that this scenario will be realized, or whether she simply hopes that Barrett will feel so confused and put-upon that he will decide to check out altogether. But, when the plan for whatever reason does not work out—the family, including Rita, all depart together for the South, and Will eventually rejoins them in Virginia—Rita continues to do everything she can to frustrate him, including playing off his commitment to Jamie against his amorous interests. She is adroit and infinitely resourceful. If Kitty, in keeping with her age and sex, is not sure from one week or month to the next exactly what she wants to do, or be, with Jamie it is one day or hour to the next. Rita, except once when she is with Sutter (p. 246), remains amazingly cool through it all—heaving to, or running quietly with the wind, when she has to, then again subtly tacking for position at the turn.

In the end, it is all for naught. Will does finally go away in pursuit of the dying Jamie, leaving Kitty behind with the field clear for Rita to work on her as she can. And it seems most unlikely that he will keep his never very firm resolve to return to the job at the Chevrolet agency and wedded bliss in "Cap'n Andy's" house. But, for all that, Rita is defeated. For she is never permitted even to try making arrangements for the further medical treatment she has proposed for Jamie. And if anyone besides the engineer might be said to exercise crucial influence in the shaping of Jamie's state of mind at death, it is not Rita, of course, but Val. Sutter, to be sure, is not really in it either, at the very end. But for Rita there is no consolation in that. For it is plain that Sutter never expected or wanted to be involved beyond setting the stage for the final scene, and assisting with the cues and the movement of props. He would as soon think of setting the priest his lines, as he would of setting Jamie his. If there might be grounds for Rita to persuade herself that she and Sutter have fought to a standoff in their struggle over Jamie, she is still defeated. For the fact is that she has all along failed to identify her real antagonist, who is Val, not Sutter. If the engineer, for his part in the final scene, can be said to act, however passively, as "agent" for anyone, it is neither for Sutter nor for Rita, but for Val.

Just as Rita wastes her strength in the struggle with Sutter over Jamie, she wastes it also in the contest with Will over Kitty. Characteristically, and no doubt annoyingly to many readers, Percy has left his novel very much open-ended on several issues, including in this instance the outcome of the central love affair. There is no way to "prove" any view of what Will and Kitty will or will not do in the future.[6] But if I am right that Will does not seem really prepared to marry Kitty, the infirmity of his resolve has little or nothing to do with Rita's schemes and maneuverings. It has to do, rather, as I have already suggested, just with his gradually developing realization that Kitty is probably not a person he could manage to live with day in and day out. In the end, it seems likely that Will and Kitty will decide for themselves, without any deference to Rita's opinions, whether to marry or not to marry. If they should decide not to, the decision would in no way guarantee Kitty's further submission to Rita. For despite her continuing uncertainty about what "role" she is best suited for, Kitty has in the few weeks preceding Will's departure already begun to show distinct signs of developing a mind of her own. More and more often, if not always firmly, she has started to disagree with Rita—even on the crucial question of Sutter's character (p. 275)—and there is no reason to assume that her impulse to independence will not continue to strengthen, with or without Will's moral support.

Will makes the conventional assumption of young men in his situation, that the solution to his problems lies in a love affair—given his "gentlemanly" predilections, a love affair with a girl who can excite him sexually at the same time that she is equipped to satisfy his need to protect and defend. And it is not hard to see why, at least at first glance, Kitty would strike him as all but ideally suited to become the wife/sister of his dreams. As we have observed, he soon discovers various causes for misgiving. Besides her susceptibility to Rita's influence, and her taste in houses, the very fact of her having so much money is deeply troubling to Will, with his instincts of the provider and protector. But the really central question is not whether this particular girl will do, but whether Will's whole notion of what he needs to do, "marry him a wife and live him a life" — as if the two were necessarily identical — is essentially mistaken.

At any rate, when before the death of Jamie in Santa Fe Will tries one last time to get advice from reluctant guru Sutter, his concern is not with what Sutter, as Kitty's brother, might be able to judge of the prospects of this particular match, but with the doctor's opinion on the general desirability of such commitments. And Sutter's perfunctory approval is hardly calculated to alleviate Will's obvious anxiety.

Will has the feeling that Rita is somehow an unwitting agent of destiny when she leads him to the hospital in Washington Heights. But, even if we grant the possibility that he is right to assume the operation of fate in his affairs, there is a further question whether he has properly identified the member of the Vaught family who is most profoundly to influence his future.

Again, the conventional assumption would be that Will's interest in Jamie is a matter of secondary significance in the story of his pursuit of Kitty. Not that anyone would for a moment suspect the honorable engineer of taking deliberate advantage of the dying youth to ingratiate himself with the family, thus covertly advancing his amorous designs on the sister. But the curious thing is that Will's taking on the job as paid companion to Jamie seems motivated by an affection for the boy which is not only genuine but, if anything, more constant and compelling than his passion for Kitty.

Not, again and further, that anyone for *more* than a moment would suspect the engineer of irregular sexual impulses. Rita's veiled suggestion (p. 160) that Will undertake introducing Jamie to the joys of sleeping with girls is absurd for a number of reasons. If nothing else, Jamie's inescapable preoccupation with his illness is hardly likely to yield to thoughts, as Will might put it, of "wantonnesse." Further, quite apart from the fact that he is dying, and knows it, Jamie like Will is a *gentleman*: a gentleman not by habit and training, but by nature, by fundamental temperament. For anyone but a person like Rita, it would be impossible to imagine two such as these fine-grained young men indulging in the kind of camaraderie of prurience she envisages, even if they were not prospective brothers-in-law. Whatever either or both might do, in the way of sexual adventure, they would surely not do it together, and surely not talk about it, either before or after the fact. Finally, there is the distinct possibility, which neither Rita nor anyone else besides Sutter perhaps, and the sentient reader, is prepared to recognize, that Will himself is still a virgin—hardly in a position to preside over anyone's sexual initiation.

Whatever other dark secrets he might have to conceal, Will is not a homosexual, either active or latent. As his actual knee-jerk reactions repeatedly testify, it is girls, like Kitty, who turn him on, whether once aroused he is able to perform or not.

Yet, repeatedly, we get the impression that he has somewhat reluctantly to remind himself of his "almost blunted purpose" as Kitty's suitor. And, after all the confusion and indecision, when he finally takes off, without Kitty, in pursuit of Jamie and Sutter, he does so not only with no very firm confidence that he will be able to rejoin his elusive "fiancée," but with no conviction even that he wants to. The only thing that is reasonably certain all along is that he wants to, and will, "see it through" with Jamie. What he wants to do about Kitty is still in doubt at the very end. To be sure, he reiterates to Sutter his ostensibly firm *intentions* in the matter. But the very fact that he feels obliged to reiterate betrays his fundamental uncertainty. What he still wants, evidently in some sense must have, before he can act, and what he never gets, is some assurance of Sutter's genuine approval of his plans. The perfunctory assent Sutter continues to offer, all it would seem that he is prepared to offer, will not serve. Will wants and needs Sutter's prophetic "blessing" on the proposed union. Perhaps that is what he means to ask for as he bounds toward the waiting Edsel at the end. But, if so, there is no reason to assume that he will receive it.

IV. Where All the White and the Black Folks Meet: Will Goes Home

Actually, of course, as we have already noted but need to remind ourselves from time to time, the whole "love story" of Will and Kitty—indeed, the whole story of Will's involvement with the Vaughts—is not the whole of the novel, nor even its principal concern. For all the brilliantly devastating comedy of Percy's satire on "sweet mother psychoanalysis," poor Dr. Gamow's insight into the nature of Will's plight is never totally discredited. As Mr. Vaught at the hospital in New York presses his proposal that Will accompany the family when they go back home, the engineer begins to think "it mightn't be a bad idea to return to the South and discover his identity, to use Dr. Gamow's expression" (p. 79). Gamow's notion of what constitutes human "identity" is, no doubt, from Percy's point of view, woefully inadequate. And the methods of "discovery" the analyst has suggested over the five years of his work with Will seem only to have led the hapless engineer farther and farther down the garden path of alienation. But there is nothing wrong with the "expression" in itself, once we have removed it, as Will is about to remove himself, from the specifically psychoanalytic context. It hardly matters what descriptive phrase we choose—"quest for identity," perhaps, or "journey of self-discovery," would serve as well—so long as we recognize the fact that Will's primary purpose in undertaking the trip, back "home" to the South, and thence to Santa Fe, his primary purpose whether or not he himself always sees it as such, is to seek some insight into the order of his own existence. Alliances with others, actualized or in prospect, or rejections of such alliances, are important only as they assist or hinder him in his search for self-knowledge.

On first reading, the narrative of the engineer's adventures on the first stage of his journey south, between New York and Virginia, might seem designed just as a vehicle for some incidental satire that Percy wanted to work in on such American cultural phenomena of the fifties and sixties as "the Negro question" and the operations of "the higher journalism." The episodes might appear to be only flimsily connected to the "main plot," of Will's involvement with the Vaughts, as a series of distractions which test the strength of the hero's honorable resolve in his pursuit of the beloved. And, indeed, this section of the narrative—as well as the later account of Will's visits to Ithaca and Uncle Fannin's place—is a vehicle of satire, and does furnish the sort of tests indicated. But the satire is not merely incidental. And Will Barrett is tested on more, and more fundamental, issues than that of his devotion either to the fair Kitty or to Jamie.

Forney Aiken and friends, in their feckless championship of various "liberationist" causes, are immediately recognizable as soul siblings of Rita Vaught. Rita's manner and sensibilities retain, to be sure, curious vestiges of gentility. Under her toughness and swagger, her "gypsy" shrewdness, there lurks a piteous yearning to play the lady. A touching undertone of old-fashioned feminine romanticism sounds in her literary allusions. And there can be little doubt — although it would be for her a fate worse than death to be forced to admit it, and notwithstanding the fact her own behavior has encouraged Sutter — that what she cannot forgive Sutter in his sexual high jinks is the offense to her wifely modesty. Rita, in short, would be none too comfortable in the sweaty company of such as Mort Prince and the "pseudo-Negro." Nonetheless, in the larger philosophical perspective of Percy's "novel of the ultimate road" here, Forney's group and Rita are plainly fellow travelers, unwitting apostles of despair who out of the essential emptiness of their own lives go forth among the ignorant and oppressed as false prophets of enlightenment and progress. Rita, for the time being, is distracted by her preoccupation with the Vaughts' family problems; but the likeness of her sometime mission to the Indians and Forney's to the southern Negroes, "behind the cotton curtain," is readily apparent. The shibboleths of their conversation, the air of indulgent moral and intellectual superiority, the phony folksiness and companionability, the flawed structures of sociological doctrine grounded in a religion of sex, the quest for the epiphanic orgasm (see the description of Mort Prince's novel, p. 138), all are depressingly interchangeable. And to the progress of our hero in his true pilgrimage, the more or less conscious effort to re-enter the world of his personal past and the all but wholly intuitive quest for something beyond time in the New Mexico desert, Rita and the firkin-makers pose much the same kind of deceitfully seductive threat.

Although not without difficulty, especially in the matter of subduing his lust for Forney's daughter, Will escapes the evil enchantment of the farmhouse in Bucks County, of course, just as he is later to escape the spell of the purple castle on the golf links. He escapes with his virtue intact — the firkin he takes with him the perfect symbol of his indomitable innocence, something valued for its own solid, well-made, objective and particular material self, something in lieu of a suitcase to stow his gear in, not for its status as the phony folk-craft-revival product which Forney had vainly hoped to promote commercially. Will escapes, and when he encounters the bumbling band of missionaries again in Ithaca (pp. 305, 316ff.), he is doubly vindicated in helping them to escape the consequences of their own folly at the same time, and with the same blow, that he defends his own dignity. All this he achieves, without ever the slightest suggestion of malicious self-appreciation.

The disguise of the "pseudo-Negro" is so flimsy—the partial skin-blacking job with the easily discoverable white patch a little way up his sleeve, the unconvincing speech patterns, "for all the world like a shaky white man's" (p. 127)—that it is downright embarrassing. The wretched Aiken, planning to pose as a black insurance man in the South, has not even bothered to learn how his prospective pseudo-clients would expect him to pronounce the word "insurance." His venality and cowardice (the latter demonstrated no farther south than Levittown, when at the first threat of physical violence he is ready to show his white patch, pp. 146–47) are matched only by his pretentious ignorance. At this excruciating farce, one hardly knows whether to laugh or to cry. And the fact that the redoubtable engineer does neither is not much help.

But, to the extent that the entire affair can be taken at all seriously as a representation of real human behavior in what it must be admitted is this generally farcical period of our actual social history, it is important first that we properly identify the targets of Percy's satire, and second that we not lose sight of his extrasocial concerns in the novel as a whole.

As Luschei has pointed out, one of the most important things that Southern gentleman Barrett learns, or re-learns, in the course of his father-searching return to Ithaca, is the fact that communication between black and white in the South has been, not improved, but if anything impeded by the celebrated official advances in integrationist policy achieved since "Lawyer Ed" Barrett, one and only local champion in his time of Negro rights, pacified his mind in the attic room (p. 331) with a twelve-gauge. Yet, if the new Southerner (Will) does not know much about his black compatriots, the new Yankee (Forney) surely knows even less.

Sweet Evening Breeze, the reputedly gay Negro proprietor of the Dew Drop Inn in Ithaca, is to Will an authentic individual. Will does not, in his encounter with the cops (one of them a former high school football teammate), make Breeze in any sense a "cause" to defend. As soon as he enters the Dew Drop, "Beans" Ellis, the older policeman, routinely blackjacks Breeze (p. 324). With a punch to the head from behind, Will then lays Beans out cold. When the other cop protests, Will replies: "I know, but look at Breeze." In the way of signs of common human recognition, it might seem to Breeze (had he been awake to receive it) the most valuable of all just that Will's "explanation" is so succinct and casual.

But Breeze is not awake. It might well appear that the episode was designed to illustrate an all too familiar kind of Southern apologetics. When push comes to shove in defense of the poor black man against white police abuse, it is not the ignorant and essentially cowardly outlanders who can do him any good. The Negro's true and only effective champion is still the one he has always depended upon, the white Southern *gentleman*, at once uniquely sensitive and superbly strong, who "speaks the language" of both the oppressed and the oppressors, and who knows exactly when it is time to speak with words and when with his fists. So goes the thin and wearisome old tune.

But we would do well not to oversimplify. To repeat, Breeze is not awake to enjoy Beans's discomfiture; and there is little solace in thinking of what may happen when the two of them come back to consciousness, with Barrett no longer on the scene. Moreover, the knockout punch Will so gratifyingly delivers to the back of Beans's thick head is in the first place frankly an act of self-vindication. The engineer strikes in defense of the particular sanctity of his own private parts, after Beans has given him a painful finger-snap on the fly of his pants (p. 325). To the extent that Will's blow is also effective in championing Breeze's "civil rights," so to speak, our adventurer is only cooperating with history. He has not actively sought the opportunity. And neither here nor in other situations involving Negroes does he fancy himself a hero of social revolution.

Within the requirements of the comic mode in which this novel is conceived, Percy nowhere blinks the facts of the real social injustice and deprivation which Southern blacks have suffered. But for Will Barrett the fact that his suicide father was in a sense a martyr to the Negro cause has, if anything, made the engineer understandably wary of any "official," doctrinaire commitment.

Charming as it is in the main, the account (p. 337ff.) of Uncle Fannin's backwoods life with his faithful black companion, Merriam, is still a flawed idyll. The young dog Rock, for one, repeatedly peppered with birdshot for his blunders in the hunt, could hardly regard this as the best of all possible worlds. The self-consciousness of the two old men in the presence of the visitor, having to pretend that they do not ordinarily sit together while watching TV after supper, is cause but for most melancholy amusement. And the episode is not in any case, I think, meant to be representative of ordinary black-white relations in the modern South. It is, precisely, a "backwater" idyll, a rare and isolated instance of human brotherhood, outside the polluted mainstream of social history.

Earlier in Ithaca, when Will is sitting at night in front of the old house where he grew up, where his father left him for the last time with the false promise that he would return, a young Negro man strolling along the sidewalk catches sight of him in the shadows and pauses for a moment.

> They looked at each other. There was nothing to say. Their fathers would have had much to say . . . But the sons had nothing to say. The engineer looked at the other . . . [thinking] you may be in a fix and I know that but what you don't know and won't believe and must find out for yourself is that I'm in a fix too and you got to get where I am before you even know what I'm talking about and I know that and that's why there is nothing to say now. Meanwhile I wish you well. (pp. 332–33)

There is little reason to doubt that hero, narrator, and author are all pretty much of one mind here. And, as Luschei has suggested, what the passage seems to be saying is that the civil rights revolution, if its primary purpose was to foster black-white communication, has failed. Will may or may not be right about the essential differences between the "fixes" blacks and whites are in, and about the limitations of the black's understanding in such matters of cultural history, but the main point is clear. Through Will, Percy is saying that young whites and blacks—not just Will and this particular black, but probably all young whites and blacks in the South, if not in the entire United States—have even less to say to each other now, since the official establishment of integrationist policy, than their fathers had to say before. Yet, this is still not to say that Will (or Percy) endorses segregation. To say that any revolution has failed, even that it has in some or all respects worsened the situation it was meant to correct, is not, at least necessarily, to say that it should never have been attempted.

Whatever else may or may not be wrong with Will Barrett's or Walker Percy's thinking about the history of black-white relations in the South, there is no grounds here for inferring that either Barrett or Percy would want to see blacks sent to the back of the bus again. We may, I think, take Will's "meanwhile I wish you well" at good face value.

On the other hand—"meanwhile"—it is most important that we not miss the novelist's design to transcend *all* social issues, the racial one most troublesomely included. For a time Will is inclined to think, and the reader with him, that his mission on the journey from New York, besides running Kitty to earth, is to come to terms with "the changing South." He has thought to "return to the South and discover his identity" (p. 79). But the trouble is that the South he comes back to—except geographically, which is itself a pretty chancy business in an age of such mighty technology as ours—is not the South he left, so that he cannot really "return" to it. The change involves much more than race relations. "The South he came home to . . . was happy, victorious, Christian, rich, patriotic and Republican" (p. 185). Especially, it is the *happiness* that baffles him:

> He had felt good in the North because everyone else felt so bad. True, there was a happiness in the North. That is to say, nearly everyone would have denied that he was unhappy. But . . . they were solitary and shut-off to themselves and he, the engineer, had got used to living among them. . . . And his own happiness had come from being onto the unhappiness beneath their happiness. It was possible for him to be at home in the North because the North was homeless. (pp. 185–86)

But the happiness of the new South is much more difficult to accommodate:

> It defied you to call it anything else. Everyone was in fact happy. The women were beautiful and charming. The men were healthy and

successful and funny; they knew how to tell stories. They had every-thing the North had and more. They had a history, they had a place redolent with memories, they had good conversation, they believed in God and defended the Constitution, and they were getting rich in the bargain. They had the best of victory and defeat. (p. 186)

The new Southerners are happy, and they are "at home," in a way that does not relieve but only intensifies the pain of exile Will has felt in the North. "There are many things worse than being homeless in a homeless place," the narrator comments (p. 186). "For example, it is much worse to be homeless and then to go home where everyone is at home and then still be homeless."

Percy's account of recent U.S. social history is obviously not meant to be taken quite literally. The mumbling prose of the last sentence I have quoted, if nothing else, is hardly excusable except on the assumption that the narrator is speaking tongue-in-cheek. Will's vision is inevitably clouded by his personal needs and desires. The reader, on the other hand, is expected to understand that the hap-piness of the new Southerners, their confident "at homeness," is actually quite as superficial as the pathetic pretensions of the North-erners. And, in fact, well before he takes off for New Mexico, Will himself is beginning to "get onto" the essential *malaise* of the South as acutely as ever he tuned into the secret despair of the North. But whereas in the North, no doubt because he never expected too much in the first place, his understanding at least for a time made some kind of workable accommodation possible (the room at the YMCA, the underground job at Macy's), back in the South, where he sup-posedly "belongs," the more he knows the more hopeless his situa-tion becomes.

For as long as he was in the North he could always entertain, at some level of consciousness, the idea of returning to the South. But once he actually has returned, and the truth begins to emerge, that the South too *is* unhappy, with an unhappiness perhaps not essentially unlike that of the North but only the worse for the new Southerners' naiveté, their still hardier, more aggressive capacity for self-deception—the truth that, whatever else it may be, the new South is most grimly and assuredly "no place like home"—there is, then, simply no place left for Will to go.

The South as a whole has changed, but changed in a way, Percy obviously means to suggest, that at least as early as World War II it would not too severely have taxed the powers of any competent social historian to predict. Moreover, the changes are at least as much the consequence of indigenous processes, traceable as far back in the regional history as the Civil War and beyond, as they are the result of recent external pressures. There is, after all, something peculiarly Southern even in the quality of the local unhappiness that Will observes. The Reb-colonel hats and canes of Poppy Vaught's unproductive Chevrolet salesmen (pp. 261–64) may be altogether spurious symbols of regional identity, something as like as not generated in a Madison Avenue advertising agency. And the customer who gets away, the "I'll be back" type, is not unknown in the showrooms of Cicero and Hartford and Tucumcari. But in the case of poor Poppy's generally feckless staff, these unaccountably "mis'able" colonels who can never "close," who are letting virtually all the customers get away, it seems unlikely that anyone except some reincarnation of General Lee would be prepared to define the exact cause of the spiritual malady that afflicts them, not to speak of a possible remedy.

And in Will's more particular South, back in his hometown of Ithaca, a few things remain rather eerily unchanged. There are the two old friends who meet him in the bank (p. 310ff.), Spicer CoCo and Ben Huger, acting for all the world as if it had been at the most a few months rather than five years since they last saw him; the loose board in the fence through which he escapes after the episode in Breeze's cafe, everything exactly as he remembers it from his boyhood (p. 326), down to Miss Mamie Billups calling to him from her porch; the black servant D'Lo looking up from her grits and batter boilers to greet him with perfunctory surprise as he enters the kitchen of the old family house (p. 334). But all these things, things that are merely *not yet* changed, are only enough to guide him finally to the one thing which, having once changed, some five years before, he must now realize is beyond all further change.

The shotgun with which his father took his own life lies in the attic room (pp. 333–34) untouched, not even cleaned, powder grains from the last charge still visible in the barrel. "The South," including even Ithaca still a going concern, all things and all places still within the control of the living, having changed many times before, can be expected to change again—perhaps, even if not necessarily, change for the better. But, for better or worse, Will's father has no further say in the matter. The change he effected in himself is beyond repair.

Try as Will may and must—sitting outside the old house in the darkness, with his hand on the tiny iron horsehead embedded in the tree, hearing again in his mind's ear the old "victorious music" of Brahms on the old 78s while the sounds of the TV giveaway program his aunts are watching on the porch drift out upon the present and palpable air, saying again with his mind's voice *Wait*, and again *Wait* (p. 332)—he cannot call his father back to answer, to explain. The old man, being dead, is literally irrevocable.

Will had said to him, as his father started to walk away in the darkness toward the street corner (p. 331): "*Don't leave.*" And his father had said: "I'm not leaving, son." And, indeed, he did return to the steps for a moment, and put his hand on his son's shoulder—but without saying a word, and turned then again, and entered the house for the last time. Clearly, although Will does not at this point put it to himself in so many words, the suicide might be regarded as a deliberate betrayal—the least forgivable of all human betrayals. The fact that Will does not permit himself openly to define it as such, that he so clearly wants to forgive, wants to understand in order to forgive—wants to give his dead father the benefit of any possibly discernible doubt, ambiguity, in the remembered exchange ("*Don't leave.*" "I'm not leaving, son.")—surely endears the anguished engineer to the reader as nothing else could.

But however all that may be—the moral situation is at best, like most or all human situations, ambiguous—the fact of ultimate importance is just that the father is now dead, unanswerable to any of the living, even to his son. At least in this novel, as Will himself seems obscurely to recognize, there is nothing further to be learned in one-way "dialogue" with the dead. If the "father search"[7] is to continue, as it does and must—for if the dead father is "irrevocable" in the literal sense that he cannot be called back again, he is also uncancelable, unerasable from the memory, unsatisfiable as the creditor of all our debts both contracted and applied-for—Will must from this point be content to deal with surrogates.

In New York he was, with the purchase of the telescope, "cut adrift from Dr. Gamow, a father of sorts" (p. 41). Now, beyond Poppy Vaught, with whom as dubious representative of the new and future South Will has already entered upon tentative, preliminary negotiations, there is Uncle Fannin, last co-beneficiary of the engineer's dubious "inheritance." But in the final stage of his quest, which essentially begins with his flight aboard the collapsible boat that he finds in the same attic room where his father's shotgun is stored (p. 334), Will departs the South altogether.

Martin Luschei has commented at some length on the frequent allusions in this novel to Twain's *The Adventures of Huckleberry Finn*, noting chiefly the Trav-L-Aire as updated, landborne version of the famous raft (p. 142). In mathematical and Kierkegaardian terms borrowed in part from Percy's essay "The Man on the Train," Luschei accounts for Will's brief trip aboard the actual watercraft as "Huck Finn raised to the second power, in a sense, a rotation within a rotation, since the Trav-L-Aire is the original raft." Actually, no very exact parallels are discoverable anywhere in the pattern of allusion. If, for example, the Trav-L-Aire is readily identifiable with the raft, the occupants of the two craft are quite another matter. Luschei appears to see Will as consistently resembling Huck. But in his relationship to Jamie, first but not solely with regard to their respective ages, Will can be quite as plausibly identified with Nigger Jim as with Huck. And the situation is further complicated by the elusive "pseudo-Negro" of *The Last Gentleman*, with what might be called his pseudo-raft, the old Chevrolet.[8] At one time and another, Forney Aiken vaguely resembles a half dozen different characters in Twain's novel.

So long as we keep it firmly in mind that our first concern is with the intrinsic order of character and event in Percy's novel, not with the question of how consistent or inconsistent that order is with any supposed "model" furnished by Twain, it may be helpful now and again to recall Huck's adventures as we follow Will's. But the temptation to rigidify parallels must be sternly resisted. Will Barrett's boat, the "English contraption of silvery zeppelin fabric with varnished spruce spars" (p. 334), which except that it is designed to move over water no more closely resembles the crudely sturdy affair put together by Huck and Jim than it does the Trav-L-Aire itself, is plainly a vessel of merely temporary symbolic expedience, as readily "collapsible," precisely, as Percy apparently wants the reader to find all his allusions to Twain. For Percy's central concern with the identity theme, and the related motifs of disguise and play-acting, Twain's book is at least one of the major sources. Huck and Will have a lot in common, including a love of travel, truth, and freedom, an innocence and generosity of spirit that makes them prey to exploitation by rascals of varied stripe, and much trouble with fathers and Negroes. But, except for being an outdoorsman, and giving his son a bad time, old Ed Barrett surely bears little resemblance to "Pap" Finn. Especially with reference to the father search, and the involvement of that with racial issues, the critical method and vocabulary required to deal with Twain's novel are very different from those we need for Percy's.

Although it would appear that Will's father was a man capable of compassion, certainly, one who had an instinct of brotherhood, an ability simply to "talk to" blacks on the basis of an unforced assumption of shared humanity, there is nothing to suggest that such sympathies provided the primary motive for his championship of the Negro cause.[9] Nothing we are told of him would indicate that he had any really passionate need and desire to see the wrongs of the past righted, the oppressed race granted their fair share of the world's goods. As for admitting the blacks to full participation in the glorious benefits of American civilization, it is quite clear that he had in the first place so little regard for the accomplishments of that civilization, so little joy in his own participation, that he could hardly have seen it as any great favor to the blacks simply to put them on an equal footing with whites as citizens. Nor is there the slightest evidence, on the other hand, that he subscribed to any newfangled notions of the blacks' African heritage as qualifying them for a uniquely valuable contribution to the development of American culture.

He was a brave man, perhaps in a measure vain of his courage. The sheer danger of his defiance of the Klan obviously had its appeal. But that, too, is not quite the whole story. He loved danger, and what finally provoked him to suicide—what he recognized as final and irrevocable defeat rather than victory—was his enemies' refusal to fight. His melancholy conviction that the reason they would not fight, did not have to fight any longer, was that the "they" of the old dispensation, "the fornicators and the bribers and the takers of bribes" (p. 330), had in the new age become indistinguishable from the "we"—the conviction, in effect, that he stood alone, with no morally creditable allies—does not essentially affect the issue of courage. So long as he could identify the enemy, it is clear, he was not afraid of being alone.

The "trouble," finally, with the elder Barrett's heroic posture—its flaw, that is, from the viewpoint of latter-day purist apologetics in the cause of racial equality—is not that it was either false or indiscriminately reckless bravado. The courage was real, and the enemy, at least in theory, carefully chosen. The trouble, rather, was just that he acted more out of hatred and contempt for the enemy than out of love or respect for those he defended (p. 237)—and, perhaps most important of all, that the grounds for the contempt were inappropriately defined. It is significant that, in the moment of his final despair, Will's father did not speak at all of racial conflict, but of fornication and bribery.

Such as these, to him, were the ultimate social sins, the crimes with which men *dishonored* themselves. He would have no truck with anyone, any white man, who willingly dishonored himself, no matter what his stand on the racial issue. And since it appeared to him that no one in his time was guiltless—that the only reliable basis for white championship of Negro rights was the principle of *noblesse oblige*, and that in those degenerate times one could no longer distinguish the nobility from the canaille—there was to his stoic mind no way out but suicide.

Now, of course, from the standpoint of our present splendid enlightenment, it is easy to see the imperfection of old Ed Barrett's vision in matters of social morality. And, implicitly, Percy excuses that imperfection as an effect of history. If Ed Barrett died leaving his son ill equipped to deal with the complexities of race relations in the South of the post–World War II era—with, for example, the emergence of a whole new class of invading troublemakers, intellectual carpetbaggers, such as Forney Aiken and his fellow "faithless pilgrims," who have nothing whatever in common with any of the native parties, white or black—it is equally apparent that Ed, in his earlier turn, had been similarly deprived. The principles of personal honor which he found inapplicable to the new alignment of forces in his own time, and his romantic nostalgia for a lost "golden age" of heroic virtue, were in large part only the notions which he had inherited from *his* father.

But these are the commonplace holdings and deprivations of mankind, of fathers and sons from generation to generation. And Will Barrett is about as sensibly disposed as any of us is to accept them as such. Will thinks (p. 332), "I think he was wrong and that he was looking in the wrong place. No, not he but the times. The times were wrong and one looked in the wrong place." But then he realizes that he too is "looking in the wrong place"—that the question of whether his father's ideas about honor and social justice were right or wrong has nothing to do with his, the son's, anguish in the memory of the suicide. Will's peculiar pain is in his sense of *personal* betrayal.

His complaint is not that his father died leaving him with a set of principles and ideas inadequate for the future. Everyone's father does that. But Will's father died by his own hand, died willingly and deliberately before his time, died depriving his son not of any "rightful inheritance," material or intellectual, but of *himself*—died so, moreover, in defiance of the son's direct and loving appeal to him to stay. "*Wait*," Will had said. "*Don't leave.*" But not only did his father leave, he left deliberately lying—left saying "I'm not leaving, son."

But did he? After saying "I'm not leaving, son," he in fact returned to the steps for a moment. Had he, strictly speaking, in that moment kept his earlier promise? And Will did not, after all, at any rate audibly, appeal to him again before he entered the house.

It is difficult to imagine anything much harder to live with than the memory of a father who could prate of "honor" right up to the end, and still go to his death lying about his intentions. In such a situation, the son's pain in the loss of filial respect and affection is exceeded, perhaps, only by the damage to his self-esteem. How worthless he must be, if the strongest appeal he could make to his father, out of his simple love and need, could yet be refused. But worse still, so terrible that he never quite consciously contemplates it, is the implicit burden of *guilt* in Will's recollections. He did not, when his father returned for a moment to the steps, renew his appeal, did not say again: "Wait. Don't leave." Who, in the end, betrayed whom? Throughout the account of Will's recollections here, the narrator refers to him as "the boy." But we may well see this as reflecting Will's own desire to make excuses for himself. For he was at the time of his father's suicide at least nineteen or twenty years old, hardly any longer a "boy" in the sense that he could not have been expected at all to understand his father's plight and to take some responsibility for trying to help him.[10]

In any event, once the horrors of that night are even partly revealed—at a point more than three-fourths of the way through the novel—we can only wonder that Will has managed to reach the age of twenty-five[11] with no worse afflictions than the continuing manifestations of what he quaintly calls his "nervous condition": fugues and nose-swellings, kneejerks, compulsive buying habits and all.

Just before the laughter of the studio audience in the TV giveaway program his aunts are watching distracts him from his meditations, and the young black man walks into view under the streetlight (p. 332), Will seems to be on the verge of some further, perhaps crucial breakthrough in his effort to understand his father's actions and their effect upon him. But, if promised at all, the revelation must be deferred. "Wait," Will keeps saying, "wait"—to his father's ghost, who will not, and to himself, in his baffled eagerness. The word is also the author's word, to the impatient reader.

In the episodes of his visit to Ithaca, the phase of Will's active concern with "the Negro question"—at no time a matter of really obsessive interest for him—is effectively closed. As we have briefly observed, his short stay with Uncle Fannin and Merriam, near the town in Louisiana appropriately named Shut Off, yields no insights relevant to the problems of the outer world, unless we are to count the two old men's common citizenship with Will's aunts in the "global village" of TV. Once Will has made arrangements, by telephone, to get Forney and friends out of jail and on the bus to Memphis (p. 347)—"free, clear of danger, but free and clear of him too"—we are to hear little more of Negroes, real or pseudo.

Indeed, we hear little more of "the South" in general beyond this point. Only a few days before, back at the Vaughts' place reading Freeman's book on Robert E. Lee (pp. 225–26), the engineer had still been doing his best to change the course of the Civil War: "moving his shoulder in the old body-English of correcting the hor-

rific Confederate foul-ups, in this case the foul-up before Sharpsburg when Lee's battle orders had been found by a Union sergeant,
the paper wrapped around three cigars and lying in a ditch in Mary-
land. I'll pick it up before he gets there, thought the engineer[,] and
stooped slightly."

By the time he reads the inscription on the Union monument in
Santa Fe (p. 358)—"To the heroes of the Federal Army who fell at
the Battle of Valverde fought with Rebels   February 21, 1862"—
all has changed. He is ready to accept history. "Strangely, there
occurred no stirring within him, no body English toward the reversing of that evil day at Valverde. . . . he felt only the cold."

As we have further noted, his courtship of Kitty, if not altogether
abandoned, proceeds with ever diminishing ardor. It is certainly to
Will's moral credit that in the midst of all the confusions of his visit
to Ithaca he had the courage and good sense to notify Poppy Vaught
of the loss of Kitty's $100,000 check. But there can be little doubt
that, having concluded his business at the bank and with Uncle
Fannin to assure himself once more of independent means, Will is
more than happy to be rid of the compromising "dowry." From
time to time, when he has a moment's leisure away from his other
more pressing concerns on the trip to Santa Fe, he earnestly assures
himself, and Sutter, that he fully intends to marry Kitty. But all too
plainly, no matter whether Sutter is present or not, it is *only* himself
that he is trying to convince.

V. Reunion in the Desert

Beyond Shut Off, only the father search, more and more clearly theological in its ultimate implications, continues unabated. Although
he dreams of him again in exhausted sleep in the Trav-L-Aire, parked
at a truckstop in Longview, Texas (pp. 347–48), Will's memories
of his natural father yield no further enlightenment. The surrogate
of last resort is Sutter Vaught.

Again as in *The Moviegoer*, there are covert but persistent hints
at the workings of a benign Providence in the events of this novel.
Even those people who in the course of Will's pilgrimage first appear
to him in the guise of Deceivers or Tempters, like Forney Aiken and
Rita Vaught, seem strangely compelled—often by the very way of

their best efforts to distract him—only to lead the hero at last back to the path of salvation. Only Valerie Vaught, perhaps, "Sister Val," is immediately recognizable (to the reader, that is, not to Will) as fully accredited Guide, appointed Helper. But, among the male characters, consciously if not willingly—wrongheaded even in his consciousness, but never with malign intent—it is Sutter who enjoys the dubious distinction of seeming chosen both by Providence and by our muddleheaded hero.

It may be that Sutter was merely careless in leaving the marked Esso map and the notebook at his apartment. And, no doubt, the engineer could have found his way—first to Val's mission and then to Santa Fe—by some other means. Sutter insists (p. 380) that the notebook, which has greatly impressed Will, is of no importance; "crap, excreta," he calls it, something he had merely "written to be rid of it." But the facts are, no matter why, that Sutter did leave the two documents, and that Will has chosen to use them in charting his course.

Will is consistently wary of Val. In his very first meeting with her, he had felt annoyed and put off by her presumption in attempting to make him promise (p. 210) that he would see to it Jamie was informed of "the economy of salvation" before death. And the trip to the mission has done little or nothing to relieve his uneasiness. As always scrupulously polite, in accepting her invitation to take the "ten-dollar tour" of the facilities, but anxious only to be on his way once he has learned that Sutter and Jamie have departed for New Mexico, Will has felt if anything only the more irritated by the "prankish perverse manner" (p. 297) of her religiousness. But, notwithstanding whatever sympathy we might have for Will, at first glance, in his fastidious reaction to this grubbily arrogant nun and her equally deplorable Southern chicken hawk—the latter shabby specimen an altogether depressing, contrary reminder of the glorious falcon in Central Park—readers at all well-versed in the conventions of modern Catholic fiction (Graham Greene, Flannery O'Connor, et al.) will soon have recognized both woman and bedraggled bird as truest emissaries of the divine. Val does indeed, as he suspects (p. 302), "have her hooks out" for Will. She does not, at the mission, mention the matter of Jamie's salvation again. But it should come as no surprise either that when Will telephones her from Santa

Fe (pp. 390–93) she explicitly "charges" him to see that Jamie is baptized before death, or that despite his resentments he ends up doing as she wishes. Will thinks: "To the devil with this exotic pair, Sutter and Val, the absentee experts who would deputize him, one to practice medicine, the other to practice priestcraft. Charge him indeed. Who were they to charge anybody?" (p. 393).

Who indeed? But charge him they do, and he performs. Sutter goes back to "work" at the dude ranch for grass widows, leaving Will with only a few hasty instructions on how to tell when Jamie is about to die. But, when the time comes, it turns out as Sutter presumably anticipated, that all the engineer really needs, in addition to the benefit of his peculiar "radar," is a modicum of common sense. And Val has only to threaten him with the duty of performing the baptismal rite himself, in order to be certain that he will find a priest.[12]

Valerie, of course, at least for the time being, is interested in Will primarily on Jamie's account. Obviously, she has her own "radar," by which she has identified the gentlemanly engineer as one who can—and will, when the time comes—probably do more than she herself could do to see that Jamie is prepared for death. If she has any notion of "getting her hooks into" Will for the sake of his own soul, we may assume that she is shrewd enough to know she must be patient, that *his* time has not yet come.

And Will and Sutter, however passionately they may be otherwise involved, both in sympathy and in hostility, with each other and with Val, are entirely cooperative in deferring concern for their own affairs until Jamie's death is accomplished. Sutter may or may not, after that, be going back to the dude ranch to corral one more "grass widow" before he blows his brains out; Will may or may not be going back to marry Kitty and take charge of Poppy's mis'able colonels at the Chevrolet agency—perhaps preparatory to blowing *his* brains out. For a few days, both yield center stage to Jamie.

There is no reason to suppose that Sutter was saying either more or less than he meant when he confided to his notebook (p. 373) his concern for Jamie, that the boy should have the chance to "know what he was doing" when he died, instead of being "eased out in an oxygen tent, tranquilized and with no sweat to anyone." And if in a sense "mixed"—in that he feels bound to Jamie both by personal affection and by the responsibilities of his position as hired companion—the engineer's motives for tracking the brothers down would seem to be at least as selfless as Sutter's are. Neither Will nor Sutter deliberately attempts to set Jamie his lines in the death scene. Both, in the dialogue, serve the dying boy merely as respondents and interpreters.

On the other hand, it is still Barrett, of course, who is the hero of the novel; and Jamie's death is primarily significant for the way it affects Will's attitude in his final dealings with Sutter. Repeatedly, there are hints that the "business" which has drawn Will to Santa Fe, even if he cannot precisely define it, is something beyond discharging his final responsibility to Jamie. As he has put the matter to Kitty, by long-distance telephone from Dallas (p. 351), his immediate purpose in the journey has been "to find, ah, Jamie." But the distracted and uncertain "ah" is a clear indication that he has something, or someone, on his mind besides Jamie.

The reasons for Will's fixation on Sutter Vaught are not altogether clear either to the engineer or to the derelict physician. In part, no doubt, the attraction is what Sutter's exasperated remarks (p. 381) obliquely suggest: the simple fascination that the older man's example, of a kind of positively *dedicated* social irresponsibility, of failure elevated to the status of *Weltanschauung*, inevitably holds for the confused and inarticulate younger "dropout," with his desperate need of some intellectually responsible way at least to account for, if not to justify, his own persistent fecklessness.

Notwithstanding the naive and touching embarrassment he shows whenever the subject of sex comes up, Will is also fascinated by Sutter's heroic prowess with women. The poor engineer solemnly confesses his having long suffered "a consuming desire for girls, for the coarsest possible relations with them, without knowing how to treat them as human beings" (p. 385). But the pathetic fact is that the entire novel offers no certain evidence that Barrett has enjoyed actual satisfaction even of his purely carnal desires, not to speak of his vague yearning to know the "girls" as "human beings." Sutter, on the other hand, even if we make allowances for probable exaggeration in both his own and Rita's stories, has almost certainly "known" a goodly number of women—women, not girls—at least in body. And at least one woman, Rita herself, to the extent that she qualifies as a real "human being," he has known in that way as well. On these grounds alone, it is no great wonder that Will has chosen Dr. Vaught as guru, "pissant wise man" (p. 381), whom he will continue doggedly to follow despite all that Sutter can do to discourage him.

But the attraction is still more deeply rooted in Will's continuing and all-consuming need to overcome the effects of his father's suicide. It is not difficult to guess why Will has failed to tell Sutter about that event; apparently, he never told Dr. Gamow either. In the account of his private reflections, indeed, there is no indication that Will himself has consciously recognized what is unquestionably the most important of all his motives in his desperate pursuit of Sutter. But, for the reader, the fact of Will's obvious repressions only underscores the significance of the terms in which he addresses his final appeal to Sutter.

" 'Wait,' he shouted in a dead run." (p. 409) And, just in case anyone could possibly miss the point, the word is repeated in the last line of the novel. "The Edsel *waited* for him" (emphasis added).

The echo of Ithaca is clear.[13] Once again, Will calls out to his "father," asking him to "wait," imploring him not to abandon him, not to die. Dr. Vaught and the defunct lawyer Barrett have a good many things in common, including, of course, the credentials of their two traditionally authoritative professions, which help to account for Will's choice of Sutter as father surrogate. But the one essential likeness is their suicidal disposition. In Will's melancholy experience, the father *is* the self-destroyer.

But experience is one thing, need another. Will's continuing need is—true to his name, his unrelenting *will* is—that the old image of the father be altered. He needs, wants, is determined that he will find, in Sutter, the father who chooses not to die but to live. The question is, of course, whether he will prevail. The key word is the same: "wait." Beyond the circumstantial particulars of time and place, and the choice of weapons—Ed Barrett's Greener twelve-gauge, Sutter's Colt .45—is there any compelling reason for us to view the final episode in Santa Fe as anything more than Will's compulsive reenactment, mere restaging, so to speak, of the original scene in Ithaca?

Sutter does wait, to be sure; Ed Barrett did not. Or at any rate—

it is essential that we speak precisely in these matters—Sutter's car waits. Perhaps the dubious vehicle—the Edsel, the "fake Ford" [14]—can safely be regarded as only, in McLuhanese, an "extension" of the driver, waiting at his bidding. Perhaps in "the Edsel waited . . ." Percy is simply employing a species of metonymy, container-for-the-thing-contained. In any case, the general effect is surely to raise serious doubts about the reliability of Sutter's final intentions. He waits. But for how long? Everything depends, presumably, upon what it is that Barrett may find to say next, once his "great joyous ten-foot antelope bounds" have carried him again to the car.

Nothing, in short, can be definitely concluded simply on the evidence of Sutter's stopping the car. On the other hand, it is not as if nothing had been said or done earlier which might lead us to anticipate his stopping. Until now, we have noted almost exclusively the evidence of *Will's* need. But in the dialogue that immediately precedes the final action—Will's last call of "wait," the car's stopping, his running after it—it is hard to say which of the two men is the more reluctant to break away.

Earlier at the dude ranch, at their last private interview before Jamie's death, Sutter has stated his intentions pretty clearly (p. 389), saying that "if [he does] outlive Jamie it will not be by more than two hours." The effect is slightly blurred, perhaps, by the rhetorical questions that follow: "What in Christ's name do you think I'm doing out here? Do you think I'm staying? Do you think I'm going back?" But it seems reasonable to assume that he means he is going to kill himself as soon as possible after Jamie dies. That, presumably, is what it so "astonishes" the engineer to hear. And the narrator's concluding remarks on the episode might briefly tempt us to suppose that from this point forward neither Will himself nor we the readers are to be troubled with any further doubts concerning his fate: "Perhaps this moment more than any other, the moment of his first astonishment, marked the beginning for the engineer of what is called a normal life. From that time forward it was possible to meet him and after a few minutes form a clear notion of what sort of fellow he was and how he would spend the rest of his life" (p. 389).

But if we are tempted to accept at face value this enthusiastic evaluation of the therapeutic effect of Will's "astonishment," we had better remind ourselves of the fact that third-person narrators are as notoriously "unreliable" as first-person narrators. By the time we get to Will's final encounter with Sutter, following Jamie's death, the engineer's words and behavior again raise serious doubts concerning his own future, not to speak of the doctor's. Indeed, it remains highly questionable whether we ever *can*, in a critically responsible fashion, consider the two separately. To repeat, neither of the two characters makes a really convincing show of wanting to separate.

Presumably harking back to their last previous interview, Will asks (pp. 407–8) *which* ranch it is where Sutter means to keep his "date"—the dude ranch, where the grass widows are, or Sutter's own place, Rancho la Merced—and, when he learns it is the latter, apparently assumes that the assignation is with death, not with a woman, and begs Sutter not to go. Again, on the surface, Will is doing all the urging. But the curious thing is that once they have got to the point of Will's trying to involve Sutter in the "arrangements" for Jamie's funeral, and, when Sutter declines, countering that with his own refusal to accept the money that Sutter offers—suddenly the shoe is on the other foot. Suddenly, it is Will who "backs away," and Sutter who has to ask: "Anything else?"

Surely here, if not long before, it becomes clear that Sutter is *at least* as much in need of Will's help as Will is of Sutter's. Condescend as he must to the poor engineer, being as self-ruined physician self-condemned to the role of supreme ironist—"You kill me, Barrett"—Sutter is yet, and all the while, begging Will to tell him something ("anything else") that might give him a reason for living beyond Jamie's end.

Notwithstanding his denials that the entries in the casebook were written for Val or Will or anyone in particular, there can be little doubt that Sutter quite deliberately left the book as well as the map in his apartment in Alabama, for Will to find. When he says (p. 360) "I didn't forget it," he *could* mean that he simply abandoned it. But the statement could at least as plausibly be interpreted as an admission that he left the book as a clue. We have abundant evidence that he had "been expecting" Barrett long before the telephone conversation with Kitty which he mentions (p. 360), and it makes sense on a variety of grounds that he should want Will to study the casebook before arriving in Santa Fe.

There is one all-important difference between Ed Barrett and

Sutter Vaught in the matter of suicide. Sutter is willing to talk about it. In direct conversation with Will as well as in the casebook entries, he makes no effort to conceal the fact either of his previous attempt or of his intention to try it again. It is impossible to imagine the intellectually arrogant and fastidious Sutter's ever dialing a "Crisis Hotline" number. But the casebook, the marked roadmap, his irritating and embarrassingly childish games with the loaded pistol, his final question to Will—"Anything else?"—all add up to what any competent Sunday Supplement psychologist would recognize as a "cry for help."

Ed Barrett emitted such a cry too, of course, but a very faint one: far too faint for his confused and inexperienced son to identify with any certainty, what with civil rights and the majestic noise of Brahms and all. But Will is a little older and more sophisticated now, and has survived various uproars with unimpaired hearing in one ear at least—surely sufficient equipment to pick up the blatant signals that Sutter is broadcasting.

"Selfish" as he may be (p. 386), the engineer, once he is past the distractions of Jamie's final illness, can hardly continue for long to miss the truth that the last thing Sutter really wants is that Will should (p. 382) "be done with [him]." By the time Sutter starts back to the ranch—presumably his own ranch, La Merced, to keep his ultimate "date"—he has already done all he can for Will. It takes a little time, naturally, for Barrett to get used to the idea, but in their brief conversation (p. 407) concerning Jamie's deathbed encounter with the priest, Sutter has quietly but irrevocably liberated Will—or goaded him into liberating himself—from the degrading intellectual and emotional dependence (or deference) which had earlier made it impossible for him to command the sardonic doctor's full sympathy.

> "What happened back there?" [Will asked].
> "In the hospital room? You were there."
> "I know, but what did you think? I could tell you were thinking something."
> "Do you have to know what I think before you know what you think?"
> "That does not mean that I would necessarily agree with you," said the engineer, trying to see Sutter's expression. Suddenly the

engineer felt his face flush. "No, you're right. I don't need to know what you think. . . ."

After that exchange, the two men are on a new footing. Will can still say "wait," "wait." He can still say, with all conventional deference in the use of the title:

"Dr. Vaught, I need you. I, Will Barrett—" and he actually pointed to himself lest there be a mistake, "need you and want you to come back. I need you more than Jamie needed you. Jamie had Val too." (p. 409)

Sutter, true to form, can still respond with sardonic humor, "You kill me, Barrett." But in the next breath he adds, "I'll think about it." And the reason he is willing to "think about it" (whatever "it" may be precisely) is pretty clearly just that he now knows that when the engineer says "I, Will Barrett" the speaker has at last begun to identify himself. Barrett finally has some idea who he is. That in itself lends a new authority to anything he may have to say, or ask.

Sutter has done all he can do for Will. Now, in the end, it is Will's turn. Doctor and patient seem to be reversing roles. Sutter waits, perhaps, for Will to tell *him* what to do. Perhaps. As most critics have agreed, the ending of the novel is "ambiguous." Nothing can be asserted with absolute certainty, except that the end *is* the end. Strictly speaking, fictional characters have no future. If any of them "lives" beyond the last page, it is wholly within the imagination of the reader, without further guidance from the author. But, imagining the two men with whom I have become acquainted in the novel to be real persons, and choosing among possible and more and less probable courses of action for them in the future, it seems to me a good deal more likely that Will might come to some understanding with Sutter—an understanding that could at least keep them both alive for a while longer, whether in New Mexico, Alabama, or elsewhere, severally or together—than that the engineer could return to wedded bliss, "in a cottage small by a waterfall," with Kitty. Will keeps compulsively-conventionally talking about it, to be sure; but the theme of conjugal love is simply of no real importance in the novel's ending. The epigraph quotation from Guardini, with its reference to "that love which flows from one lonely person to another . . . ," has been all along much more clearly relevant to the relationship between Will and Jamie than to Will's and Kitty's fantasies about each other; beyond Jamie's death, it is relevant only to what passes between Will and Sutter.

But, having lured Will out to the desert and there at least started the process of liberating him from his own false expectations, what is it precisely that Sutter wants or expects from the poor engineer in return? Not, surely, any enlightenment on the purely philosophical issues—of "immanence and transcendence," and the way back and forth from one to the other—with which the celebrated casebook is concerned. "My God, what is all this stuff, thought the poor bemused shivering engineer," when he started to read it in the cab of the camper (p. 293) the morning after the campus riot. The passages immediately in question have to do with covert lewdness in contemporary American popular culture; but Will is little more at ease with other parts of the notes. To adapt a line from the early Robert Penn Warren, "[his] breed ain't metaphysical." [15] When he is not fidgeting and blushing over all the "pornographic" references, his head is set spinning with the philosophical jargon in which Sutter so delights.

Even so, Will rightly interprets the argument with Val that Sutter carried on in the casebook as evidence that the doctor has by no means closed his mind to the possible truth of Christian faith. But if Sutter had ever seriously hoped that Will might somehow serve him in the office of "evangelist"—the bearer of the "good news" which is beyond argument—Barrett's apparently total failure even to comprehend the joke about Philip and the eunuch in the Gaza desert (p. 359) is profoundly discouraging. And, if that were not enough, then the engineer's explicit comments on religion (p. 383)—his reference to "an awareness of the prime importance of the religious dimension of life" which Sutter has shown in the casebook reflections—must be something near the final blow. For an instant, Sutter is tempted to think that Will is now having his own joke. But no such luck:

> "The religious dimension of life?" Sutter looked at him suspiciously.
> "Barrett, are you putting me on?"
> "No sir."

"Then if you're not, you're doing something worse."

"Sir?" asked the engineer politely.

"Never mind."

Indeed, "never mind." Poor Sutter called for a Philip, and they have sent him instead some humorlessly eager neophyte assistant to Norman Vincent Peale.

Against the background of this dismaying conversation, it is little wonder that Sutter should be reluctant later, when they have left the hospital together following Jamie's death, to try talking to Will about "what happened back there." Luschei, for one—distressed by the attitude of the "umpirelike priest administering baptism from a 'clouded plastic glass' and holding Jamie's hand while awaiting his death with a 'workaday five-o'clock-in-the-afternoon expression' . . ." —has lingering doubts about the authenticity of the deathbed conversion, despite his admission that Percy's design in the scene may be to "stress the centrality of the rite over the instruments." [16] I am inclined to agree with other critics who are less skeptical of the proceedings. As Panthea Reid Broughton puts it: "Though he may seem like a 'storekeeper over his counter' (*LG*, 396), Father Boomer serves as a messenger of Truth." [17]

What we have here is another version of "the uncontrollable mystery on the bestial floor" that we observed in the case of grubby Sister Val and her bedraggled hawk at the mission in Tyree County. Again, one must wonder how it is that the earlier examples of Joyce, Greene, O'Connor et al. have failed to prepare Percy's critics for this kind of Catholic fiction.

Father Boomer's credentials are not in question. Boomer—with his name reminiscent of the University of Oklahoma fight song—is, precisely and simply, your basic "workaday" priest. One may find his insensitively self-assured, cliché-ridden manner of speaking ("I would say it is a 'must,'" p. 399) both aesthetically deplorable and spiritually unedifying. But Boomer's clichés, unlike the kind of phraseological horrors Will has taken up ("the religious dimension of life," p. 383), are not doctrinally compromising. Boomer, presumably, is a duly ordained Roman Catholic priest. Either one takes the authority of such ordination seriously, or one does not.

The drinking cup of clouded plastic will serve as well as any other vessel for the baptismal water. "For now we see through a glass, darkly." Either the prescribed, sacred formula of the priest's words and gestures is efficacious, or it is not. (It is understandable that the poor innocent engineer should think "surely it was to be expected that the priest have a kit of some sort" [p. 405]; but surely Percy expected his professional readers to know better.)

The fact that Jamie accepts baptism *in extremis*, and unable to speak for himself audibly in words—having to depend upon Will, the reputed nonbeliever, "who did not know how he knew" (p. 406), to interpret his signals to the priest—is of no consequence in determining the validity of the acceptance. Will is right in his interpretation of the boy's mutterings and gestures, his smiles and frowns, or he is wrong. Either the most eloquent man alive, in full possession of his mature faculties, has experienced the miracle of faith, or he has not. As these affairs ordinarily go in the experience of such a man as Father Boomer, it seems likely that Jamie's *credo* would strike him if anything as rather more convincing than most he has heard. We may well imagine that Val, when Barrett has the opportunity to report to her, will feel that the engineer has quite satisfactorily met the terms of the "charge" she laid upon him concerning Jamie's end.

It is only with respect to the survivors, Will himself and Sutter, that issues remain which cannot be reduced to the either/or formula. Again, as in the case of the *The Moviegoer*, some of Percy's own comments in the interview with John Carr seem curiously to oversimplify the situation in this novel.

According to Percy, "Barrett has eliminated Christianity. That is gone. That is no longer even to be considered. It's not even to be spoken of, taken seriously, or anything else." With his "acute radar," Will

> . . . knows what people are feeling. And he is aware of something going on between the dying boy Jamie and Sutter there across the room and the priest. And he is aware that Sutter is taking this seriously. So after the boy dies they leave and Barrett . . . asks Sutter, "What happened there?" . . . [But] Sutter brushes him off as usual. . . . [and the novel] ends, unlike *The Moviegoer*, with Barrett missing it, like Kate missed it. He *misses* it! . . . Barrett, who existed in a

religious mode of search, repetition, and going into the desert, which are all in Kierkegaard's religious mode, at the end misses it. Whereas Binx, who exists in the aesthetic mode . . . in the end becomes a believer, in his own rather laconic style." [18]

Kierkegaard and Binx and Kate aside for the moment—let us first try looking directly at what happens in the particular novel under consideration, and without any such philosophical apparatus as the Kierkegaardian categories, which for critical purposes I find more trouble than help most of the time—it is as if Percy and I had read two different versions of the book called *The Last Gentleman*. I referred to Percy's remarks as an "oversimplification" of the fictional situation as I perceive it; "distortion," perhaps, is more accurate.

The muddleheaded modernist conception of Christianity that Will is trying to sell himself on in the course of the last extended conversation he has with Sutter prior to Jamie's death—the notion of some vaguely defined body of traditional beliefs and practices, conveniently variable according to one's "denominational" preference, which is due consideration simply as one possible way of expressing awareness of "the prime importance of the religious dimension of life" (p. 383)—is certainly itself a grotesque distortion of what Percy, as Catholic existentialist, means by Christianity. But, however wrongheadedly, what Barrett conceives as Christianity he certainly does not fail to "take seriously." He is more than a little *embarrassed* by it, to be sure. It is part of the same bill of goods that includes Kitty and Cap'n Andy's house and the job at the Chevrolet agency; and he is having a hard time persuading himself to buy any of it. The embarrassment, as evidence that he has the capacity eventually to figure out for himself just how vain and silly all his hopes for the future are, is the one thing that continues to sustain our sympathy for the engineer in the face of Sutter's scorn. But, however confused, however complicatedly *uneasy* he is about Christianity and the way it has affected relationships among members of the Vaught family, Will surely does not ignore the subject, as one "not even to be spoken of." He speaks of it to others—and, what is more important, to himself—several times, and always quite seriously. He takes Christianity as seriously as he takes anything which affects the Vaughts: and that is very seriously indeed. Poor Barrett's principal "trouble" in life, I should think, is that he takes everything so seriously.

Moreover, *in the novel*—i.e., in the pattern of Will's personal experience, whatever might be the case in the ultimate order of theological truth—the engineer's conception of Christianity is not totally irrelevant to what happens, and what he partly perceives as happening, in Jamie's deathbed conversion. It seems to me absurd to suggest, as Percy does, that Will's famous "radar" is operating there quite independently of the thinking he has been doing in recent days about "religion"—about Val and the "charge" she has given him, about what he found in Sutter's casebook. And, whatever it is that happens to Jamie, we must not forget that Will has an essential part in *making* it happen. Perhaps it could have happened without his assistance. But, again, the facts of the novel are all that we can legitimately be concerned with: and those facts are that it is Will who fetches the priest, and Will who, in the final moments (even though he "did not know how he knew" [p. 406]) interprets for the priest what Jamie is trying to say.

Percy said, repeatedly, that Will "misses it." Misses what? The true nature—as something simply to be perceived, understood—of what happens to Jamie? His own (Will's) salvation? The obscurity of the pronominal reference is, I suppose, excusable in the unrehearsed interview. Let us give Percy the benefit of the doubt, so to speak, and assume that he meant both: "it," the truth of Jamie's experience, and "it," Will's own salvation.

With respect to the former, I find it possible to grant, at best, only qualified assent to Percy's assertion: that Will "misses it." By the time of the interview with John Carr, it would seem that Percy had simply forgotten those facts that I regard as crucial—the facts of Will's *participation* in the baptismal process, a participation which is so intimate that I have the greatest difficulty in focusing on the engineer as the mere perceiver (or misperceiver) that Percy would make him out to be. What he is called in the novel (p. 404), "the interpreter," designates a much more active and vital role. "Again the youth's lips moved and again the priest turned to the interpreter." Obviously, Percy is right in a sense. If Will had not to some extent "missed it," there would be no point in his later asking Sutter about the episode. But if Will inevitably misses something of what is happening—he has part of his mind the whole time on his own troubles, and this is, after all, his first experience as witness to a deathbed baptism—I would insist nonetheless that it is, in the curious old phrase, a "near miss," i.e., a near hit.

If Percy means, by Barrett's "missing it," that he misses his own salvation, one must surely agree that he is not converted on the spot. He does not, to be sure, ask Father Boomer to wait while he fills up the plastic cup a second time. Nor is there any indication that he intends, as soon as he has concluded his business with Sutter, to pursue the priest to the rectory. For the time being, although he is "embarrassed" again (pp. 406–7), Barrett is not disposed to dissent when Sutter "curtly" assures the priest that they won't be needing him anymore.

But neither is there anything to indicate that Will's keen interest in "what happened back there" (p. 407) is permanently discouraged by Sutter's "brushing him off," as Percy rather oddly put it in the interview with Carr. In speaking of Will's awareness during the final scene in the hospital that "something [is] going on between the dying boy Jamie and Sutter there across the room and the priest,"[19] Percy would seem to imply that Sutter, unlike Will, has somehow *not* "missed it." And again, obviously, the distinction makes a certain sense. On the matter simply of perceptions, once more, Sutter is obviously better prepared by experience than Will is to see what is going on. As a physician, he is familiar with the phenomena of dying; and it is probably not the first time he has witnessed a priest's attendance upon the dying. He and the priest have a kind of "interprofessional" understanding of each other from which Will is necessarily excluded. Further, as we already know from the casebook entries, and the narrator's account of Will's reactions to that curious document, Sutter is far more sophisticated than Will is in his understanding both of the theological issues and of the phenomena of metaphysical consciousness involved in the baptism, is better equipped to "take it seriously" in this sense than Will is. He also has, of course, the simple advantage of longer acquaintance with Jamie.

It is fairly clear that Sutter has all along wanted it to be Val whom Will calls when Jamie is approaching death. When the priest asks Sutter whether he concurs, as Jamie's brother, in Val's request

103

that the sacrament be administered (p. 401), Sutter's response—simply inviting the priest, "by all means," to "stay"—might be regarded as equivocal. But, since Jamie is still conscious at that moment, the suggestion that the priest's questions should be put directly to him seems not unreasonable. And, in various practical ways—repeatedly urging the priest not to waste time, holding Jamie down with the bedsheet (p. 407) when the boy appears to be trying at the last moment to get out of bed once more—Sutter helps to see that the baptism is accomplished. On the other hand, as we have noted, it is Will, not Sutter, who serves as *interpreter* to the priest. Sutter does not presume, as Will does, actually to speak for his brother. It was Sutter, not Will, whom Val first specifically asked (p. 223) to have Jamie baptized before death.[20] But, in the end, it is Will, not Sutter, who plays the more prominent role in carrying out Val's charge.

When we come again to the second aspect of the question—the matter of participation, of possible sharing, in the act of salvation—it seems to me Sutter is, if anything, even farther off the mark than Will is. Surely it is Sutter, if either of the two, who has the more clearly "missed" his own chance for salvation in witnessing Jamie's death. If he had not missed it, he could not be afterwards on his way out to his own ranch, presumably to keep his "date" with the Colt. "I won't miss next time," he wrote in the casebook (p. 373); and the name of his ranch is *La Merced*. But if the irony here is not consistently dependable, then nothing is—either in the novel or in Percy's Catholicism. Not to miss with the pistol, especially on the second and therefore unequivocally premeditated attempt, even to contemplate such a deed, is surely not only to miss but to *reject* Christian salvation: surely to make a mockery of the "Gift," the "Grace," for which the ranch was named.

Of course, the mercy of God is infinite, and inscrutable. But all the humanly available evidence would suggest that if *Will's* last appeal does not work, then Sutter is done for, both in this world and in the next. Again, Percy's remarks to Carr are strangely misleading:[21] "So after the boy dies they leave and Barrett catches up with Sutter and he asks Sutter, 'What happened there? Something happened. What happened?' And Sutter brushes him off as usual. 'What do you think happened? You were there.' Well, it ends . . .

with Barrett missing it. . . . He *misses* it! He says something to Sutter like 'Why don't you come back to a town in the South and make a contribution, however small?' "[22]

The crucial fact is that Will's fatuous talk of the "contribution" comes *before* Jamie's death (pp. 384–87)—not, as Percy's comments suggest, afterwards.

When Will and Sutter have left the hospital, and Will is begging him not to go back to the ranch, *Sutter* sarcastically recalls the earlier conversation:

"Dr. Vaught, I want you to come back with me."
"Why? To make this contribution you speak of?"

But nothing could be plainer, or more plainly significant, than that Will declines the gambit. He does *not* repeat himself. His response (p. 409)—" 'Dr. Vaught, I need you. I, Will Barrett'—and he actually pointed to himself lest there be a mistake, 'need you and want you to come back' "—is something entirely new.

If either man has learned anything back there in the hospital, it would appear to be the engineer, not the doctor.

4

Love in the Ruins

I. Character and Genre

In his vaguely futuristic third novel, Percy returns to the first-person-present narrative technique of *The Moviegoer*. But *Love in the Ruins*, with its middle-aged, alcoholic rake of a hero, is surprisingly different from either of the two earlier books.

Don Juan/Faustus Dr. Thomas More, who claims as a collateral ancestor his celebrated sixteenth-century namesake, is in many ways the most attractive of all Percy's heroes. His virtues are palpable. Although he accuses himself of deficiency in love of his fellow man, his actions acquit him of the charge: witness the late night visit to the "love couple's" camp in the swamp (p. 46ff.), for the unsullied purpose of doing what he can to restore a dehydrated infant to healthy life. His unanticipated encounter with the lovely Hester in no way compromises the essential charity of his first intention. And, just as an example of his generosity in his medical practice, there is nothing unusual about this particular case. He is in the habit of treating any and all "denizens of the swamp," with all manner of ailments, for the good and simple reason that "nobody else will treat them" (p. 46).

Even in his many vices, everything from simple carnal lust to the most subtle delectations of intellectual pride, he is genial and un-affected. Obviously, he means his "girls" no harm, and is ever at great pains to please them as well as himself. He is reluctant to take unfair advantage of anyone, even of the devil himself if he appear in reasonably convincing human form. Unlike Binx Bolling's self-

106

deprecations, which ring always a bit hollow, poorly concealing a smug assumption of innate superiority, More's seem entirely sincere in most instances. More really is superior, and freely admits it. His assessment of himself as "a genius nevertheless" (p. 11) is offered with the same offhand and charming candor that marks the catalogue of shortcomings provided in his dossier, so that we are readily disposed to take him at his word. We may occasionally feel that he is too hard on himself, but seldom if ever that he is not hard enough.

His sorrows, too, are real and heavy. He has lost a daughter that he loved—if imperfectly, still genuinely and deeply loved—to a dreadful and grotesquely disfiguring disease; and, partly as a consequence of that, lost as well a wife that he loved, again genuinely and deeply if imperfectly. Worse, he has had to face the fact that in both cases he deliberately refused even to try such measures as he might have taken to prevent the disaster.

More's narrative is nearly ended before we learn the dreadful secret of his bad conscience concerning his daughter Samantha's death (p. 374). Doris, the faithless ex-Episcopalian mother, wanted to take Samantha to Lourdes. Tom, the bad but still practising Roman Catholic, demurred—not, he suspects, so much because he did not believe in the possibility of a miraculous cure as because he was afraid one might occur. And the fact that Samantha herself did not want to try it has in no way diminished his sense of guilt. Later, when Doris told him she was leaving him, he did not pursue the only course, of direct personal appeal, that might have dissuaded her, but—all the while "*knowing* [he] was wrong" (p. 69)—wasted his energy in abusing her spiritual "seducer," Fuchs-Forbes.

The loss of the child and the wife is a burden heavy enough to bear; the inescapable truth about himself is heavier still. The wonder is not that he has become a drunkard, and that he attempted suicide, but that he has, after all, survived: and survived sufficiently in possession of his powers not only to work on the Lapsometer and to keep up a reasonably effective if desultory medical practice, but to tell his story, to recall and analyze and dramatically recreate his experience.

For all his forgetfulness and bumbling, he is tough, resilient, cannily resourceful when he needs to be, and physically courageous. His personal vanities are artless, almost boyishly naive. He never stands on false dignity, in either professional or private dealings. Occasionally, he shows a certain cunning in playing upon the predictable feelings of friends and colleagues who happen to be in a position to help or hinder him in his designs, but there is no real guile in his maneuverings. His characteristic way of overcoming opposition is by a disarming candor rather than deceit or intimidation. Utterly shameless in his dependence upon what he believes to be the essential good will of his fellow mortals, he literally owes his life to at least four people: to Lola Rhoades and her father and another physician, Max Gottlieb, in the matter of the ill-fated rendezvous with Lola in the bunker and his subsequent attempt at suicide; then, twice or more during the present Fourth of July goings-on, to Victor Charles, the black veterinary assistant who joins the Bantu revolutionaries but retains a lifelong affection for the More family.

When Tom, drunk on an empty stomach during the morning of July 1, faints and falls down in a ditch near the animal shelter, Victor takes him into the treatment room, stretches him out on the big-dog table and revives him, gives him some friendly advice about protecting himself when the shooting starts, and accompanies him the rest of the way to the Little Napoleon tavern where he can rest and get something to eat. Later, when More has been captured (p. 296ff.) and the conspirator who calls himself Uru, a tough ex-pro athlete from Michigan, is bent on having him shot, Victor again intervenes to save him. Badly disordered as the society is—torn with racial and religious tensions and the fears and hatreds born of economic injustice, rotten with greed and intellectual hypocrisy— still, for tottery Tom More, the woods are full of Good Samaritans, black or white, male or female, Gentile or Jew, Knothead or Left, ready to pick him up every time he falls. Moreover, he has the grace somehow to accept everyone's aid without presuming upon it. He is frankly dependent, but neither arrogant nor groveling. He can accept help from a man or a woman, be properly grateful for it, and yet keep his emotional and moral perspective, never yielding to that subtlest and most dangerous form of ingratitude, the impulse to exaggerate the nobility of the benefactor.

But for all the fascination of More's personality, and the suspenseful interest we must take in the story of his successes and failures, this book is obviously not primarily concerned with the personal life of the hero: or, at any rate, not in the senses of the "personal" which are operative in conventional, basically realistic fiction of everyday life, fiction in the tradition of what Northrop Frye, for example, calls the "novel." [1] To be sure, all the conventional novelistic questions are raised about what will happen to Tom More—raised, and in due time either settled or pointedly left unsettled. Will he successfully complete his research on the Lapsometer? Will he be committed to the mental hospital again? Whom, if anyone, will he choose for his second wife? Will he and she be happy? We are keenly interested also in all the moral and psychological subtleties of his motives and actions, in his aesthetic responses—in everything, in short, concerning his mind and sensibility as they interact with his social and physical environment. Nonetheless, it is clear throughout that this is not what the book is centrally "about."

In the first place, a fiction which is centered in the personal life of the hero requires depiction of his involvement with *other* characters developed in considerable depth, characters who engage our sustained interest to some extent in their own right, not as types but as individuals, whose lives seem significant apart from their immediate importance to the protagonist. In Percy's two earlier novels, there are several such characters. In *The Last Gentleman*, there are Val and Sutter, and even Poppy Vaught and Kitty, not to speak of Rita. In *The Moviegoer*, despite the conspicuously egocentric narrator-hero, Aunt Emily and Kate repeatedly threaten to break out on their own. In *Love in the Ruins*, only the briefest hints of a few other characters' independent existences are allowable—one thinks of Colley Wilkes and Victor Charles and Max Gottlieb, perhaps of Father Smith—just enough to remind us that there *is* another kind of fiction, another way of looking at life, and that the author is aware of it.

But further, *Love in the Ruins* is frankly unrealistic in another sense. We can figure it out that the time of the central action is July of 1983. [2] But the fact of our having to "figure it out" is obviously significant. Nineteen eighty-three is one year before 1984; surely we are expected to make the connection. But Percy seems to have done his best to avoid being misinterpreted, as Orwell so often is, by literal-minded readers who are encouraged by the title to mistake satire on contemporary society for an effort to foretell the future.

The time-present of Dr. More's narrative—Christmas and the Fourth of July, and, with the firecrackers and the children's joyous salutes ("Hurrah for Jesus Christ! . . . Hurrah for the United States!"), the two made one at the end (p. 400)—is deliberately a "time out of time," myth time, not historic time. What Percy is trying to do is not to predict what might actually happen in the next fifteen years or so following publication of the book (1972), but to examine the fate of the American myth—the myth of our special, divinely ordained status and mission as a nation, the myth of "the New Eden"—as it affects, and is affected by, the processes of modern history in general. The seasons of the Fourth of July and Christmas—the one a commemoration of an historical event, a mere *holiday*, which over the course of two centuries has been elevated by the power of nationalist piety to the status of *holy day*, the other a notorious example of the workings of an opposite cultural process, the gradual secularization of the divine, whereby holy day is converted not simply to holiday, but to the most grossly commercialized of all our holidays—are exactly suited to Percy's design. No other national celebration is so expressive as the Fourth of July is of our presumptuous confidence in God's favor, our unwillingness to admit our radical involvement in the historical process which engages the rest of mankind—our unwillingness essentially, Percy suggests, to admit that the effects of original sin are universal. And Christmas—in the liturgical calendar the feast of the Incarnation, birth of the god-man, from eternity entering time to redeem fallen humanity—we have transformed into a strange festival of gluttony, reckless spending, and tasteless sentimentality which has as little significant connection with the ancient pagan ceremonies attending the winter solstice as with what happened in Bethlehem.

Love in the Ruins is primarily satire, in the mode of the picaresque mock-confession, with elements of virtually every other kind of fiction ever devised: melodrama, sentimental farce, anatomy, pseudo-history, utopian and dystopian sci-fi fantasy both repeatedly undercut by the narrator's anti-utopian skepticism,[3] comedy of manners, mock-epic, burlesque, and musical comedy. There is a tone of elaborate spoofing in all of it. Dr. More makes fun of everything and everybody—including not only, of course, himself, but his author as well, Walker Percy. He jibes, he capers and cuts the fool, he sets himself up for pratfalls. But he is adept at provoking all manner of smiles as well as laughter. Tiring of buffoonery, he turns ironist, exposing the follies and vices of others, the absurdity of their prejudices and pretensions, in a simple and straightforward report of their actions. Or he comments with wry amusement, a witty play on words or an outrageously misappropriated quotation, in the manner of T. S. Eliot, say, on the melancholy spectacle of his own infirmities and indignities. Or another turn, and he becomes simply healthy and exuberant, frolicking in his joy. And yet again, without warning, rarely but the more strikingly for the rarity, the comic mask will briefly drop altogether—as in the passages concerning Samantha's death—and we stare for a moment into the abyss of human suffering and ignorance.

In any event, through use of the wild mixture of fictional modes and the holiday time-settings, not to speak of his choice of a drunkard and sometime madman as narrator, Percy frees himself of all narrowly restrictive requirements of probability and logical continuity in telling his tale. To repeat, the book is predominantly satire, a purposive mode in which all sorts of exaggerations, distortions, oversimplifications, outrageous inventions in the way of events, institutions, and even geography, are traditionally acceptable. Most of the characters are types of one sort and another—representatives of social or professional classes, absurd mouthpieces for prejudices and pernicious ideologies—rather than fully individualized human beings. But that is what characters in satire are supposed to be.

We are meant to recognize the society Percy is satirizing as essentially, and in general, the society "of our own time." For example, when More speaks of how people behaved in "the old Auto Age," the age of motor hotels and travel on the interstate superhighways, we are expected to register the fact that that age has still not ended, and in all probability will not end for the time of at least another generation or two. In actuality, the major political parties in the United States did not alter their names before the elections of 1984; and it is unlikely that Percy anticipated such a development when he published the book in 1972. But what we also have to acknowledge is the fact that the Knotheads, as More describes them, and their opponents in the Left party, are just what conservative Republicans and liberal Democrats are and have been for at least a half century,

that the fictional names are after all *truer* names than the traditional
ones. The art of the satirist, like all art, distorts, enlarges and mini-
mizes, gives to the familiar an unfamiliar name, mingles invention
with convention, so that we may see into the essence of things which
have dulled and clouded in the eyes of custom. But satire is art in its
most active and conscious *critical* function; and it is essential to the
critical purpose that the satirist maintain within the structure of his
bizarre invention a solid framework of reference to the familiar. The
satirist, however exuberant of fancy he may be, is not simply having
fun. He is poking fun. And the reader, of course, must know what
he is poking it at.

The targets of satire here are all traditional: false religion, the
abuse of love, the vainglory of learning, the arrogance of power, the
inhumanity of the rich and the gullibility of the poor, the cruel folly
of racial conflict, the absurdity of social pretensions and the quest
for status, the universal corruption of taste, the inordinate veneration
of sports, the injustice of the law. In keeping with the promise of its
title, the book is much concerned with love, in many kinds—sexual
love, parental love, love of neighbor and god and country, self-love,
love of nature and art and learning—and with the abuses and per-
versions of them all. As might be expected in a book whose author
as well as its hero was educated as a physician, the *philosophes*
whom Percy holds up to scorn and ridicule—the wicked wise men,
learned fools, vain and quibbling "doctors" of the tradition—are all
members of the medical profession. Perhaps it is more than a simple
matter of the author's preferring to work within the area of his and
his hero's expertise; in our society the medical doctor is, in fact,
generally regarded as the only "real" doctor, perhaps the only one
whose abuse of his authority is really worth satirizing. In any event,
those anciently favorite butts of satire, the clergy and the legal profession, are less in evidence here. The only practicing clergyman
dealt with at any length, Father Smith, is a humble parish priest,
except for a few failings of the flesh a virtuous if undistinguished
man with no intellectual pretensions. Alistair Fuchs-Forbes is a
"holy man" of sorts; but he appears only in More's reminiscences.
And the ex-priest Kev Kevin, who works in the Love Clinic as
chaplain and "counselor," sometimes filling in also as operator of

the "vaginal console" (p. 123), is little more than a crude caricature. The workings and misworkings of the legal system are mentioned now and again, but no lawyers figure in the central action.

In the background, there is the war in Ecuador, and we are told of draft-dodgers, foreign and domestic, and of the sinister workings of the military-industrial complex. But in the way of the traditional *miles gloriosus* we have only the low- and lower-comic figures of the Bantu guerrilla leader Uru on one side and, on the other, Colonel Ringo, sometime officer of the Alabama National Guard, who commands a rearguard action in defense of the white community (p. 281ff.) after the fall of the Paradise Country Club. Despite all the references to political history and the unholy collusion of government and the "private sector" in the promotion of exploitative and corruptive enterprises, we see little or nothing of politicians in action. Besides the uneasily anticipated visit of the President and Vice President at the golf tournament (p. 356), there is only Victor Charles's announcement, in the epilogue, of his intention to run for the U.S. Senate.

But we cannot judge the relative importance of the various satiric themes simply by reference to the number of persons representative of this or that class or profession who appear in the forefront of the action. Notwithstanding the fact that very few clergymen appear on stage, the corruption of religion in our society is clearly Percy's central and overriding concern throughout. All the themes, all the degenerative forces in the society, are ultimately interrelated. And the central principle of that interrelationship—according to Percy the one seat and center of the malady, symptomatically so complex and bewildering, that afflicts our age—is clearly indicated in the very first sentence of Dr. More's narrative. "Now in these dread latter days of the old violent beloved U.S.A. and of the *Christ-forgetting Christ-haunted* death-dealing Western world. . ." (emphasis added).

II. Blacks and the "Jew-Christian" Tradition

A bit later (p. 57), More reflects upon the possible centrality of the "nigger business" in the history of America's and the white man's

113

decline. God had set us a final test, perhaps, after He gave us "Israel and Greece and science and art and the lordship of the earth, and finally even . . . the new world that [he] blessed for [us]":

> One little test: here's a helpless man in Africa, all you have to do is not violate him. That's all.
> One little test: you flunk!

But no, that is not it, after all. The thesis is plausible at first glance, and attractive for obvious reasons. Perhaps we could *un*violate the black man, so to speak. Pass some antidiscriminatory legislation, about educational and employment opportunities, seats on the bus, toilet facilities, etc. Work through the U.N. for Third World development and sanctions against South Africa, etc., etc. Difficult maybe, but not impossible. And, theses and the question of their validity aside for the moment, Dr. More certainly spends more time and energy on "the nigger business" than on anything else, except looking after his "girls."

But to the alert reader, if not to sleepy Tom More, the fallacies are apparent at no more than brief second glance. *If* God did, indeed, set such a test, what reason have we to assume that He will grant us a retake—at the U.N. or anywhere else? Or is there not, indeed, a patent presumption in the very notion of the "testing"? Who are "we"—"Israel and Greece and science and art and the lordship of the earth" and all—that we should assume the "helpless man in Africa" is or ever was helpless, was created simply to test our worthiness? God, for all we know, being God and therefore inscrutable, might just as well have created us as a test for the black man. Or created either for neither, for that matter.

If I read rightly what Percy is saying in the book as a whole, the "nigger business" is simply the most conspicuous example of our failure as a nation to keep Christ's commandments—first and foremost, as the title again suggests, those *two* commandments (Matt. 22:39–40) upon which "hang all the law and the prophets": 1) that we love God, 2) that we love our neighbors "as ourselves." To suggest that the white man's "violation" of the black, however abominable it may be, is distinct and separate from all other sins against charity—that the ills of our society could be cured if only whites would start to love blacks, while feeling free to go on hating each other, "peckerwoods" and "rednecks" hating "hebes" and "bohunks" and vice versa, and all together getting off on the "chinks" and "russkies," not to speak of the mutual contempt of husbands and wives, parents and children, the old and the young, the myriad spites and envies we conceive against each other in every conceivable human relationship—is worst and most dangerous folly. Worse than folly, it is rank impiety.

In this book, as everywhere in his writings, Percy recognizes the black-white conflict as a very special case. According to his lights, he tries earnestly to define the problem, and to understand the point of view and motivations of everyone concerned, while refusing finally to excuse anyone. But the case, although special, is not unique. The problem, and its solution if any, like all other problems of human enmity, is rooted most deeply in the individual, personal conscience.

There is nothing to suggest that, at the time Dr. More begins his narrative, the old civil rights legislation has been repealed. At Fedville, as the position of Dr. Colley Wilkes testifies, an official policy of racial equality is in force. But racial harmony is not wholly established even there. And in the local community beyond the walls of the government complex, things remain much the same as they have actually been in the deep South (and many other parts of the country) throughout the past twenty-five years and more of our supposed enlightenment. Official "integration" simply has not been established *de facto* in most aspects of daily life. The Valley Forge Academy (p. 12) is one of the pseudoreligious, pseudoprivate institutions for whites which were established all over the South to prevent effective integration of the public schools. And the management of the Paradise Bowling Lanes and the Little Napoleon tavern, where any Negro who attempts to exercise his officially guaranteed civil rights can do so only at the risk of a cracked skull or a kick in the kidneys, is typical of the way such local "neighborhood" establishments have been run all along. But the only real hope, ever, even for minimal improvement of the situation, Percy suggests, lies still just where it has always lain, in the persistent personal faith and personal, intensely individual goodwill of such men as Victor Charles and Tom More.

The frustrated and disgusted black ideologist Uru (whom More

recognizes [p. 300] as the former Elijah Washington, sometime professional football player) sees that his need to depend upon the likes
of Victor Charles for support in the local black community presents
an even greater threat to the revolutionary cause than the outright
hostility of the whites. Despite everything Uru can say to disenchant
him, Victor stubbornly clings to his simpleminded Christianity and
to his personal loyalties—refusing to forget that when his "auntee"
was mortally sick Dr. More not only gave the old black woman the
same professional attention he would have given to any white patient
but "sat up" with her through long nights of her final suffering. It is
difficult to determine how much Victor's maneuverings during the
Fourth of July troubles did or did not have to do with the failure of
the Bantu uprising at that time. But, in the epilogue, it is clear that
his proposal to run for the U.S. Senate, with More as his campaign
manager, represents the best hope that the newly reorganized community has for survival, not to speak of the establishment of a just
society.

The superficially happy outcome of the racial conflict, in the epilogue, with the oil-rich blacks having peacefully established their
dominance over the whites—blacks now owning the country club
and gravely deliberating whether to start opening membership to a
few whites, blacks getting up gift funds to provide Christmas baskets
for poor "peckerwood" children, etc.—is clearly intended to be
seen as fantasy. And, further, the essential thing to be noted about
the situation, from Percy's usual sociotheological point of view, is
that nothing has really changed. Whether whites are up and blacks
down, or vice versa, social inequity is social inequity, racial discrimination is racial discrimination.

Colley Wilkes and his wife, finding themselves members now of
the newly dominant race, are in no way essentially different from
the white liberals of the earlier dispensation. They are broad-minded
and generous in their support of the new progressive programs—
broad-minded and mealymouthed, just like their white predecessors,
gently reminding their old friend Tom More, when they mistakenly
see him as disposed to "rock the boat" in agitation for the cause of
integration, that "these things take time"—only, if anything, pro-
viding with the dignity of their educated blackness a new and dangerous authority to certain kinds of false faith which had begun to

flourish in the decades of the sixties and seventies. It is not so much the culture of the new American blacks in particular, as it is the corruptibility, in Percy's view, of the liberal intelligence in general, that is satirized in Colley's and his wife's conversion to the fad-cults of nature- and primitive ancestor-worship represented (pp. 388–90) in the quest of the ivory-billed woodpecker and the veneration of Longhu6, "Bantu god of the winter solstice."

That blacks such as Uru (the former Elijah Washington), and, in their more refined fashion, Colley and Fran Wilkes, should rebel against the dominant culture of the society into which they were born, rejecting the "white man's religion" along with names and other aspects of the hated "Jew-Christian" tradition (p. 300), is certainly understandable. Dr. More obviously understands, and, to the extent that his own ineradicable whiteness will permit, sympathizes. Even his amusement at the blacks' solemn antics — in which affectations of Bantu tradition are mingled with pathetic imitations of white customs, as most hilariously in the revival of old-fashioned British golfing dress and nomenclature at the country club (p. 385),[4] along with the roastbeef and Yorkshire pudding of the holiday menu — is more sympathetic than scornful. But to understand and sympathize is one thing; to abandon faith and principle is another.

No matter what revolutionary measures they may take, the American blacks can do no more than their neopagan white compatriots can to expel Christ and the Jews from their cultural heritage. Much as they might like to, the neohumanist Skinnerians at Fedville — including Colley Wilkes, for all the power of his super-blackness — cannot deny the creator of *Utopia*, Christian Sir Thomas More, Catholic *Saint* Thomas More, his place in their intellectual history. For better or worse, all Americans, blacks included, share the same "Christ-forgetting Christ-haunted death-dealing Western world," and there is no choice for anyone regarding Christ, no choice now any more than there ever was, but to believe or not to believe.

But that choice is, of course, from Percy's point of view, the one essential choice. Willy-nilly, we share the same complex cultural heritage, of which the pagan elements are still as ineradicable as the Judeo-Christian, and we rejoice in the liberties of a pluralist social and political system, and, as a practical necessity in the interest of preserving that system, we all try to live in peace with our neighbors,

117

whether they share our beliefs or not. But to understand, to sympathize, to live in peace with, to be prepared to "see" everybody else's "point of view"—to seek the democratic humanist order of social and political "consensus"—is something very different from what is required by the Christian commandment that we *love* our neighbor: love our neighbor *as ourselves*. The false ideal of *consensus*—false not in itself, and in the areas of conduct in which it is properly applicable, but false when represented as effectively *superseding* the Christian virtue of charity—is, as Luschei has pointed out, a central target of Percy's satire here. (Luschei's chapter on *Love in the Ruins* is entitled "The Ruins of Consensus.") The suburb of *Paradise Estates*, the false Eden where liberal infidel scientists and conservative Christian businessmen, Knotheads and Lefts—anybody and everybody *except* blacks, of course (p. 18)—live side by side in complete and wondrous bourgeois harmony, is one of the more obviously dubious achievements of consensus. Another takeoff on the ideal is the lengthy catalogue of culture-hero Tom More's ailments: "It is my misfortune—and blessing—that I suffer from both liberal and conservative complaints, e.g., both morning terror and large-bowel disorders, excessive abstraction and unseasonable rages, alternating impotence and satyriasis. So that at one and the same time I have great sympathy for my patients and lead a fairly miserable life" (p. 20).

III. Doctors and Demons in The Pit: The Case of the Speechless Linguist

The crucial test of the ideal, and of Dr. More's ability to transcend it, comes in the scene of his "trial," ordeal, in the debate at The Pit. The central illogicality of the "humanist" doctrine represented by Dr. Buddy Brown is obvious enough. In the familiar specious jargon of his school, full of pretentiously "scientific" phrases which are all the more odious for their perverse echoes of a terminology once respectably used by moral theologians, Dr. Brown tries in advance of the debate (pp. 196–98) to ingratiate himself with More and to minimize the importance of their philosophical differences. He hopes that they will be able to "give them a real show" in The Pit.

But, oblivious of the fact that much of his own vocabulary is "religious" in origin, he first accuses More of having allowed "nonscientific"—i.e., religious—considerations to influence his judgment in Mr. Ives's case, and then, reversing his tactics, concludes with an effort to persuade his opponent that they have not, after all, any real quarrel with each other. Both, says Buddy, agree that "it's the quality of life that counts. . . . the right of the individual to control his own body. . . . above all a man's sacred right to choose his own destiny and realize his own potential." Babbling in tautologous enthusiasm, he assures Tom that he "knows" him: "I know . . . you place a supreme value on human values. . . . we believe in the same things, differing only in the best way to achieve them."

Momentarily taken aback by Buddy's buddiness, Tom is reduced to agreeable and feebly protesting mumbles, "Yes. . . , well . . . we do?" But, in the official confrontation in The Pit, he is more than a match for his presumptuous colleague. Brown's position regarding Mr. Ives—whom he proposes mercifully to "terminate" at the "Happy Isles Separation Center," by way presumably of recognizing the old man's "sacred rights" aforementioned—is plainly insupportable. If a man is to have no life at all, it is useless to talk of the "quality of life"; it is useless to defend a dead man's right to control his body. Buddy Brown's kind of talk makes no sense of any kind: as morality, theology, medicine, or social planning. It makes no sense either as "religion" or as "science." If Brown represents a "consensus" of the faculty, then it is a consensus of nonsense.

In the showdown, More refuses to compromise, insists that the real issue, of life or death for Ives, be clearly defined—calls a spade a spade—and brings down the house. When he refers to the Happy Isles Separation Center as an "anteroom to the funeral parlor" (p. 223), the students blush and gasp, girls pull their skirts down over their knees. We see that in this latter-day brave new world the scientistic notion of the ultimate perfectibility of man flourishes, if a little less openly, still as strongly as ever it did in Huxley's day. Death, or the name of anything associated with it, is a dirty word.

Having received a reprimand from the Director, and a warning that he must be careful of his language or risk being sent back to the psychiatric ward, More proceeds to demonstrate that Mr. Ives is in full possession of his faculties, by no means a candidate for euthanasia, and Buddy Brown is routed. But it is essential to note that More does not triumph by the power of rational argument alone.

Just before the debate, drunk, demoralized, and incoherent with fatigue, he was approached by Art Immelmann in the men's room, where, in a grotesque, unwitting parody of an indecent sexual encounter, he not only signed the contract for development of the Lapsometer and sharing of patent rights, but submitted to a quick "treatment" (p. 211ff.) with one of the instruments fitted with Immelmann's special attachment. The treatment promptly relieved all his tensions and anxieties, restoring his confidence in anticipation of the debate. And, on stage, More himself twice uses the modified Lapsometer, first to disable the inhibitions of the unsuspecting Dr. Brown (pp. 226–27)—so that Buddy can be depended upon to "be what he is" and focus his attention on the charms of Helga Heine and nurse Winnie Gunn—and then to stimulate Mr. Ives to talk.

Sometime alienist Dr. More takes on the role of exorcist, driving demons out of poor Mr. Ives into the swinish doctors and students. But how does he drive them out? If it is not exactly in the *name* of Beelzebub—since he does, after all, try to keep Immelmann from distributing the Lapsometers among the audience at large—still, he knows where he got the one that he uses on Brown and Ives, and he obviously knows what it can do. When More tells Immelmann that he is "cancelling the contract" (p. 241), any fair-minded observer would be inclined to give the devil his due. Offhand, Art seems entirely justified in his friendly dismissal of the threat, airily assuring "Doc" that he will be "right as rain tomorrow."

What Tom More has to recognize, before he can hope to rectify matters, is his *complicity* in whatever evil it is that is let loose in The Pit and that may, as he fears, spread to the surrounding community and beyond, whether through a chain reaction in the heavy-sodium deposits or by other agencies as yet undefined. He wants to "cancel the contract" with Immelmann, and recover his Lapsometers. But the devil did not, in the first place, appear unbidden.

Tom was in his office, listening to a recording of *Don Giovanni* while a spectacular thunderstorm raged outside, when Immelmann paid his first call. It is surely no accident that, in the instant before the office lights went out, More had been thinking, "If only my Lapsometer could treat as well as diagnose, I wouldn't be caught up in these farces" (p. 165).

Like Faust's, it is More's intellectual pride that first calls up the devil—pride, and the impatience of pride. No matter that, besides his more obviously self-seeking ambitions—for prestigious publication, research funding, and, vanity of vanities, perhaps a Nobel prize—he also has worthy humanitarian intentions to justify his desire. In the field of the kind of maladies he is proposing to treat, "cure" is a term that is very difficult to distinguish from "save." And the story of where that kind of humanitarianism leads—the story of the physician with delusions of priestly power—is an old and sad one indeed, as old and sad as any in the long history of creaturely pride.

Where it leads, in Percy's fable, is straight to The Pit: to the devil again. To be sure, poor Tom is drunk, disheartened, weary with good works (chiefly in the interest of his girlfriends, perhaps, but still, good works), intimidated with the threat of being returned to the madhouse, etc., etc., when he meets Immelmann again in the men's room. But who ever went to the devil without excuses of much the same kind?

There is no getting around the fact that he does sign the contract, does take the modified Lapsometer on stage with him for the debate, and does use it—without being *really* sure in advance how it will work—both on his adversary, Dr. Brown, and on the patient, Mr. Ives, neither of whom has been apprised in advance of the highly experimental character of the procedure.

Regardless of the truth about the "scientific" procedure, it should not be difficult to define how seriously More has compromised his moral position in the use of such tactics. Dr. More implicitly accuses Dr. Brown of hypocrisy in charging him (More) with allowing "religious considerations" to affect his scientific judgment (p. 197). And More is surely right; a hypocrite Brown is, and always will be. But, when we come to the showdown in The Pit, it must appear that Brown had a point, after all. More, too, is a hypocrite; maybe a better-natured, better-intentioned hypocrite, maybe only now and again a hypocrite, but a hypocrite.

Dr. More, with judicious use of the Lapsometer, shows Dr. Brown up for all to see as a coarse-minded lecher, shouting from the stage his ribald greetings and gesturing obscenely at Winnie Gunn and Helga Heine. But what, we must ask, of our hero's own propensities? A trifle more decorous, perhaps, as befits a gentleman of courtly English ancestry, more "reserved," our good Doctor Tom. He does it in golf course bunkers and ruined motels, out of the public eye more or less. And there is the question of relative refinement of taste in the choice of partners. Lola, at least, with her cello, is a good deal classier even than Dr. Heine, not to speak of Nurse Gunn. But, then, alas, there is Moira, who for her part really does not seem to appreciate these fine distinctions: who, in fact, has the effrontery finally to *marry* Buddy Brown, notwithstanding her memories of rapture in Tom's embraces.

Only More's deliverance of Mr. Ives will stand more than a moment's scrutiny as a justification for his performance in The Pit. We recognize in Ives—the learned amateur linguist who in thrall to the evil Skinnerians at Gerry Rehab has lapsed into total silence as the most effective way of showing his contempt for his captors, who in fact would literally rather die than cooperate with these desecrators of humanist tradition—a hero of Language, student of that one faculty of man which in the order of nature most clearly distinguishes him from the beasts.[5] When Buddy Brown and his nefarious colleagues and students in The Pit, his fellow jargonists, are momentarily transformed into beasts by the power of the Lapsometers, it is, allegorically, a punishment for their abuse of Ives as guardian of the sacred "word-horde." (The "fountain of youth" Ives was seeking in Florida is, of course, the eternal fountain, or spring, of language itself.) In championing Ives, More confers upon himself something of the mysterious power that belongs to the old man. But even in that case, his resorting to use of the modified Lapsometer raises serious questions about More's motives. Does he do it for Ives's sake, or for his own, for the sake of his own freedom and his own ambitions?

The answer is, I think, for both. The case of Mr. Ives presents a curious parallel—parallel by way of contrast—to that of More's daughter, Samantha.

IV. The Complicities of Tom More

When Doris proposed that they take Samantha to Lourdes, as a last resort to try saving her life, Tom refused. Much later, in his reflections on the matter (p. 374), he concludes in effect that he refused, not simply because Samantha herself did not want to go, but also because he was afraid to make a compact with God to secure the miracle. "Suppose you ask God for a miracle and God says yes, very well. How do you live the rest of your life?" On the other hand, he is not nearly so afraid of making a compact with the devil, Immelmann. Why?

At least one of the important differences between the two cases is that his motives for dealing with Immelmann are much more frankly self-interested. The development of the Lapsometer, with which Immelmann pretends to be assisting him, promises some ultimate benefit to humanity at large. But when More finally consents to sign the contract, it is fairly obvious that he has nothing immediately in mind except saving himself from the threat of being sent back to the hospital as a mental patient. The modified Lapsometer provided by Immelmann is essential to his success in the debate with Buddy Brown, and thus to the rescue of Mr. Ives. More could not, or would not, obligate himself to God to save his daughter's life; but, using the instruments he has obtained in his dealings with the devil, he exerts himself to save an old man who is all but a total stranger to him.

But the point we must keep in mind is precisely this, that he was not thinking of Ives's welfare when he encountered Immelmann in the men's room and signed the contract: was not, that is to say, using the prospective opportunity to help Ives as an *excuse* for dealing with Immelmann. In a curious way, More seems to end up endowed with virtue, the power to save Ives and thereby to "justify" himself, precisely because he has not sought justification.

More's decision to sign the contract is hardly, in fact, a real decision, a real choice, at all. It is the kind of "choice," rather, the kind of "decision," which is a function of total intellectual resignation, of mental *despair*. But, theologically, that despair is the beginning of hope. More's resignation, in the men's room, his submission to

Immelmann, his losing his *fear* of the devil, is not after all abject surrender, but—however still unwitting, befuddled, and confused—an essential act of faith. He does not fear the devil, and a compact with him, as he once feared God and a compact with Him, for the simple reason that he knows (no matter how) that the devil has no such power as God's—that no contract with the devil is enforceable except by the will of God and that, while we continue in this life, such will is not to be anticipated. Man is, in short, free to defraud the devil if he can.

On the other hand, and by the same token of God's inscrutable will, there is no guarantee that More can contrive the "flaw in the indenture" with Immelmann. More is no lawyer, but a physician. And Who knows what Art is?

To put the matter still another way, More must admit complicity —sign, in effect, a contract of complicity, confessing that he *deserves* no better fate than Immelmann may lead him to—before he can hope for release. Then, when the time comes, beside the burning bunker when he feels himself strongly compelled to follow Immelmann—when Ellen, echoing Milton's Eve facing expulsion from the Garden, suggests that if they "both go . . . maybe it will be all right" (p. 376)—Tom is able to make the one kind of appeal, with no false pride, no taint of self-assertion, which is sure to be effective. In his helplessness, he calls upon his sainted ancestor—which is to say, upon the communion of saints, upon the grace of God—and he is delivered.

As Luschei has pointed out, the *Lapsometer*—literally, a device for measuring lapses—is designed to diagnose a kind of "second fall" which modern man has presumably suffered. Man first fell by his pride from a state of humble dependence upon the will of God which is perfect wisdom, into the need to pursue knowledge by the strength of his own imperfect intelligence. Having over the ages scored impressive gains in knowledge and control of his environment, even of his own body as a functioning organism within that environment, man faces now—in a more intense and frightening form than ever before—the experience of self-alienation, the disabling sense of being a stranger, not only to God and the angels, but to himself. This is the "second fall." And it is entirely appropriate that Percy should choose the phenomenon of atomic "fall*out*" as metaphoric vehicle for this new spiritual "fall*in*," as it might more properly be called. As More describes the probable effects of exposure to the "noxious particles" (p. 5), the worst suffering is to be expected by the man who is "already *abstracted* from himself." Such a man, after the impending catastrophe, will be totally "*sundered* from himself and roam the world like Ishmael" (emphasis added).

There can be little doubt that we are meant to see in these catastrophic events something akin to the phenomena prophesied as preceding the "second coming" of Christ. Besides the reference to the "bad times," in which "principalities and powers are everywhere victorious [and] wickedness flourishes in high places" (p. 5), just in case anyone should miss the point Percy runs in an allusion (p. 18) to W. B. Yeats's celebrated poem "The Second Coming"—which presents, of course, a somewhat heterodox view of what may be expected at the end of the second millennium since the birth of Christ: "The center did not hold." It is extremely interesting that another allusion to the same poem appears in the epilogue chapter, in connection with More's account of his meeting with Colley and Fran Wilkes as they are on their way to report to the Bird-Watching Society their sighting of an ivory-billed woodpecker. The alert reader will already have spotted the elusive ivory-bill—commonly thought to be extinct—as a satiric secular parody of the returning Christ. But, again just in case, Percy nails it down (p. 387): "This morning, hauling up a great unclassified beast of a fish, I thought of Christ coming again at the end of the world. . . ." ("And what rough beast, its hour come round at last / Slouches towards Bethlehem to be born?")[6]

The trouble with Tom More's, as with most if not all millenarian thinking, is in his evident impatience to see the end. The "diagnostic" uses of the Lapsometer are, from a theological point of view, hardly less presumptuous than the therapeutic. The notion of a Second Fall, requiring the invention of such an instrument merely to measure its effects, is false doctrine, necessarily implying a certain weakening of belief in the First Fall, and serving, whether consciously or not, as an excuse for actively promoting the disorders which portend the Second Coming. The devil, Art Immelmann, is much more orthodox; confident of the powers granted to him under

125

the old dispensation, "he doesn't even need the lapsometer" (p. 376), although he knows how to use it when it suits his convenience. As "shaky" in faith as in bodily health, Dr. More appears never to be fully convinced that the prophecies will be fulfilled without his direct intervention, that all he really has to do is to "watch and wait."

He does, however, have a series of partial awakenings to his complicity in the evil which afflicts him and the society at large. One such recognition comes in his reflections upon Doris's having left him. Although he says that the notion she had of going to Cozumel for a life of "meditating and making things" was "not a bad idea really"—and that "[he'd] have gone with her . . . and made pots" (p. 67)—there is nothing to indicate that he ever made any systematic effort to explain his attitude to her, much less ever *insisted* that he be allowed to accompany her when she went. The implication is clear that what he took to was the idea of the making, not the meditating. And perhaps she would not have suffered his companionship in the one without the other. But he never gave himself the chance to find out.

Although he acknowledges his "mistake" (p. 69), and presumably recognized it as such even at the time, in taking out his rage and frustration on Fuchs-Forbes instead of making some positive effort to come to terms with Doris herself and the reasons—reasons antecedent to the coming of Fuchs-Forbes—for the failure of their love, he was still somehow unable to act upon the knowledge, but yielded as under a kind of compulsion to the self-destructive anger. He too, like Doris, "wanted out from the bad thing" (p. 64) their life had become. What he says he "*didn't* know at the time" (emphasis added) was that he himself, in Doris's eyes, was "part of the bad thing." We may legitimately question, in the light of his other recollections of their conversations, whether he was in fact totally unaware of her attitude before she left him. In any event, at some later time—he does not say precisely when—he did realize how Doris had seen him. And the whole import of his account of the affair is to suggest that he has come to agree with her. The implication is clear that he sees it as impossible for him to get "out from the bad thing" precisely *because* he was, and is, "part of the bad thing."

Another important recognition of complicity comes in the episode of his arrival at the Little Napoleon in the company of Victor

Charles (p. 149ff.). Because Tom allows Victor to go with him inside the barroom, but then lets go of his arm an instant before the proprieter, Leroy Ledbetter, turns and sees them, Ledbetter mistakenly assumes at first that the black man has "forgotten his place" and mutters an admonition, directing him to a side window where Negroes are permitted to make carry-out purchases. When Tom then says "thank you, Victor, for helping me up the hill" (p. 150), Leroy recognizes his error, and attempts to make amends with a ritual remark about the weather spoken "in Victor's direction." But it is, though only by a split second, too late. All three men, while "keeping their cool," are obviously aware—each in his own fashion and with his own particular mixture of emotions—that the situation is irredeemable.

At least on the surface, it would appear that no great damage has been done in this particular encounter. But it reminds Tom of another and more violent episode five years before, when Ledbetter physically attacked a Negro couple who tried to patronize the bowling lanes he was managing at the time, thereby touching off the riots during which the shopping center was burned and the motel and St. Michael's church were abandoned. Almost in passing, with so little emphasis that the casual reader might miss it altogether, More mentions the fact that at that time he and Ledbetter were business partners, co-owners of the Paradise Bowling Lanes (p. 152). Although Tom never specifically states the facts, we may assume that the partnership was dissolved following the riots, or even earlier, as soon as Ledbetter had told him what he did to the Negro bowlers. But, in any case, there is no getting around the fact that Tom still frequents Leroy's present establishment, the Little Napoleon, and that, as he ponders his role in the past incidents, he admits the possibility at least that he was "*glad* [he] had not been there" (emphasis added) when Leroy used his "learner" (most likely a blackjack) on the Negro intruders—glad, because he suspects he would not have had the skill or the courage to prevent the assault.

There is, in short, no getting around the fact of his past, and continuing, complicity. If his marriage to Doris became a "bad thing," he was part of the bad thing. If racism is a "bad thing," he was and is a part of that bad thing too. Not wholly passive victim, but, in both cases, part perpetrator. In both cases, his complicity is in a sense "negative," perhaps, but it is nonetheless complicity, *knowing* complicity, whether positive or negative.

But the "lesson" of complicity is one that Tom More finds it difficult to remember; and he has to be taught it over and over again. The crucial recognition, as I have already suggested, in preparation for his final confrontation with Immelmann, comes in his recollection of Samantha's death, and his refusal to take her to Lourdes.

Savoring his remorse, he asks himself (p. 374) "is there not also a compensation, a secret satisfaction to be taken in her death, a delectation of tragedy, a license for drink, a taste of both for taste's sake?" And a final question: "Is it possible to live without feasting on death?"

V. Conclusion: "Who was then the gentleman?"

Complex but unequivocal, an answer to Tom's question emerges in the epilogue. On the purely natural plane, which is the plane of *fallen* nature, the answer is no. Although the picture of Tom soaking up the morning sun in his kitchen garden is at first glance unrelievedly cheery (pp. 381–83)—in marked contrast to the picture we got of him at the outset of the novel, gin-soaked reprobate, desperate hunter and hunted, "broken out in hives and waiting for the end of the world" in the scruffy non-place of the highway intersection, "eyed for meat" by the circling buzzard at sundown—the briefest second look will discover that in the dawn of this new day too, life in the natural state is still a matter of feasting on death.

"In the corner of the wall a garden spider pumps its web back and forth like a child on a swing" (p. 382). The simile presents the spider in deceptively benign aspect. E. B. White notwithstanding, we all know what that pretty web is for; here is no child's play. "A kingfisher goes ringing down the bayou," with overtones of a Hopkinsean celebration of nature as sacramental being. But for the hapless fish he is after, there is little to rejoice at in the winged blue fire of the diving bird. The kingfisher inhabits with the marsh hawk and the buzzard of the novel's opening scene, with man indeed, the same world of Hobbesian nature, where life for all alike is "nasty, brutish, and short."

Nor is there much if anything in the world of human society here to relieve the grimness of nature. If the triumph of the local blacks, for example, as we have previously observed, has done nothing to worsen the situation of five years before, neither has it worked any notable improvement. When Tom More catches a ride into town with Colley Wilkes (p. 387ff.)—presumably representative of all that is best in the new culture of black dominance—the scene is reminiscent of nothing so much as that in Dusty Rhoades's car back in the "July First" chapter five years earlier (p. 74ff.).

Dusty's car was a new black Toyota; Colley's is a new orange Toyota.[7] Dusty listened to Viennese waltzes on the tape deck; Colley, more eclectic in taste, favors "a Treasury of the World's Great Music, which has the good parts of a hundred famous symphonies, ballets, and operas." Dusty urged Tom to attend the Pro-Am prayer breakfast, honoring Jesus Christ, "the greatest pro of them all"; Colley and Fran proselytize for the ivory-billed woodpecker and Longhu6. *Plus ça change*. More of a natural gentleman than Dusty, and certainly a superior scientist, super-Bantu and arch-liberal Colley is finally as intolerant as their erstwhile Knothead colleague in his attitude toward Tom's continuing research on the Lapsometer. He asks about it mostly out of politeness, and reacts with obvious distaste when Tom persists in speaking of "diabolical abuse" and "angelism, bestialism, and other perturbations of the soul" (p. 389). As blind still as any of the crowd who gathered beside the burning bunkers five years before, Colley still cannot break free of his "scientific" prejudices to acknowledge the plain evidence of his senses. Tom asks him what he thinks was responsible for "the Troubles" five years before (p. 390). " 'The usual reasons, I suppose,' says Colley mournfully. 'People resorting to violence instead of using democratic processes to resolve their differences.' " When Tom responds with an obscene exclamation and the question—"what about the yellow cloud?"—Colley simply refuses to answer. The ride is over, and, so far as Dr. More's request for support among his scientific colleagues is concerned, he is obviously right back where he started with the Lapsometer, if not indeed farther from his goal than he was just after the Vieux Carré Project.

Rejoicing in the simple treasures of his fine new boots and new family, his modest but charming apartment in the old slave quarters,[8]

Tom More might seem now best advised simply to "cultivate his garden." But, as I have tried to suggest, Percy's attitude toward *that* project, too, is at least as complex as Voltaire's.

Even without the daily distractions of his continuing involvement with the corrupt intellectual, economic, and political institutions of the larger community, Tom's retreat on the banks of the bayou could hardly be regarded as the best of all possible worlds. And besides, it is quite apparent that his maintaining contact with the community is a practical necessity. For better or worse, both his private and his professional life must be pursued in an imperfect world, a world where all life, human and non-human, feasts on death.

Yet, for all that, More *is* better off in this Christmas season than he was on the Fourth of July five years before, and not simply in such obvious ways as the improvement of his health and of his domestic situation. He is better off also in being closer to—in having, shall we say, ever stronger intimations of—a life that does not feast on death.

I see no point in hedging, as many of Percy's critics have done, on the question of his Catholicism. This book, even more plainly than his other works of fiction, plainly and purely if by no means simply, concludes with an assertion of orthodox Christian faith.

Hedging is one thing, however, and discrimination is another. When I speak of More's new intimations in the events of the epilogue, what I emphatically do *not* mean is that he appears finally as a prophet of the Millennium. That indeed, it seems to me, is the role he is in the process of repudiating at the end of his narrative.

More's preoccupation with eschatological matters is apparent from the very beginning. He sits in the pine grove "waiting for the end of the world" (p. 3). In terms of the biblical prophecies (p. 5), "principalities and powers are everywhere victorious. Wickedness flourishes in high places." But "a clearer and more present danger" is that of the "unprecedented fallout of noxious particles . . . a catastrophe whose cause and effects—and prevention—are known only to [him]." Reinforced by the unconscious irony of his echoing the legalistic phrase "clear and present danger," which refers specifically to the kind of danger that is obvious to any normally intelligent and unbiased observer, his claim to exclusive knowledge of the nature of the impending disaster is unmistakable evidence of his intellectual pride. Ordinary mortals may have to depend on such ambiguous portents as the Bible identifies in predicting the end of the world. He, Tom More, Super-Scientist, has something much more reliable. He can tell you almost to the hour when the end will come, and what form the destructive power will take. Moreover, if you want protection against it, again you need not trouble yourself with the slipshod, notoriously unreliable methods of theologians. Call for an appointment with Dr. More. He, and he alone, has the one sure technique of prevention and cure.

The allusions to Yeats's "The Second Coming," early in the novel and again in the epilogue, could be seen as a concession on Percy's part to traditionalists of the "post-Christian" intellectual era and persuasion, the kind of modern heathen who might either have missed or have chosen to ignore the biblical references. But Colley and Fran Wilkes, with their excitement over the sighting of the ivory-billed woodpecker, are in this episode an obvious satiric caricature of the type. And Tom's unspoken response to their remarks—remembering the "great unclassified beast of a fish" he had caught that morning, and thinking specifically of "Christ coming again at the end of the world" (p. 387)—emphasizes both More's spiritual estrangement from the Wilkeses, the estrangement of belief that goes much deeper than race, and the continuing danger he is in of sinning through intellectual pride.

All but completely tuning out Colley's and Fran's patter, he continues musing on "how it is that in every age there is the temptation to see signs of the end and that, even knowing this, there is nevertheless some reason, what with the spirit of the new age being the spirit of watching and waiting, to believe that—."

At this point he breaks off (p. 387), watching Colley's hand straying restlessly over the tape deck; but what it is that he is *still* tempted to believe is fairly obvious. The Wilkeses' ivory-bill, Tom's own mysterious fish, along with all the rest—"principalities and powers . . . wickedness flourish[ing] in high places"—are but obscure "signs and portents." Whatever others may read in such phenomena, More watches and waits only for Christ—and not with much patience.

But he has thought of all this before—notably during the Fourth of July "troubles" five years earlier, to which he refers in the conversation with the Wilkeses—and, in view of how things turned out then, there is reason to hope that he will be more cautious about yielding to the excitement of such notions again. It takes no great acumen to detect in his statement at the beginning of the narrative, that he is "*waiting* for the end of the world" (emphasis added), a concealed wish for the catastrophe. His allowing for the possibility of error—"either I am right and a catastrophe will occur, or it won't and I'm crazy"—is no real concession at all to the virtue of rational dialogue. It is the standard "either-or" formula of fanaticism, allowing for no compromises of response. Such impatience, and the refusal to countenance any response that seeks a middle ground between conviction and doubt, is typical of millenarian thinking. The notions of the "ultimate catastrophe," Armageddon, and of the Second Coming, the institution of the Millennium, obviously exercise much of their seductive appeal as a promise of relief from the wearisome responsibilities of everyday faith and judgment —above all, perhaps, from the tedium and indignities of human love. For any number of reasons, Tom More, as we see him at the beginning of the novel, is exceptionally vulnerable to that appeal. His involvement with Immelmann is a direct expression of the typical millenarian impatience. He is, precisely, *not* disposed to "wait" for the end of the world. Rather, he will go to any lengths necessary, including a compact with the devil, to insure the catastrophe, to force God, as it were, to get on with it.

But, either despite or in some sense because of More's best efforts —the question is arguable either way—the world did not, after all, come to an end that Fourth of July. And, as we see him in the epilogue, he seems on the whole much better reconciled to the possibility of its indefinite continuance.

With the local ascendancy of the Bantus, many whites of both Knothead and Left persuasion have departed for other states and cities more rigorously definable in ideological terms. More gives his own reasons for having stayed (p. 386): "because it's home and I like its easygoing ways, its religious confusion, racial hodgepodge, misty green woods, and sleepy bayous."

The renewed sense of *place* here, place as something related to but still distinct from time, that survives somehow radically unchanged through the changes of era and institution, the shifting of ideological and racial boundaries, is of a piece with More's renewed spirit of self-acceptance. Along with the "*misty* green woods" and the "*sleepy* bayous"—south Louisiana remains south Louisiana, the *country* of south Louisiana endures, no matter who is in charge with what ideas—he likes the "religious *confusion*," the "racial *hodgepodge*" (emphases mine). The words I have italicized are of crucial importance, it seems to me. To pick up again the key word of Luschei's analysis, "consensus"—that euphemism for unprincipled compromise in all matters of governance both intellectual and political, the unprincipled itself falsely elevated to the status of principle—was and remains intellectually *unacceptable* to More, although he suffers the effects of it in the combination of typical Knothead and Left bodily ailments to which he is subject. The kind of complicity in evil of which he is guilty, as in the case of Ledbetter and the black bowlers, has nothing to do with the "consensus" of which Luschei speaks. And his fondness for certain qualities of life in south Louisiana—the "confusion" and "hodgepodge," the "easygoing" ways of the local citizens—is not to be mistaken for tolerance of muddleheadedness on certain essential issues of both scientific and religious doctrine. Confusion and hodgepodge, the misty and the sleepy, are simply definitive of the human condition, of the imperfections and uncertainty of vision, the *lapses* of understanding, which we cannot choose but accept—and which, therefore, it behooves us to accept with good grace, with "liking." If we reject these uncertainties, we reject ourselves.

Father Rinaldo Smith, the pastor of the minuscule Roman Catholic congregation, appears as a somewhat shadowy figure on the fringes of the action in the main part of the novel. The first mention of him does not even include his name. He is referred to simply as "an obscure curate, who remained faithful to Rome" (p. 6). But in view of the role he assumes in the epilogue, as Tom's confessor, it is worthwhile noting the rest of the information about him we are given earlier.

Following the schism, we are told, when some of the local Catholics allied themselves with the Dutch separatist group and others, the majority, with the American Catholic Church, Father Smith "could not support himself and had to hire out as a fire-watcher. It is his job to climb the fire tower by night and watch for brushfires below and for signs and portents in the skies" (p. 6).

Later, we learn several other things about the priest that might help to account for his greater than ordinary pastoral interest in More. For example, Smith is a fellow alcoholic, who over a number of years has been sent off periodically to diocesan hospitals for drying-out sessions. And, during More's stay at the Fedville psychiatric facility following his suicide attempt, Father Smith was also admitted as a patient—for treatment of a disorder which involved, according to the account of his experiences elicited by Max Gottlieb and other doctors, close encounters with demonic powers.

Early in the development of the Bantu plot for the Fourth of July takeover, Father Smith tries to warn More that he is in danger and offers to share his apartment in the old slave quarters as a refuge (p. 187). For any number of readily apparent reasons, including most obviously the assignation with Moira at the ruined motel, More declines the offer. And, in general, he seems disposed to keep the priest at arm's length, regarding him with a kind of indulgently respectful, mildly amused condescension.

In the confessional (epilogue, p. 398), when Smith hints that he himself may have some experience of womanizing as well as the other sinful dispositions they share, Don Juan More gets downright irritable at what he sees as the priest's "patronizing" attempt to win his confidence. "How can he lump the two of us together, him a gray ghost of a cleric and me the spirit of the musical-erotic?"

But Father Smith, meanwhile having extracted the information that More has not, after all, actually committed any sexual sins lately, but has only thought about them, goes on with exquisite and devastating courtesy to chasten the reluctant penitent for his vanity (p. 399):

> . . . forgive me but there are other things we must think about: like doing our jobs, you being a better doctor, I being a better priest, showing a bit of ordinary kindness to people, particularly our own families—unkindness to those close to us is such a pitiful thing— doing what we can for our poor unhappy country—things which, please forgive me, sometimes seem to me more important than dwelling on a few middle-aged daydreams.

Feeling "instantly scalded," More says: "You're right. I'm sorry." And Father Smith, closing in for the kill, picks up immediately on the word "sorry."

"You're sorry for your sins?"
"Yes. Ashamed rather."
"That will do. Now say the act of contrition. . . ."

So far as the efficacy of the particular sacrament is concerned, that indeed "will do." More, at long last, has actively returned to the faith. He is once more "in communion."

No matter that the local community of the faithful is still pitiably small—in fact, even smaller than it was five years before—and sharing its shabby "briar-patch"[9] quarters with other congregations, not only with a motley company of Protestants, but even with Jews (p. 396). In the time of the old "Troubles," five years before and earlier, "the center did not hold." Now, the crowded communal chapel in the slave quarters, where the beginnings and endings of the various services overlap, gives promise of becoming a new center, for religious and social reunification. On Christmas Eve, just before the midnight Mass "there is some confusion in the chapel. The Jews are leaving—it is their Sabbath. The Protestants are singing. Catholics are lining up for confession. *We have no ecumenical movement* (emphasis added). No minutes of the previous meeting are read. The services overlap. Jews wait for the Lord, Protestants sing hymns to him, Catholics say mass and eat him."

Again, the implication is clear, that the best promise for unity—not only among the various Christian congregations, black and white, but among Christians and non-Christians—is precisely the "confusion." Ecumenical *movements* as such, rationally contrived plans for unity, whether in the religious or any other order, are in More's view (obviously coincident with Percy's here) automatically suspect. "Ecumenism" is but another name for "consensus." If unity is ever to be achieved—whether it is the reunification of the United States or of the Christian church, or the ultimate reunification of Christians and Jews—it must come, not of conscious planning, the achievement of a "consensus" which inevitably involves the deliberate surrender of all distinguishing principle, but of the concatenation of individual commitments of faith, the almost haphazard building, in circumstances of practical necessity and a common economic adversity, of a community of goodwill.

What all these people have in common, with each other and notably with Tom More, is that they have been brought low. The visible power and dignity of all their religious establishments has been destroyed. Each in his own way, like Tom More by the words of the priest in the confessional, has been "scalded." This, if there is a way, is the way of their salvation. Especially with regard to the Roman Catholic Church, Percy's prophecy is clear. If it is ultimately to survive, and prevail against the powers of darkness, it must first be destroyed.

As for Tom More himself, in his personal fate, the "scalding" is essential to his recognizing the *limitations* of his mind and will if he is effectively to exercise them at all. In his admonitions prefatory to granting absolution, Father Smith speaks specifically only of More's sins of drunkenness and sexual promiscuity—and quite properly so, since these are the only matters which More himself brings up—but in his *way* of handling these offenses, the priest strikes at what he knows to be the real root of the trouble, More's personal *pride*. Smith says nothing of the Lapsometer, and of More's presumptions as millenarian prophet, but it will be the worse for More if he does not accept the chastening as applicable also to his intellectual pretensions.

Twice in the course of Tom's description of his session in the confessional (pp. 396, 398) there are references to Father Smith's part-time job as fire-watcher. We would do well to recall More's first description of the priest's duties in the firetower (p. 6): "It is his job to . . . watch for brushfires below *and for signs and portents in the skies*" (emphasis added). Precisely, the priest's job; not the physician's.

An important feature of the gentle remonstrance Father Smith administers to Tom in the confessional is his stress (p. 399) upon the duty of attention to professional responsibilities: "doing our jobs, you being a better doctor, I being a better priest." And, a few minutes before, having extracted Tom's promise to "pray that God will give [him] a true knowledge of [his] sins and a true contrition," he further remarks: "You are a doctor and it is your business to help people, not harm them."

Again, there is no specific reference to the Lapsometer project, or to the notoriously mischievous pride of the self-anointed prophet. In his generalized self-accusation (p. 397) More has spoken only of his "delight in the misfortunes of others, and of loving [himself] better than God and other men"; and Smith does not press him for details. But even the most casually attentive reader should have little difficulty in identifying the notable occasions of More's *Schadenfreude* and his overweening self-esteem. Both are rooted in his *intellectual* pride, his all-consuming devotion to the project of perfecting the Lapsometer, and, at any expense that might prove necessary, including the destruction of the earth, proving himself right and his academic enemies wrong.

Remembering the Fourth of July fiasco (More's own word for it, p. 383) five years before, one is likely to feel the hair rise on the back of his neck when, only a few hours before going to confession and communion, our mad scientist reveals the fact that he is *still* working on the Lapsometer, still believes it can "save the world"—if only he can "get it right": "Even now I can diagnose and shall one day cure: cure the new plague, the modern Black Death, the current hermaphroditism of the spirit, namely: More's syndrome, or: chronic angelism-bestialism. . . . Some day a man will walk into my office as ghost or beast or ghost-beast and walk out as a man, which is to say sovereign wanderer, lordly exile, worker and waiter and watcher."

It is the old familiar harangue all over again, with only minor changes in the phrasing—perhaps improvements, perhaps not. No doubt the desire for curative powers seems laudable enough at first glance, quite nobly altruistic. But, then, this is *not* the first glance, not the first time we have heard the piece. It sounded good five years ago, too; and look what happened. No doubt the devil will not show up again as Art Immelmann. But who is to say another disguise would not work?

The only real reason for hope we may have, hope for More as for the rest of us, is that all this does come before the confession and communion: not long before, to be sure, but still before. We can only hope at the end that More has truly got the message from Father Smith, in his talk of what their respective responsibilities are as priest and physician.

"Time to get locked in the box," Father Smith says (p. 396). The only real alternative to the Skinner box, for physicians or anybody else, is the Smith box, the confessional. And as for "signs and portents in the skies," the watching for those is also the priest's job, not the physician's—now as it always was.

The situation in the epilogue is precisely that, an allegory of a return, to things *as they always were* in the era of the Christian dispensation, not a prophetic vision of things to come "at a time near the end of the world." The unity of the church, as well as the unity of the United States, has been and is, always, in the making, always at a new beginning.

If Tom More's situation has at all changed, and improved, since the Troubles of five years before, it is just that he is now in a situation which renders him more *susceptible* of Grace. But Grace, as it works however obscurely through the agency of the church's sacraments—themselves necessarily imperfect since they must be administered by the imperfect, human priest—is the only recourse he has, just as it always was. No science of Tom's own, or any other man's own, can work the necessary miracle of redemption.

It does not matter, really, that Tom has got the hair shirt on outside his sports jacket (p. 399). (St. Thomas More is reputed to have worn a hair shirt, more appropriately, *under* his outer clothing.) And it matters really only a little more that Tom's "lusty Presbyterian" wife should judiciously (half-approvingly, half-warningly) raise her eyebrows at this display of public penance—silently reminding him of what happened once before when "you Catholics" got sanctity too much mixed up with "things." As More's simply *having* a Presbyterian wife, with Father Smith's tacit approval, sufficiently testifies, the Reformation—as far as it goes, or has gone or can go—is undoubtedly in Percy's view "a good thing" for the Catholic Church.

All outward signs, all workings of the divine will through human agency—pre- and post-Reformation—are necessarily imperfect, necessarily and properly suspect. But some are more suspect than others, as attesting a deliberate attempt to thwart that will, or turn it to special advantage.

And the most suspect of all, which is like all else a working of the divine will but refuses to recognize itself as such, is the veneration of Idea. Presbyterian Ellen warns Catholic Tom against a corruptive fascination with physical "things"; but the processes of abstraction pose a far greater danger for him. The "ruins" of Percy's novel are simply the world itself of man's customary habitation, a world ruled and ruined *by* the false worship of human intelligence.

The only way out of the ruin is by love. Divine love, of course. But divine love as manifested in lesser loves. For example, the love of woman. *Woman*, as distinct from *women*.

Tom More quotes his celebrated ancestor Sir Thomas (p. 383) to the effect that "knowing, not women, . . . is man's happiness." It is a remark to make feminists bristle, no doubt, at the implications of the plural "women" and the singular "man" if nothing else. Perhaps Sir T. spoke only from his own experience. But, however that may be, it is interesting to observe that Percy's novel ends, not with any talk of the Lapsometer, or of "signs and portents," but with Tom's taking Ellen off to bed.[10] There, it appears, at least for *this* man, with *this* woman, is the only happiness available.

5

Lancelot

I. Monologue and Madness: Some Questions of Competence

Like *The Moviegoer* and *Love in the Ruins*, *Lancelot* has a first-person narrator who is also the protagonist. But only in the "frame situation," of Percival's[1] visits to Lance in the prison/hospital, do we find anything resembling the present-tense convention of the two earlier novels. And that resemblance is largely superficial.

Except for Percival's monosyllabic, italicized responses at the very end—and two other less obtrusive devices which we shall discuss later—everything in this novel belongs to the form of the dramatic monologue. The principal action of *Lancelot* is contained in the protagonist's *past*-tense narrative, of the last days at Belle Isle and of events in his earlier personal history which are significant in foreshadowing the disaster. Use of the present tense in *Lancelot* is something altogether different from either Binx Bolling's or Tom More's way of telling his story. Here, it is a function of dramatic presentation, exclusively confined to what happens, as it were "on stage," during Percival's visits to Lance's cell.

Binx Bolling, in the epilogue chapter of *The Moviegoer*, speaks vaguely of a "document" he is producing, perhaps a book; near the beginning of *Love in the Ruins*, Tom More tells us he is using a tape recorder. In neither case is the narrative addressed to anyone in particular. On the other hand, everything that Lance Lamar says is most precisely and particularly addressed to Percival.

Thus, the reader is obliged not only to attend to what Lance is saying—try to keep up with plot and characters, analyze motives, react appropriately to the madman's philosophical rantings—but constantly to consider why he is saying these things, in the precise way he says them, to Percival. One must constantly attend to Percival, but attend to him—until the last two pages—without ever hearing him speak in his own right. Percival is the Tyrolian emissary to Lance's Duke of Ferrara.[2] Everything that we "know" about Percival, including the very fact of his presence in the cell, we know only by inference, from Lancelot's promptings and responses. Even the final series of italicized monosyllables is intelligible, if at all, only as linked to the long chain of inference we have to construct from Lancelot's monologue. Except inferentially, we could not so much as identify the italicized voice as Percival's.

Many of the reader's difficulties derive simply from the conventions of the dramatic monologue. But Percy has further complicated our task by presenting a madman as monologist. To be sure, Lance says at the end that he has been pronounced cured, that all arrangements have been made for his release. But the delusions of the accomplished "cure" and of imminent discharge are pathetically commonplace among inmates of mental institutions. If we are to read the book with any kind of critical responsibility, certain discriminations are called for: concerning, first of all, the nature of Lance's disorder.

We must begin by accepting the fictional "reality" of the opening scene. Perhaps, once we have got the first hint that the speaker is a lunatic, we shall want to reserve judgment on the question of Percival's presence. But the cell itself, we must assume, is just as Lance describes it: i.e., as Percy has determined he should describe it. The scene outside the window is what Lance describes. He has got the time of year right, too. The old women are dressing up the cemetery, scrubbing the tombstones, for All Souls Day: November 2 or 3. As Percy explains in a brief foreword, he has altered the map of New Orleans to suit his fictional purposes. The foreword serves to assure the reader that the liberties taken are part of the author's design for the whole fictional "world" of his novel, not distortions attributable to Lance's madness.

From the beginning, Lance exhibits no obvious symptoms of mental impairment. He is not disoriented. He is certainly not suffering from aphasia. He does not babble. He rants and raves, but that right eloquently. On the first day, he says that he "thinks" he recognizes Percival. The next day, he says that the initial uncertainty was all pretense: "I have a confession to make . . . I knew you perfectly well. There's nothing wrong with my memory. It's just that I don't like to remember" (p. 9). In short, it must soon appear, to the reader and we may assume to Percival as well, that Lance, if mad at all, is "but mad north-northwest."[3] There is little point in our going on with the book at all, beyond the first few pages, if we are disposed to keep raising the question of Lance's mental competence, to keep wondering whether the whole story of Belle Isle, as well as of the events in the prison/hospital, might not be the product of hallucination. Lance is certainly a type of the "unreliable narrator." His unreliability, although different in various important ways from both Binx Bolling's and Tom More's, is like More's in being in some aspects clearly related to his illness. But again in Lance's case as in More's, the unreliability cannot be conceived as total.

A few experiences Lance describes—notably his interview with "Our Lady of the Camellias" (p. 210ff.), and his watching and hearing the little girl who danced and sang a Cajun song on the levee (pp. 216–17) just before the storm struck—have the character either of vision or of hallucination. But these episodes are readily distinguishable, both for the reader and for Lance, from the commonplace, purely factual events of the same day.

Finally, although I tentatively granted the reader's right to "reserve judgment" on the question of Percival's real presence in the frame situation, it seems to me that we must, from some point very near the beginning, proceed on the assumption that he is actually there—for the simple reason that Lance's monologue is not consistently explicable on the basis of any other assumption. If we are not convinced that the silent Percival is present all along, his "speaking loud and clear" at the end will not remove our doubts.

But to be convinced that Lance in his cell is not simply talking to himself, and that he is accurately representing the basic facts of what happened at Belle Isle, is only a first step toward critical understanding of Percy's design. A number of troublesome uncertainties persist.

142

At the beginning of his last interview with Percival (p. 249), Lance says that he has been declared "psychiatrically fit and legally innocent." Even if we assume that he has not imagined the whole thing, that someone in authority has actually told him he will be discharged later that day, the legal situation is not very clear. Without specifics, the reference to "a writ of habeas corpus" (p. 250) does not explain either what has already happened in the courts, or what might happen in the future. The only thing we can infer with any confidence is that the question of Lance's sanity—specifically, the question whether he was legally sane or insane at the time the house at Belle Isle was destroyed—has been all along an issue of major importance for determination of his criminal liability.

And it appears that the state has had no valid grounds for holding him, except the same grounds on which he must be, or has already been, found innocent of the crimes at Belle Isle: i.e., the grounds of insanity. Once he is "cured," he must be released. To repeat, the precise nature of the writ his lawyer has obtained is not revealed. But Lance would appear to believe that he is no longer in legal jeopardy, that his impending release is final and unqualified. In the absence of any evidence to the contrary—and noting that Lance himself is a lawyer who has practiced in Louisiana—we have no choice but to take him at his word, no reason to hope, or fear, that the discharge will be cancelled.

Percival apparently thinks that the decision to release Lance is unwise (pp. 249–50). And, knowing what he knows just from listening to Lance, most readers will probably agree. But Percival as psychiatrist is no longer, if he ever was, officially connected with the case. And in any event, strictly on the basis of his medical expertise and experience, he would probably have to "agree" with the official decision: that, within the legal definition, Lance is now sane.

We might well imagine that Percival's dilemma is shared by all the experts, both legal and medical, who *are* officially involved in the case. All might agree, *as experts*, but privately, that a very dangerous man is being loosed, that he will probably do again, but on a much larger scale, what he has done before. On the other hand— still professionally, but publicly and officially—the very same experts must agree that the dreadful fellow is entitled to his freedom.

Society, meanwhile, which created both professions, both companies of "experts," presumably for its own protection and improvement, is left helpless, victimized by its own creation. In all essentials, the predicament is one with which we are depressingly familiar in the everyday experience of real life. How are we to account for it? And what is our recourse?

The "answers," I think, implicit in Percy's book, are approximately these. There is no accounting for the quandary presented by such a case as Lance's so long as we regard it as stemming from specific flaws in the system of justice, such as might be corrected by specific modifications of the legal code. What is wrong in cases like this, Percy suggests, is wrong with the *whole* system of justice; and the ills of that system are symptomatic of a deep-seated malady that infects the entire social body. We cannot understand the problem, and we cannot protect ourselves from the miscarriage of justice, so long as we depend upon the various "experts"—legal, medical, or other—to make all our decisions for us.

The very name of the institution in which Lance is confined suggests the nature of the problem. *Lancelot* is not primarily a satire, and not notably futuristic; but the "Center for Aberrant Behavior" sounds like something belonging to the false utopia of *Love in the Ruins*. Fancy jargon in the naming of institutions and projects is always a sign of the pernicious reign of "expertism," of course. And it looks as if the particular company of experts who have set up shop here are none other than our old friends the super-Skinnerians from Fedville. The plea of innocence by reason of insanity in cases of "capital offense" has been around for a long time; and we long ago all but totally abandoned the use of words like "prison" and "jail" in official designation of those unpleasant institutions. Both phenomena are representative of the tendency, inherent in pernicious expertism, to try coping with the bad thing by calling it something else. Certain crimes are not crimes at all; they are manifestations of illness, and we put the perpetrators in hospitals, not prisons. Once we have got the notion of crime as a function of illness into our heads, it is hard to get it out. Perhaps, we begin to suspect, there is really no such thing as a crime. If the perpetrator is not sick, then the society which produced him must be.

If, in practice, we still find it necessary to "convict" a considerable number of bad doers, we commit them to a "house of detention" or a "correctional facility." Of course, everybody knows, or strongly suspects, that the place is still a house of horrors. But at least for those of us who do not have to go there, the naming itself makes us feel better, somehow. We pay the experts, not to do anything about the problems, but just to provide new terminology.

"Center for Aberrant Behavior" carries the familiar process one step further. It would appear that, in Lance's world, not only "crime" and "prison" but "sickness" and "hospital" as well are dirty words. What was once a crime or a manifestation of insanity is now merely a type of "behavior." Not even *errant* behavior, but *ab*errant behavior. The uninitiated observer—the "plain reader," shall we say—might well wonder what is done in such a place. Do they "center" the "aberrant behavior" there for the purpose of confining it, correcting it, observing it, or what? Fostering it, perhaps? In any event, it is a fascinating feature of the institution that its admissions policy apparently makes no distinction between perpetrators and victims. Lance's "aberrant behavior" consisted in part of blowing a house and four people in it to kingdom come. Anna, on the other hand, got herself gang-raped, slashed and beaten up, and left for dead on the river bank. But here they are at the Center in unlocked neighboring rooms. Perhaps, if we insist on distinctions, it would be permissible to designate Lance's aberrance as active and Anna's as passive. He and she are both "behavers," nothing more or less.

One of Lance's more attractive, or admirable, characteristics is his unaffected scorn for his captors and their jargon (p. 3). "Is this a prison or a hospital or a prison hospital? A Center for Aberrant Behavior? So that's it. I have behaved aberrantly. In short, I'm in the nuthouse." At first, feistily refusing to cooperate—"After all, what is there to talk about?"—he must remind us a good deal of old Mr. Ives at Gerry Rehab. But the differences, between the two men and their quests and between the two situations they are up against, are at least as important as the likenesses.

For example, it appears that at the Center for Aberrant Behavior the inmates are not only permitted but encouraged to consult clergymen as well as medical doctors. And Percival's dubious dual creden-

tials, as "screwed-up priest [and] half-assed physician" (p. 10),
reflect a general confusion of values that goes beyond what is represented in the image of Kev Kevin at the vaginal console.

In Lance's view, the prevailing secular doctrine, according to
which there are no such things as crime and criminals, has its
analogy in modern theology, Catholic as well as Protestant. Not
only has crime been philosophically eliminated, but so has sin. This
is Lancelot's great theme in his haranguing of Percival, the theme of
the Quest which he says he conceived in pursuit of proof of his
wife's infidelity. He came to think of his investigation as a search for
the Unholy Grail, an appropriate modern inversion of the quest
undertaken by his legendary medieval namesake.

II. Lance and the Myth of Aristocracy

The scholarly quest for the origins of the Grail legend has taken its
pursuers into terrain as obscure and dangerous as any the Lancelots
and Percivals and Galahads themselves had to venture upon. As all
readers of T. S. Eliot know, Jessie L. Weston wrote a book called
From Ritual to Romance,[4] which purports to offer "a genuine
Elucidation of the Grail problem"—such elucidation consisting
primarily, as the title suggests, of studies exploring the connection
between ancient fertility rituals and the Grail legend as it appeared
in medieval romances. A spirit of the anti-ecclesiastical, as it might
be called, is obvious from beginning to end of Weston's book. In
chapter 13, "The Perilous Chapel," she theorizes, or rhapsodizes:
"The Grail romances repose eventually . . . upon the ruins of an
august and ancient ritual. . . . Driven from its high estate by the
relentless force of religious evolution . . . it yet lingered on . . . where
those who craved for a more sensible (not necessarily sensuous) contact with the unseen Spiritual forces of Life than the orthodox development of Christianity afforded, might, and did, find satisfaction" (p. 187).

Weston suggests that medieval authors made various efforts to
Christianize the quest story—one of the cruder examples being "the
identification of the sex Symbols, Lance and Cup, with the weapon
of the Crucifixion, and the Cup of the Last Supper"—but "the

Christianization was merely external, the tale, as a whole, retaining its pre-Christian character" (p. 205).

Sir Lancelot du Lac, as seeker of the Grail, belongs to the more thoroughly Christianized adaptation of the story. Thus there is justification for Lancelot Lamar's referring to him as a "Catholic" hero. Lance explains his notion of why his father named him as he did: "The Andrewes was tacked on by him to give it Episcopal sanction, but what he really had in mind and in his heart wanted to be and couldn't have been more different from was that old nonexistent Catholic brawler and adulterer, Lancelot du Lac, King Ban of Benwick's son, knight of the Round Table . . ." (p. 116).

Nothing that Lance Lamar says would indicate his own awareness of anything other than the Christian interpretations of the Grail stories. And I am not primarily interested here in pursuing the question of what Percy might or might not have "intended" in the system of allusions. But Weston's theory, of the origins of the Grail story and of continuing conflict between the medieval church and the secret fertility cults, provides an extremely valuable background for analysis of what happens in Lance's personal quest for the "Unholy Grail."

Starting out with some notion of a fairly simple *parody*, or simple inversion, of the Christian symbolism—and failing, then, in that quest, as he tells Percival—Lance ends up with a vision of a "new life," a new order of the world, from which it seems likely that traditional Christianity will be excluded altogether. If, as Lance says he has discovered to his satisfaction in the disaster at Belle Isle, there is, in fact, simply no such thing as Sin, original or otherwise, then it follows that there is no need for redemptive Grace. Christianity can be written off; and anyone, such as Lance, who simply knows what he wants, is free to start over from scratch. He proposes, in other words, to found a rival cult, one not simply "heretical," but based on entirely different principles, an entirely different worldview: in short, something that would, like the medieval fertility cults hypothesized by Weston, "str[ike] at the very root and vitals of Christianity" (p. 187).

I do not mean that the society of new-worlders envisaged by Lance Lamar, *except* in its radical opposition to institutionalized

Christianity, in any way resembles the cults of which Weston speaks. The principal points I want to make, about Percy's allusions in this novel to the Arthurian romances, are that 1) it is all too easy to oversimplify the nature of the literature to which he alludes, and 2) it is all too easy both to oversimplify and at the same time to exaggerate the significance of those allusions as a key to the structure of the novel.

It will not do, I think, simply to pick out some version of the Grail story—say that of Tennyson, or of Malory, or of Chrétien de Troie—and set about defining all the possible parallels between the source and Percy's novel. That way, and not a long way, madness lies.

In this kind of game, it hardly matters where one starts. The pigeonnier looks tempting, perhaps, as a "Perilous Chapel." But perilous in more ways than one, unfortunately. So many things happen there. In their youth, Lancelot and Percival read "dirty books" there (*Ulysses* and *Tropic of Cancer*, etc.) and resurrected the old Bowie knife; Lance first made love to Margot there; there, later, he made his great "discovery," of Margot's infidelity; there he met the visionary Lady of the Camellias. Have we, in the dining room where Margot and the movie folk met for late supper and talk, their company briefly joined by Lance, a version of the Round Table? The notion is hard to resist, with both a Lancelot and a Merlin present. But where is Arthur, and who is presiding in his absence? Who is Jacoby? An alter-Merlin? Jacoby is, after all, a person of obscure origins, unknown parentage. Lance did, after all, guy Merlin about his "assistant." Who was really directing the film, the grizzled master magician or the upstart underling? *Hm*, as Lance is wont to mutter so often. What of Margot? Guinevere? Twice, at least, Lance toys with that notion, but is forced to admit, on the fundamental question of cuckoldry, that the comparison will not work. Lancelot du Lac was the queen's lover; King Arthur, the cuckold. Here, Lancelot himself is the cuckold—to the second power, as it turns out, since Jacoby as well as Merlin had "known" Margot.

Lance (p. 116) speaks of Lancelot du Lac as "one of only two knights to see the Grail (you, Percival, the other)." According to Malory and Tennyson, the authors Lance Lamar would be most likely to know, neither Lancelot nor Percival was able to look directly at the Grail.[5] Lancelot, because of his sin with Guinevere, saw it only in a kind of dream, half waking and half sleeping.[6] Purer Percival achieved a genuine vision, but not the closest. Only the flawlessly virgin Sir Galahad, with a power beyond all human intelligence, was privileged to look directly upon the vessel, beholding its unspeakable mysteries. Some readers have been tempted to see this "mistake" of Lance's as significant; and the temptation is certainly understandable. Lance's failure to distinguish between Lancelot's and Percival's way of seeing the Grail, and his neglecting Galahad altogether, could well be taken as symptomatic of the spiritual malady he suffers which foredooms his own "quest" to failure. Like his legendary namesake's, but even more severely, his spiritual insight is impaired in his preoccupation with sex. So "engrossed" is his mind with the subject of sexual sin that he cannot conceive of higher orders of inquiry, of what it might be like to see into the "heart of light" which is the true Grail.

But the moment we begin to notice how many obscurities there are in Lance's references to Arthurian literature, we are wise to use caution in making very much of any of them. I cannot see that there is any comprehensive, consistent system in the handling of the allusions: anything resembling, say, the strict pattern of correspondences in Joyce's *Ulysses* between the events of everyday life in modern Dublin and the episodes of the Homeric epic.

It seems to me the Arthurian allusions might "work" best, for critical purposes, if we viewed them simply as the most flamboyant evidences of Lance Lamar's general disposition to self-aggrandizement. First, there is the matter of his family pride.

Few critics of the novel have paid much attention to Lance's "aristocratic" consciousness. But a preoccupation with his lineage radically affects everything that he does. In the final analysis, none of the other critical issues—aesthetic, moral, theological, psychological, social, and political—can be adequately examined without reference to the Lamar family heritage.

If there is anything that has given Lance more trouble all his life than sex—and the two cannot really be separated—it is his ancestry. He makes fun of himself for it, of course. He is too intelligent not to make fun. How droll he is, remembering himself as the "master of Belle Isle," made over by Margot into a living movie version of the "Southern gent," sipping his "toddy" from a silver goblet, in the restored old house now surrounded by a wilderness of gas flares and pipery. But the self-mockery is actually a device of self-protection, against the real pain of the guilt he feels as an unworthy "scion." He makes fun of the family pride, but he dotes on it all the same. How melancholy he is, withal, as he talks of his father's "dishonor" in taking the kickback money from the crooked politicians.

The family had denied the rumors about his father, because the Lamars "were an honorable family with an honorable name." As Lance uses the word, "honor" is clearly a property of hereditary social status. What his father did would have been for a man of undistinguished lineage merely *dishonest*. *Dishonor* is reserved for those who are judged—by others and by themselves—according to an ancestral code.

When Lance tells of his finding the ten thousand dollars in his father's sock drawer, he stresses the strange, secret delight he took in the discovery, the sense of personal liberation it gave him: "*Ah, then, things are not so nice*, I said to myself. But you see, that was an important discovery. For if there is one thing harder to bear than dishonor, it is honor, being brought up in a family where everything is so nice, perfect in fact, except of course oneself" (pp. 41–42). But the rest of the novel makes it plain that the sense of liberation was deceptive. The "old world" did not, after all, fall apart. The sweet new thing he savored so, "dishonor," was no new thing at all. "Dishonor" and "honor" are but the two socks of one pair, superior to ordinary socks only in this: that if, having somehow misplaced one of the pair, you keep the other, its mate is *sure* to turn up sooner or later. If Lance seems at times to have entertained the notion of throwing off his burden of family consciousness, it is important to realize that he has got exactly nowhere with that project by the time he addresses his last question to Percival.

When he tells the story of how, back in the sixties, he got the local Kluxers to lay off the Buells (Elgin's family) and their black Baptist church, Lance is wearing his customary mask of self-deprecation (pp. 92–93). In old Ellis Buell's TV-fevered imagination, "Mr. Lance" had "called out" the "white trash" Kleagle of the Klan and, "in the grand mythic Lamar tradition," simply threatened to shoot him if the harassment did not stop.

Wryly referring to the "slightly bogus-liberal fashion" of his thought and behavior at the time, Lance confesses to Percival that he really did not threaten, or even berate, the Kleagle—an old high school classmate of Lance's named J.B. Jenkins. What he did was simply to "give his word" to J.B., knowing it would be accepted, that nothing subversive was going on at the Buells' church. When Jenkins continued feebly to protest that even if Ellis were no Communist he was certainly "one more uppity nigger," all Lance had to say further (p. 93) was "Yeah, but he's *my* nigger, J.B." The encounter ended with the amiable pair toasting their meeting of minds with a slug of J. B.'s best three-dollar whiskey.

Regardless of method, and "bogus-liberal" or not, Lance was effective in his immediate purpose, of protecting the Buells and their church building, which the Klansmen had threatened to burn down. And the surface candor of the revelation, what I have called "the mask of self-deprecation" he wears in the telling, is charming enough in its way.

But the mask *is* a mask, however charming. "Bogus-liberal" in his thinking on black civil rights, Lance is by the same token a "bogus buddy" in his dealings with J.B. What Lance essentially was in his visit to the Kleagle—a lord of the manor, stepping in to settle a troublesome dispute between one of his domestic servants and some obstreperous townsman, serenely confident of his benevolent superiority to both—he remains to the end, except that he loses the benevolence.

The best that can be said for Lance's conduct in these affairs is that he acted on a principle of *noblesse oblige*. By the time he got around to "collecting" on the deal by engaging Elgin, Ellis's son, as his confederate in spying on Margot and her friends—proving that the son too, far more "uppity" than old Ellis could ever have been, was still "[his] nigger" (p. 181)—there was little left of the *noblesse* but arrogance. Telling Percival about it, Lance drops the genial mask altogether: "Ha. Then he was my nigger after all, and if he could look [at the films he had made of the white folks' sexual capers], wouldn't, didn't. Or better, he looked for technical reasons, but forebore to see. He was the perfect nigger."

Lance insists to Percival that his discovery of Margot's infidelity, although it reminded him of the money in his father's sock drawer, was really "something quite different" (p. 42). But disguise it as he would, the old sense of the family "honor" was obviously very much alive in his responses as knowing cuckold. The first, intensely personal, pain he felt in imagining Margot's "ecstasy" with another man—and, again despite his denials, it is clear that he did feel such pain—gave way to a growing sense of dismay, not at what Margot had *done*, but at what she *was*.

Repeatedly, beneath all his finespun theorizing, Lance's narrative of the events at Belle Isle reveals the deepening *embarrassment* he felt in the anomalous position to which he had consigned himself, allowed Margot to consign him, in his ancestral house. As he watched Margot with the movie people, she fawning upon them almost as obviously as teenager Lucy fawned, courting their vulgarly pretentious favor, knowingly and shamelessly permitting herself to be exploited, both for sex *and* for money—above all, for money—Lance came to the sickening realization that he had been not only cuckolded, but cuckolded in a marriage that was beneath him. His house had been taken over, he himself shunted aside, by a band of ragtag mountebanks, insufferable trash. But the worst of it was that his wife herself, in heart and desire if not in performance (he realized, seeing her before the cameras, that she was not even a good actress), was one of their company. His first wife, Lucy, for whom the daughter was named, had been a proper mate for a Lamar, not only virgin as a bride, but fruit of a more than acceptable Georgia family tree. But Margot—he suppressed the knowledge at first, ravenous as he was for sex, nose down on the trail of the bitch scent and oblivious to all else—Margot was in no sense acceptable. Rich, to be sure, and with a certain brash, home-on-the-range Texas charm, at least in youth, but Margot was trash.[7] By comparison not only to Janos Jacoby but to Margot herself, the chief mountebank Robert Merlin came to appear in Lance's eyes a kind of "nature's gentleman."

Very early in their acquaintance, Lance noted and mused upon the odd rapport that he and Merlin had established and that was not damaged, but if anything enhanced, by Lance's "discovery" that Merlin had fathered Siobhan. Recalling a conversation about certain dialectal peculiarities Merlin had observed in local speech patterns, Lance tells Percival:

His blue gaze engaged me with a lively intimacy, establishing a bond between us and excluding the others. Somehow his offense against me was also an occasion of intimacy between us. . . . Things were understood and unspoken between us. . . . Not even Margot followed us when we spoke of Tate's "Ode to the Confederate Dead" and Hemingway's nastiness to Fitzgerald.

It was as if we were old hands at something or other. But at what? Why should there be a bond between us? . . . (p. 47)

The sympathy of intellectual interests, and the shared sense of intellectual superiority to the others, are obvious enough, and apparently did not account to Lance's satisfaction for the strength of the affinity he sensed. Neither, it would appear, while acknowledging the ironic fact of its being an additional "occasion of intimacy," did Lance regard their having shared Margot's sexual favors as quite explaining his and Merlin's interest in each other. Later, when Lance learned that Jacoby had replaced Merlin as Margot's lover, that in effect both he and Merlin had been "jilted," perhaps that discovery provided still further grounds for his sympathizing with the man who had first put the horns on his head. But this too is not quite enough when it comes to explaining why Lance decided in the end to spare Merlin, encouraging him to leave Belle Isle before the house was destroyed. The essential "bond" between Lance and Merlin, which Lance has such difficulty in defining, is one that finally has little to do with Margot's infidelities.

The episode that provides perhaps the best clue to the nature of the affinity is that in which Jacoby ignored (or simply failed to notice) Lance's offering to shake hands, and the embarrassed Merlin was at pains to try making amends (pp. 148–49). The all important difference between Merlin and Jacoby, from Lance's point of view —the difference that made Merlin, Margot's first seducer, worth sparing, while Jacoby, the second offender, must be destroyed—is simply that Merlin had a right sense of manners and their value, of how a guest ought to behave in the presence of his host, and Jacoby did not. Although neither he nor Lance, presumably, sensed it at the time, it is clear in retrospect that Jacoby had sealed his own death warrant when he failed to grasp Lance's outstretched hand.

"That wretched Jacoby," as Lance calls him (p. 253), is the complete interloper. Lance did not hate Jacoby, but loathed and despised him, less because he had entered Margot's bed—there was, after all, no longer any telling how many had taken their turns there— than because he was the guttersnipe who had dared to enter the *house* without proper respect.

The House of Lamar. With the ancestral weapon, the much-celebrated old Bowie knife[8]—presented to him by his mother in the second phase of his vision in the pigeonnier—Lance killed Jacoby. Of his father's dishonor in the matter of thievery, Lance had been convinced since childhood that there was tangible "proof" in the shape of the money in the sock drawer. But he had long suspected something more: that his father was also a cuckold, probably a knowing and cooperative one. When Lance was a child, his mother often went off on long drives, "joyriding," with "a distant cousin . . . a handsome beefy Schenley salesman" known at Belle Isle as "Uncle Harry" or "Buster" (p. 96). In later years, naturally, Lance brooded much upon the dark possibilities of the situation; and at least once, as a young man, he entertained the horrid thought (p. 214) even that this walking cartoon, the archetypal "traveling salesman," might be his father. Perhaps he, Lance, was not a Lamar at all.

But the more the family honor was sullied, and the grounds of his own right and duty in the matter eroded almost beyond recognition, the more desperately determined he was to redeem it all. In the first phase of the vision in the pigeonnier, the "Lady of the Camellias" informed him that at least one of his old suspicions was justified: yes, Harry Wills was Lily Lamar's lover. Then, in the second phase of the vision, the Lady became Lance's mother: who, handing him the Bowie knife, plainly commissioned him to take revenge upon those who had desecrated his ancestral house. This, despite the fact that she herself, with Wills, had added cuckoldry to the dishonor of her husband's thievery. Under the circumstances, it hardly seems important that the question of Lance's paternity was not even brought up in the course of the visionary interviews.

Taking the newly "consecrated" knife from his mother's hands, and making his way back to the house through the storm, Lance, it appears, was not in the least disturbed by the moral incongruity of his mission in light of his own and his parents' complicity in dishonor. By the time he had rigged the connection of gas well to air-conditioning system and got to Jacoby, whom he dispatched with

154

no compunction and hardly more feeling than he might have had in killing a large rat, Lance had reverted completely to the ancestral type.

Moreover, there is still a good deal of artistocratic arrogance and complacency of the simplest form in Lance's presumptuous approach to Anna. Why should she not be attracted by the prospect of so splendid a "catch" as he is—madness, ruined fortunes, bastard daughter and all? The attitude is, of course, in part a function of madness. But the madness only intensifies a habit of mind which is frequently characteristic of "normal" class-consciousness.

Talking to Margot just before he lighted the lamp, and pathetically thinking that somehow they might still repair their broken marriage, Lance completely forgot about the gas. And presumably he intended—or, at any rate, was willing—to blow himself up along with the others. Had that happened, the parallel between the Houses of Lamar and Usher—which Percy has obviously invited the reader to consider—would have been all too patly established.

But it did not happen. With the demise of Roderick Usher, the last of his line, the House Genealogical presumably perished with the House Architectural. But Lancelot Lamar survived—survived, moreover, with living issue.

It might well have been that Lance, at some point in the final days of the moviemakers' visit, sank so deep in despair that he felt the honor of his house could be redeemed only by its destruction. Or before he rigged the mansion to explode—making the house itself the bomb, the instrument of its own destruction, thus ingeniously suiting the physical to the moral situation in which the human beings had conspired, knowingly or unknowingly, in their own ruin —perhaps despair had already yielded to madness. The chronology of the development, or disintegration, of his mental life is never quite clear. It is possible that both his "theological" speculations and the "mythologizing," in which he seems at times to have conceived of himself as an actual reincarnation of Lancelot du Lac, were well advanced *before* he blew up the house, rather than being entirely the product of his broodings in his cell at the Center.

Either way, it is obvious that any notion he might have had of totally destroying the House of Lamar has not worked out. In the first place, he has apparently given little thought to his older children's future. He speaks repeatedly of his plans for Siobhan. Since it would appear that the facts about her parentage are not known to anyone who would care to challenge Lance's legal status as her father, he is probably correct in assuming that he can reclaim custody once he has established a new residence. But it is hard to make any sense of his one remark concerning the others in his final conversation with Percival (p. 255): "I do not propose to live in Sodom or to raise my son and daughters in Sodom." Actually, he will probably have little to say about what happens to his daughter Lucy from now on, and nothing at all in the case of the son. For better or worse, these two are already "raised" long since.

Lucy is mentioned by name only once after Lance's account of his sending her back to school to escape the hurricane. It was the sight of Lucy's sorority ring on the actress's finger (p. 235) which confirmed Lance in his final murderous hatred of Raine Robinette. Perhaps we may take it as one of the surer signs of Lance's madness that, in the light of subsequent events, he can still assume that his daughter will accept his moral guidance when he emerges from his cell at the Center.

In the entire novel, there are only a few brief references to the grown son—a former draft-dodger, now turned homosexual—who was Lance's and his wife Lucy's first-born. Lance is obviously ashamed of his son, and reluctant to talk of him; emotionally, he seems close to disowning him. But on the matter of legal rights of inheritance we are given no information. And Lance's account of the young man's sex life is at best unconvincing even with regard to the past and present, not to speak of the future.

When Lance first mentions him to Percival (p. 17), he says that his son simply "got enough of women before he was twenty," adding rather vaguely that "presently he appears to be a mild homosexual." On later telling (p. 177), the story has changed a bit. Lance has, he says to Percival, a "confession" to make: his son became a homosexual—and not, it appears after all, quite so "mild" a one—because he was *frightened* rather than merely worn out by the insatiable lust of all the girls he knew. In the final reference, having mainly to do with the war records of the Lamar men of different generations, sex is mentioned only as one item in a list of the son's renegade activities (p. 217). "My son refused to go to Vietnam, went underground instead in New Orleans, lived in an old streetcar, wrote poetry, and made various kinds of love."

It is difficult to reconcile the two earlier accounts; and the last does nothing to clarify the situation. That the supremely "laid-back" young man of the episode first described should be capable of entertaining boyfriends as well as girlfriends is certainly not hard to believe. What seems highly doubtful is that he could become the "scared little prick" Lance later describes, turned homosexual out of sheer terror of women. Lance says that this is the story he got from the young man himself (p. 177). And, by introducing it as part of a "confession" he is now making, as it were to *correct* misrepresentations in the earlier account, Lance obviously hopes to establish its credibility with Percival. But, in addition to numerous other improbabilities in the case history as Lance presents it, the trouble with the idea of his son's homosexual alliance as mere refuge, from the terrors of the heterosexual life, is just that such an explanation is so plainly what a father like Lance would *want* to believe. It appears that the one possibility Lance cannot finally accept—anxious and guilt-ridden as he obviously is about all his own sexual problems, including his never quite successfully repressed bisexual tendencies— is what he first suggested to Percival (p. 17), that his son, whether "hetero or homo," simply never has been "hung up on" sex in the way he himself is.

In any event, nothing that Lance says about his son definitely rules out the possibility of the young man's marrying at some time in the future, and perhaps begetting a son of his own—so that the family may be continued in the direct, male line of descent. It is by no means established that the younger Lamar's conversion to homosexuality is permanent. And besides, the time-setting of the novel's principal action, beginning in 1976, is well within the American social era in which avowed homosexuals, both male and female, have more and more frequently contracted marriages with members of the opposite sex—"marriages of convenience," or "mixed marriages," as they might be called—for the primary or sole purpose of reproduction.

Genealogically, the House of Lamar survives. And it is important to note that even the House Architectural is not completely destroyed. Nothing more is made of it in later conversations, but in assessing Lance's plans for the future we should not forget his disclosure that the pigeonnier was not destroyed in the explosion and fire (p. 31), and his portentously casual remark to Percival that the complete and careful records he kept in his files there are probably still intact. Though non-contiguous with the main house at Belle Isle, the pigeonnier survives as an essential part of the Lamar estate: estate legal, estate psychological, estate moral, estate mythological, estate theological.

In spite of all, the family history continues, and so does Lance's preoccupation with it. Early in the course of Percival's visits to the cell, family- and class-consciousness—the sense of heriditary superiority their two families shared as "an enclave of the English gentry set down among hordes of good docile Negroes and comical French peasants" (p. 14)—is of central significance in Lance's reminiscences. And the same consciousness, essentially unaltered, radically informs his ranting prophecies at the end.

Not that Lance has never thought of the terms on which his aristocratic claims might be challenged. Indeed, he is both painstaking and eloquent, at times scathingly self-mocking, in his own critique of the tradition.

Neither the house at Belle Isle, isolated in an industrial wasteland, nor the "scion" himself, with his quaint notions of honor and dishonor, had been for a long time worth anything to anybody except as either or both might be briefly exploited for profit—first by the gas producers, then by the tourists and movie people, and finally, after the fire, by sensation-mongering journalists. The attitudes of a degenerate and ignorant public are not in themselves enough to invalidate the heritage. And neither are Lance's own misdeeds. But beyond and back of all that, Lance is obviously aware of the possibility that the "heritage," at least in its American phase, never amounted to much.

One of Lance's forebears was supposed to have known Jim Bowie, and to have "had a part in the notorious Vidalia sand-bar duel in which Bowie actually carved a fellow limb from limb" (p. 18). Another one was said to have fought his own duel: "in fact on the same sand bar," and remarkably similar to Bowie's adventure in other respects (pp. 154–55). Were the two ancestors actually the same man? To add to the general dubiety of the situation, it might be noted that the story of *Bowie's* duel is not a matter of undisputed historical fact. Nor, for that matter, is it certain even that he was the inventor of the so-called "Bowie knife." But in what is known of his life—that he was a low-born Kentuckian, sometime fortune-hunter, interloper in New Orleans society, clever and ambitious and unscrupulous entrepreneur in the sugarcane processing business, slave trader withal, something on the order of a real-life Thomas Sutpen—there is nothing to suggest that he was incapable of the barbaric acts attributed to him in the legend of the sand bar.

If Lance must look to men like Jim Bowie for an ancestral "role model," he is in sad case. There was no "honor" in what Bowie is said to have done on the Vidalia sand bar, and none that Lance can praise with much conviction in his ancestor's behavior in the same setting. The latter exploit, indeed, as Lance tells Percival (p. 154), was precisely *not* an "*affaire d'honneur*." A traditional measure of a family's nobility is its contribution to the making of history, and one great-great-grandfather, Manson Maury Lamar (p. 217), did something definitely heroic in the Battle of Sharpsburg. But he was only *Captain* Lamar and his career seems to have been otherwise unremarkable. Another ancestor, a private, came home on leave to Belle Isle in 1862 and hid out from a Yankee patrol in a fireplace warming oven (p. 45). Another (p. 237) was a friend of John C. Calhoun, way back in the 1840s. But this is a connection, never very clearly defined, to a man who was in any sense an "aristocrat" only by marriage, and "honorable" chiefly in vain defense of the extreme Southern position on slaveholding in the Senate debates preceding passage of the famous Compromise of 1850.

The picture that gradually emerges is of a Lance suffering lifelong anxiety about the family heritage. Aristocrats? One of the principal traditional criteria is hereditary ownership of land. At least in the past, the Lamars had the land. No matter that, at some point unspecified, they seem to have lost it. At least up to Lance's generation—which is to say, up to the point that most people ceased to care much one way or the other about the definition of aristocracy—the South loved losing. But it would appear that a number of Lamars of earlier generations also had dealings, in business and politics and sex, with low-born interlopers and fortune hunters, the "Uncle Harrys" and "Margots" of their various times, some of whom, with their get and kin, even became members of the family. If nothing worse, we know that the *ethnic* purity of the strain was compromised many generations back. It is doubtful from the context that Lance has anything of that in mind when he speaks self-mockingly of his "sweet Louisiana Anglo-Saxon aristocracy gone to pot" (p. 81). But since he has at least once before mentioned the family's pride in its status as "English gentry" (p. 14), it seems worthwhile noting that the knife-wielding great-great-grandfather was son to a woman who—if a "lady" and "very white"—was of Creole[9] ancestry, "a d'Arbouche from New Roads" (p. 154), most certainly not Anglo-Saxon. There is in the Lamar family chronicles no consistent record of substantial public service; no record of consistent moral rectitude, of adherence in any sphere of activity to a reliable code of ethics; no reliable tradition of manners or ceremony in social conduct. Although he speaks also of their gregariousness and anti-Long political activism (p. 15), by Lance's account the men of his family, before his father, were notable chiefly for their violence. And, while violence is by no means alien to the aristocratic tradition in any society, it is no less commonly characteristic of lower-class behavior. About the only thing that dependably identifies the Lamars of all eras as gentry—an aptitude otherwise consistently observable only in pimps and big-city municipal employees—is their ability to sustain life without working.

Lance is well aware of all this. When he says (p. 121), concerning Margot's romantic notions of what she was getting in marrying him, "of course we were not . . . aristocratic,"[10] he is speaking primarily of himself and others of his generation. But we may assume, from the evidence of the whole novel, that the thought has more than once crossed his mind that the Lamars, throughout their history in this country, are typical of American gentry in the essential fraudulence of their hereditary claims to special status. And yet, no matter how often and unmistakably the falsity of the aristocratic ideal is revealed to him, he is unable to relinquish it.

When he made his first great discovery, in his father's sock drawer, that things were not after all so "perfect" in the family—made the discovery and relished it—the experience might have been the beginning of true wisdom. But the wisdom has never come. Instead of rejecting the false ideal altogether, and seeking some workable alternative faith, he has spent his life in a series of attempts somehow to "redeem" the discredited heritage.

His fascination with his first name, his notion that the "Andrewes" was simply "tacked on" by his father as a concession to Episcopal respectability, the temptation to see mysterious "correspondences" between his own experiences and those of Arthur's knight: all represent what might be called a "sublimation" of the aristocratic impulses which he sees as intellectually indefensible, but which he is still unable to subdue. What Lance likes about Lancelot du Lac is first of all that he is "nonexistent" (p. 116). "Lamar" and "Andrewes" are names compromised and tainted by history, by the world of time. "Lancelot" speaks to something beyond time, incorruptible. The nobility of the company to which Lancelot du Lac belongs, the Order of the Round Table, is a nobility—unlike that of a mere Lamar or Andrewes—which cannot be compromised, regardless of what crimes and follies the knights and their ladies are charged with.

But Lance's effort to create a kind of invulnerable mythic identity for himself, on the strength of his name, does not work. First, he has no very reliable knowledge of the Arthurian legends. At least twice he asserts (pp. 116, 176), as we have noted, that Lancelot and Percival were the only two knights who saw the Holy Grail. He has forgotten not only "good Sir Bors" but, more significantly, Sir Galahad: the Knight of Perfect Chastity, the only one—in the version of the legend which has come down to us through Malory and Tennyson—who was found worthy to look directly upon the sacred vessel.[11] Further, Lance is consciously embarrassed by the improbability of the parallels which he tries to draw between his situation and Sir Lancelot's: "it was not so much the case of my screwing the queen as the queen getting screwed by somebody else" (p. 64). It is just as well that Lance was willing to play any or all of the parts himself—Arthur to his own Lancelot, if not the queen to both or either—for no one else present at Belle Isle seems even to have been aware of his attempt to reenact the legend.

The attempt failed, first because Lance does not very well understand either this particular legend or the relationship in general of legend to history. But further, it failed because the others knew no more, and cared no more, about Lance as Lancelot du Lac than they knew or cared about Lance as Lamar. If they had been asked to consider the matter (and they were not asked), we may safely assume that all would have been one to them: Camelot and Belle Isle, Knights of the Round Table and Uncle Harry at the Mardi Gras, all undifferentiated grist for their cinematic Instant-Myth-Mix machine.

III. Cinema, Sex, and Revolution: The Cuckold's Revenge

When Lance was told (pp. 25–26) that the film's plot involved a scheme by the "master of the house" to steal a sharecropper's land, his "only contribution to the story discussions was to point out that the land could not belong to the sharecropper if he was a share-cropper." There are several layers of irony here, some of them visible to Lance and some not; but the point I want to emphasize is that the dry and lawyerly reserve of Lance's comment perfectly expressed his contempt for the whole undertaking. In his view, it is only on such a precise point of legal definition that the "story" makes even a mistaken connection with reality. All the rest—the "half-caste swamp girl" and the "Christlike hippy" who helps blacks and whites among the fantastical band of refugees to "discover their common humanity"—is so phony that Lance would hardly have known where to start attacking it, nor would have deigned to try.

Only with Merlin was he able to take even the most tentative steps toward communication, and that primarily on matters of litera-ture and language which had no immediate relevance to the film project. He and the other invaders had nothing to say to each other. Though together for a few fateful days in the same house, they inhabited different worlds.

Yet, in spite of himself, Lance could not quite sustain his first casual indifference to the film (p. 25): "Margot had told me about it but I didn't pay much attention." On several occasions, he made detailed and acute observations on plot and characters as well as technical problems. Most obviously significant is his exchange with Merlin about the fate of Lipscomb (p. 153), the "master of the house" in the film story. A bit earlier (p. 148), Merlin had explained that Lipscomb "has lost his ties with the land, nature, his own sexuality." In the end, Lance learned (p. 153), the script called for his "gently subsid[ing] into booze and Chopin." It is not difficult to imagine the vindictive delight Lance must have taken in writing a very different part for himself as master of Belle Isle.

But the point is that he did merely substitute one "script" for another. The moviemakers had, indeed, "invaded" his house, callously turned it into a "location." But Margot—with Lance's passive consent—had already turned Belle Isle into a movie set, long before the arrival of Merlin and his company. When Lance speaks of "dress[ing] the part," and "playing up to the role" of Southern gentleman Margot had assigned him (p. 121), it is primarily if not exclusively a *movie* role he is talking about. And, Lance was dismayed to discover, once the professionals were on the scene the whole town was ready and willing to join the action at a moment's notice.

The major in-town location, with ironic appropriateness, was the public library. "Miss Maude," the librarian, played by Margot in the movie, was rewarded by Jacoby for her cooperation with a brief "walk-on." [12] Beside herself with gratitude, the wretched woman urged them to consider using her house, too, as a set.

> Town folk, not just Maude, acted as if they lived out their entire lives in a dim charade, a shadowplay in which they were the shadows, and now all at once to have appear miraculously in their midst these resplendent larger-than-life beings. She, Maude, couldn't get over it: not only had they turned up in *her* library, burnishing the dim shelves with their golden light; she had for a moment been one of them!
>
> Presently Mrs. Robichaux, a dentist's wife, whom all these years I had taken to be a mild comely content little body, showed up from nowhere and told Raine she would do anything, *anything*, for the company: "even carry klieg lights!" (p. 152)

Implicitly acknowledging his shameful kinship with Mrs. Robichaux and the other moviestruck townspeople, Lance goes on ironically to Percival: "The world had gone nutty, said the crazy man in his cell. What was nutty was that the movie folk were trafficking in illusions in a real world but the real world thought that its reality could only be found in the illusions. Two sets of maniacs." Not simply had he lived for a few days in his house with people who inhabited another world and yet seemed strangely akin to him, but he had lived all his life, unsuspectingly, with another company of familiar aliens in the local community. The final pathos—involving paradoxes which his own faculty of irony is not quite able to accommodate—was that he could at last find no way to deal with the invaders but to try outdoing them at their own game.

Engaging Elgin—who was also taking a bit part in the "official" film under Merlin's directorship—Lance constructed a "set-within-the-set" peopled with a "cast-within-the-cast," and launched his own clandestine, subversive career as producer-director. Lance's project—videotape, not film—is a marvel of parodic self-containment.

Lance was not only producer and director, but the whole audience. (Elgin, we will remember, "looked but forebore to see.") The production was only another means of preventing the communication Lance wanted (or should have wanted) with Margot. As for actors, there were none. The personae in Lance's "double feature" —Margot and Merlin and Jacoby, Lucy and Raine and Dana— were unaware that their "lines" *were* lines. Moreover, the director-producer-audience is indifferent to the most egregious lapses in the dialogue. Knowing beforehand what the non-actors must have been saying—i.e., what he had decided they should say—he was more than tolerant of their shortcomings in following the script, quite willing to fill in the gaps for himself. Had the cameraman proved inefficient, so that sound and images were fantastically distorted— light and dark values reversed, the figures of men and women flowing into and out of each other like flames? No matter. In apology for the technical defects, Elgin spoke of the "images" as "nothing but electrons, of course" (p. 181). Poor lad, poor sorcerer's apprentice, he had no sinister intent of philosophical ambiguity. We may assume that the distinction between person and image was still clear in Elgin's mind. But Lance's mind is quite another matter. By the time he began his private viewing of the tapes, he was already far gone toward losing all sense of distinction between appearance and reality. Unconsciously substituting "figures" for Elgin's "images," he thought (p. 186): "Didn't Elgin say the figures were nothing but electrons?" In context, the casual error may be seen as additional evidence of the increasingly solipsistic tendency in Lance's thinking.

What was he thinking, as he "stared" (p. 186) at the minuscule commotion going on in his "tiny Trinitron" that "great skyey afternoon" (p. 185)—or, if not thinking, then tempted to think? That in fact there was no valid distinction to be made between the person and the image? That the people themselves might be "nothing but electrons," or something else whose distinct existence, if any, is understandable only to a physicist?

Lance does not literally believe this. And before setting the final stage for demolition of Belle Isle he was careful—on various grounds of affection and moral judgment—to select those whom he would send away to safety. At least two of the "images," or "figures," even of the videotape—Merlin and Lucy—he was able to recreate as human beings. But aside from the general arrogance of his taking upon himself to decide who deserved to live and who to die, once he had composed the death list the people on it became, for him, in a radical sense unreal. A partial exception, perhaps, must be made for Margot, but from the others who remained in the house he was totally sealed off. As he tells Percival later, what he remembers of his feelings is only a profound *coldness*. Emotionally and morally, he could not see or hear his victims. They spoke, Raine and Jacoby, and intellectually he understood them. Some of the things Raine told him—"she was talking about her childhood" (p. 233)—might ordinarily have stirred a faint sympathy even in the hardest of men. But beyond the intellect, in the ear of his affective consciousness, Lance remained quite deaf.

Nor had the deafness come upon him suddenly, with the shock of the revelations in Elgin's "dirty movie" (p. 180). There was nothing in the tapes which really surprised Lance. Some time before the videotape surveillance system was set up, he had collected evidence that Jacoby had replaced Merlin as Margot's lover. And he must at least have suspected, before seeing the tapes, that Raine and Dana would not stop with talk in their "initiation" of Lucy as novice love cultist.

The elaborate gathering of evidence is not what Lance sometimes pretends it was, an unprejudiced and objective search to determine whether he had grounds for charging Margot and the others with specific offenses. He had determined their guilt on the first shred of evidence. Whatever Elgin produced, Lance would find satisfactory.

Elgin sensed this, saying "I think you may still have what you want" (p. 181). The ritual of evidence-gathering merely gave Lance time to exercise his perverse ingenuity at self-dramatization: first in relishing his disgrace, and then in deciding what if anything he might do by way of appropriate revenge.

Just as the physicians in Percy's novels are wont to neglect and abuse their own health, so Lance the lawyer is convinced, in determining what he should do in his personal affairs, by evidence and a line of reasoning to which he would surely never submit in court.

As he describes it to Percival, Lance sees his life as a series of grand awakenings, beginning with his finding the money in his father's sock drawer. The second such experience was his discovery that he could not have fathered Siobhan. This led to the realization that he had, for many years, been leading a kind of half-life, without design or serious purpose (p. 60): "fiddl[ing] at law, fiddl[ing] at history, keep[ing] up with the news . . . and drink[ing him]self into unconsciousness every night." Feeling much rejuvenated by the shock of facing the truth, he conceived the "quest of the unholy Grail," set about gathering evidence against Margot and the moviemakers, and then, just as it seemed his "almost blunted purpose" must fail again, took final courage in the vision of the Lady of the Camellias, and swept to his revenge.

But this is no traditional revenge tragedy, in which we are moved by the death of the innocent along with the guilty. No innocent people died at Belle Isle. His excusing Merlin—who was as guilty as the others—is the first obvious sign of the pathetic, in no sense tragic, weakness of Lance's moral posture as avenger. If excuses could be made for Merlin, why not for the others? Lance himself hasn't a moral leg to stand on. His house had been desecrated by the Hollywooders. But he invited the desecration. And then, fed up with it, instead of throwing the desecrators out he further implicated himself by trying to outdo them at their own game, making his "dirty movie" in secret while they proceeded openly with theirs.

Had Raine and Dana corrupted Lucy, with their brainless neo-mysticism and the three-way sexual exercises so exactly described and diagrammed by Lance? Well . . . yes. Lucy was a college student, and old enough to be legally classified, perhaps, as a "consenting adult." But most American fathers of Lance's generation probably would not regard him as abnormal for feeling outraged by the conduct of houseguests who used his daughter in this fashion. The trouble is that Lance seems to have been not so much outraged as simply fascinated by the intricate figure, the "rough swastikaed triangle" (p. 192), which the three bodies formed in their impersonal intimacy. Further, although we are given little information about the kind of father-daughter relationship that Lance and Lucy had in earlier years, it seems safe to assume that it was not much different from what we see in his notably "permissive"—i.e., slothful and neglectful—dealings with Siobhan. He had deplored her grandfather's influence on the child—not only feeling that Tex was retarding the growth of her mind and imagination with too much TV-watching and the juvenile vulgarity of his verbal humor (the "runny babbitts" and "koinkidinkies"), but even suspecting (p. 55) that the old man could be guilty of improperly fondling her—and yet had taken no practical steps to correct the situation. Lance had neither the energy nor the patience to assign himself an active part in Siobhan's rearing; the best he could think of, even as a possibility, was to turn her over to Suellen Buell, the long-suffering black "mammy" of the family. About the only thing, in fact, that we do know about Lucy's upbringing is just that this same Suellen was in charge of it: as she was in charge of Lance's son's, and, before that, of Lance's own.

All in all, no very impressive picture of Lance's responsibility as a parent emerges. It is to his credit that, in talking to Percival (p. 55), he makes no excuses for himself in his neglect of Siobhan. "Why didn't I do something about Siobhan earlier? . . . Because I didn't really care. . . . Why couldn't I take care of her? To tell you the truth, she got on my nerves." But the candor of his "confession" in no way alters the fact of the neglect. Lance says to Percival, concerning his anxiety for Siobhan—"and here's the strangest thing of all, it was only after my discovery, after I found out that Siobhan was not my child, that I was able to do something about it" (p. 55) —but the truth is that nothing was ever done. He *thought* about kicking Tex out and turning Siobhan over to Suellen. But thinking was as far as he ever went with that project. Instead, what he finally did, before the hurricane hit, was to send Tex and Siobhan away together. And he does not even try to convince Percival that he had the interests of any of his children in mind when he decided to blow up the house and, if need be, himself as well as Margot with it.

Except as they affect his view of himself, the truth is that Lance has never cared much about any of his children, and still does not when he talks to Percival. The truth is that in the series of great "discoveries" he has only awakened, over and over again, into ever more dreadful nightmares.

At Belle Isle, from sock drawer to the big bang, nothing worked. And the situation of his last days at the Center for Aberrant Behavior seems scarcely more promising.

It would appear that he still has hardly a glimmer of insight either into his psychological history or into the essential hypocrisy of his moral judgments. His narrative of the first "great awakening," the episode of the money in the sock drawer, furnishes one of the more obvious examples of his extraordinary capacity for self-deception: the way he has of so belaboring one "truth" of a complex experience that it blinds him — and at least momentarily, perhaps, his listener — to other and equally significant facts of the event.

All Lance wants to talk about, with a fine show of candor and analytical precision, is the dark joy and the sense of liberation he felt in contemplating the evidence of his *father's* dishonor. But we would do well not to overlook, as he apparently has overlooked, or repressed, the significance of the information he casually supplies at the beginning of the anecdote, explaining why he opened the drawer in the first place (p. 41): "My mother was going shopping and had sent me up to swipe some of his pocket money from his sock drawer." He discovered the evidence of his father's dishonesty, then, in the process of his own act of petty thieving, in which he was serving as accomplice to his mother: the same mother whom he later (?) suspected of adultery.

That drawer, obviously, has a lot more in it than just the socks and the neat bundle of bills. A pretty kettle of fish, indeed; can of worms; Pandora's box. We should be wary of lingering overlong to rummage about there. This is the kind of trap prankster Percy is notoriously fond of setting for psychoanalytic critics, just for the fun of watching their hairy scurryings. One is reluctant to encourage him. But there are at least two matters of unavoidable, and inextricably interrelated, interest here.

One—which is half, but only half, apparent in that aspect of the event which Lance himself emphasizes, the discovery of his father's moral imperfection—is his tendency to shift responsibility for his own actions to someone else. He, too, was a thief; but, then, "[he] was a child," and his mother put him up to it. The other matter of importance, of course, is the specific identity of the person to whom Lance shifts responsibility in this instance: his mother. A woman, the first woman in his life. If the discovery of the money in his father's drawer constituted, in some sense, as Lance obviously wants or needs to think it did, a "loss of innocence," it was his mother, "the woman," who directed him to it.

If nothing else is obvious in Lance's account of what happened at Belle Isle, and of the "new world" he intends to bring into being after he leaves the hospital, it is that he despises and fears women. He recognizes the need for them in the process of procreation, of course. And, to put it mildly, he desires them. But he loathes himself *for* the desiring; and the self-loathing is inevitably projected back upon the object of the desire. In taking his revenge upon Raine, he needed not only to murder her, but first, while she was still conscious, to violate and humiliate her sexually. Both initially and continuingly, a major element of his attraction to Anna is a morbid fascination with the story of the gang-rape she suffered. If in some sense he truly believes in his paradoxical theory of her restoration to purity, exaltation to a kind of "super-virginity," as a consequence of the rape, we may still fear that he wants to marry her only to see whether *he* can somehow accomplish what the sailors, in their crude and thoughtless fashion, failed to do: i.e., to violate her wholly and permanently, humiliate her utterly, in body and soul. The sinister tone that Lance's story of his "courtship" of Anna has from the beginning—with the mock-childishness of the knocking code they use in starting to communicate, then in their first face-to-face encounter his adopting the classic stratagem of the child-molester, enticing her with candy (p. 109)—still distinctly persists, it seems to me, at the end. Is it cause for hope, or for dread, that Percival predicts Anna and Siobhan will join Lance in Virginia?

Lance's inordinate hostility to homosexuals, to whom he most often refers with the crudest epithets of contempt—"fag," "queer," —is explicable partly as a defense against recognition of his own questionable sexual tendencies. The open admission to Percival of the desire he had sometimes felt in their youth, to "grab [him] and hug those skinny bones" (p. 74)—followed by the challenging question, "does that shock you?"—is probably to be read more as a disarming tactic than as anything else, calculated to distract attention from the really more "damaging" evidence of his preoccupations in later life. Still, he remains predominantly heterosexual in his overt behavior. And his antihomosexuality is probably attributable primarily to *envy* of the fully committed homosexual male, as someone who has managed to get away altogether from degrading contact with females.

But we need not attempt to explore all aspects of the problem in order to establish the main point, that the radical ambivalence of Lance's attitude toward women—the fear and contempt which is inseparable from the relentless desire—is at the center of the vast web of hopeless contradictions in which he has involved himself in his account of his past life, and from which his vision of the future seems to promise no escape.

Apparently, Percival prods him repeatedly on the question of what the role of women will be in the new world he envisages. The badgered Lance responds: "Women? What about women? . . . Freedom? The New Woman will have perfect freedom. She will be free to be a lady or a whore" (p. 179). The absurdity of the notion that such a choice constitutes "perfect freedom" is, in any case, immediately apparent. But, when Percival continues to press him, Lance abandons all pretense to rational consistency, and in the course of a few short sentences flatly contradicts himself: "*Don't women have any say in this? Of course.* And we will value them exactly as they value themselves. They won't like it much, you say? *The hell with them. They won't have anything to say about it*" (p. 179, emphasis added). And he is off again, with Queen Guinevere as his predictable example, on women and their natural tendency to impurity. "Guinevere didn't think twice about adultery. It was Lancelot, poor bastard, who went off and brooded in the woods."

From this, perhaps, all the rest of the "consistent inconsistency," the desperate circularity, of Lance's thinking proceeds. And, from a psychoanalytic point of view, it is difficult to avoid attaching some importance to his report of the sock drawer adventure. The analyst, or psychoanalytic critic, would be inclined to find that episode still somehow vitally significant, even if he should suspect that Lance's "memory" of the event could be either deliberately or inadvertently distorted.

But the problem is complicated by the fact that we are presented with a *character* in the novel, Percival, who is a psychiatrist, and who does not appear to be much interested in the sock drawer story one way or another. I would not suggest that the presence of such a character, even in such an obviously crucial role as Percival's—the role of sole listener to Lance's monologue—necessarily invalidates a psychoanalytic critical approach to the novel. But, at the very least, the critic who takes that approach must somehow "get around" Percival. And, at least tentatively, it strikes me as a more promising course simply to follow the lead of Percival's attitude—his implied responses, questions, and comments—rather than to try outguessing him from the start.

Percival does not appear to be much interested in the sock drawer story, or, indeed, in any of the more routinely fascinating features of Lance's psychological history. Lance does not say what *kind* of psychiatrist—other, that is, than a "half-assed" one—Percival is. But, professionally and otherwise, he seems largely indifferent, at the most only politely attentive, not only to Lance's recollections of childhood but to many other details of his "life story," including the influence of the Lamar family history on his personal development. It is much the same with all the other topics—social, religious, artistic—on which Lance tries repeatedly to engage Percival.

Lance is, ever enthusiastically if not always expertly, a considerable "literary gent." His narrative bristles with literary allusions, direct and indirect, ancient, medieval, and "modern" in all senses of the term. For the reader inclined to source-and-analogue hunting, there is God's plenty here. And the use of the allusions also interestingly complicates the problems of narrative strategy. It is often difficult to tell in the case of covert allusions—such as those to Hopkins and Eliot, which figure as importantly in this novel as in the others— whether Lance himself is aware of the echoes or whether Percy is making signals to the reader from somewhere behind his bemused narrator's back. But, regardless of what game we may decide it is that author and narrator/monologist are playing, my point at the moment is that Percival does not participate. Lance reminds him that in their youth they read books together—James Joyce and Henry Miller, etc.—and suggests that the fantasy of identification with the heroes of Arthurian romance was in the beginning as much of Percival's making as his own. But nowhere is there an indication that Percival now shares his old friend's keen nostalgia for those days.

Neither does Percival seem disposed to let Lance draw him into an argument about religion and social history. "You don't like my theology. I see," Lance says (p. 224), apparently in response to Percival's prompting him to get back to the account of the last day's events at Belle Isle. One suspects it is not so much that Percival *dislikes* Lance's ideas as that he finds them embarrassingly sophomoric as well as harebrained. No matter what Lance might have been saying, most readers would probably sympathize with Percival's eagerness to have him leave off the prophesying and get on with his story. After all the mighty to-do of anticipation, it is hard to imagine anyone's reacting otherwise to "THE GREAT SECRET OF LIFE" Lance is finally able to reveal (p. 224).

But beyond the purely secular good sense of it, Percival's attitude is eminently *priestly*. Notwithstanding the obvious differences of personalities and circumstances, sophisticated Percival's attitude in his response to the horrors of Lance's narrative is oddly reminiscent of the salutary put-down the guileless Father Smith administers to Tom More in the confessional (*Love in the Ruins*, p. 399).

Sometime-madman More's relatively amiable vanity shows itself in his making too much of his "middle-aged daydreams" of sexual sin; the monstrous pride of Lance Lamar's blasphemies is of another order, calling, it would seem, for much sterner measures of chastisement than those Father Smith uses to "scald" poor Tom to repentance. Lance repeatedly and scornfully rejects in advance any redemptive forgiveness, any "absolution," which Percival may be disposed to offer. Lance, we are repeatedly reminded, is not even "a bad Catholic." He is not any kind of Catholic, and has no intention of becoming one, unless the church, and God himself, will consent to mend their ways to suit him. (See, for example, pp. 176–79 and 255–56.) Although he has several times earlier spoken of having "a confession to make," he takes care in their final interview to be certain that Percival does not misunderstand (p. 253). "No, no confession forthcoming, Father, as you well know." He does not seek sacramental aid.

Yet, despite all discouragements, Percival has at the end decisively reassumed his priestly role. And, in retrospect, we might see as an early sign of his regeneration in that office, simply his consistent preoccupation with the "bare facts" of Lance's narrative. Regardless of what Lance chooses to call his confidences, Percival receives them —almost without exception from beginning to end—with exactly the customary air (always so disappointing to the imaginative penitent) of the priest in the confessional. Like Father Smith with Tom More, Percival is not interested in "fantasies" of any kind. Perhaps Lance is not, as he insists, a penitent in any sense. Nonetheless, Percival treats him as if he were one. Every time Lance strays from his story of what happened at Belle Isle—wandering off into accounts of his dreams and visions, or philosophical musings, or rantings and ravings against the evils of the modern world—Percival soon calls him back. "Just tell me," he says in effect, "what you *did*. What sins have you committed? How many times? With whom?"

But there is nothing to show that the exercise has had any redeeming effect except upon Percival himself. On the last day, Lance says to Percival (p. 254): "I have the feeling that while I was talking and changing, you were listening and changing." Of the change in Percival, there is some tangible evidence. When he first visits the cell, he is wearing clothing that Lance contemptuously refers to as "phony casuals" (p. 5). The next day Lance mentions having seen him: 1) stopped by an old woman in the cemetery (p. 11), and shaking his head in evident refusal of what could only have been a request that he say a prayer for the dead; 2) on the levee (p. 20) talking to a beautiful young woman with whom Lance suspects him of being in love. Percival appears to say nothing to dispute Lance's interpretation of either encounter.

Some days later, as Lance approaches the end of his story of the events at Belle Isle, we learn that Percival has doffed the "phony casuals" and is once again dressed as a priest (p. 163). And on the final day (p. 254), Lance speaks of having seen him again in the cemetery: but this time alone, and this time pausing before a tomb to say a prayer.

On the strength of all this, it seems reasonable to assume that

Percival *has* changed, has conquered his doubts and renewed his priestly vows. There is no good reason not to take him at his unqualified word—"*Yes*"—when he assures Lance that he intends to become pastor of the "little church in Alabama" (p. 257). It may or may not be that Lance's talking, as he with his characteristic vanity wants to suppose, is chiefly responsible for it; but the change in Percival is evident before he speaks for himself.[13]

But in Lance's own case, we have *only* his words for it (words, not word, and they are "but wild and whirling words") that anything he has experienced in his entire adult life has worked real change in him. On the basis of what we have already seen, it would seem reasonably safe to predict a future for Percival in which he will at least do no great harm to anyone. For Lance, the outlook is hardly so promising.

The man who once made a religion of his oral/genital joys with Margot before they were married—glorying in the "sweet dark sanctuary" of her private parts, in a "communion" of cunnilingus (p. 171)—now emerges as self-anointed prophet and scourge of the new "Sodom" of the modern world (p. 255). Outside his cell window, posters advertising movies with titles like *The 69ers* (p. 22) and *Deep Throat* (p. 255) offend his holy and wrathful eye. Dreaming of beautiful young men with rifles, marching and singing,[14] he is ready to set forth for Virginia to lead a Third Revolution which will bring death and destruction to our unholy "cocksucking cuntlapping . . . Happyland U.S.A." (p. 158) and usher in the sternly virtuous reign of the "strong and brave and pure of heart" (p. 179), men who are willing to "den[y themselves] to be strong," when (p. 158) "if there cannot be love . . . there will be a tight-lipped courtesy between men" and "chivalry toward women."

As we have previously noted, there will be in Lance's New World only two kinds of women, Ladies and Whores. It would appear that a Gentleman will be entitled to use a Whore in any way that suits his fancy. A Lady, presumably, will be sexually approachable only in wedlock and face-to-face, with the Gentleman (her husband) assuming the so-called "missionary position" to accomplish penetration. It goes without saying that there will be no lascivious touching of any description between Lady and Lady, much less between one tight-lipped Gentleman and another.

Gangsters, crooked and lying politicians and labor leaders, muggers and bribers and incompetent educators and sundry false religionists are mentioned contemptuously in passing (p. 220), but sex is Lance's obsession from first to last. In the storm of his ravings on that subject, it is all too easy for the reader, as presumably it is for Percival, to overlook the fact that Lance's "puritan" revolution is also racist and neo-fascist. "The Nazis," he says (p. 156), "were clods, thugs," and the Klan "poor ignorant bastards." "Blacks, Jews, Catholics," all will be welcome to join the Third Revolution. But in the end he makes it plain (p. 256), as we might have expected, that the line must be drawn somewhere: there will be, if he has his way, "no Russkies or Chinks in the Shenandoah Valley." The deep and deadly ambivalence of his social vision is all of a twisted piece with the unconscious hypocrisy of his sexual attitudes.

His new Revolution, "new Reformation" as he calls it once (p. 177), promises no more genuine a *change* than the "reform" he has effected in his personal life. His revenge at Belle Isle was a sordid crime, nothing more, bringing him no enlightenment, no relief of any kind. Nor, in the absence of a penitential spirit, is there any salvation either in his imprisonment or in his "confession" of his crimes to Percival. There is little or no reason to suppose that living in Virginia, with or without Anna and Siobhan, will succeed where all else has failed, to make him any happier and wiser, or any less dangerous, than he has ever been. His two religious ardors, first as himself a devout 69er and then as the prophet of doom to all who practice such foulness, are but two different phases of the same mouthy obsession.

If we can manage for a moment to forget the horrors of the prospect, there is a certain dark amusement here, especially in the picture of a "tight-lipped" Lance Lamar heading the crusade. The Lance we have come to know is hard to imagine holding his tongue in a context either sexual or revolutionary.

IV. Conclusion: The Limits of Text

But I have spoken of what Lance says—about "Russkies" and "Chinks"—"in the end." The question is, where or what *is* the end?

All Percy's novels are to some extent "open-ended." That is, they all leave us looking to the future, wondering what is to become of the main characters. Even the "epilogue" chapters of *The Moviegoer* and *Love in the Ruins* do not quite resolve all the issues raised in the preceding parts of the narratives. And *The Second Coming*, a kind of "sequel" to *The Last Gentleman* which answers some of the questions left dangling at the end of the earlier novel, generates equally troublesome new mysteries of its own. Appropriately enough, in view of the protagonist's madness and the all but unrelieved darkness of his vision of the modern world, *Lancelot* is most enigmatic of all in its conclusion.

The final sense of profound uncertainty is reinforced by two formal devices involving departures from the conventions of the dramatic monologue. These are: 1) special graphic aids such as all-capitalized titles for certain subsections of the numbered chapters (e.g., OUR LADY OF THE CAMELLIAS), drawings (pp. 189, 192) representing the relationships of Margot and her men and the positions assumed by Troy, Raine, and Lucy in their love making, the reproduction of Lance's hardware shopping list (p. 194), and, most important of all, the sketch of the partially obscured sign outside Lance's cell window to which he twice calls Percival's attention, during their first interview (p. 4) and again during the last (p. 250); 2) the concluding "dialogue," in which Percival responds to Lance's questions with a series of monosyllables.

The sign outside the window is inevitably tempting—and frustrating—to readers in search of a "key" to the novel.

Free &
Ma
B

The sign's first visible word clearly suggests the central issue of Percival's concern about the new society Lance envisages. Lance looks forward to securing his own freedom. But what he wants the freedom to *do* is to set up a system for restricting the freedom of others—not only freedom of sexual behavior but, perhaps still more significantly in the context of reference to the *sign*, freedom of speech. The dangling ampersand then tempts us, with Lance, to supply a further word or words in the first line. The words we choose, in association with "free," may reveal something of how we are accustomed to defining freedom and (&) our notion of what freedom (moral freedom, political freedom) entails.

Percival would appear to be especially concerned for the freedom of women in Lance's ideal society. And we have noted at length the significance of Lance's feelings about his *mother* for understanding the whole pattern of his sexual behavior and attitudes. Hence, we may want to consider the possibilities of "Ma" as a word in itself. A good many readers may feel that the final concern of the novel is not, after all, with sex and society, but with metaphysics. Perhaps, then—ma(y)be—"B" is to be taken as equivalent, semantically as phonologically, to "be." What, in short, are we as human beings free to be . . . once we have got clear, if we ever do, of Ma?[15]

But in pursuing such questions as these, we as readers claim, perhaps, more freedom than the circumstances immediately warrant. Let us go back to have another look at the sign: first as it appears to Lance from his cell window, and then as it is shown to us on the printed page.

With reference to Lance's present situation, the irony of the sign's first visible word—"Free"—is obvious enough. We understand, of course, from Lance's words to Percival (p. 4), that the righthand portion of the sign is arbitrarily cut off from the prisoner's view by the edge of the cell's window embrasure. We assume, with Lance, that what he can see is only a fragment of some rationally intelligible whole, a "complete" verbal text, inscribed on the total surface of the sign (sign-board, or banner, or marked-off section of a building's wall) as such.

The arbitrary limitation of Lance's field of view by the cell wall exactly defines the nature of his deprivation. Human freedom, the freedom of man "the talking animal," is precisely and uniquely the opportunity to *read* without externally imposed restrictions, to observe and interpret "complete texts." Thus, on the day before he is to be released, Lance poignantly anticipates seeing the *Free & Ma B* sign whole (p. 250). "At last I shall know what it says," he reflects solemnly, as if seeing those words, apprehending them in their total order—grammatical, logical, rhythmic, rhetorical, and so on— might somehow reveal to him the whole meaning of life. Of course, we might well choose to regard Lance's solemnity as, in the first place, *mock* solemnity, characteristic of his customary sardonic humor. The chances are, as we may assume Lance himself actually anticipates, that the sign presents some such totally innocuous message or notice as those he has suggested earlier (p. 4), merely identifying the establishment to which the board or banner is attached: "Free & Easy Mac's Bowling" or "Free & Accepted Masons' Bar."

On the other hand, the overtones of the occult in the reference to "Masons" might seem to accord with somewhat disturbing tendencies we have elsewhere observed in Lance's thinking. In the way of "signs," he is certainly serious enough in his eschatological reading of the movie posters and the bumper stickers on the Volkswagen (pp. 254–55). Perhaps he is, after all, at least half-serious about the possibilities of the *Free & Ma B* sign as well.

In any event, the important point is simply that he cannot *know* what the full text of the sign is—what it "says"—and neither can we. At first glance, Percy seems to challenge the reader to speculation. And it is amusing to try coming up with plausible alternatives to Lance's suggestions.

But the trouble is, paradoxically, that Percy has left the reader entirely *too much* "freedom" in the matter. For example, Lance's two hypothetical texts suggest that the first line of the sign—*Free &*—must be completed with *one* additional word. Thus, in seeking alternatives to his phrases ("Free & Easy," "Free & Accepted") we might feel obliged to follow the same formula: with "Free & Equal," perhaps, or, if we envisage a different kind of establishment with which the sign is associated, "Free & Frisky."

But—before we go any further with this exercise—*why*, we might ask, does Lance assume that there are only two words joined by the ampersand in the first line of the sign? We may surmise that the portion he can see gives him some notion of the size and shape of the whole sign. But no information is provided that would help the reader of the novel to assess the accuracy of Lance's calculations.

The case is quite different with other signs to which he calls Percival's attention: the Volkswagen's bumper stickers, the movie posters, the blackboard at LaBranche's (Zweig's) bar. It is hard to imagine a reader who would not know what a bumper sticker or a movie poster looks like. And the ones mentioned here are plainly legible. Lance and Percival may disagree about what, in the larger context of cultural history, the movie titles and the bumper-sticker slogans "signify," and different readers may have still other widely variant opinions on that head; but what these signs literally "say," as well as the fact that the stickers are affixed to the bumper of a battered Volkswagen (not a Chevrolet or a Mercedes) and that the movie titles are posted at what was once the "colored entrance" of the theater, is information we all share. Lance is too far away, apparently, to read the chalked words on the blackboard at Zweig-LaBranche's. But even the comparatively rare reader who has never actually seen such a sign should have little difficulty in envisaging it, and little or no reason to question Lance's guesses at the "Today's Special" menu that might be posted there. Concerning these signs, we are "assured of certain certainties." It is not so with "Free & Ma B."

What does Lance make of the indentations?

Free &

Ma

B

Assuming that the lettering and spacing are uniform, the first of the two texts he suggests comes out pretty ragged looking.

Free & Easy

Mac's

Bowling

The second yields a design more nearly symmetrical.

Free & Accepted

Masons'

Bar

But, in the absence of answers to the other questions we have raised, its superior symmetry alone does little to recommend the second text. Not only do we have no reliable information on the size and shape of the whole sign, and no information on whether the lettering appears on a freestanding signboard or a banner or the surface of a wall or what, but there is nothing in Lance's comments to indicate why he assumes that the building with which it is associated houses a place of entertainment. With only the one unmistakably whole word to go on, why should we not think of a lecture or concert hall, or a storefront church, or the headquarters of a political party?

I have said that the references to the sign involve a violation of the strict conventions of the dramatic monologue. The violation occurs when the italicized fragment of the sign's text is graphically isolated from the text of the monologue:

Free &

Ma

B

Lance's narrative, we must remember, is represented as an *oral* performance, addressed to Percival. The graphic representation of the sign fragment is not something provided by Lance for Percival's benefit. We might imagine Lance's picking up pencil and paper to sketch out for Percival "the rough swastikaed triangle" formed by the bodies of Lucy, Raine, and Dana in their three-way sexual capers (p. 192), or the other triangles representative of Margot's infidelities (p. 189). Perhaps, with his passion for detail in his recollections, he might even have written out again the hardware shopping list. The capitalized subheadings in his account of his "dirty movie" and of his visions in the pigeonnier may be taken to represent oral "announcements" addressed to Percival in a dramatic mode of elaborate self-mockery. But the graphic representation of the *Free & Ma B* sign, like the triangle sketches strictly a "visual aid," is an aid that *Percival* does not need in order to understand Lance's comments, since what is present outside the cell window is equally visible to both men.

The graphic representation, then, is provided by the *author*, for the *reader's* benefit. It is, strictly speaking, not a part of the monologue.

But since it does not in the least help us to guess the wording of the whole sign, what exactly are we to make of the device? The way it works, I think, is simply to underscore very sharply—near the beginning of the novel, and again near the end—certain essential facts of the fictional situation.

First, the graphic representation *shows* us, to reinforce what Lance *tells* Percival, that the whole sign is not visible from the window of the cell. Second, the device serves to remind us that Lance's "point of view" in the novel is limited in other ways than physically. Lance, we are reminded, is only one *character* in the story. He is the main character, and the monologist-narrator. But, as such, he is clearly and essentially distinguishable, not only from another character, Percival—who is present in the cell, and to whom the entire monologue is specifically addressed—but from the author. The play on Walker Percy's family name involved here should not distract us from the fact that the "implied author's" point of view is no more to be identified with Percival's than with Lance's. Finally, and most importantly of all, we are reminded that all three (or four)— monologist, listener, and author(s)—are distinct from the reader.

Thus, the final reference to the sign, with the graphic representation which interrupts the monologue, serves its principal purpose: to prepare us for the startling intrusion of Percival's voice, in the series of italicized monosyllables, at the end. We are "prepared" in the sense that we are forewarned: not to accept Percival's words as necessarily any more reliable a "key" to the meaning of the whole novel than the sign outside the window is.

Lance's reactions to the sign furnish an important, if not unique, clue to the way his mind works. He is always on the lookout for "signs" in the sense of omens, foreshadowings. One of the first things the alert reader is likely to note is the fact that, since Percival is free to come and go as he pleases, Lance need not wait for his own release to find out what the complete text of the *Free & Ma B* sign is. He could simply ask Percival to read it and tell him. Certainly, Lance's reluctance to take that easy way is understandable. Any man who had been looking at such a thing for a year or more, in anticipation of the day he could walk out into the street and clear up the mystery, might well feel it would be cheating himself to appoint someone else to bring him the information a few days in advance. Up to a point, we can sympathize with his perfectly "normal" attitude. We may surmise that Percival sympathizes, in this simple human way, and, since Lance has not asked him for it, does not volunteer the information. But, in the light of many other evidences of Lance's habitual need to "have everything his own way," we might well be inclined to see something a good deal more than normally self-indulgent in his attitude here.

He does not simply ask what the sign "says," perhaps because in a sense he does not *want* to know; or, at any rate, does not want to know so long as Percival is still there. So long as he does not know the wording of the sign—does not have to share that knowledge with Percival—he is free to continue making something portentous of it, without having to *argue* with his visitor about it, as he does about the movie titles and the bumper stickers. The bland arrogance of Lance's assertion that Anna is like Lucy (his first wife) simply because he wants her to be—"want[s] the same thing of her [he] wanted of Lucy" (p. 86)—is only a more obvious expression of the tendency, to see everybody and everything in the world as created to assist or hinder him in fulfilling his destiny, which is covertly apparent in his reaction to the *Free & Ma B* sign.

But the sign itself, remaining as it does unintelligible in its incompleteness, tells us precisely nothing. And much the same can be said of the "last word" Percy has vouchsafed to Percival in the pseudo-dialogue with which the novel ends.

Lance, we are sometimes tempted to forget, but should not, is a lawyer. The final exchange with Percival has, at second glance, much the look of a courtroom "interrogation." And, as is unfortunately the case with a great many such exchanges in real life, questions of the kind Lance asks do not rationally admit of the "yes or no" answers which the formula of legal process demands.

What, for example, does it mean that Percival should answer "*yes*" when Lance asks whether Anna and Siobhan will join him in Virginia? Lance has said a moment before: "One last question— and somehow I know you know the answer" (p. 257). He then proceeds to ask, in fact, *four* more questions, the first two merely inquiring whether, and if so, how well, Percival knows Anna. Presumably we are meant to carry forward the "somehow I know you know the answer" as applicable to the *third* question of the series— actually, two questions in one—"Will she join me in Virginia and will she and I and Siobhan begin a new life there?" But, again, what are we to make of Percival's "*yes*"? In what *sense* does he "know the answer"?

Is Lance suggesting that Percival is able to foretell the future? Or does he simply mean that he "has a hunch" that Anna has told Percival what her intentions are, and that Percival, with his experience as both priest and psychiatrist, is better able than most people are to judge the likelihood of her carrying out those intentions?

Lance has shown recently a few signs of failing confidence in his own prophetic gifts, especially since Anna surprised him with her vehement rejection of his ideas about the "violation" she had suffered (p. 251). Perhaps he does need and want now to attribute occult powers to Percival. It seems much less likely, from what little we know of him, that Percival has got so carried away, in the enthusiasm of his regeneration, that he would see himself as a prophet. But even if he does, there is nothing in the context to require that the reader share his view.

We are entirely free to go on regarding Percival as having—beyond the qualifications of his professional training and experience in psychiatry, and the qualifications of his personal acquaintance with both Lance and Anna—nothing more than the ordinary authority of the priest. It appears that his listening to Lance has had much to do with restoring Percival's own faith in that authority, but there is nothing to suggest that he has also taken from Lance the mantle of the prophet. We are entirely free to regard Percival's "*yes*" as merely his "educated guess" that Anna and Siobhan will join Lance in Virginia. We are dealing with rational assessments of the *probabilities* in a human situation, not with the certainties of divine revelation.

It is most important of all that we remember the *Free & Ma B* sign when we come to Lance's final question—"Is there anything you wish to tell me before I leave?"—and Percival's final "*Yes*." While it is distinctly a whole word—neither a non-alphabetical character standing for a word nor a letter or group of letters which might or might not be regarded as merely part of a word—that "*Yes*," left enigmatically dangling above the blank space at the bottom of the page, is much like the *&*, the *Ma*, and the *B* of the sign in that it seems to refer the reader to something that is simply not there. Since nothing literally *follows* it, we cannot be sure what, if anything, follows *from* it. All texts are, of course, in various respects incomplete. This one seems incomplete in a rather special way.

Percival has something to tell Lance—*possibly* something of vital importance—but Percy has decided not to reveal it, whatever it is.

Here is the point at which we, as readers, must accept the responsibility of freedom. The text may not look to us "finished," but we cannot look around the corner, turn the page, to read the rest of it. There is no "rest." All that we can do, if we are so disposed, is speculate on what such a man as Percival, as we have come to know him, in the circumstances described, *might* have to say to one like Lance: might have to say, that is, if the pair were real persons rather than characters in fiction.

Different readers, or even the same reader, might find a number of different possibilities consistent with Percival's character as it has been revealed. Perhaps he might intend saying to Lance: "Yes . . . I have listened to your story. Now, before you go, I want to tell you mine." Or: "Yes . . . you insufferable ass, I do indeed *know* Anna, in more senses than one. Yes, she wants to join you in Virginia. But I won't permit you to take up your new life with her thinking that you are the first who has been her lover since she was raped by the sailors." Or: "Yes . . . I believe Anna and Siobhan will join you in Virginia. But you still have a responsibility to your daughter Lucy and to your son. Before you leave Lousiana, you must seek understanding and reconciliation with them."

I imagine that Jerome Christensen is representative of a majority of readers in seeing Percival's unspoken "message" to Lance as the Good News of Christian salvation.[16] Most probably, the newly re-dedicated priest would want to try convincing the suffering sinner — now that the latter seems, if not yet repentant, at least disposed finally to *listen* instead of talk — that only love, not vengeance, can redeem the world.

Repeatedly, but never in a way to suggest that he would stay for an answer, Lance has challenged Percival to stop acting like a psychiatrist — for whom all ideas and actions of the patient are morally indifferent — and play his priestly part, to explain to him what a sin is, so that he may know how to judge the things he did at Belle Isle. Actually, as we have noted, much of Percival's attitude throughout is reminiscent of priestly behavior in the confessional. Lance has not had enough experience of priests' company to know how they act. But perhaps Percival is ready now, at the end, to accept the challenge to talk, to teach and to exhort, as well as to listen.

184

Repeatedly (e.g., p. 179), Lance has scorned Percival's "whispering" of love. "Don't talk to me of love until we shovel out the shit." Perhaps Percival is at last emboldened to speak the word "love" aloud, and to explain to Lance that if we wait until all the shit has been shoveled out it will be in all the world as it was in the pigeonnier, too late for love.[17]

Repeatedly, Lance has demanded that Percival show him evidence of God's redemptive love. "Look out there," he says (p. 224). "Does it look like we are redeemed?" We have seen at least circumstantial evidence that Percival himself is redeemed; redeemed again, one might say, in the effect of Lance's story upon him. Perhaps the restored priest feels himself competent at last to explain to Lance, in turn, that it is not "out there," in the street, that one must look for the signs of Grace, but inside oneself.

Perhaps. But we cannot be certain. There are two reasons for my having suggested, besides the Good News, other things that Percival might have in mind to say to Lance. First, I have wanted simply to stress the fact that *anything* we might come up with is only an inference, from what went before the final "*Yes*," since nothing comes after it. In preferring one speculation to another, among alternatives none of which is totally inconsistent with the text we have been reading, we must consider simply the *extent* of the consistency.

Second, and in every sense finally, I have wanted to drive home the point that Percival and Lance are *not* real people. They are fictional characters. It is not that we cannot "look into the future" to determine what they will say or do. Like all characters in all fiction, they have no future.

Walker Percy has often spoken of the limits of the Christian novelist's role. He is not "authorized," it is not his business, as artist, to bring the Good News to his readers. Whether or not that is necessarily and universally true, it is true of *this* novel that Percy has stopped short of having Percival "speak the Word" for which both the reader and, in the reader's imagination, Lance may be thirsting. And in thus "stopping short" it seems to me Percy has, regardless of considerations of religious truth, observed a principle of the art of fiction which *is* universally supreme. I mean the principle of dramatic consistency.

We may feel, as anxious and troubled citizens of the modern

world, which we see all too accurately reflected in this novel, a profound need for consolation and hope. We may find Lance's view of the trouble and the prospect of remedy, in Charles Marlow's words for Mr. Kurtz's pronouncements, "too dark altogether." We may devoutly wish for Percival to "take over" before the end.

But Percy has rightly sensed that such a turn would be dramatically inappropriate. The dominant mode of the novel is that of dramatic monologue, and no extended departure from the monologue conventions would be possible without hopeless confusion. The monologist, Lance Lamar, is for better or worse the established central figure of the dramatic action, the established "protagonist." It is, as we say, "his story" regardless of whether we do or do not approve of him and his ideas. Percival is, in the novel as a whole, only the listener, a *foil* to Lance in his madness. The strength and conviction of Percival's role is precisely in his silence. Percy can risk having Percival say, aloud, only enough to remind the reader that Lance's is but one point of view: that, though dominant, he is like Percival only a fictional creation. To have given Percival a larger voice would have been simply to encourage further confusion on the question of authorial sympathies.

That a good many readers, including publishing critics, have been confused anyway—choosing up sides on the issue of whether Lance or Percival represents Percy's views on sex, faith, and freedom in the world of quotidian reality—is hardly Percy's fault. Even more than the judge or the physician, all the more stringently for the fact that no institutional sanctions are in force, the novelist is under obligation to do equal justice to all his characters. At least in this novel, Percy has fully discharged that obligation.

6

The Second Coming

I. Old Hero, New Heroine

The ambiguous title of Percy's fifth novel reflects its thematic and tonal complexity. There is no disjoining here the bawdy and the sacred significances of the word "coming."[1] And this is the second time Will Barrett has appeared in Percy's fiction, a fact of considerable importance for all readers of *The Second Coming*: important in one way for those who have read *The Last Gentleman*, important in another way for those who have not. The matter of final import, no doubt, is the reference to biblical prophecies of Christ's second coming, and to other writings ancient and modern on the same subject—notably including William Butler Yeats's poem of identical title. But as Barrett's experience, like Tom More's, again amply demonstrates, it is useless to get in a hurry for enlightenment on that notoriously hazardous topic. Last things are best left to last.

Percy's *The Second Coming* is in the first place a love story, a story of earthly love, and quite a beautiful love story. Beautiful love stories, plausibly "affirmative" love stories, are extremely rare in fiction that purports to treat in any way realistically the life of our unhappy times. Percy himself has not given us anything much like this story before. In three of the earlier novels, he was consistently very good at representing amorous activity in its more genially laughable aspects, and very good with marriage and the family in both joy and sorrow. Especially in *Lancelot*, he showed himself also capable of handling, to something more than merely sensationalist effect, the madness and horror of sex. Everywhere, his satire on the celebrated "sexual revolution" in modern American society is brilliantly incisive, excoriating and marvelously entertaining at the same time. But before *The Second Coming* there is no successful representation of the love of a man and a woman that is at once solemn and full of delight.[2]

The Second Coming has something of everything notable in the preceding novels, including the association of sex with terror and violence and death. There are insistent and frequently sinister sexual overtones in Will Barrett's feelings about virtually everyone with whom he comes in contact—not only Kitty, but his daughter Leslie, and Jimmy Rogers and Ewell McBee, even the old men at St. Mark's convalescent home—as well as in his ugly little habit of playing with guns when he is alone. But the love affair with Allison somehow *redeems*, in several senses of the word, all the rest.

Behind the brilliant satire on the abuses and follies of sex, it was difficult in the earlier novels to define what positive values the author might be thought to espouse. The act of love was most often represented as a painful and in one way or another degrading or frustrating, if sometimes moderately amusing, experience. On the rare occasions when sexual desire neither failed nor was thwarted, its end was achieved in a mood either of bawdy hilarity, genial but hardly edifying, or of a cold, totally impersonal and dehumanizing gratification.

Will's and Allison's loving is something all but wholly new. In the moments of physical intimacy neither partner maintains any of the attitudes of emotional and intellectual detachment, ironically observant or self-bemused, that characterized the couplings and noncouplings described in the earlier novels. There are no "theorish bold" experiments here, and no pathetic comedy of frustration and impotence: no hysterical phenomena such as the young Will's noseswellings and knee-jerks in his encounters with Kitty, or Tom More's outbreak of hives in the sandtrap with Lola. With Will and Kitty it was always hard to tell what if anything they had accomplished in their fumbling embraces. About Will's and Allison's exertions—once they have got to the Holiday Inn, at any rate—there is no such doubt. The physical act is completed, over and over again. And it is great fun for both of them. They like what they are doing, and they like talking about it, in language that is earthy without obscenity.

Unlike most of the other lovers in Percy's fiction, Will and Allison are not disposed in any sense merely to "use" each other, in the satisfaction of an indifferent lust, or as the substitute objects of indefinable emotional needs. Neither is already fired with desire when they meet; they are in the strictest and most intensely personal sense aroused by each other. Their ecstasy, their "coming together," is no swoon of mindless self-forgetting, but a mutual surrender of selves, each to the other, in which all their human faculties are intensified and heightened, none suspended or obliterated.

But if Will and Allison are easily the most attractive pair of lovers Percy has created, their story also involves the most difficult problems in the morality and psychology of sex with which he has attempted to deal. Most of the other people with whom they have to contend are so sorry or ridiculous a lot, a company of manifest knaves and fools, that it is easy for the reader caught up in the excitement of the lovers' adventures, their hairbreadth escapes from the threat of exploitation, capture and confinement, to overlook at times the troublesome aspects of Will's own behavior. But one does not exactly have to "take sides" with Kitty or Leslie, let alone Dr. Duk or Jack Curl, to question Will's virtue in his pursuit of Allison.

Allison is of age. And she is not a virgin. She has had a lover of sorts, the redoubtable jewelry salesman called "Sarge," with his illustrated sex manual (p. 94). Still, not only is Will "old enough to be her father," but the disturbing question is raised, and never quite satisfactorily answered (pp. 167, 360), whether he might actually have begotten her.[3] And, even if we choose to ignore the hint of incest, the history of Will's association with Kitty gives rise to other doubts concerning his attraction to Allison. It is not unreasonable to suspect him of taking a certain malicious pleasure in his old girlfriend's discomfiture when she learns who it is that has, in her own favorite old-fashioned slang phrase, "beat her time" with him. Finally, there is the fact of Allison's mental illness.

The reader knows, of course, that Will has not "tak[en] advantage of a psychotic girl" in the sense that Kitty accuses him of it (p. 316). No doubt, Kitty is wrong about the prospects for her daughter's recovery. Far from assuring a regression, Will's love probably offers Allison her only real hope for continuing sanity. And Kitty's maternal concern, while genuine enough up to a point and certainly understandable, is hopelessly compromised by her patent jealousy and her exploitative designs on both Allie and Will. Still, one must continue to wonder to what extent Allison's infirmity may account for Will's attraction to her. If, as the lifelong pattern of his loves might suggest, he is at least in part interested in her because of, rather than in spite of, her affliction, it bodes ill for their marriage.[4]

Allison is in almost every respect a woman both more admirable and more lovable than Kate Cutrer, and the middle-aged but still bumbling Will Barrett a more admirable and lovable man than the Binx Bolling of either the main narrative or the smug epilogue in *The Moviegoer*. But more than a trace of the morbidity that tainted the love story of the first novel is still detectable in *The Second Coming*. And, notwithstanding the fact that, for the first time, Percy has chosen in the case of Allison Huger to tell a good part of his story from the viewpoint of a female protagonist, neither Will Barrett nor the third-person narrator of *The Second Coming* is essentially any less the male supremacist than Binx Bolling is.[5]

I find the representation of Allison's consciousness fascinating and all but totally convincing. The inanity of her non-dialogue with Dr. Duk—"no buzzin' cousin," the "knock knock" jokes—strikes me at times as a bit overdone, although Percy's obvious satiric intent is valid enough. Dr. Duk is a ridiculous man; Allison herself deplores the silliness to which she is reduced in trying to deal with him. Where such as Duk (and his name is legion) is appointed as gatekeeper to the world of the "sane," it is little wonder that a woman of Allison's intelligence should often feel the effort to gain readmission is hardly worthwhile. But the point is frequently obscured. Percy tends to get carried away, perversely relishing the childish word-games for their own sake. Further, in the account of Allison's mental illness, I find the quest of the white dwarf a rather annoyingly precious motif, again tending to distract attention from the serious business at hand.

The rest of Allison's story, however, is marvelous: Her encounter with the stout policeman of the hat-dented hair (part 1, chapter 2), when she is trying to get her bearings and find her way from Linwood to the old Kemp place. Her matter-of-fact acceptance of her responsibility to the big stray dog who shows up to share her refuge in the abandoned greenhouse. The dog's reliable, exquisitely discriminating sense of his reciprocal duty as her guardian, relenting at the last instant in his impulse to bite Will's hand (p. 107), but firmly and without a shadow of self-doubt (p. 240), "his eyes turning red as a bull's," discouraging the presumptuous hiker who takes hold of Allison's unwilling thigh. The saga of her struggles with the enormous old wood-burning stove which she finds in the thicketed former basement of the burned-out mansion. Her discovery, in the process of moving the relic to the greenhouse, of her rare and previously unsuspected talent for "hoisting."

Most compelling of all, of course, is her strange, beautiful and disturbing utterance, a way of speaking that seems at times almost a reinvention of language.[6] There are moments when the jaded reader must feel Percy could hardly do better by Will Barrett than to marry him to Allison solely for the undisturbed opportunity to study her personality, the whole complex "phenomenon" of her mind and sensibility. But such, for better or worse, is not the design of the novel. Once Will and Allison meet, and have worked out the doubts and suspicions of their first encounter, her fate becomes a matter of continuing interest primarily as it affects his.

The final outlook for marriage here—assuming that the wedding is actually to take place[7]—is certainly better than it was for Binx and Kate at the end of *The Moviegoer*. Will's and Allison's plans appear to involve something more closely approaching an active and equal partnership, an equal sharing of both money and talents. And, although there is no account of his having directly spoken to her of his spiritual quest prior to his interview with the old priest at the end of the novel, there is also nothing to suggest that he will try to avoid talking to her about it in due time, or that she will be (like Kate) incapable of understanding when he does speak.

But neither can there be any doubt who is to "chair" the marriage, define the ultimate goals, determine fundamental policy, make all the crucial decisions. The man is in charge.

II. Tiger-, Treasure-, and Father-Hunting

In any event, it is essential that we see the story of human love, whatever its quality in and of itself, as in the larger design of the novel defining only a stage in the lifelong quest for religious faith.

Allison is not what Will gets *instead of* the revelation he sought when he entered the cave. During his sojourn with her in the greenhouse, and later in their premarital "honeymoon" at the Holiday Inn, it might appear that he finds the delights of her company all-sufficient and has abandoned the search for God. But in the end he comes to see Allison, rather, as "a gift and therefore a sign of a giver," and is determined, however "crazy" it may be, that he must and will have both.

God has not, the implication is, refused altogether the revelation that Will sought. It is only that He declines, as is His wont, to let the human seeker determine the time, place, and manner of His appearing. God appears, not in the cave, and not in any such fabulous shape as the Blakean whimsies of Will's note to Lewis Peckham might tempt us to anticipate — in the form, perhaps, of some glorious and terrible reincarnation of the fossilized tiger — but at various times later in the greenhouse, the Holiday Inn, and the nursing home, and in thoroughly believable, if by no means commonplace, human guise, i.e., in the persons of Allison herself[8] and Father Weatherbee. It is, of course, no accident that in the instant before he sees in the "simple silly holy face" of the old priest a mask of the Lord (p. 360), Will has caught Father Weatherbee's thin wrists in his hands, eliciting an "odd expression" that somehow strangely reminded him of "Allie in her greenhouse, her wide gray eyes, her lean muscled boy's arms, her strong quick hands." When Jack Curl speaks of how he has "found God . . . in other people" (p. 137), it is a cant phrase, thrown out as a way of avoiding the issue of Will's embarrassingly direct theological inquiry. And the kind of "other people" Curl has in mind are hardly such as Allison and Father Weatherbee, but the sort of business and professional men who gather for the "ecumenical weekends" at Montreat. Yet, for all that the chaplain is a foolish prating knave, as spiritual leader about as competent and inspiring as your average Scoutmaster, he is curiously vindicated in the final outcome of Will's quest.

When Will spells "tiger" with a "y" in his note to Lewis Peckham (p. 183) — "I have a sudden hankering to visit the haunt of the saber-tooth tyger you discovered" — Percy makes sure that the reader of his novel does not miss the allusion to Blake (p. 184). There is no way to tell whether Will himself has any other poet in mind, at that moment or later. But in this novel, as elsewhere in Percy's fiction, intricately ironic echoes of T. S. Eliot abound. Will Barrett, finding himself admitted as a patient to the convalescent home over which, as his wife's heir, he exercises precarious ownership, is surely some version of Eliot's "ruined millionaire." [9] And, but for the grace of Allison's coming, he is patently a man in imminent danger of failing in any way to distinguish his life from the lives of all the other "decent godless people" in the local country-club set, "their only monument the asphalt road / and a thousand lost golfballs." [10] In such a context, regardless of the question of Will's own literary awareness, as distinguished from Percy's or the narrator's, it is difficult to avoid sensing a kinship of Gerontion's "Christ the tiger" with the beast whose lair Will seeks in the cave.

Eliot and Blake draw on a common tradition, of course. But the allusion to "Gerontion" is more directly relevant to certain central themes of Percy's novel: the problems of age and aging, and of the failure of desire; questions of the nature of man's tenancy of the earth and of his own body; the uncertainties of the quest for sacramental aid and for understanding of the universality of the church, notably including the mystery of Christ's mission to the Jews.

Like Gerontion's, Will Barrett's concern with his personal life history, and the life histories of other people he knows and has known as individuals—Kitty, Marion, Allison, Leslie, his father, Ewell McBee—is inevitably, and inextricably, related to his concern with public history, the history of civilization, and, beyond and beneath that, with the "natural history" of man, history of mankind as an organic species whose existence is related in certain more and less easily identifiable ways to the existence of other species extinct and extant: such as sabertooth tigers, anvil-headed dogs, and cave bats. Like Eliot in all his major poetry, Percy is concerned, centrally and primarily, with understanding of the relationship of past and present as key to the future. His satire on the degeneracy of contemporary society is no less savage here than in the earlier novels. But over and over again we are reminded of the falsity, and the moral futility, of any simplistic celebration of the past at the expense of the present. Allison's magnificent stove is a major exhibit. She has, she feels, truly "found a treasure" (p. 92) in the old Grand Crown: "big and black and iron" (p. 91) with its "oven and firebox as big as a dollhouse and capped by iron lids the size of dinner plates and a balcony of warming compartments . . . even . . . a water tank," its "mica windows crazed and brown and glittering with crystals [which] let into the dark room of the oven." Merely to read of such a thing is enough to rob any but the dullest-witted slave of progress of all pride or pleasure in owning the latest microwave equipment, whether "built-in" or a readily portable "countertop" model. But admirable as the Grand Crown may be simply to look at, and to contemplate as relic of a technological age in which utilitarian and aesthetic values were better harmonized than they are in ours, Allison wants more of it than that. She wants it actually to perform all the functions for which it was so happily designed: to cook her food, warm her dwelling space in the greenhouse when "le cool" of autumn comes, keep her supplied with hot water for bathing and for washing dishes and clothes. And if it is to do all that, to be something other than a ponderous "collectible" for her, it must be somehow "hooked up" to the here and now of her household. Beyond the formidable task of moving the thing from its resting place in the cellar-hole of the burned mansion to the greenhouse—a job which by her own devices Allison can only half accomplish—there is the question of how the stove's piping system is to be connected to an adequate, renewable water supply.

Similarly, the three old men whom Will befriends at St. Mark's have to be willing to try adapting their traditional skills to changed conditions if they hope to "make it" again in the outside world. They are "old men but good" (p. 34), and Will and Allison can make them a legitimate and attractive offer of partnerships in the housing development on Allison's land. But to get the job done, considering among other matters the cost and availability of labor and materials, Mr. Arnold will have to forego his longstanding preference for such things as handsplit roofing shingles and chinking plaster made of river clay and hog's blood for the cabins he will "notch up"; and Ryan the contractor, who has lost both feet and one leg in amputations, must reconcile himself to the prospect of getting about in a car equipped with newfangled hand controls.

There are a number of subtle ironies in Percy's comic treatment of the theme. While Mr. Arnold is all but unbelievably outmoded, Ryan rather prides himself on being up-to-date and yet seems touchingly unaware that there is nothing really novel either about hand controls for disabled drivers or about "hippies" as workers (pp. 319–20). The novel was first published in 1980, and internal evidence generally suggests a contemporary time-setting. But automobile hand controls have been commonplace for a quarter of a century, and were available, if comparatively rare, in the thirties or earlier. And, since the late seventies, any young person even vaguely resembling what used to be called a "hippie" has been hard to find *except* in working-class society. Finally, Percy works a neat reversal on the formula for updating the oldsters' skills when he has Barrett suggest to the sometime gardener, Mr. Eberhart, not that he try some ultra-modern technique of greenhouse-atmosphere control, but just the opposite: a revival of the cave-air utilization system devised by the original owner of Allison's place, old Judge Kemp.

Allison's love affair with Will is obviously a case of closing the celebrated "generation gap." As we have noted, Will is at first disposed to stereotype her as quickly as possible as "one of them," one of the new gypsies, new breed of "vagrant dwellers in the houseless woods," with whom it is impossible to establish rational communication.

There is something familiar about her, about those "fond hazed eyes" (p. 77), but he does not want to waste any time in trying to identify it. "Oh well. She was on something and couldn't focus her eyes." And a little later (pp. 77–78), in a momentary mood of insincere and fatuous sympathy: "Maybe they're better off, after all. At least they are unburdened by the past. They don't remember anything because there is nothing to remember. They crawl under the nearest bush when they're tired, they eat seeds when they're hungry, they pop a pill when they feel bad. Maybe it does come down to chemistry after all."

Even her strange way of speaking he tries to account for as part of the stereotype: "Again the slow scanning speech. He looked at her. Yes, she was on something" (p. 77).

Actually, Allison's language has at least as much in common with *Paradise Lost*, *Through the Looking-Glass*, and *Finnegans Wake* as with the commonplace inanities of post-Beat "head" talk. On the quality of her speech as on almost every other point concerning her, Will is in his first assessment badly wrong. Chapter 3 ends with the sentence: "He remembered everything" (p. 79). Chapter 4 begins: "She remembered nothing" (p. 80). However, as the reader already knows, and Will is soon to learn, Allison is very much burdened by the past. Moreover, the past she is burdened with is in considerable part—namely, Kitty's part—intricately entangled with Will's past. If Allison cannot remember anything, or has a hard time remembering, it is not, as Will rather contemptuously assumes, because for people like her "there is nothing to remember," but because the memories are too painful or bewildering to tolerate. At the time Will meets her she is not, in the sense he means it, "on something." On the contrary, she is for the first time in quite a while *off* all the bad stuff. Will's mistaken perceptions are certainly understandable. The reader has the advantage of him, of course, in already knowing a good deal about Allison before she encounters Will. And Allison has the advantage of him—seems superior to him, in more quickly perceiving the true quality, if not the precise causes, of his emotional state, in sensing *his* individuality, his essential nonconformity to the stereotype signified by his golfer's gear, before he can "see" her without prejudice—on two accounts. First, she has the advantage of her long training in the mental hospital, where the danger of permanent loss of personal identity is a terrifying daily reality, and survival radically depends upon zealous cultivation of an ability to penetrate disguises and of an extraordinary sense for what it is that distinguishes one person from another. The second advantage she has over Will is just in literally having seen him, his approach heralded by the two golf balls, so that she had a few moments to study his attitude and gestures, before he was aware of her presence.

During their first encounter, Will obviously never quite gets over his embarrassed resentment of her "watching" him (p. 77), despite her assurances that her failure to reveal herself sooner was not a matter of either "spying or denying," but simply of fear. By the time of his second visit to the greenhouse, he is past his initial petulance, and much more disposed to take her at her word—at least to the extent that he can make out what she is saying.

Her eyes may be hazed, unfocused, and yet the gaze in which she holds him from her hiding place in the bushes is more penetrating than any other ever turned upon him. There is no mistaking the significance of the fact that later she sees *his* eyes as unfocused

(p. 115). For something even partially to match the kind of insight she has developed at Valleyhead, Will has to await his own brief experience of "commitment," and the fear that it might become permanent.

But in the "outer world," the "real" world of everyday social responsibility, which Allison is taking the first timorous steps toward reentering and Will is attempting rather desperately to retain a foothold in when they first meet, the primary requirement for survival is often the opposite of the skills one needs in the world of the mental hospital. In the workaday world, one cannot go about attempting to assess the unique personal qualities of everybody one encounters. The habit of promptly classifying people, together with a willingness to be classified, is a matter of practical necessity, an essential device of self-preservation.

Will's first perceptions of Allison are understandable. And they are not, after all, entirely mistaken. She is, and is not, like other young women of her generation in America, just as she is, and is not, like her mother (p. 279). (Just as Will is, and is not, "one of them"—the Linwood country-clubbers.) Perhaps in the eyes of God human individuality is pure and absolute. But to each other we are, except in moments of most rare intuition, recognizable or definable as individuals only on the basis of those minute particulars of behavior, appearance, and attitude in which each of us departs from the norms of group identity: the identity we have as male or female, black or white, learned or illiterate, patrician or bourgeois, Jewish or Christian, and so on.

Another theme explored at length in the novel is that of the conflict between the virtues of charity and self-reliance. Early in her acquaintance with Will, Allison is wary of asking or accepting his help in moving the big stove. Immediately after his first visit to the greenhouse she asks herself why she had let the opportunity slip:

> . . . for the reason that he was, she saw at once, out of it, out of his life, he'd have been glad to do anything at all except whatever it was he was doing or not doing . . . he'd have done it, not for her, not even seeing her, but for the pleasure, the faint ironic pleasure of the irrelevance of it, helping a stranger move a stove in the woods . . . [But] no, she hadn't asked him because she didn't want to ask anybody. Asking is losing, she might have said. Or getting help is behelt.

197

It is not that a debt is incurred to a person for a thing as [*sic*] that the thing itself loses value. . . . She had found a treasure. You don't ask a stranger to help you move a treasure. You don't ask friends either. And you certainly don't ask family. (p. 92)

And on his second visit, when she has already managed by herself, with a complex system of ropes and pulleys, to raise the thing from the ruined cellar, but has not yet quite figured out how to get it the rest of the way to the greenhouse, she balks at his rather inept offer simply to come back with a couple of men and a golf cart to finish the job (p. 111). She can, although with some misgivings (p. 112), accept his gift of avocados and a can of olive oil once she sees that he understands her reluctance to incur a debt of gratitude; but the task of moving her "treasure," the stove, is still quite another matter. She has now learned that he knows something of her history, and she is desperately afraid that he must be in some way connected with her parents' schemes. In such a context, his very "understanding" itself is suspect. As she succinctly puts it (p. 113): "Understanding can also be a demand. De man. Le mans." For all his undeniable charm, Will has begun to act most distressingly like the other "mans" in her life—her father, her lover "Sarge," Dr. Duk— whose "understanding" has brought her nothing but pain and madness and the terrors of solitude.

At last, she is able to acknowledge the fact that she needs assistance, and takes Will up on his offer to supply her, from the Ford agency he owns, with one of the devices called "creepers"—used by mechanics for pushing themselves about underneath automobiles— which it occurs to him might serve her purpose in moving the stove. Allison constantly delights in all manner of equipment and tools— all "gear and tackle and trim" [11]—and in the names of such things. But she accepts the offer only on the strict condition that she be left alone to secure the creeper, figure out precisely how to use it, and do the actual work. Moreover, Will risks making the offer, and she is able to accept, only after she has given *him* assistance when he falls down in one of his "petty mall" seizures—thus in some way "evening the score" for the avocados and olive oil.

Again, the situation in Will's dealings with the old men at St. Mark's is somewhat similar. Arnold's and Ryan's and Eberhart's need of Barrett's help, in the form of the jobs he offers them, to escape the debilitating routine at the nursing home, is more obvious at first glance than his need of them. But, as we have already noted, Barrett is in part inspired to his own new self-assertiveness by their example. And there is no reason to assume anything but that he expects them to contribute to the business enterprise the most expert and efficient services available.

The point that Barrett's experience keeps driving home to him—a point that multimillionaires, presumably, have a harder time keeping in mind than the rest of us have—is that no one can accomplish much of anything without some kind of assistance from somebody, and that the positions of assister and assisted are readily reversible from moment to moment. Even on a strictly secular-humanist view of the matter, it is plain why one might think it worthwhile, as Barrett does with the three old men, to avoid offering help in such a way as to damage the recipient's self-esteem.

But, besides failing to accommodate the emotional complexities of a personal relationship such as Will's and Allison's, a secular-humanist theory of altruism—theory of "enlightened self-interest" —can appear thoroughly convincing only to the person whose sense of the "other" does not exceed the limits of the human community and the time-bound universe of its environment. Such a theory can make satisfactory sense only to the man who is reconciled to his personal mortality, content to see death not as passage to another life but only as end to this one. The crucial question raised in the account of Will's continuing struggle with his dead father is whether it is actually possible to be so reconciled—whether those who pretend to be are not, in fact, grossly self-deceived, whether they do not in truth passionately desire that death which they make a show merely to accept as inevitable.

In any event, the father becomes, in Will's obsession with his memory, little more than a ghostly personification of the son's own death wish. Even with the best and wisest of parents, any sensible man is likely to experience occasional dismay in contemplation of the state of affairs on planet Earth in the late twentieth century, but it is obvious that his father's attitudes have profoundly influenced Will's rather special revulsion from contemporary society.

The elder Barrett, whose character we have examined at some length in discussing *The Last Gentleman*, soured Southern stoic and sometime champion of black civil rights on the paradoxical principle of *noblesse oblige*, had found the degeneracy of the modern world already intolerable in "the Eisenhower years" (p. 126), the period of troubled social conscience and growing dread of atomic power which followed so soon upon the dubious triumph of the Allied forces in World War II and the subsequent disgrace of Korea. That era of our national history—all too appropriately, perhaps, presided over by the great hero of the war against Nazi Germany—was assuredly a bad time. It was a time which must have seemed to any man of spirit, any man with any plausible ideal of human dignity, Christian, stoic, or what you will, a time of "death in life" (p. 126). Yet, by the time Will reaches middle age—"here in rich reborn Christian Carolina with its condos and 450 SELs and old folks rolling pills and cackling at *Hee Haw*" (pp. 131–32)—the corruptions his father lamented have multiplied tenfold. And even after Will has been able to cut through the elaborate structure of repressions he has built up over half a lifetime, at last clearly to remember what happened on the bird hunt in the Georgia woods, to face the probability that the old man himself, at least in that instance, was the would-be agent of death, he is unable immediately to repudiate his father's values.

Even appalled as he is in the growing suspicion that his father, for all his own heroics in the struggle against the Nazis, in the end brought home the gods of the enemy—wrote a history of the Third Army's actions in World War II which contained "not one word about Buchenwald" (p. 132), while he kept as an apparently cherished memento certain photographs of a German SS colonel, with the death's-head insignia on his cap, standing in the hatch of a Tiger tank—Will is not prepared simply to turn his back on the ethical tradition in which he was reared, dismissing it all as rankest hypocrisy. Beyond the mysteries of filial love, which is well known often to survive, however irrationally, under the most extreme stress of abuse and betrayal, there are several possible considerations at work in Will's reluctance to forswear all allegiance to his father.

If, for example, he is justified in suggesting (in the somewhat ambiguous syntax of a parenthesized rhetorical question) that the horror of Buchenwald may be where such "humanism" as his father espoused inevitably "ends in the end" (p. 132), he could hardly fail to recognize the fact that the culture of the condos and SELs and pill-popping oldsters also derives from the "humanist" tradition. And he knows quite well that his father, if he were alive, "wouldn't put up with that either" (p. 132), perhaps the more certainly for the fact that this particular lot of neohumanist hypocrites make such a point of styling themselves "reborn Christians." Thus, it appears that certain finer distinctions are in order.

In the first place, notwithstanding the disturbing fact of the elder Barrett's failure ever to mention the fate of the Jews in Nazi Germany, and the evidence of a morbid fascination with the sinister SS colonel, there are other apparent facts about his father's performance in World War II that Will is hardly likely to forget so long as he is able to maintain any rational perspective in the matter. Perhaps his father had a touch of sympathy with the Nazis, a certain admiration for their disciplined death worship; perhaps his silence on the horrors of Buchenwald indicated covert anti-Semitic leanings. Perhaps. But what appears to be undeniable is that, however he felt about them, he fought effectively against the German soldiers, and was, therefore, an effective practical champion of the Jews, however he felt about *them*. All forms of racism are reprehensible; some are more reprehensible than others. A plausible case could be made against old lawyer Barrett as essentially a racist even in his advocacy of black civil rights in postwar Mississippi. On the other hand, it would be extremely difficult to show that the impurity of his motives and principles so compromised the moral position of his clients that they would have been better off without his aid.

But whether Will is right or wrong about anything his father did or thought, either on the bird hunt in Georgia or during World War II in Europe and back in America in the troubled postwar years, the fact of first importance, with which Will must come to terms before he can save himself, is that the old man is dead. It does not matter whether Will approves or disapproves of whatever it is he thinks his father did or thought, or failed to do or think: his father is dead, beyond praise or reproach.

"Old mole," Will is whimsically pleased to call him from time to time (e.g., p. 162), echoing Prince Hamlet's antic epithet for the murdered king's ghost as it returns (act 1, scene 5) to the underworld. But while Will Barrett's character and situation are in some ways reminiscent of the moody Dane's—he is nothing if not distracted, and given to melancholy and inconclusive soliloquizing upon the defects of his own temperament and the sorry state of the world in general, he is subject to strange fits and wild utterances that raise serious questions concerning his sanity, he is beset by jealous and scheming flatterers, false friends, prating fools, smiling villains—yet in at least as many respects, like Eliot's Prufrock, he is "not Prince Hamlet, nor was meant to be." Perhaps the most significant dissimilarity is precisely in the matter of his relationship to the "old mole."

For except Will himself, no one has so much as seen this ghost even in his mind's eye. Prince Hamlet is the only one privileged to hear his father's story, and to receive his charge for revenge. But Bernardo and Marcellus, and then Horatio, all have repeatedly seen the apparition before the prince himself greets it for the first time. And Marcellus and Horatio (along with the theater audience) presumably hear the voice from beneath the earth which seconds the prince in his demand that they swear themselves to secrecy. Will, on the other hand, is in every sense entirely on his own in his efforts to communicate with his father.

Not only does no one else "see" or "hear" the departed lawyer, but in the mental colloquies Will holds with him the old man volunteers no information concerning his experiences either in this life or in the next. Nor will he answer any questions. "But what about the Jews?" Will demands. "What to make, father, of the Jews?" (pp. 133–34). But there is no response. Will must figure out the probable facts as best he can, by deduction and intuition. Neither—being, as Will already knows, dead by his own hand—has the old man any commission of revenge to impose upon his son. The ghost of the dead king fairly plainly urges Prince Hamlet to go and kill Claudius. So far as Will Barrett can make it out, *his* father has nothing to suggest but that he follow the parental example and kill himself.

In the "dialogue" that Will carries on with his dead father, he is, literally and in all other senses, really talking to himself: arguing with himself, trying to explain, and in some way to justify, his own behavior. Regardless of what the truth might have been about his father's attitudes, and how they might originally have influenced the son's thinking, it is now Will who decidedly "has a thing about the Jews"—his fantasy (pp. 11–12 and elsewhere) of their exodus from

202

North Carolina and its possible significance as a sign that the Last Days are at hand, his strangely vivid recollection of the brief but desperate love he had felt for a Jewish girl he knew in high school (pp. 7–8 and elsewhere), the mad commission he gives to Sutter Vaught in the letter he writes before entering the cave. And as for the Germans, and his father's disturbing fascination with the SS colonel, Will's habitual and lascivious fondling of the Luger pistol the old man brought home as a war trophy is no very promising sign. (The chief mementoes of his father Will has kept are the Luger and the suicide weapon, an English-made Greener shotgun.) The point is reinforced in the multiple ironies of Will's reference to the prevalence of 450 SELs—along with drug-taking and *Hee Haw*-watching oldsters—as evidence of the degeneracy of contemporary society in North Carolina. Will's own favorite car, in which he luxuriates, often simultaneously, with the same lascivious excitement he has in fondling the old Luger, is that much celebrated product of German engineering, a Mercedes 450 SEL.[12] To the extent that it helps him simply to *understand* himself, his relentless probing of his memories of his father is a good and necessary procedure. But, beyond that, it serves only to exacerbate, and literally to implement, in the shape of the guns and the automobile, the morbid tendencies of his mind.

Having discovered the worst about his father, or, more accurately, having found the courage to face the possibility of the worst—for nothing can be proved beyond doubt—Will is still left with the responsibility to defeat his own death wish, somehow to come to terms, on his own, with the miseries and terrors of existence in a world that is little to his liking. Perhaps it is true, as he suspects, that his father meant to kill them both in the Georgia woods. But the only facts of present and continuing importance are that for whatever reason—"was it love or failure of love" (p. 148)—he "missed" with the shot from the Greener presumably intended for Will, and that, many years later when he took his own life with the same gun, he did not try again to shoot his son. The father is dead, the son lives. The choice is now Will's, and his alone, whether he will die or go on living.

The first essential step for Will, then, is simply to recognize his freedom of choice. But recognition is *only* the first step. The act of choice is another matter. What prompts him to decide as he does: i.e., to live rather than to die?

The bizarre "litany" of his renunciation of death in all its forms (pp. 272–74), as well as his throwing the pistol and shotgun down the mountainside (p. 338), is primarily a ritual performance, celebrating a decision already made. There has been no fundamental change in his view of the ills of the contemporary world; in this, he remains as much his father's son as ever. The state of the world as he continues to see it is still a state of "death in life." Writing to Sutter Vaught [13] before setting out for the cave, Will ranted at length on the "bankruptcy" of both the company of the believers and the company of the unbelievers in our time.

The believers, "who think they know the reason why we find ourselves in this ludicrous predicament"—i.e., the predicament of mortality—"yet act for all the world as if they don't" (p. 190), "are repellent precisely to the degree that they embrace and advertise" their faith (p. 188). The unbelievers, although often more attractive than the believers in being more effectively concerned for the welfare of their fellowman—"they generally perform good works, help niggers, pore whites, etc." (p. 190)—are nonetheless, as Will sees it, obviously "crazy" in no longer bothering even to seek an explanation for the "preposterous" situation (p. 189) of their mortality.

Obliged to count himself as one of the unbelievers, and yet appalled by the "insanity" of their customary intellectual acquiescence, Will had for a time considered "the famous wager of Pascal" as offering a way out of his dilemma (p. 191). Pascal's proposal, the only really "practical" one ever made before—"a proposal of which the rare sane unbeliever could at least make a modicum of sense"— Will nonetheless rejected, on the grounds of its essential "frivolity."

"My father knew all about this," Will wrote to Sutter (p. 191), "about believers and unbelievers and Pascal's bettor." In committing suicide, "what he said was I'm having no part of any of you. Excuse me but I won't have it. Good day, gentlemen."

"The trouble with Pascal's wager is its frivolity," Will concluded (p. 191). "The trouble with my father's exit is that it yields no answers. It does not even ask a question."

However absurdly and presumptuously, Will was convinced, of course, at the time he wrote to Sutter, that his own approach, the demand for a confrontation with God in the cave, remedied the defects of both his father's and Pascal's strategies. Besides all the other complexities of historical, geological, psychological, and anthropological significance involved, Percy's design draws upon a long tradition of association of caves with the pursuit of wisdom and with practices of ascetic self-discipline.[14] It is hard to say how much of that tradition we are meant to assume Will had in mind when he set out alone for Lost Cove Cave. In any event, the toothache and the nausea and the battering he suffered slipping and falling about in the darkness quickly defeated his pride as upstart theologian.

Yet, without notably altering his opinion of the generality either of believers or of unbelievers—or, presumably, his opinion of Pascal's proposal—Will does not despair and in the end is somehow able to throw off his morbid preoccupation with his father's memory. He never really repudiates his father's bitterly pessimistic view of the modern world. Still, he is able to resist the temptation to suicide. Why? What makes the difference? That is the crucial question, I think, for evaluating the final success of the novel: the essential *dramatic probability* of its conclusion.

III. No Second Eden, No Second Coming

As the TV and bumper-sticker evangelists have it, "Christ is the difference," presumably, or "Christ is the answer." Rather uncomfortably for nearly all readers, I imagine, regardless of whether our own settled workaday persuasions favor or oppose Percy's Catholic fundamentalism in general, there can be little doubt that this novel is centrally "about" Christ-hunting.

But which Christ? Newly escaped from the mental hospital and looking about her at the marvels of the country of the sane, Allison sees a car in Linwood with the familiar bumper sticker: I FOUND IT. "Found what? she wondered" (p. 22). As we get to know her, we can hardly imagine that her wonder is likely to be satisfied with the kind of answer she might get from the driver of the slogan-bearing car. That Christ, surely, is not the one Barrett has in mind at the end as the "giver" signified by Allison herself.

Whose Christ? Marion Peabody Barrett's Christ? Jack Curl's? Leslie Barrett's? Curl assures Barrett that "what [Marion] wanted more than anything else was [Will's] coming into the church" (p. 137). And it would seem that Will himself had something of that in mind from the beginning of the marriage (p. 156), that he had, indeed, tried for some time to convince himself that he actually shared Marion's faith, even though he stopped short of a formal commitment.

But whatever direct influence Marion might once have had upon him is no longer available, perhaps had been dissipated long before her death, indeed. The ludicrous and self-serving Jack Curl, as chief spokesman for the Episcopal church in the circle of Will's local acquaintance, is hardly likely to persuade him to the commitment that he failed to make while Marion lived. The hope he had, before entering the cave, that he might eventually find "common ground" with Leslie (p. 197), was obviously at best forlorn; and, besides, the "experiment" of the cave does *not* work out. In the way of "love-and-faith community" projects, the residential development Will begins planning with Allison and the three "old men but good" is clearly nothing in which either Jack Curl or Leslie would want to participate.

If the animosity one kind of Christer feels toward another—e.g., Leslie's angry contempt for "shaman" Curl (p. 144)—is dismaying to Will in his search for faith, later instances of interfactional fellowship, such as the collaboration of Leslie and Jack with Dr. Battle in stowing him away at St. Mark's, are hardly reassuring (pp. 312–14). In short, professing Christians of any description seem to have nothing to offer Will, at least until the final episode of the novel.

The principal human agent of his salvation, of course, the one who not only nurses him back to physical health after his misadventure in the cave but gives him, in the simplest emotional sense, "something to live for" again, is Allison. And, if there can be little doubt that we are meant to see her finally as Christ-surrogate, or Christ-bearer, in her service to Will, it seems to me very important that she does not see *herself* in that light. Still more plainly, perhaps, Will is Allison's savior. But again, while various features of the "Christ figure" may be discernible in descriptions of Will,[15] especially in his encounters with Allison, there is no evidence that he consciously plays the role.

Initially, Will's and Allison's loving solicitude for each other, without any theological sanctions or implications of which they are aware, is sufficient to account for both his and her rejuvenation. The pattern of the essential Christian mysteries, Percy suggests, survives in the modern world not in the activities and observances of any institutional body—it is, perhaps, least of all discernible in deliberately "religious" usages—but primarily in the most intensely private, most uncalculated, purely personal encounters. The *phrase* "personal encounter" is the one Leslie uses to describe her way of knowing Christ; but like Jack Curl's talk of "finding God in other people" it seems more accurately descriptive of something quite different in the relationship of Will and Allison.

In the churches, whether of Jack Curl's sold-out Episcopalianism or Leslie's self-consciously iconoclastic fellowship, a man like Will Barrett can see little evidence of God's presence. But in the forest and the cave, in the abandoned greenhouse, in the bizarre love affair which by any conventional standard is surely "out of bounds," Will's and Allison's words and actions insistently hint at a pattern of sacred significance: as if, all unconsciously, they were striving to follow some defaced and fragmentary dramatic text, text of an ancient cycle of mystery plays, in which the original sequence of actions is blurred and confused, roles are so uncertainly differentiated as to seem at times wholly interchangeable, low-comic matter is freely intermingled with the holy, and yet the sense of supreme seriousness is never lost. In the setting of the forest and the greenhouse, images of Eden are suddenly and all but imperceptibly altered to a Nativity scene, or scenes of the Crucifixion and Resurrection. At one moment, walking in the woods, Will has the look of an Adam to Allison's Eve; at the next, or simultaneously, he might seem the Lord God Himself, out for a stroll in the cool of the evening. When he tumbles out of the cave into the greenhouse, the description of the grotesque mess he has made of himself and of Allison's ministrations to him —his body "smeared head to toe with a whitish grease" (the excrement of the cave bats), and "smell[ing] of a grave" (p. 234), her lifting him, washing him with hot water from the reservoir of her newly installed stove, wrapping him in her sleeping bag (pp. 234–35)—is deliberately and obviously ambiguous, combining elements of scenes of birth, resurrection (resurrection as rebirth), and preparation of the dead for burial.

It is difficult to avoid thinking of Mary Magdalene with the risen Christ (John 20) when Allison, telling Will of how he fell into the greenhouse (*The Second Coming*, p. 229), remarks "To see you was not to believe you," and then recalls (pp. 233–34) the strange way in which for a moment she both had and had not "recognized" him. But on the complex issues of seeing and believing, faith and evidence, not to speak of the issue of personal recognition involved in the Gospel story, Percy's allusion is deliberately somewhat "skewed," to say the least: with Allison's "To see you was not to believe you," and Will's request to her (p. 229, the final page of part 1), "Don't tell anybody I'm here." [16]

Besides, the circumstances of Will's escape from the cave into Allison's care, and their subsequent dialogue, perhaps as readily suggest a likeness to the return of Lazarus from the grave (John 11), the story of which merely foreshadows that of Jesus's own resurrection. It is quite impossible, on the other hand, to ignore the one direct, explicitly stated comparison of Will to Christ which is attributed to Allison herself. As she tries to figure out the best way to grasp and turn the unconscious man while she washes him, she thinks how the inert body, "the abdomen dropping away hollow under his ribs, the thin arms and legs with their heavy slack straps of muscle, cold as clay, reminded her of some paintings of the body of Christ taken down from the crucifix [*sic*], the white flesh gone blue with death" (p. 236). But since it is unclear whether the kind of painting she has in mind is a "Descent from the Cross" (a "Deposition") or a "Pietà," the role she herself might be seen as assuming in the total composition remains also extremely difficult to define.

In sum, the various uncertainties and confusions seem too numerous to be regarded as anything but a matter of conscious design on Percy's part. On the part of the actors themselves, Will and Allison, there is presumably no deliberate intention to imitate the divine drama. I have suggested that it is as if they were striving "all unconsciously" to act out parts in a mystery play; and the impression of their unawareness is absolutely essential to Percy's design. Even the one conscious comparison Allison makes of Will to the dead Christ may strike many readers as heavyhanded. But it is notable that Percy at least does not compound the mistake, if mistake it is, by having Allison assign herself a role in the scene, as either the

Blessed Mother or Mary Magdalene. And Will, of course, is literally and totally unconscious at the time.

Moreover, lest we be tempted to make too much of the solemnity of Allison's vision of Will, we should not miss the fact that she also sees in the hand of the presumptuously amorous hiker (p. 240) a likeness to the hand of Adam, his forefinger touching God's, in Michelangelo's Sistine Chapel painting of the Creation. Allison seems rather habitually fascinated by representations of the male anatomy in paintings on sacred subjects, and ready whenever possible to see imitations of such art in everyday life. Will as the dead Christ, perhaps, is in this regard no very special case.

To represent the man and woman as consciously imitating any of the biblical personages, or, regardless of the state of their awareness, even to structure their actions in such a way as to suggest to the reader an exact, point-for-point parallel between any episode of the novel's surface narrative and an episode of the lives of Christ and his followers, or the lives of our first parents, would be contrary to Percy's purposes both as novelist and as Christian apologist. What Percy wants to do, as I see it, with the series of deliberately obscure and ambiguous allusions, is just enough to indicate the persistent vitality of the Christian myth in the modern world, its continuing "relevance" to the needs of anyone who seeks a conviction of purpose in his existence and cannot find it in any of the "isms and asms" (p. 273) of false faith Barrett lists in his catalogue of rejections. The Christian myth is still valid, still "makes sense" of the experience of human existence as nothing else does; and the Christian redemption is still available, on the same terms as always. Will imagines, or remembers, his father's describing his life in the years following World War II as a state of "death in life," and wondering "if it ever happened in history before" (p. 126). In the imaginary conversation, Will replies "I don't know." But the implicit answer of the novel as a whole is pretty clearly "yes." To those capable of seeing, those who refuse to deceive themselves, the true state of affairs is perhaps more obvious now than it was in any earlier period of our history. But, essentially, nothing has changed. The state of "death in life" that Will's father tried to define can never be fully explained, Percy suggests, as the consequence of purely historical processes. Neither can it be explained in purely "scientific" terms, as a matter of the responses of the human organism to alterations of the environment. Rather, that state of radical alienation, our sense of our being never and nowhere "at home" in the world, is the inevitable and permanent human condition—the condition of *fallen* man, man suffering the effects of original sin.

The particular manifestations of original sin may differ from culture to culture, and from one historical age to another, even as they differ from stage to stage of the lifetime of the individual. But the ultimate source of the evil is the same, whether for the child or the middle-aged man in twentieth-century America or the stripling in Renaissance Rome. So too, the essential nature of Christ's redemption remains constant, through myriad changes in the immediate circumstances of its offering.

Will Barrett and Tom More have quite a good deal in common, notably including their penchant for eschatology and their unsteadiness on their feet. At the beginning of both *Love in the Ruins* and *The Second Coming*, the hero is in apparent danger of being picked off by a sniper. But neither the "Bantu" revolutionary nor Barrett's old Covite buddy Ewell McBee is responsible for the general evil of the times. "Was not the shot expected after all? Is this not in fact the very nature of the times, . . . a concealed dread and expectation which, only after the shot is fired, we knew had been there all along?" (*The Second Coming*, pp. 15–16). But further, the "times" in question, "after all," are all the times of man.

In his repeated "seizures," whatever the precise nature of the physical malady they manifest, his many falls—in sandtraps, in the forest, off the moving bus, from the cave into Allison's greenhouse —Will Barrett enacts over and over again a parable of the Great Fall. And each time he is lifted up, most especially, of course, in Allison's lifting his bruised and unconscious body onto the table of the potting room after his startling rebirth from the cave, we are reminded of that grand paradox of the "Fortunate Fall," the idea that the sin of Adam and Eve, inasmuch as it has made necessary the redemption of man through Christ's love, is indeed the "happy fault," a cause not for repining but for greatest rejoicing.

If in the description of the greenhouse and environs, and Will's and Allison's actions there, it is impossible to miss "a strain of the earth's sweet being in the beginning / In Eden garden . . .",[17] it is

210

essential also that we not fail to recognize the illusory character of the likeness. Like Milton's Eve in prospect of the expulsion from the garden, Allison is reluctant to give up her greenhouse, but must yield to the practical requirements of a future with Will. She could no more realistically hope to return to life in the greenhouse than she can propose to go on living in the obviously ersatz paradise of the Holiday Inn (p. 343). Not only will they "need more than one room eventually," as Will points out, but in all probability Allison will not really want even to spend weekends at the motel once they are into the routine of marriage. And the greenhouse, if it is to figure in their future, must like the rest of her property be "developed," not as a retreat for them alone, but as a functioning part of their enterprises which will involve many more people and which, by the same token, must be *profitable*. "I could make money," Allison says (p. 344), rejoicing in her newfound knowledge of the price of lettuce and tomatoes.

The final point is not that, in the prospect of marriage, they have decided to *return* to the world of fallen man—the world of time, of disease and death and taxes, of the laws of property and the marketplace—but that they realize they never were really out of that world. Their woodland idyll has really been only another case of "love in the ruins." Neither the forest nor the lovers are virgin. Even the cave, not to speak of the greenhouse, has never been more than partially cut off from the mainstream of time, a kind of temporal backwater which can serve briefly as appropriate setting for discovery of the *signs* of man's immortal destiny, but in which the fundamental conditions of his temporal existence are in no way changed. There is no reliable *escape* for Allison and Will in the "enchanted" precincts of the forest; and when, in the prospect of their marriage, they prepare to "reenter" the workaday world, they do so in possession of no new and special faculties, but only with the beginnings of a new understanding of, and a new willingness to accept, the conditions of their existence there.

Perhaps the willingness to *accept* is, indeed, of first importance. For one of the conditions of human existence, according to the Christian doctrine I think Percy follows here, remains something beyond rational understanding: an irreducible paradox, in short, a mystery. I mean, the fact of our being at once radically free and radically dependent. As we have already noted, a partial analogy is provided in the purely secular sphere of human experience: we cannot act in any way in total independence of other human beings and of the non-human physical environment, but we are, within certain variable limits, free to choose whom and what we will depend upon. There is no real mystery here. No logical contradiction is involved in the assertion of such qualified dependence and qualified freedom. The truth of the Christian doctrine, on the other hand—the mystery of fallen man's absolute and total dependence upon divine Grace, upon a power which he is yet totally and absolutely free to accept or reject, the same mystery which is involved in that "grand paradox" of the *Felix Culpa*—is a truth of which we can be convinced only by Faith. And at the novel's end, although Will is clearly and directly *grasping* for it in his colloquy with the old priest, neither he nor Allison has yet achieved the vision of faith. But what they have achieved in their secular experience, the new knowledge and acceptance of their mutual need, the "grace" (lowercase) of their personal love, has equipped them at least with what theologians call a "right disposition" to faith.

Short of the final conviction of faith, one of the surest indications of Will's new insight into the nature of moral freedom is his acceptance of responsibility for the choices he has already made in his past life. Leslie, in common with a number of others in Will's circle of acquaintance, is quite confident that she knows why he married her mother (p. 220)—purely and simply "to get the Peabody fortune"—and is, with the irritating smugness that characterizes all her charitable actions, willing to "forgive" him for it. Will himself, like most of us in our retrospective reflections upon such matters, upon the decisions, the choices that have "made all the difference" in our lives, is never quite sure what he had in mind with his first marriage (pp. 155–56). But the important thing for him now, in prospect of his marrying again, is just that he accepts the fact he did choose Marion the first time, for whatever reason—married her of his own free will, without coercion or deception of any kind—and that the choice has had certain consequences: consequences which require him to make still further choices in his present situation. Regardless of whether Leslie is or is not right about his original intentions, he has, through Marion's will, come into control of the Peabody fortune. A good many people pretend that they know what Marion wanted done with the money; but the only documented fact in the matter, as he points out to Vance Battle (p. 313), is that Will is her sole legal heir. For reasons which ought to be clear enough without elaborate analysis, he decides that he does not want to use the Peabody money for his and Allison's support after they are married. He has not, he tells Allison (p. 343), decided yet just how the inheritance should be used. But the implication is clear that he has reserved to himself, as his exclusive right and responsibility, both legal and moral, the task of making that decision—without necessary further consultation with Leslie, Jack Curl, or anyone else.

Additional evidence of Will's new receptivity to an orthodox Christian view of the world is his qualified willingness to accept medical aid. In *Love in the Ruins*, Percy satirized the legalized and government-sponsored practices of the medical profession at Fedville as something little different, in moral-theological terms, from the observances of the cannabis-smoking dropouts in Honey Island Swamp. Both were seen as essentially rooted in the same hedonist-humanist doctrine which at once debases man, in denying the divine endowment of his sovereign will, and falsely exalts him, in denying the effects of the Fall. *The Second Coming* presents, in a less heavily satiric mode, a set of variations on the same theme.

Early in his acquaintance with Allison, when he still takes her to be a typical representative of the youthful drug culture, Will muses on the lifestyle of her set as he conceives it (pp. 77–78): "They crawl under the nearest bush when they're tired, they eat seeds when they're hungry, they pop a pill when they feel bad." "Maybe," he is for a moment tempted despairingly to concede, "they are better off, after all. . . . Maybe it does come down to chemistry after all." Later, when we are treated to a view of the goings-on at St. Mark's, it is apparent that except for the regimentation and the fact that the church itself is the sponsoring institution—both of which considerations only compound the disgrace—there is little to distinguish the irresponsible half-life of the elderly patients there from the degraded nirvana of the youthful "heads" as Will envisages it. Certainly, there is no evidence that Jack Curl would find anything radically offensive to his version of Christian truth in the notion that the problem of human happiness might "come down to chemistry after all": or, at any rate, chemistry plus golf and television, and maybe an occasional "retreat at Montreat."

Will vigorously resists the "conspiracy" of Leslie and Curl and company to have him institutionalized, but so long as he can handle matters on an out-patient basis he seems little disturbed by the diagnosis of his falling fits as a case of "Hausmann's syndrome,"[18] and the prospect of regular monitoring and dosing, for the rest of his life if necessary, to see that his blood pH level is properly maintained. It is a question, of course, of his seeing things in a different perspective now. In the state of mind he was in at the time he first met Allison, and brooding on the terrible memories of his father, he could see the notion of the chemical basis of human well-being only in absolute terms, the standard "all or nothing" formula of despair. Either *everything* "comes down to chemistry after all," or nothing does. But once he has known Allison, and wants to marry her, the falsity of that formula becomes apparent.

The implied idea of the limited validity of scientific knowledge is familiar from Percy's earlier fiction. To the extent that Will's problem is with staying conscious and on his feet, analysis and manipulation of the processes of his body chemistry can probably help a good deal. But whether it is *worthwhile* standing up in such a world as this, walking about upon such an earth as ours, is a question of a different order.

Again, Milton comes to mind. Reflecting upon the nature of his life after the Fall, Adam speaks to the Archangel Michael (*Paradise Lost*, book 12) of how he is now content to "have [his] fill / Of knowledge, what this vessel can contain; / Beyond which was [his] folly to aspire." As Arnold Stein argues in *Answerable Style*:

> Before the Fall the highest value is knowledge (including self-knowledge) under which are subsumed obedience and love. Through Adam's faith in knowledge, and the irrational disobedience of knowledge through love, man is re-created into an order that makes a strength of his accepted weakness. After the Fall the highest value is love, by which man fell. The violation of knowledge by love is reconstituted as the ground of possible true knowledge through love. (Though love, through grace and enlarged freedom, transcends obedience, it is not independent of knowledge and the virtues, but is rather the "soul of all the rest"....)[19]

Allison too must be disabused of her own naively charming but faulty notions of the power of scientific reasoning. Flushed with the pride of her first success as self-taught master of hoisting, she muses on the question of why "scientists had not long ago solved the problems of the world" (p. 234). A kind of latter-day Archimedes, she is convinced that "with pulleys and ropes and time to plan, one could move anything." "Were they, the scientists, serious?" she wonders. Perhaps that is it; she can think of no other reason. "Perhaps they ... were *not* serious."

But no, of course, that is not it. Scientists are serious enough, all right—*too* serious, as like as not. A bit later (p. 240), in the encounter with the amorous hiker, she comes close to the true reason without realizing it. "She knew a great deal about pulleys and hoists but nothing about love." There, precisely, is the seat not only of her trouble, but of the trouble with scientists as well. But she does not, of course, recognize the connection at the moment. And she is, understandably, only the more confused when she goes to the library (pp. 240–41) in an effort to find out something about love, just as she had gone there to find out about the principles of hoisting, but discovers that although much has been written on the subject of love, none of it has any practical value.

We will recall that "Sarge," her first lover, made use of illustrated sex manuals for their exercises in bed. But there is, Allison at length discovers with Will, no way of learning about love—"being in love," that is, as distinguished from "making love"—but by firsthand experience. Nor can the experience be anticipated, or its occasion deliberately sought after. And yet love is, above all things, the one thing *necessary* for the descendants of Adam and Eve, including scientists.

There is, then, no "Second Eden" for Allison and Will. And neither do they witness the Second Coming.

When the latter subject first comes up, in Will's conversation with Vance Battle about the Jews (pp. 11–12), the doctor is obviously inclined to regard the preoccupation as a symptom of mental illness. Will has suggested that there are remarkably few Jews still living in North Carolina, that a kind of latter-day exodus appears to be underway, and that this phenomenon might be interpreted as a prophetic "sign" of some nature. "Hm," says the embarrassed and skeptical Battle. And the narrator adds, in an aside to the reader: "It is not at all uncommon for persons suffering from certain psychoses and depressions of middle age to exhibit 'ideas of reference,' that is, all manner of odd and irrational notions about Jews, Bildebergers, gypsies, outer space, UFOs, international conspiracies, and whatnot. Needless to say, the Jews were not and are not leaving North Carolina" (p. 12).

Much later, in a conversation at the Duke University hospital following Will's fall from the bus and the subsequent diagnosis of his ailment, Battle again raises the question of the "exodus" and related matters (pp. 304–5), and is plainly relieved to discover that his patient, presumably as a consequence of the correction of his blood pH level, has all but forgotten their earlier talk.

Now, I do not mean to suggest that Percy would regard any and all kinds of interest in prophecies of the Last Days as necessarily, and simply, a manifestation of mental illness. Even the narrator's remarks I have quoted do not unequivocally support such a view. And the narrator's voice, we must repeatedly remind ourselves, is not always identifiable as Percy's. Certainly there is no indication that Percy supports Dr. Battle's hope that "the hydrogen ion may even solve the Jewish question" (p. 304). Obviously, Battle himself is mostly kidding about that, if not about finding a cure for the golf slice.

But there are excellent theological grounds, as well as medical, for skepticism concerning both the reasoning and the motives of anyone who is much preoccupied with thoughts of the end of the world, especially if a fascination with the fate of the Jews figures prominently in his search for "signs" that the Last Days are at hand. The biblical writings are full of warnings against the dangers of listening to false prophets and the folly of attempting to calculate the schedule of impending events. All this, besides the well-known mischief that apocalyptic thinking habitually works when it is allied with political and economic power.

At the very end of the novel, in his interview with Father Weatherbee, Will grows excited by the old man's words about Christian faith and love and speaks once more of the prophetic "signs." The very word is enough to provoke in the sympathetic reader a shudder of apprehension, that the poor fellow may, after all, be about to set out on still another solitary spiritual quest — if not in a cave again, perhaps this time undertaking on his own the mission in the deserts of the Holy Land for which he had previously tried to recruit Sutter Vaught. But there is a considerable measure of reassurance in the final paragraph, when his thoughts return to Allison, and it is only *she* then whom he has in mind as a "sign":[20] "a gift and therefore a sign of a giver." So far as Christ is concerned, Barrett is at least for the moment content to detect His presence in the person of the old priest.

All this is quite in order under the old dispensation. To regard human marriage as a sacramental union, typifying the marriage of Christ and His church, is thoroughly orthodox. And so is the view of the priest as living embodiment of the Lord he serves. Will Barrett's way of apprehending these truths may be somewhat eccentric, but there is no compelling evidence either of lunacy or of apocalyptic vision.

IV. Conclusion: A Question of Authority

I imagine a great many professing religionists among Percy's readers —Roman Catholics, Episcopalians, and persons of various other persuasions—will find reason for continuing dissatisfaction with *The Second Coming*. And so, no doubt, will many of the more secular-minded, including some admirers of Percy's earlier novels. Some, for example, who were charmed by the reticent and modest Will Barrett of *The Last Gentleman* may well find him considerably less attractive as the coarser-grained millionaire in middle age.

Paul Gray, in his *Time* magazine review of *The Second Coming*, found fault with the characterization of Barrett on other grounds, merely noting in passing that the same hero had appeared in the earlier novel, and fixing instead on traits which he saw the older Will as having in common with all Percy's protagonists. "From *The Moviegoer* (1961) on, his heroes have been thinking animals, unencumbered by the routines and demands of daily life. They are either feckless or rich. The hero of *The Second Coming* is emphatically both."[21] The charge of fecklessness is, it seems to me, at least in the present case misdirected. One of the things *The Second Coming* is centrally concerned with is Will's progress toward victory

over his fecklessness. At the beginning, he is assuredly weak, inde-
cisive, ineffectual; at the end, strengthened by his love for Allison, he
is beginning to make decisions, accept responsibility for his choices
and actions. But rich he is at the beginning, and rich he remains to
the end. To be sure, he has decided that he and Allison will not
depend upon the inheritance from Marion. But he still has considerable assets of his own earning. He clearly proposes to earn a great
deal more, once he has reestablished himself as a lawyer. And Allison
too, at least potentially, is wealthy in her own right. One way or
another, Will seems likely to continue enjoying considerable freedom
as the "thinking animal."

Indeed, even among the minor characters in Percy's fiction there
are very few ordinary wage and salary earners, people whose jobs
are neither in any sense "professional" positions—desirable at least
as much for their intangible rewards as for monetary gain—nor
positions, such as some in domestic service, guaranteed by family
tradition or personal affection. We get only fleeting glimpses of those
who work every day, according to a prescribed schedule, at whatever jobs they have managed to find, not to satisfy some deeply felt
personal yearning or sense of duty, the demands of God-given talent
or vision, nor yet surely to escape mere boredom with the activities
of excess leisure time, but simply to meet the commonplace needs of
the human organism. It would appear to be all but beyond Percy's
imagining what life is like for such people.[22] Among his major characters, there are none at all who must face life without some material
legacy, however small, and without as good a formal education as
they are willing to accept.

Such, obviously, is a severe limitation of the novelist's imagination, the more surprising in a novel, like this one, centrally concerned
with original sin—one of the chief effects of which, in the traditional doctrine, is the necessity of labor. And it is a limitation all of
a piece with other defects of Percy's social vision in *The Second
Coming*. Notwithstanding the great subtlety of the novel's artistic
design, and our primary responsibility as students and critics of
literature to attend to that, the plain fact remains that the book
deliberately addresses certain fundamental social issues of our time.
The book is a novel, neither a sociological study nor a volume of
essays designed to promote social reform. We do not demand of the

novelist either a rigorous adherence to scholarly method or a forth-right statement of his practical position on such issues as the rights of mental patients. But we do expect at least a realistic representation of the social conditions he is criticizing.

Consider what happens at the convalescent center and the psychiatric hospital. Both St. Mark's and Valleyhead are, in the first place, institutions of the privileged classes. Yet the novel provides no adequate picture of the real horrors of life even in such places as these, not to speak of what goes on in the state-supported facilities to which the helpless aged and the insane of the lower orders are committed. Real-life counterparts of Messrs. Arnold, Ryan, and Eberhart can have little hope for deliverance by a fairy godson like our hero here. If it is not at all improbable that the owner of such a place as St. Mark's, in the extra-fictional world, should enter it as a patient, what unmistakably stamps Will's institution as never-never land is his having to be told by a fellow patient that he doesn't charge enough (p. 351).

Finally, there is the matter of the church's role in Will's prospective redemption. If I am right that a major sign of his new disposition to faith is precisely his diminishing interest in "signs and wonders"—giving over his impatience to witness the "Second Coming," and resigning the quest for a special and private revelation which took him into the cave—then it might reasonably be expected that his final interview with Father Weatherbee would show him in an act of definite submission to the authority of the church, humbly seeking admission to the sacramental community. What a nice piece of comic irony it would be if Allison, without having had the slightest conscious intention of doing so, should succeed where Marion failed and bring him into the church.

But, in fact, nothing is definitely settled between Barrett and Weatherbee. At the end of *The Last Gentleman* we had good reason to doubt the firmness of Will's resolve to marry Kitty Vaught. Here, it seems much more likely that he and Allison will legalize their union. But it must remain questionable whether the priest can be persuaded to officiate. Will first says that he will not take instructions, that he is "not a believer and [does] not wish to enter the church" (p. 357). Within a few moments he has considerably modified his stand. Speaking both for himself and for Allison he says "we are . . . willing to take instructions, as long as you recognize I cannot and will not accept all of your dogmas. Unless of course you have the authority to tell me something I don't know. Do you?" (p. 358). Any experienced clergyman worth his salt ought to be able to recognize the signs of Will's readiness for salvation at this point, and be prepared to respond to his questions with ardent confidence.

But aside from the fact that poor old Weatherbee, while no doubt sufficiently experienced, simply is *not* any longer capable of priestly ardor, and does his best to persuade Will that "Father Curl is [his] man" (p. 358), the question Will puts to the old man about his "authority" is extremely troublesome. In the first place, we may feel prompted to wonder what authority Will himself has here, to speak for Allison too in the matter of willingness to take instructions. Further, the question of the priest's authority must be considered in the total context not only of this novel and its design as a whole but of the entire body of Percy's work.

When Jack Curl introduces Will to the group of old men who entertain themselves with the model railroad, he speaks in a tone of absurdly condescending jollity of Father Weatherbee's "believ[ing] in two things in this world . . . the Seaboard Air Line Railroad and . . . Apostolic Succession" (p. 311). To "new church" clergyman Curl, the latter "sounds more like the ancestor worship of [the] Mindanao tribesmen," whom Weatherbee had once served as a missionary priest, than like anything of serious concern for modern Christians. Nonetheless, Curl is able accurately if minimally to explain to Will what the phrase "Apostolic Succession" refers to—"a laying on of hands which goes back to the Apostles"—and it is very interesting that Barrett, apparently having forgotten who gave him the information, presents it as his own "hunch" in the later interview with Weatherbee which concludes the novel (p. 357).

The repeated references to the ceremony of the "laying on of hands" belong to an elaborate motif of "touching" which is developed throughout this novel, and which gives rise to a number of questions of psychological as well as theological interest.[23] But the theological implications are, in every sense, of *final* importance. No matter how either of them came by the notion, both Curl and Barrett are right that the Apostolic Succession has to do with a laying on of hands. But also "involved," to use Barrett's word, is a matter of crucial concern for him in his apparent need for a spiritual mentor who can speak with "authority."

The doctrine of Apostolic Succession—specifically, the question whether the Succession, as the basis of episcopal authority and therefore of the validity of priestly orders, continued unbroken in the Church of England—is, or used to be, a central issue in relations between Rome and Canterbury. In view of Percy's much-publicized status as convert to Roman Catholicism, one must wonder just what he is up to with the kind of ending he has written for *The Second Coming*. In all his other novels, including *The Last Gentleman*, the Roman Catholic church is the only religious organization whose claims to sanctity and doctrinal soundness are treated very seriously. Here, the hero is presented in the final scene seeking guidance of an Episcopalian priest—one who just happens to be in some way especially interested in the doctrine of Apostolic Succession—and making a particular point of inquiring whether that priest has authority to instruct in matters of faith. Will certainly seems disposed to believe that Father Weatherbee can "tell him something he doesn't know." He, Will, "perceives" that the old man knows something of vital importance (p. 358), and perceives "by the same token" that Jack Curl does not know.

But this kind of radical personalism, Barrett's claim to a special intuition in judging between the two clergymen, only underscores the importance of his reference to *authority*. Paraphrasing Kierkegaard, Percy spoke in the interview with Carr of a special kind of spiritual "authority" which distinguishes the role of the "apostle"—as bearer of the Good News—from that of either the "genius" (philosopher or novelist, presumably) or the ordinary "preacher." [24] Perhaps it is some such meaning of the word "authority" that Barrett has in mind in his question to Father Weatherbee here. But, in the immediate context, the reader is at least as likely to think first of a different kind of religious authority—one based on official doctrine and respect for tradition rather than upon individual inspiration.

The practical question at issue is whether Barrett, and Allison, must "take instruction"—i.e., enter the Episcopal church—in order to have Weatherbee officiate in the marriage ceremony. If Weatherbee does have the authority to instruct, in this context, then he has it as a consequence of his ordination; and, "by the same token," Jack

Curl has identical authority, Barrett's intuitions notwithstanding. If Curl does not have authority, it is because his ordination is invalid, not because Barrett considers him a twit. And if Curl's ordination is invalid, so is the ordination of all Episcopal clergymen, including Weatherbee; if the Apostolic Succession was broken in the Anglican church, then Weatherbee too, regardless of his personal sanctity, cannot speak with authority.

In short, the question of whether Will and Allison will or will not enter "the church" is not the only one left unsettled at the end. There is also the question whether that church to which Weatherbee might admit them, the Episcopal Church, is still a part of The Church.[25]

On the day he introduces Will to the model railroaders, Jack Curl is "leaving for Hilton Head and an ecumenical meeting between a Greek Orthodox archimandrate, a Maronite patriarch, and the Episcopal bishop of North Carolina, a meeting suggested in fact by Jack Curl." Presumably, it is Jack himself who asks the rhetorical question (p. 309) — "Could Jack Curl reunite Christendom?" — and then answers it with another: "Why not? Isn't it just the sort of damn fool thing God might favor?" In any event, it is very interesting that the subject of ecumenism should be introduced in such close context with the first reference to Father Weatherbee's preoccupation with Apostolic Succession, and that the list of participants at the Hilton Head conference does not include a representative either of the Latin-rite Roman Catholic hierarchy or of any major Protestant group.[26]

The point is not that a novelist who is a Roman Catholic is obliged to make religion the central concern in his fiction, or, if he chooses to do so, to write sympathetically only of the kind of religious experience that unequivocally affirms the truth of Roman Catholic teaching. He is not obliged even to mention Roman Catholics, certainly not to limit himself to protagonists who are already members of the Roman Church or on their way to entering it. What is troublesome here is the elaborately oblique way Percy has contrived to avoid the subject, so that Barrett's not thinking about Roman Catholicism is the best way to assure that the reader *will* think about it.

Strict constructionists of aesthetic formalism might argue that each novel is self-contained with respect to questions of consistency and probability in the characters' actions. But novels that belong to "cycles," such as Faulkner's Yoknapatawpha chronicles, and "sequels" such as *Rabbit Redux* and *The Second Coming*, are notoriously difficult to account for in formalist terms. Reaching the end of the present story, anyone who has read *The Last Gentleman* is likely to find it very hard to put out of mind the concluding scenes of that novel, in which the young Will Barrett and Sutter Vaught witness the Roman priest's attentions to the dying Jamie and then, a few minutes later outside the hospital, discuss the question of "what happened back there" (*The Last Gentleman*, pp. 402–7).

The middle-aged Will Barrett is brought into contact with Curl and Weatherbee as a consequence of his marriage to Marion. We may also assume that there are very few Roman Catholics among the circle of his everyday acquaintance.[27] But his intense interest in the problems of faith did not begin with his first marriage. And, although for most *readers* the scenes in the Santa Fe hospital are likely to be literally unforgettable—if anything in the earlier novel is—for the hero, when he talks to Father Weatherbee, it is as if he remembers nothing of the quest that took him to the desert in pursuit of Jamie. Indeed, there is little if anything in *The Second Coming* to indicate that Will gave much thought to his earlier experience throughout the years of his life with Marion. It is as if, so far as Will is permanently concerned, precisely *nothing* "happened back there" when Father Boomer called at the hospital.[28]

Once more, we will recall Percy's remarks to Carr, that Will "missed it" in witnessing the miracle of Jamie's dying-into-life.[29] Perhaps Barrett's forgetfulness twenty years later only attests the consistency of the characterization. But I was not persuaded by Percy's reading of the situation in the earlier novel, and it does nothing now to explain, or at any rate to justify, the middle-aged Will's behavior in his dealings with the clergymen. Regardless of other meanings of the word which Percy might have in mind in various contexts, what I am primarily concerned with here is "authority" in its root sense of a power belonging to the "author" of something. And the something in question here is the novels themselves. As novelist, Percy speaks with "authority" *in the novels*—there and there only—not in interpretive remarks, whether in interviews or in formal essays, before or after the fact of the fiction.

Nor is the voice of authority, in this fundamental sense of the word, necessarily an unequivocal voice.[30] What so fascinatingly troubles me is not the question whether Will's behavior at any juncture is or is not consistent with Percy's critical interpretation of either of the two novels. I am, and must be, concerned finally only to judge whether the hero's actions at any point seem consistent with his character as *I* see it revealed in the fictions as a composite whole, and with what I conceive as the essential and universal nature of the adventure, or spiritual enterprise, in which he is engaged.

On these grounds, a large measure of paradox is supportable. Nothing seems to me certain about the ending of *The Second Coming*, indeed, except the dubiety. In this, at least, Percy is consistent with his practice in all the earlier novels. All, as we have observed, are in one way or another open-ended.[31] Most of the essential questions of the hero's fate—especially the fate of his thinking and feeling and knowing, fate of believing—are typically left unresolved. Faith is the central and final issue in all the fiction. And faith is a mystery. To find it is an undertaking quite as dangerous and absurd, as fraught with endless terror and uncertainty, as "preposterous," as that situation of man's mortality which can be corrected in no way except by faith.

It is difficult to imagine how such a subject could be treated at all in a fiction which did not sometimes risk the so-called "fallacy of imitative form." Percy risks it time and time again. But the risk is inseparable from his authorial strength.

Few novelists of any time have presented so convincingly, so tellingly I should think for believers and unbelievers alike who have any considerable faculty of sympathetic imagination and a capacity for self-criticism, the essential drama of the search for faith. Among Percy's contemporaries, there are none to equal him in this, and only a small company who may be counted his peers in any practices of the art of fiction.

7

The Thanatos Syndrome

I. Time and Place

I have mentioned in the Introduction the special circumstances of my reading *The Thanatos Syndrome*. But if in having no access to the opinions of other critics I am relieved here of one set of contextual responsibilities, all the others are still in force.

We may look first to the context that Percy's other novels constitute. For one thing, his italicized prefatory remarks clearly present *The Thanatos Syndrome* as a continuation of his long-term project, reminiscent of the labors of a Thomas Hardy or a William Faulkner, to create a quasi-mythical territory, the "Feliciana" country.[1] Further, this latest novel is, like *The Second Coming* but probably more deliberately designed as such from the beginning, a "sequel" to an earlier work, *Love in the Ruins*.

I am sure that readers who are not acquainted either with *Love in the Ruins* or with any of the critical commentaries on it will have little difficulty in viewing *The Thanatos Syndrome* as a distinct artistic whole, to be evaluated on its own terms. But we who do know the earlier novel, and that includes Percy himself, cannot avoid making comparisons.

If the personality of the hero is somewhat altered, the causes of the change are not immediately apparent. As in all the earlier novels, deliberately in some instances and carelessly in others, Percy has again made it difficult to establish a chronology. Internally here, at least until very near the end, the obscurities are not especially troublesome. But precisely how much older Tom More is supposed to be at the beginning of this novel than he was at the end of *Love in the Ruins* is hard to figure. When we first see him in *The Thanatos Syndrome* he has just returned from serving a two-year prison term in Alabama, but the problem is with calculating how many years had already elapsed between the final action of *Love in the Ruins* and the time of his sentencing.

He is old enough that when he and Ellen take a family trip to Disney World, in Leroy Ledbetter's big RV, their neighbors in a KOA campground think Meg and little Tom are his grandchildren (p. 336). But at the beginning neither his sexual nor his intellectual energy seems significantly diminished. If he is not quite so frenetic and imprudent a lover now as he was in *Love in the Ruins*, nor so ambitious a researcher—having apparently abandoned his dream of finding a cure for all the ills of modern man, and thereby of winning a Nobel prize—the new modesty might be the product more of loyalty to Ellen and of self-chastening reflections during his imprisonment than merely of failing powers.

We learn as early as the account of Donna's provocative behavior in his office that he is still capable at least of intense sexual excitement (p. 21). And there can be little doubt of his potency with Ellen in their first love-making after he comes home from prison (pp. 52–53). So far as the new "smaller scale" of his intellectual aspirations is concerned, the explanation he gives (p. 67) sounds frank and, at least for the moment, plausible enough.

If I am right that the main events of *Love in the Ruins* take place in a fictional 1983,[2] and therefore that the year of that novel's final section, "Five Years Later," must be 1988, then the beginning of *The Thanatos Syndrome*, because Tom More has just spent two years in prison, cannot be dated *earlier* than 1990; and the apparent ages of More's children in the latter novel would seem to require adding a few more years.[3] Further, when Father Smith comments on an apparition of the Blessed Virgin "in Yugoslavia a few years ago," it would seem that "this one hundred years" of which he speaks, "the twentieth century . . . this dread century," is still in progress (pp. 364–65). Thus, we get at a probable time in the middle to late 1990s that seems to square with other references such as that to the way Lucy Lipscomb's ancestors probably reacted "when the Americans came down the river two hundred years ago in 1796" (p. 161).

Father Smith appears to have been about sixteen (p. 247), a recent high school graduate (p. 240), when he met eighteen-year-old Helmut Jäger (p. 239) in Germany. The year of the trip to Germany is identified only as sometime "in the 1930s" (p. 239). But a date not later than 1935 is indicated, since Huey Long was assassinated in September of that year, and it appears that he was still alive (p. 251) when Smith and his father returned to America. Later we are told that, at least by the time Father Smith's failing health forces him to retire from the hospice directorship, Tom More can reject Max Gottlieb's diagnosis of Alzheimer's dementia on the grounds that Smith is "too old" for the onset of that disease, which normally occurs "in the fifties or sixties" (p. 367). Thus, it appears that he must be in his seventies or older. Assuming, for the sake of the argument and as a way of explaining why Gottlieb might have thought his diagnosis at all plausible, that Smith is still in his seventies, and counting back then to an age of sixteen for him in the early to middle 1930s, again we get at the middle to late 1990s for *The Thanatos Syndrome*.

But such calculations do not finally hold up very well. Beginning with chapter 2 of part 5 (p. 334ff.), much of the action is presented retrospectively, with bewildering jumps back and forth from narrative past tense to present tense, so that it is all but impossible to keep up with the order of events, or to tell just how much time is supposed to have elapsed between one episode and another. Was it (is it), for example, a few weeks, months, years, or what, that Father Smith was (is) in charge of the reopened hospice (p. 363) before he had (has) to be committed there as a patient (p. 367)? Probably a few months at the most. Probably the end of the century is still several years ahead when Mickey LaFaye shows up again at Tom's office (p. 370ff.) for the concluding scene of the novel. But we cannot be sure. And while sometimes it is clear that Percy does not *want* us to be sure about the chronologies, now and again it seems he has fallen victim to his own deceptive purpose.

More's claim that he served a residency under Harry Stack Sullivan (p. 16) raises further questions about the relationship of fictional and "real" time which are potentially of great interest to anyone proposing an investigation of the author psychology of Walker Percy. In *Love in the Ruins* (p. 156), we are plainly told that Tom More is forty-five years old. Assuming, again, that the year of the main action of that novel is a fictional 1983—and nobody, to my knowledge, has suggested an *earlier* date—More would have been born in 1938. Since Harry Stack Sullivan died in January, 1949, Tom More, at the age of ten years or less, must have been one of the youngest medical residents on record. In *The Thanatos Syndrome* (p. 55) it is "fifty years" since Bruno Hauptmann was executed (1936), but also (p. 143) "fifty years" since the end of World War II (1945). All this, like the difficulties we encountered (chapter 2) in trying to square Binx Bolling's life story with the dates of the Korean War, hardly has the look of confusion by design.[4]

One of the curiosities of this novel as "futuristic" fiction is that the culture it represents, both in social and in technological and scientific developments, seems in some respects less rather than more advanced than the one dealt with in *Love in the Ruins*. There is little mention of politics, but what there is seems to suggest fairly stable governmental institutions—local, state, and federal. Not only have the mysterious and sinister vines that sprout everywhere in and out of doors in the earlier novel disappeared here, but we hear little or nothing more of such latter-day social phenomena as the establishment of squatter camps in Honey Island swamp or the Bantu ascendancy in Paradise Estates that first sent Tom More to live in the old slave-quarter apartments. The crime rate, in some categories and locations, is or until very lately has been high, but neither in that nor in the dismal picture of the school system is there anything that would have startled an observer at least as far back as the 1970s. There is some evidence of serious, continuing deterioration of the older industrial economy. Tom More notes that on I-12 a little east of Baton Rouge "the rest stops are crowded by pitched tents, seedy Winnebagos, and Michigan jalopies heading west from the cold smokestacks" (p. 133). But we hear nothing of mass starvation; and the few specific references to salaries and to the prices of various things—such as houses, automobiles, and guns—do not suggest runaway inflation.

Fedville doctors still legally practice euthanasia, as they did in the time of *Love in the Ruins*. There are a few new developments in the fields of infectious disease and related pharmacology. Otherwise, the observations and arguments on the condition of More's patients, on the status of psychoanalysis in relation to neuropsychiatry, on the psychopathologies of fascism and child-abuse, etc., all reflect now-current fashions in theoretical controversy established by such writers as Bruno Bettelheim, J. M. Masson, Oliver Sacks, and Frederic Wertham. Nothing much new seems to have happened in nuclear technology and public debate over regulation of its uses.

Transportation and communications also figure prominently in milieu and plot development; yet neither the automobiles nor the computer systems, for example, seem very different from ours. The fabulous Toyotas of *Love in the Ruins*, machines with one moving part, are nowhere to be seen. Tom More's Caprice and his cousin Lucy's Chevy pickup, although quite serviceable, are conspicuously out of date, but there is nothing to suggest that their fellow physicians' later-model Mercedeses and BMWs (p. 13) are vehicles of entirely different automotive design. For lack of any information to the contrary, we may assume that both the cars and the huge trucks that crowd the crumbling but still usable interstate highways operate on internal-combustion engines, requiring either gasoline or, for the diesels of varying size, distillates of one sort or another that might be produced at the same refinery. Despite the reference (p. 213) to dried-up oil wells in the vicinity, it remains a puzzle why such a long-established facility as the huge Exxon refinery at Baton Rouge is "deserted" (p. 133), presumably shut down. The highway vehicles and the tugboats and other commercial and pleasure craft on the rivers and bayous must get fuel from somewhere, and we are not told why crude oil as well as already refined products could not still be brought in, as for a long time in the past, by pipeline or aboard barges and seagoing tankers.

Problems concerning "time sense" and those concerning "sense of place" in this novel are about equally important and equally complex, and, as always, difficult to distinguish. In the italicized preface, Percy speaks of the history of "Feliciana," its settlement and brief period of political independence, and goes on finally to forewarn the reader that "in what follows [i.e., the novel itself], the geography of the place has been somewhat scrambled." It is fascinating, if not notably rewarding in the long run, to look out for details of the "scrambling." For example, in *Love in the Ruins* the principal settings of Tom More's adventures—among them the "Fedville" complex, the old town where Tom keeps his office, and the waterfront block of several times "restored" slave-quarter apartments where he and Ellen went to live after the Bantu takeover and where she and the children have stayed on while he was in prison—all were very close together, within walking distance or at most a drive of a few minutes in an automobile. In *The Thanatos Syndrome*, the windows of Bob Comeaux's office in Fedville command a view of the Mississippi River, "from the haze of Baton Rouge to the south to the wooded loess hills of St. Francisville to the north" (p. 23). Yet when Tom takes Van Dorn fishing, presumably starting out from a dock very near the Mores' place in the old slave quarters, they go skimming along in Tom's venerable Arkansas Traveler "down the Bogue Falaya" (p. 57). In reality, the little Bogue Falaya River runs alongside Walker Percy's property near the town of Covington, Louisiana, some seventy miles east of Baton Rouge.[5] Then there is Pantherburn, the old family plantation not far from St. Francisville, Louisiana, where Lucy Lipscomb, Tom More's cousin, lives with Uncle Hugh Bob. If there is or ever was a real Pantherburn in Louisiana—anything so named, a plantation, a town, a creek or other small waterway, perhaps—I have so far been unable to discover it. There is, however, a Panther Burn, Mississippi, on U.S. Highway 61, up in the delta country near Greenville. Just three miles north of Panther Burn is the town of Percy, Mississippi; and, according to Lewis Baker (*The Percys of Mississippi*, pp. 109, 132), Leroy Percy once operated a plantation called Panther Burn.

Not all the scramblings have such readily discernible associations with the lives of Walker Percy and others of his clan, with the places on maps of the "real" world where they have left their mark. It may be that there is some such connection I have overlooked in the account, for example, of Tom More's jaunt down the Mississippi with Vergil Bon (cf. Charles Bon, of Faulkner's *Absalom, Absalom!*) and Uncle Hugh Bob in the pirogue (p. 277ff.) on their way to rescue the children at Belle Ame; but the main thing is just that Tom and his crew have one hell of a time keeping up with "where they're at" from one moment to the next, and so does the reader. The reader has a hard time even if he is content simply to keep Percy's text in front of him. If he decides to seek help from Rand McNally, he is in worse trouble.

Tom and Vergil and Hugh Bob spend a good deal of their time in the pirogue alternately checking their bearings and swapping Ol' Man River stories—about the Mississippi's capricious changes of course, and the ghosts of lost steamboats, and towns and plantations that once had landings on the main channel becoming isolated on newly formed islands and the banks of blind lakes—Vergil one-upping Hugh Bob's superstitious folklore with geological observations and vice versa, all with a confident show of esoteric place-name dropping that effectively obscures the bewildering meanderings and cutoffs of the central narrative. Back near the beginning of part 3, (p. 133), when Tom drives past Baton Rouge and notices the deserted refineries he plainly takes care to inform us at the beginning of the next paragraph that he is headed "upriver" to get to Panther-burn, which it appears is somewhere a bit north and west of St. Francisville, on up toward Tunica, Louisiana. Much farther along in the story (part 4, p. 281) when the rescue party are about to come ashore for their raid on Belle Ame, the smell of old oil fields and the sight of a tank farm and a deserted refinery are mentioned again, in a passage so strikingly reminiscent of the earlier account (pp. 133–34) that it is hard to imagine a reader's not immediately assuming that the industrial wasteland is the same in both instances: i.e., that Tom and his friends have simply worked their way back *downstream* in the pirogue, albeit with highly improbable speed (in twenty to thirty minutes, p. 275) from Pantherburn and environs to the outskirts of Baton Rouge. But if some faint further shadow of incredulity should prompt us to check back a bit, to Tom's instructions to Vergil and Hugh Bob just before they set out from Old Tunica Landing, we shall surely find it a disquieting exercise. For Tom's plan is that, after the visit to Belle Ame, Hugh Bob and Claude "can take the pirogue [presumably in the water, with them aboard it] on *down* to Pantherburn" (p. 275, emphasis added). The fact that Tom decides, after all, to leave the magical pirogue at Belle Ame for a while—he doesn't "think anybody feels like fooling with it" just then, what with their exhausting adventures at the school, and Vergil can come back later to pick it up—will hardly serve to relieve the bedeviled reader's anxieties as he must get back in the car with the escaped-

231

jailbird narrator and, after a brief stop-off at Popeye's for spicy chicken and a frosty, once more head off "up the Angola road" (p. 325). Talk about your blue highways.[6]

Setting aside for the moment problems with the coordination of real and fictional maps and calendars, and questions concerning the consistency of this novel with *Love in the Ruins*, considerations of time and place are intricately involved in *The Thanatos Syndrome* with all other elements of the book's total internal order as a work of fiction: plot, character, myth, language, narrative structure, structure of motif, philosophical dialectic, etc. The river provides for Tom and Vergil and Hugh Bob the best practical means of getting to Belle Ame unobserved; but in order for Tom to get back to Angola before his "escape" is discovered they must carefully calculate just how much time the journey downstream will take. Percy's putting Vergil and Hugh Bob together in the little boat—talking in their different idioms, from their different points of view, sometimes complementary and sometimes not, about the river and its history—facilitates discovery of their character both as individuals (to the extent, if any, that either is ever developed beyond the stage of caricature) and as types representative of the new social order and its pattern of ironically complicated relationships between young and old, black and white, working class and gentry. For all its multi-ethnic and polyglot social history, the devastating effects of industrial pollution on the natural environment and the general homogenization of language and customs in twentieth-century America, the "Feliciana" country still somehow survives as a distinctive region. And Tom More's unmistakable if never easily definable "belonging" gives him an enormous advantage over even the cleverest of interlopers like Bob Comeaux and John Van Dorn. Van Dorn at least claims to have been born a Southerner, in the neighboring state of Mississippi, but there is something a bit stagey about his manner and speech—"he sounds like Marlon Brando talking Southern" (p. 57)—and, even if his story of his origins should happen to be true, still he is now in spirit as much an alien as Comeaux is, a man who can never truly "belong" anywhere.

The river—not only Twain's river, but Eliot's river as "strong brown god,"[7] and Conrad's, the way into the heart of darkness that is Belle Ame—is itself a mythic presence here, of manifold significance for study both of the personal psychology of the characters and of the novel's commentary on American history, the myth of the "American dream." Tenor and vehicle are hard to distinguish most of the time, but the journeyings in this novel, both by land and by water, in daylight and dark, on the shadowy borders of consciousness between place and non-place, are metaphors of narration. It is no accident that our hero/narrator drives a car named Caprice.[8] It is, if anything, altogether too easy to see in Tom More aboard the pirogue a type of the artist, with his two companions (one of them, heaven help us, named Vergil) along as the jealous and skeptical reader-critic-guide-guardians, co-plotters and -stylists, who for all their troublesomeness are indispensable (indeed, their indispensability is what is most troublesome) not only before and after the fact of artistic creation, but throughout the process. The river itself, obviously, is no mere "setting," but the mighty flux of the prime creative energy, whose current the individual human artist may briefly ride—if he has strength, skill, patience, and daring enough—to forward his own designs.

For all the unbridled gamesomeness of his geographical "scramblings," the one thing I am inclined *not* to believe is that Walker Percy, in his authorial capacity, conceives of himself as the river: of which Hugh Bob says that once it has decided it "wants to go," and comes "piling across" a neck of ground, recklessly rearranging the landscape to suit itself, there "ain't nothing in the world is going to stop it, not the U.S. engineers, nothing" (p. 279). Respect for governmental agencies aside, Percy is simply too much the ironist to let himself get by with that kind of grandiose conceit.

II. Men, Women, Doctors, and Others

The first two words of the italicized preface are "the place." But one of the most interesting things about the novel proper, at any rate for the reader who is familiar with Percy's other novels, is the relatively abstract manner of its beginning. The first words here are "for some time now"; but the phrase is chiefly notable for its imprecision. "For *some* time now I have noticed that *something* strange is occurring in our *region*" (p. 3, emphasis added). The matter of importance, obviously, is the intellectual exercise in which the speaker is engaged.

What the reader will want next is information about the nature of the evidence the speaker has been observing, these odd occurrences. What exactly has been happening, and what is so "strange" about it? Initially, it does not much matter precisely how long the "some time" is over which the speaker has been conducting his observations. The phrase "for some time" means, simply, for a "considerable" time, a time long enough to suggest that the various occurrences in question may be significantly related in some way. Nor is it likely that the reader will give at first more than an instant's thought to the question of precisely what "region" it is in which the speaker conducts his inquiry.

Another of Percy's first-person-present narrators, Binx Bolling of *The Moviegoers*, uses only one short paragraph to tell us about the note from his aunt before starting to sketch in, with rich sensory detail, the all-important New Orleans setting of the action.[9] In all the other novels, notably including *Love in the Ruins*, with its vividly drawn opening scene of Tom More's vigil in the pine grove, the stress is on place, the place/time experience, from the very start.

The Tom Mores of *Love in the Ruins* and *The Thanatos Syndrome* have a good many things of considerable importance in common. Both have fearfully interentwined woman troubles, career troubles, religious troubles. Both are in various senses "on the run": constantly and intolerably busy trying to keep up with their conflicting commitments; anxiously conscious of being followed by sinister strangers; as parolees from mental hospital and prison, torn between prudent instincts of self-preservation, in the need to please persons who have the authority to put them away again, and the equally strong urgings of conscience, personal and professional, to go to the aid of variously threatened relatives, friends, patients, and more or less innocent sufferers among the citizenry at large.

But in *Love in the Ruins* it is Tom More the wildeyed fugitive we first see, drunk, exhausted, rifle in hand, propped against a diseased pine tree and babbling of "the dread latter days" of the world. We must go on for several pages before we learn even that the narrator speaks with some pretense to professional authority, that he is a physician and scientist. In the second sentence of *The Thanatos Syndrome*, on the other hand, More is already referring to his "patients"; and before he has bothered to tell us much of anything about himself and his own troubles—"I've been away, but that's another story" (p. 5)—he is off into the case history of Mickey LaFaye.

First and last, and predominantly throughout, it is *Doctor* More with whom we are concerned in this novel. Regardless of what his richer, more successful, and superficially more self-confident colleagues in other specializations may think of him in particular and old-fashioned Freudian shrinks in general (pp. 13–14, 88, and elsewhere), regardless of the doubtful status of his medical license since he was released from prison (pp. 25ff., 97–98), notwithstanding, and perhaps to an extent in confirmation of, the fact that his professional ambitions are much more modest now than when he was trying to perfect the MOQUOL, he is more consistently and conscientiously committed to improving his ordinary practice. He is more modest and more cautious, even about trying to define the "syndrome" he suspects he may be dealing with in the various case studies he has begun to collect, not to speak of finding a consistently effective treatment. But at the same time, having stayed off the bottle while he was in prison and being generally healthier and more alert than he was when he had to contend with Buddy Brown and Art Immelmann, he never seems in this novel in much real danger of losing out to the likes of Van Dorn and Comeaux. Obviously, the book is designed as a kind of intellectual thriller, superficially self-spoofing but deadly serious all the same.[10] As the doctor/detective/counterspy hero goes about simultaneously, and for the most part through the same procedures, solving the mystery of what his patients' cases have in common and getting the goods on his evil opponents, necessarily putting himself in extreme jeopardy, himself operating a step outside the law from time to time, what suspense there is does not involve questions even about the identity of the malefactors, not to speak of who will win. For better or worse in assessing the book's final effect, we know from the beginning—as surely as we know it about Scarecrow or Magnum or Quincy—that Tom More will triumph, or at any rate that his enemies will not. In the well-executed conventional thriller, it is essential that the reader find it at least as hard as the hero does to distinguish between the right sort and the wrong sort of people he meets, and to spot the key offender or offenders among the latter group. In *The Thanatos*

Syndrome, we need five minutes at the most in the company of Comeaux and Van Dorn to tell that they are a pair of very bad actors, and that whatever evil scheme they are conspiring in probably has something to do with the odd symptoms exhibited by Dr. More's patients.

So far as the surface action is concerned, we are kept in suspense about nothing except the details of the conspiracy, and of Tom's plan, his counter-conspiracy, to thwart it. Beyond that, at what we must assume is the heart of Percy's intention, there are only the problems of the philosophical argument, and in some sense finally, the question whether the thriller plot-vehicle—or vessel, one thinks again of Tom and his companions in the overloaded pirogue—is adequate to support the burden of ideas.

By various means, Percy rather severely tries his reader's patience at the outset, and susceptibility to distraction is one of the hero's essential characteristics, but it gradually becomes apparent that the central story will concern More's pursuit of two fairly clearly definable, by no means easy but eminently practical, personal objectives: to get his wife back, and to establish himself in a medical practice that is both financially gainful and legally, morally, and intellectually acceptable.

The two objectives are, of course, in various ways interrelated—one of the main things Tom wants his wife "back" for is to serve at his office as nurse/receptionist (p. 69)—but provisionally separable for purposes of analysis.

When we met him in *Love in the Ruins*, Tom More was both childless and wifeless. Following the all but unbearably painful experience of their only child's death, his wife first ran away, with an Englishman of doubtful sexual and religious inclination, and not long thereafter died, under somewhat obscure circumstances, on the island of Cozumel. It is understandable that Tom, having once already suffered in such wise, should be uncommonly anxious about his second wife's, and their children's, association with Van Dorn.

Despite Percy's much discussed preoccupation with the subject of death, few of the characters in his novels die in any sense "on stage." The one notable exception among sympathetic characters is Jamie Vaught, in *The Last Gentleman*, and, among the villainous, Janos Jacoby in *Lancelot*. The account even of Lonnie Smith's death, in

The Moviegoer, is essentially retrospective. Indeed, considering the dominant fictional fashions of our time, Percy is as remarkably sparing of close-up detail in representing physical violence and suffering of any kind as he is in describing sexual encounters. The outrageous comic effects in the account of Hugh Bob's pistol and shotgun marksmanship exhibition at Belle Ame more than offset the violence. Nobody dies, or is in any plausible danger of dying. And, mingled with other comic devices, Tom's and Lucy's habitual use of technical terminology in describing the evidence of the sexual assaults on the children deliberately and effectively discourages any prurient response from the reader.

Although we learn of it only in More's reminiscences, however, it is presumably certain that his first wife actually died. And, Percy being still less given to trafficking in acts of supernatural intervention than he is to the love of gore, there could be little question of Tom's playing Heracles to his own Admetus and bringing Doris/Alcestis back from the grave even had he been disposed to try. But in *The Thanatos Syndrome*, this the first of Percy's novels that uses a name of death in its title and yet as studiedly as any of the others avoids the physical spectacle of dying, the situation is, at least at first glance, somewhat more hopeful. Here, it is something closer, perhaps, to a matter of Dr. More's doing a Harcourt-Reilly to his own Edward in getting Ellen/Lavinia back, from the first stages of a kind of *living* death: the only trouble being that it is even harder in our day than it was in Eliot's to tell just where the borderline is between the states of death-in-life and what might be considered real life.[11]

In any event, having convinced himself if not necessarily the reader that he really wants and needs her, and that she is not in any ordinary sense unfaithful to him, with Van Dorn or anyone else—i.e., that the spell John Van Dorn has cast upon her, to alter her customary sex habits and to turn her into a world-class bridge player, is not essentially different from what Van Dorn and Comeaux have been doing to any number of other people with their heavy-sodium experiments—Tom does in the end win Ellen back again, if not quite as the same person she was before he went to prison. It might briefly appear that Lucy Lipscomb will succeed in her frank efforts to alienate Tom's affections. All along, she plainly has marriage in mind, not just a casual affair. One of the amusing minor ironies of the situation is that Lucy quickly takes up with Tom one of the motherly/wifely grooming habits, smoothing his unruly eyebrows with a spit-moistened fingertip, that was distinctively characteristic of Ellen's behavior in *Love in the Ruins*.[12]

But the reader who is familiar with the notions of sexual propriety shared by all Percy's heroes, their standard positional preferences, so to speak, in connubial intercourse, will know the moment Lucy gets on top, in her visit to Tom's bed his first night at Pantherburn, that marriage is at best a remote possibility for this pair. Still more clearly in this than in any of the other novels, a face-to-face positioning is designated as the uniquely *human* posture in sexual intercourse; and that is retained in Lucy's approach. Yet even Ellen's newfound delight in rearward and sixty-nining engagements, so long as she assumes a position that is in any way distinctly submissive to the male, is obviously more acceptable to Tom than Lucy's face-to-face but dominant stance.

The truth is that once Lucy has done her stuff with the computer networks, and examined the children at Belle Ame to determine that some of them have been sexually abused, she has about exhausted her usefulness to Tom, and is quietly retired to the background of his consciousness and of the action. It is no accident that for the commando trip down the river in the pirogue, Tom chooses an all-male crew.

Despite the important thematic emphasis on sex and personal identity, sex and the definition of the human, none of the women in this novel is portrayed in any depth as an individual. More's women patients, with all the complexities of their personal histories, are of interest to him and to the reader only as "cases." Even the sexual excitement they arouse in Tom is only a complication of the professional relationship. Lucy, on the other hand, occasionally treats Tom as if he were her patient (e.g., p. 103), but only in such a way as to emphasize the larger importance of their personal attraction. Yet, their love affair does not develop beyond the one occasion of weary physical intimacy at Pantherburn, when Tom is so sleepy that he can hardly be sure the next morning that the whole thing was not a dream. And we must suspect that one of the major motives of Tom's resistance thereafter—a motive *at least* as strong as that of his fidelity to Ellen—is just that he fears Lucy may be in every way too much for him to handle. It is not simply that she seems to prefer the dominant physical position in sexual intercourse. Obviously, he finds that not altogether unpleasant (p. 348 and earlier). But he is above all uncomfortable with the experience of sexual attraction to a woman as *intelligent* as Lucy is.

It is unquestionably no shortcoming but in Tom's eyes one of Ellen's chief wifely virtues that she is—Van Dorn's repeated assertions to the contrary (pp. 63, 216) and her having made a lot of money in real estate notwithstanding—a bit of a dumbbell. Both in this novel and in *Love in the Ruins*, he values her Protestant skepticism for its effect of strengthening his Catholic faith by constant testing. Yet, in their exchange on the merits of infant baptism (p. 355), Tom is more than content to note that the complex theological wit of his allusion to the story of Nicodemus (John 3:1–7) has escaped her. Plainly, it is in Tom's view no proper part of "a wife's duty" (p. 356) to attempt intellectual intercourse with her husband: even, or especially, on a theological subject.

"New Woman" Lucy Lipscomb, no doubt, would find such a doctrine of marriage ill-suited to her needs. Tom never quite gets at it in his own self-congratulatory reflections on the subject, but his decisive anxiety about the marriage with Lucy that he managed to avoid was in all probability the suspicion not that "she was the sort who likes the upper hand" (p. 348) but simply that she would have wanted, in keeping with her intelligence, an equal hand.

Although Tom's respect for Lucy's professional expertise is apparent in the kind of help he seeks from her to define his "syndrome" and then to combat Comeaux's and Van Dorn's designs in the Blue Boy project and Van Dorn's at Belle Ame, he never fully takes her into his confidence about the deeper problems of conscience and belief that are involved in the career choices he must make. When she undertakes to give him advice about it (as on p. 212), it is strictly on the basis of what she considers his practical best interest; and his perfunctory response is plainly calculated to avoid further discussion. The novel's central issues are issues either of the conflict of one man with himself or, sometimes as a consequence or extension of such inner stress, of the conflict of men with men.

In trying to reestablish himself professionally and socially, Tom has many of the typical problems of the ex-convict, not the least of them the restrictions on his freedom to choose his associates. If he had not been in prison, it is hard to imagine his having anything to do with the likes of Comeaux and Van Dorn.

But in a somewhat murky legal situation that More is in no position to insist on having clarified, Comeaux either is or effectively pretends to be, along with Tom's old friend Max Gottlieb, in charge of certifying his competence to reclaim an unrestricted medical license. It would be difficult for him to restore even his meager private practice without accepting Comeaux's referrals. And, unless the children are to remain principally or entirely dependent upon Ellen's income for support, a situation he would like to avoid for a number of fairly obvious reasons, the very best he can ever expect to earn in private practice will probably not be enough. Hence, he can hardly refuse at least to consider Comeaux's repeated offers of a high-paying job in research.

The Van Dorn connection is stickier yet. The chances are that no married man in prison—no matter what he has observed before about his wife's behavior, no matter what emotions the idea might stir in him, of fear, or rage, or pity for himself or her, perhaps even of some perverse satisfaction—can entirely escape the thought of his coming out a cuckold. Given the history of his first marriage if nothing else, we may assume that Tom More must have spent a good deal of his time at Fort Pelham reflecting upon that possibility. And, once out, he sees and hears little to reassure him. At the very least, most people seem to take it for granted that Ellen has been sleeping with Van Dorn; and for some time there is reason to doubt that her marriage to Tom can possibly last much longer.

From the first, Tom is in spite of all determined to *try* making a go of it. But even in that effort, needing as he does to find out just what kind of influence it is that Van Dorn has on Ellen before he can hope to break it—not to speak of the sad attraction to his rival the cuckold is wont to feel no matter what his intentions regarding the future of the marriage—More is compelled to suffer the companionship of the man who presumably has put the horns on his head. It is difficult to imagine a situation more grotesquely appropriate to the falsity of their relationship than the fishing trip these two take together: especially if we compare it, as Percy must have intended we should, to that other episode of difficult but precariously *achieved* male camaraderie, the journey of the three men in the pirogue to Belle Ame. For it is on that journey, of course, with Vergil and Hugh Bob, that Tom gets the final evidence he needs of Van Dorn's worst proclivities. Not content with Ellen, the man has had designs on Tom's children as well; and they are rescued, possibly, in the nick of time.

The raid on Belle Ame also provides Tom with the principal weapon he needs to defeat the Blue Boy conspiracy and thus, finally, to get Comeaux out of his hair about the medical license and the question of whether he is to continue in private practice. Each time Comeaux shows signs of trying to reassert himself, and somehow redeem Blue Boy despite both Van Dorn's disgrace and the evidence that the project never had federal authorization, all Tom has to do is to remind him (p. 331)—or wait for him to remind himself (p. 332)—that his own slightly defective little son, Ricky Comeaux, was one of the children rescued from Belle Ame.[13]

As we have noted before, there is never any doubt that Tom will be able to outwit such a pair of obvious phonies as Van Dorn and Comeaux. If not still earlier, their potential vulnerability is readily apparent in the references to Van Dorn's slightly hokey Southernism (pp. 57–60)[14] and to the secret of Bob's puzzling decision to change the spelling of his name, from Italian "Como" to French "Comeaux" (pp. 98–99).

The question of Comeaux's possible motivation for the name-change is, of course, extremely complex. The simple advantage for upper-class social acceptance in Louisiana suggested by Mickey LaFaye's story of Comeaux's admission to the Feliciana Hunt Club (p. 99) apparently does not strike More as an adequate explanation. But there may be a clue Tom is overlooking in Comeaux's false claim to French *Huguenot* ancestry. Perhaps it is an Italian *Catholic* background that the sometime "Como" needs to repudiate, more profoundly even than he needs to claim the merely "classier" ancestry of sixteenth- and seventeenth-century settlers in America. All this, by way of perplexing contrast and interaction with the eccentric ethnic-religious background and resultant mentality of Tom More, an English Catholic who in *Love in the Ruins* claims as a collateral ancestor Sir (later Saint) Thomas More, Henry VIII's martyred

Chancellor. The puzzle of John Van Dorn's hokey Southernism is further and amusingly complicated by his response to Tom's query about where he "come[s] from originally." Van Dorn answers: "Not a hundred miles from here. Port Gibson" (p. 60). The reader who knows where the town of Port Gibson, Mississippi, actually is, who recalls that this conversation is taking place on a waterway near Covington, Louisiana (see my remarks, above and in note 5, this chapter, on the location of the Bogue Falaya and connecting streams), and who proceeds then to Van Dorn's oblique claim of relationship to Confederate General Earl Van Dorn (p. 60), must wonder for a moment just where either of our two canny fishermen is, as hippie-folk used to say a while back, "coming from."

But further, the moment Tom begins to question Comeaux and Van Dorn separately about their association in Blue Boy, each is quick to try distancing himself from the other—Comeaux from Van Dorn (p. 200) and Van Dorn from Comeaux (p. 217)—and their remarks have a ring of just enough sincere hostility, a mixture of jealousy and contempt, that it must occur to Tom they might be easily maneuvered to do each other in. It may be finally, in fact, not so much phoniness of any sort as the sincerity that makes them vulnerable.

In general, the ruthless satire of *Love in the Ruins* is much tempered in this novel. While in his stereo-equipped Mercedes Duck, as he floats through the woods to the strains of Viennese waltzes (p. 201), Comeaux may momentarily remind us of that comparatively innocent ruffian in the earlier novel, the conservative proctologist "Dusty" Rhoades, more often, in the debates with Tom, it is likely to be Buddy Brown who comes to mind. But there is virtually nothing in Comeaux's case to provoke the kind of unsentimental delight with which the reader is expected to witness More's rout of Brown and his cohorts in The Pit. Van Dorn—with the doubts about his origins and his professional status (just what kind of "doctor" is he?), his intense interest in More's work with the Lapsometer on "localizing cortical function," the hint of demonic connections in his reference to the "Azazel convention" (pp. 61–64)—we might be briefly tempted to see as another incarnation of the one we knew as Immelmann in *Love in the Ruins*. But the satanic presence is more diffuse in this novel. As individual, Van Dorn is as "human" as

242

most who claim the title in his time. Although, for once, it seems doubtful that Percy had Twain in mind here, I am somehow reminded by the characterizations of Comeaux and Van Dorn of Huck Finn's phrase for the duke and the king in his final judgment of them. Those two "pitiful rascals," he calls them.

The final pathos of Comeaux's and Van Dorn's defeat lies in the fact that they somehow genuinely wanted More's approval of their schemes, that both genuinely wanted him, in Comeaux's phrase, "on the team," perhaps not solely for the purpose of keeping an eye on him but also for the opportunity to prove themselves worthy of his respect. Comeaux, we might put it, wanted to trade "certifications" with More, and there is a slight but undeniable element of regret, for More as well as for Comeaux, in their having to face the fact that the deal cannot be made.

The occasion of Huck Finn's compassionate reflections upon the fate of the king and the duke is the sight of them being ridden out of town on a rail by a mob of irate citizens, tarred and feathered almost beyond recognition as "[any]thing in the world that was human . . . like a couple of monstrous big soldier-plumes."[15] It is very important, of course, to note that neither Comeaux nor Van Dorn *is* tarred and feathered, that neither the law nor Tom More's influence in the case will permit their being quite so brutally punished as scapegoats for the community that in one way or another, either actively or passively, has collaborated in their offenses.

At the end of their fishing trip, Van Dorn's and More's exchange concerning Ellen's uncanny talents at bridge—"I really think you ought to do something about this," Van Dorn says, and Tom answers "I will, Van, I will"—certainly sounds ominous enough in itself. What Tom despises most in Van Dorn's treatment of Ellen, perhaps, is the implication that he seduced her, not out of any kind of love, but simply to *use* her in his experiments. In any event, the passage that follows, a kind of "endnote" to part 1 of the novel, further suggests that in whatever precisely Tom might decide to do there will be no fate for Van Dorn but that of one or the other of Aaron's goats.

Either he will be killed outright, or he will be driven away into the wilderness: appointed, that is to say, as the "scapegoat," the one permitted, or forced, to "escape," after being ceremonially loaded with the sins of the people, on the Day of Atonement.[16] Van Dorn is, in fact, not killed but consigned to a fate that might be considered equivalent to banishment into the wilderness, reduced for some time to an apelike existence (p. 342), one that comes at least very close to being, in Huck's phrase again, "like nothing . . . human": but only until Tom, our vacillating Aaron, hits upon a plan for rescuing him.[17]

III. "But speak the word only . . ."

Tom's plan, involving the use of an educated female gorilla named Eve to guide Van Dorn to recovery of his power of language (p. 343ff.), provides a key to the connection between the novel's two distinct plot lines: that of Tom's struggle with Comeaux and Van Dorn, and that of his communications with Father Smith. Like all of Percy's novels, this one is elaborately structured. It is easy enough to spot the motif-patterning that suggests deeper structural relationships. There is, for example, the vast exhibit of maps and charts and related paraphernalia: on one hand, the relatively primitive equipment that Father Smith uses for his divinations in the fire tower; on the other, the computerized statistical maps that Lucy calls up on her privileged terminals at Pantherburn, the mental maps that the victims of the heavy-sodium experiments carry about in their impaired, computer-like brains, the geological map of the lower-Mississippi valley that Vergil the Superblack carries about in his distinctly unimpaired mind; all somehow, but the question is precisely how, related to the big "scrambled" map of *Feliciana* with which Percy has whimsically provided his hapless hero and reader. The patterning is obvious. But pattern is not structure.

Ellen, Lucy, Max, not to speak of Comeaux, with his alleged designs on the St. Margaret's property (pp. 105–6), practically everybody wishes for one reason and another that Tom would give up on Father Smith. The old lunatic is at worst a dangerous subversive, at best an embarrassing nuisance for virtually the entire community—black and white, learned and ignorant, rich and poor, born-again and staid denominational Christians alike. Most of the Catholics even, of *their* infinitely varied latter-day stripe, don't know what to make of him, and are not much disposed to waste time in trying to find out.

I suspect that a great many readers will share the general sentiment of the fictional townspeople in this matter. Percy has taken considerable risks in developing the role of the priest here at such length. In his other novels, there are a number of interesting studies of priests, but they remain for the most part in the background. This is true even of the priest/psychiatrist "Percival" in *Lancelot*, in the sense that until the very end his only function is to *listen* to the mad narrator. In *Love in the Ruins*, it is the understatement in characterization that somehow guarantees the crucial importance of Father Smith's role. Here, in the lengthy biographical sketch with its emphasis on Smith's multiethnic heritage and his hostility to his father, in the faintly improbable tale of his trip to Germany as a teenager during the early Nazi era, in the impromptu "sermon" that he delivers at the ceremonies for the reopening of St. Margaret's, Percy risks at the very least boring the reader beyond bearing. And the use of the sermon, or homily, raises distracting questions of genre proprieties. There is, to be sure, a long tradition of the effective use of sermons in novels. But this one, perhaps only the more obviously for the fact that the narrator, Tom More, furnishes a running critique of it as it is delivered, smacks strongly of authorial *intrusion*. Walker Percy is well known to have some stubbornly held opinions on the definitions and causes of a variety of evils in modern society; and, whether we do or do not tend generally to share his ideas, we may feel at first a bit put-upon in suspecting him of using Father Smith simply as a polemic mouthpiece.

At second glance, however, if we can summon the patience to take it, the novelistic situation here looks a good deal more interestingly complicated. In the italicized prefatory notes, Percy identifies Frederic Wertham's "remarkable book *A Sign for Cain*" as the source of the "information about the Nazi doctors and their academic precursors in the Weimar Republic" (p. viii) he has used in Father Smith's account of his visit to Germany. In fact, the word "information" may be misleadingly restrictive. A central theme of Wertham's argument in that entire book, not exclusively in the part of it directly concerned with the Nazi example, is his insistence upon the fact that the propensity to violence of one sort and another is, ever increasingly in our times, characteristic of quite "ordinary" or "normal" people, of both sexes and all age and ethnic groups, all social and economic classes, all occupations. Using an account of the development of the Nazi extermination programs as but one major example—pointing out that much-respected medical authorities and other learned critics of the social process, long before Hitler appeared on the scene, had proposed elimination of variously "unfit" and "defective" citizens, and producing impressive evidence that the doctors in the Nazi era, as well as military people of all ranks, acted quite on their own in many of their crimes, not, as they later claimed, on "orders" of any kind from any of their superiors, up to and including Hitler[18]—Wertham argues for a doctrine of social responsibility, based on recognition of universal complicity, or at any rate the universal potential for complicity, that certainly has much in common with the position implicitly upheld by Tom More in his struggle with Comeaux and Van Dorn. Here we have another pair of recklessly ambitious, glib enthusiasts for "scientific" social planning, who like the respectable malefactors of the Nazi era make false claims of official authorization for actions taken on their own initiative and, when Tom begins to question them too closely on their participation in Blue Boy, alternately try to obscure the ethical issues with jargon and statistics, disparage each other, and pretend that, each having ultimately much larger or different philosophical fish to fry, they have contributed to this particular project only as technical experts.

In any event, whatever validity any of Father Smith's remarks, in the "sermon" or in private conversation, may or may not have with regard to the cultural history of Germany and the United States—past, present, and future—the story of the priest is thoroughly relevant to everything else that Tom More does and thinks about in this novel. It is at many points difficult to exclude consideration of Walker Percy's personal history, as well as questions about the implied author's use of the novel as critique of its own design. In much the same way that he appropriates part of his own family history in the references to Tom More's and Lucy Lipscomb's polygamous "common ancestor," the first master of Pantherburn, Percy incorporates in the section entitled "Father Smith's Confession" a version of the story he told an interviewer about a trip he himself made to

Germany in 1934, when he stayed for a time in the home of a family with Nazi connections.[19] The situation in *The Thanatos Syndrome* is further complicated by the strange, authentically detailed dream that Tom More has about an encounter with a girl in Germany, despite the fact that he has never actually been there, and that can be only partly accounted for by Father Smith's brief reference, earlier that day, to *his* first visit to Germany and a dream *he* has just had about "lying in bed in Tübingen and listening to church bells" (p. 138). No doubt, there is no suggestion of anything preternatural afoot in Smith's and More's sharing of dreams, anything that could not be sufficiently explained to Tom's satisfaction as psychiatrist: "old-style Freudian analyst, plus a dose of Adler and Jung" (p. 93). Besides Smith's words about the "silvery sound" of the Tübingen bells, echoed in the memory-laden "tinkle of silver against crystal" at Pantherburn (pp. 159–60), there is a good deal of other stuff floating around in Tom's consciousness of current personal experience that could serve as appropriate "dream stimulus," to use one of the Freudian terms for it, regardless of what deeper significance the dream symbolism may contain. Especially in the context of such developments as Tom describes in the medical and legal practice of his own day, it is hardly surprising that he should be set to troubled musing and dreaming by anything in any way associated with Germany and Germans: a sometime featherbed (p. 161), the name of the hapless immigrant carpenter convicted and executed in the notoriously mishandled Lindbergh kidnap/murder case (p. 24).

Given all the allusions to the Nazis and the guilt of other Germans who passively if not actively subscribed to Hitler's racist policies, people whom Father Smith directly compares to Tom's present-day "Qualitarian" colleagues, the "Louisiana Weimar psychiatrists" (p. 252), More's "Bruno Hauptmann suit" (pp. 24, 46, 55, and elsewhere simply "that suit") should remind us of the ambivalence of American attitudes toward Germany in the 1930s. The intense public hostility to Hauptmann might have been attributable in part to a current of anti-German sentiment in the United States. But that was by no means the whole story, and the irony of Charles Lindbergh's own pro-Nazi leanings cuts in several different directions. For more than a few Americans, even during and after World War

247

II, the heroic image of "the lone eagle" remained untarnished by his America First activities and persistent admiration and sympathy for the Germans.

When at one point (pp. 127–28) Father Smith identifies More himself with Comeaux and company, the company of those who will "end up killing Jews," Tom deeply resents it. But there can be little doubt that the accusation, however unfair it is, does have the good effect of alerting Tom to the dangers of passive complicity in what Comeaux and the other "Qualitarians" are doing. And once Lucy has put the name in his head with her phrase (p. 24) for his old double-breasted seersucker, it is easy to understand how ex-convict Tom—faced now with the threat of being drawn one way or another into still more dangerously suspect activity—should remind himself of Bruno Hauptmann (p. 55), a man probably innocent of the crime for which he was executed, but guilty of other, lesser offenses whose consequences helped to determine his final fate.[20]

The precise mechanisms of association—either in More's dreams and waking fantasies or in the novel as such—are for our present purposes a matter of secondary importance. What counts most is just that Tom's continuing interest in Father Smith, the objections of others and his own frequent exasperation and deeper fears and resentments notwithstanding, does not really *distract* him from his other more immediately pressing problems and responsibilities but furnishes him, instead, with an essential insight into the true nature of those quotidian concerns and the only truly "practical" way of dealing with them. Father Smith, mounting and descending his tower, often fasting but all the while keeping fit with his isometric exercises, is the essential agent of correspondence between heaven and earth, spirit and flesh, the eternal and the temporal, the sacred and the profane spheres of love. Again as in *Love in the Ruins* but still more strongly now, Percy suggests that if the Catholic church is to prevail in the world, it must first be destroyed. In Smith's own references to the name "Simon," by which he is known to most others besides Tom in this novel, he identifies its source as that of St. Simeon Stylites, whom he claims as his "patron saint."[21] But the hospice Smith runs is clearly to be seen as a prophetic model of the new church that may rise from the ruins of the old, and it can hardly be a mere coincidence that the name of the notoriously fallible head of this institution is the same as that of the man whom Jesus first whimsically chose to become the "rock" upon which He would build, Simon Peter.[22]

Father Smith's relationship with Tom is a complex system of interdependences. While Smith remains in the tower and the health of his devoted follower Milton Guidry continues to fail, Tom is obliged to take over more and more of the responsibility for the old priest's practical-nursing care. Once, having prodded him out of his meditative trance to "get on with the Mass" at the ceremony cele-brating reopening of the hospice, and discovering then that Milton is again unavailable (one suspects that Smith might deliberately have sent him away), the good doctor finds himself pressed into service as altar boy (pp. 362–63). But all this, if not quite quid pro quo, is yet somehow in return for the services Smith has rendered Tom in such media as the "confession" and the "sermon."

Perhaps a bit too obviously in the case of "Father Smith's Con-fession," Percy is up again here to his old favorite game of role exchanges. As is suggested in the very form of the word "confessor" itself, used to designate the priest not the penitent, there is always and inevitably some ambiguity in the sacramental relationship. But Percy relentlessly drives home the point, with listener Tom's impa-tience giving way to a final indulgent skepticism, in the course of "Father Smith's Footnote," everything short of assigning penance and granting absolution, in a fashion that resembles the typical manner of the weary priest in the confessional at least as closely as it does that of the psychiatrist, running behind schedule at martini time. This, after we have already seen Smith openly playing doctor to More, with his word-association tests (p. 121ff.), and, at the beginning of the "Confession" (pp. 239–40), not very surprisingly revealing that he had once actually thought of becoming a psychia-trist. So, the self-confessed "failed priest" is actually a spoiled doc-tor, and vice versa.[23]

Shortly after they have first got onto the fact that someone at Belle Ame is sexually abusing the students, Lucy is vexed with Tom for wanting to go off to attend to Father Smith (p. 227) instead of first looking after his own welfare and that of the children. But there are several things that Lucy does not fully understand about the situation at this point. She is, of course, wrong in thinking (p.

228) that Van Dorn himself has not been aware of what is going on in his school. And, in warning Tom not to keep Comeaux and Gottlieb waiting, taking the occasion even to urge him to accept Comeaux's offer of a job (p. 229), she is oversimplifying the kind of danger that Comeaux as well as Van Dorn poses. No doubt, her thinking about the other matters is to a great extent muddled simply by her preoccupation with the prospect of getting Tom away from Ellen; having mentioned Gottlieb, she also seizes the opportunity (pp. 229–30), to tell Tom that she has it on his old friend's authority that there is "not much future" in his "relationship" with Ellen, and that, while her concern is primarily for the children, she does not mind admitting that she is "a selfish woman," with her own needs. But, whatever the reasons for Lucy's misunderstandings and confusions, and regardless of the plain fact that Tom himself at this point does not fully comprehend either the external situation or his own motives, the visit to Father Smith he insists on making before he takes any other action is *not* a distraction from more pressing practical responsibilities—to himself, his family, the children at Belle Ame, or anyone else—but a necessary preparation for the other things he must do. Father Smith, who it happily turns out is not yet dying, as Tom had feared he might be, not only helps Tom to get his other responsibilities in proper emotional and intellectual perspective before he can deal with them effectively, but offers the only really practical alternative to the "programs" of Comeaux and Van Dorn.

In the cases of Ellen's uncanny prowess at the bridge table (p. 63), LSU's flawless football team (p. 195), and the happy cotton-picking "darkies" at Angola (p. 327), it is easy enough to see both the evil and the comical absurdity of Comeaux's and Van Dorn's work in the heavy-sodium experiments. There is, of course, hardly any point to a competitive game of any kind in which one of the contestants, whether an individual or a team, is absolutely unbeatable. And, obviously, what the socially "progressive" Blue Boy project has done with the docile blacks on the prison farm is simply to condemn them to a state of slavery that is if anything, "Swing Low, Sweet Chariot" and "colorful kerchiefs" notwithstanding (p. 266), still more degrading than that which their ancestors endured on the antebellum plantations.

On the other hand, Comeaux's and Van Dorn's, and even

Gottlieb's arguments from "success" in defense of the way they and their colleagues have dealt with some social problems (pp. 191, 217–18, 328, and elsewhere)—such as the high incidence of violent crime in urban areas, the abuse of public housing facilities, the disciplinary and instructional shortcomings of the school system, the runaway increase of both abortion and illegitimate births, drug abuse, teenage suicide, AIDS, the ethical and economic complexities of care for the elderly—are a bit harder to refute with either logic or laughter. But, laughter aside for the moment, the consistent, central objection that More has to Comeaux's and Van Dorn's positions on any and all of the specific issues is that the people they pretend to be trying to help simply cease to *be* people as a consequence of the "treatment" they are provided. Either they are eliminated outright, by abortion or by euthanasia in one form or another, or they are somehow dehumanized, condemned to one of a variety of states of half-life, or death-in-life. People of all ages and both sexes suffer impairments of brain function which reduce them to the status of not very complexly programmed, walking computers; one of Tom More's female patients gets into a bad state of nerves, even quits her job, over a quarrel with a robot; women develop an estrus cycle, with corresponding changes in their sexual behavior, including a marked tendency to "present" by displaying their backsides to males. When the massive dose of the heavy-sodium additive Tom persuades him to take (p. 308) reduces Van Dorn after a time (pp. 341–42ff.) to a "pongid" state so extreme that he seems likely never to recover his powers of speech, he is, of course, simply being repaid in kind for what he has done to others.

There is no implication that Percy regards the use of computers for any purposes as intrinsically dehumanizing. Indeed, it seems likely that he would agree with Wertham that what we need for the improvement of modern society is "not fewer computers but more and better ones" (*A Sign for Cain*, p. 369). There is no harm in the development of "artificial intelligence," so long as we do not mistake it for natural intelligence, or propose (as Van Dorn implicitly does, p. 63) to put the latter in the service of the former, no harm in referring to "computer languages," so long as we do not suppose that we can *converse* with computers, or they with each other, in anything like the sense that we converse with other human beings. It is only on the basis of a failure to understand such distinctions as these, a failure to understand the unique status of *homo loquens* in the world both of our own and of God's making, that the fanatics of computer science and their dupes in all other fields from education and medicine to business and politics have something essentially in common with the extreme theorists of animal communication and their cultist popular following, and are appropriately made the joint butt of Percy's satire in the allegory of Van Dorn and Eve.

Clearly, in Percy's view, it is only a short step from the legalized abortion of our own times to the government-sponsored euthanasia programs referred to both in this novel and in *Love in the Ruins*. Whether he means us to see it as a hopeful sign that the government of the 1990s still does not officially sanction such programs as Blue Boy is not quite clear. In any event, as we have noted earlier, More does not hesitate to take his own minor liberties with the law when it suits his higher moral purposes. And, once having by hook or by crook got Comeaux where he wants him, he presses his advantage relentlessly, even over Max Gottlieb's anxious objections, to get the unexpended portions of the "legitimate" funds Comeaux controls (NIH and Ford) diverted to assist Father Smith and all the "euthanasic candidates and quarantined patients from the Qualitarian Center" transferred to the hospice (p. 333). St. Margaret's, an institution that operates somehow above or beyond the province of secular law (beyond the regular jurisdiction of the organized church, for that matter), is More's answer to Blue Boy, which operated outside the secular law, though not, as Comeaux rather cogently argues, in violation of the spirit of it.

St. Margaret's, which accepts and keeps alive as long as possible all patients of all kinds, regardless of age, sex and sexual preference, race, temperament, religious persuasion or the lack of it, regardless of the nature of the disease or defect with which they are afflicted, operates on a principle directly opposed to that which rules at the highly specialized and exclusive Fedville facilities. Comeaux and crew have taken it upon themselves to decide who are fit or unfit to receive treatment, who are to live or die, and if the latter, when and by what means. Father Smith, of course, with the assistance and concurrence of More, is disposed not to meddle in such matters, not to attempt to judge of the "quality" of human life, so long as it persists in any form, and can be to any extent nourished by their care (p. 361). Both Smith and More, if with somewhat different emphases and varying certainty, share the conviction that all are *redeemable*.

The notion of *redemption* is, of course, completely foreign to Comeaux and Van Dorn, for the simple reason that they have no sense of *guilt*. They can at worst feel embarrassed, at worst admit either to themselves or to others that they have made a mistake, a tactical blunder. In their eyes, any *crime*, unless it suits their convenience to pretend to take it seriously, is only a more or less embarrassing, more or less stupid mistake; of *sin*, whether individual or universal ("original"), they have no conception whatever. (Again, Tom's friend Gottlieb shares some of these attitudes, but is at least in a workaday sense "redeemed" by his instinctive decency. Or, arguing from some of Father Smith's notions of special dispensation, one might suppose that it is Gottlieb's Jewishness that does it; his name means what it says whether he knows it, or likes it, or not.)

A "hospice," in one of the two most common contemporary senses of the word, and the one that would seem most closely applicable to Smith's operation at St. Margaret's, is an institution for the care of the terminally ill. Everyone in the world, of course, from the moment not simply of birth but of conception, is terminally ill. But the essential difference between those who are and those who are not admitted to Smith's "hospice," plainly an image of the church itself, is just that the former are truly *cared for*—in acceptance of the truth that they must quit this life, and in hope of their entering the next—while the others, those committed at last to one of the Fedville clinics, are eased in and out as quickly and with as little pain and terror as possible, with little or no consciousness of what is happening to them, and therefore without hope either. The unflinching recognition of evil, of the reality of sin and of death as its consequence, is the necessary precondition of faith.

Although Tom's own sense of contrition is defective, as we have had several occasions to note both in *Love in the Ruins* and in this novel, and so is Smith's, these two are strikingly different from Comeaux and Van Dorn in being always quick to acknowledge their own deficiencies of moral character, their responsibility for the troubles they bring upon themselves and their proper share of the blame for the sufferings of others. Of course, guilt can also be a source of pride, and an overreadiness to acknowledge it a way either of attempting to head off proper punishment or of avoiding the next occasion for responsible action. Such pride and such dodges are routine features of Tom More's behavior, and the danger of them is often apparent even in Smith's. May we not legitimately suspect that Smith's "confession" to Tom about his experiences in Germany —especially the part in which he is at such pains to distinguish between his powerful attraction to Helmut and the tradition of the Marienburg oath on the one hand, and his vague distrust of the learned doctors and outright contempt for the brownshirt Lothar on the other—is rather carefully edited? Has not the whole thing a flavor rather more of *apology* than of confession? Is there not a lurking pride in it still, a sinister vanity, more than a faint note of name-dropping in the references to Jäger and his distinguished guests? Certainly, the pride is there in the sardonic remarks addressed to his guilt-free audience at the ceremonies reopening St. Margaret's: pride in his very lowliness, his status as "old drunk," "failed priest," as a modern-day poor imitation of his fifth-century Syrian namesake, the ascetic St. Simeon Stylites, whose original tower-standing act perfectly symbolizes the paradox of arrogant humility that is at the center of all saintly practice.[24]

Nonetheless, whatever his own more subtle culpabilities, we may assume that Father Smith is dead right about his audience at the reopening ceremonies, that "everyone looks justified," that there is "not a guilty face" in the crowd (pp. 360–61), and that that is going to be his biggest problem in trying to reach them. Another manifestation of this same spirit of the age is the reluctance everyone has to look at the lewd photographs Tom collects at Belle Ame, showing Van Dorn and members of his staff cavorting with the children. Not only is it known from the start that photographic evidence will be declared "inadmissible" in court proceedings— Tom is keeping the pictures for other purposes, anticipating that they may come in handy for his scheduled interview with Comeaux back in Angola—but, except for Tom, even the people on the immediate scene, perpetrators and captors alike, and later, Comeaux and Gottlieb, refuse quite to credit the plain evidence of their senses. One after another, and repeatedly, they will venture only sidelong glances at the photographs; even if the look is lingering, and troubled or toughly appraising, it is still somehow asquint and aslant, never a direct and candid gaze.

Besides the obvious one that nobody wants to act as if he or she might be *enjoying* the pornography, the motives are many and diverse. Perhaps people like Mr. and Mrs. Brunette, hardened repeat offenders, are totally "out of it" in matters of conscience, mindlessly and solely preoccupied with the questions of legal admissibility. Mrs. Cheney essentially may be the decent old body practically everyone wants to think she is; simply not very bright, especially when under the influence of the doctored drinking water, and perhaps genuinely *offended* by the photographs. Perhaps she could, in properly friendly and jolly company, be induced to *do* the things she is pictured as doing. But to be required to *look* at herself doing them, long after the fact and in the presence of comparative strangers: that, now, is just a little more than a respectable woman has to put up with. Uncle Hugh Bob, his previously settled prejudices against people who "mess with children" notwithstanding, finds Mrs. Cheney in her "presenting" posture "some kind of woman," and certainly is not going to waste much of his time looking at any kind of pictures of the old girl when he has the real thing right in front of him. Vergil, perhaps, as a black man, is a bit like Elgin in *Lancelot*, who "looked but forebore to see" the videotape evidence that he himself had gathered against the guilty white folks, his attitude a mixture of fear and detached contempt. But all to some extent share the malady that most notably afflicts the master of Belle Ame himself, Van Dorn, that radical incapacity not only for self-knowledge or self-examination but even for self-recognition which Percy sees as essentially characteristic already of our own age. In the futuristic satire here, the Blue Boy experiments produce effects that only minimally exaggerate the kind of monstrous behavior we have all become quite accustomed to reading about in our daily newspapers. If Van Dorn is intelligent enough to know when the jig is up, give over protesting, and drink the big glass of his own medicine with which Tom presents him, but at the same time is still somehow unable to recognize himself in the offending photographs, it is in a very real sense because he *has* no self.

It is as champions of the self, on the other hand, champions of the cause to restore our all but lost sense of self, that More and Smith emerge from their struggle with the Blue Boy conspirators and their more or less like-minded fellow professionals at Fedville. In More's professional sphere, the self is that *psyche*—or spirit, soul, German *Seele*—of which, according to Tom, Freud himself was a "champion . . . even though he spent his life pretending there was no such thing" (p. 16). Unquestionably, it is this paradoxical character of Freud's thinking, as much as anything else, that determines Tom's basic professional commitment first of all to the Freudian teachings, and, after that, to the "psychiatric faith" he got from Harry Stack Sullivan.

Although he qualifies it from time to time—with nods of acknowledgment, for example, to Jung and Adler (pp. 67, 88)—the general tone of loyal approbation, not to say veneration, is unmistakable in More's remarks about Freud in this novel. He is "our mentor Dr. Freud" (p. 13) and "a genius and a champion of the psyche" (p. 16). Jung had some valid ideas, but "in the end Dr. Jung turned out to be something of a nut, the source of all manner of occult nonsense. . . . [while] Dr. Freud was not. [Freud] was a scientist, wrong at times, but a scientist nonetheless." All this represents something of a switch from the predominance of an overtly hostile, at times even contemptuous, attitude in the direct references to Freud that Percy has made both in essays and in his fiction before now. William Allen goes so far, a bit farther than I would ever have gone, as to speak of Percy's having "*rejected* the Freudian interpretation of the human condition" (Allen, *Walker Percy*, p. xix, emphasis added; see Bibliography). Perhaps in *The Thanatos Syndrome* Percy has found his way through the worst troubles of that career-long struggle with Freud as "father figure" that Allen so astutely analyzes. Perhaps, by coincidence or as another part of the same process, Percy has been prompted to the new and forthright defense of Freud in adverse reaction to the many books and papers of recent years that in various ways seek to discredit the man and his influence—notably including, for present purposes of our concern with the theme of sexual abuse, J. M. Masson's *The Assault on Truth: Freud's Suppression of the Seduction Theory* (see Bibliography). It is hard to say. And whether anything about the new attitude can be interpreted as Percy's licensing Freudian or any other brand of psychoanalytic *criticism* of his novel is another and still knottier question: we can be certain only that such criticism will be attempted, whether Percy approves of it or not. (Like "shrinks" [p. 17]—and implicitly novelists, a good many readers will undoubtedly think—critics too, of all persuasions, are going to demand being dealt a hand anytime it comes to the "rendering the unspeakable speakable" game.) But Harry Stack Sullivan is another obvious case of the kind of habitual double-mindedness that More seems to admire in Freud.

For Sullivan too, although his "interpersonalist" doctrine is the very thing that most sharply separates him from more orthodox Freudians, inevitably had a hard time reconciling that doctrine with the belief in the self-curative powers of mental patients, " '*even some psychotics*' " which More attributes to him (p. 16). "Now, I don't know where he got this," More goes on, "from Ramakrishna, Dr. Jung, or Matthew 13:44. Or from his own sardonic Irish soul. But there it is." In any event, wherever *he* got it, More's essential faith in the existence of that "pearl of great price," the "buried treasure" of "the patient's truest unique self," which it is the psychiatrist's responsibility simply to "help him reach" (pp. 16–17), unmistakably allies the doctor with the priest.

And the unique self in question is the individual human self, the self of that creature whom Percy identifies, again and unmistakably, as *homo loquens*. The self, the soul, whether with the aid of the priest or of the psychiatrist, is reachable only by willing consent of that same self, the individual penitent or patient, and, in appropriately differentiated modes, by that power of language which manifests his/her unique creaturely status.

Father Smith it is who repeatedly insists that "words no longer signify" (p. 118). Yet he not only goes on celebrating in the Mass the mystery of the incarnate Word, but on occasion even preaches, and, if for a time only to Milton Guidry, offers in the confessional the words of divine absolution. Dr. More—in his central adherence, though with modifications, to Freudian doctrine, the teachings of the medical practitioner who did more than many professional linguists to shape our modern notions of the nature and function of language—follows first and last the method of helping his patients to "talk it out." Comeaux and Van Dorn have wanted Tom on their "team" primarily for his other talents, as the inventor of the Lapsometer, as the one who may be "going down in history as the father of isotope brain pharmacology" (p. 200). But Tom has consistently resisted their blandishments, even before he learned of Blue Boy, asserting that since his ambitious days of the MOQUOL research he has learned that "there's more to it than neurones" (p. 88).[25] And at the end he is still resisting, still intent as he was at the beginning on helping his patients to "speak the unspeakable" to him (p. 17). Now that Ellen has put the children in a Pentecostal school with high tuition, and at the same time "given away all her money to the Baton Rouge evangelist" (p. 367), he may be obliged either to go in with Max Gottlieb at Mandeville or to take the fulltime but low-salaried job as director of St. Margaret's hospice. But the chances are that he will always find some way to work with a few private patients like the suggestively named and otherwise fascinating Mickey LaFaye, whose case in his judgment is one of those that in the end can be handled, if at all, only by the techniques of psychoanalysis. It is not, as we have seen, from contemptuous ignorance but from a thorough professional understanding of their work that More questions the practices of the "brain engineers, neuropharmacologists, chemists of the synapses" who have "mostly [but not quite] superseded" the Freudians (p. 13), and knows that the new breed can never have anything effective to *say* to a patient like Mickey.

Mickey, we will remember, was the first of Tom's patients to whom we were introduced at the beginning of the novel. She was referred to him by Dr. Comeaux, but Comeaux soon felt his own prior neurological interests in the case threatened by the kind of tests More wanted to run on her, and warned Tom (pp. 96–97) that if he hoped to get the restrictions removed from his medical license he had better stay in line. We may regard Mickey, perhaps, as part of the professional "spoils" Tom claims in his victory over Comeaux. As the novel ends, she is "back on the couch as she used to be, facing the window," having come all but full circle from her voluptuous "Duchess of Alba" phase, almost now to the emaciated image again of the woman in Wyeth's *Christina's World*. Almost, but not quite. Percy insistently repeats the qualification. "She's *almost* Christina again . . . beautiful actually, but *beginning* to be ravaged again, thin, cheeks shadowed under her French-Indian cheekbones, but not yet *too* thin, not yet *wholly* Christina" (p. 370, emphasis added).[26]

The qualifications in the physical description are important in pointing up certain essential differences between her psychological disposition now and that one she showed in her first visit to Tom's office after he returned from prison. Perhaps having had quite enough recently of back views of women, Tom now asks her to leave the couch and come over to sit where they can see each other. She does, and "doesn't mind looking at [him]" (p. 370), but it is notable also that all the old arch seductiveness is gone now from her manner. Rather, she wants simply to "talk about" what is bothering her. She wants to talk, and the first thing she wants specifically to talk about is the old recurrent dream: "of [her] grandmother's farmhouse in Vermont and the smell of winter apples and the stranger coming" (p. 371). Early on, Tom in his own reflections had tentatively identified the stranger as a part of Mickey herself. ("A visitor was coming and would tell her a secret. . . . What was she, her visitor-self, trying to tell her solitary cellar-bound self? What part of herself was the deep winter-apple-bound self?" [p. 6].) Now she too, but independently, is inclined to that view.

"Do you know who the stranger is?" she asks Tom. His reply is to put the question back to her: "Who do you think he is?" And she responds: "I think the stranger is part of myself" (p. 371). And again she asks: "Could I talk about it?" And he replies: "Yes."

To be sure, she looks at Tom "searching [his] eyes as if [he] were the mirror of her very self." But that is not, I think, to suggest any confusion of Tom with the stranger, i.e., with that "part of herself" who is the stranger. The mirror, the mind of the psychiatrist, holds only an *image* of her distinct self. And when the analysis is finished, however long that may take, she will have no further need of the mirror.

Tom's first fear had been of "some odd suppression of cortical function" (p. 22) that Mickey and Donna were suffering, a fear that has been all too well confirmed in his later discoveries about the heavy-sodium experiments. Comeaux and Van Dorn and company have been working such suppressions—amounting to suppression, in fact, of the specifically *human* functions, an impairment of those speech faculties, among others, which define the human self—on countless numbers of people, including Donna and Mickey. Now that Tom has won Mickey back, has her fully and consciously, imaginatively starting to talk again, it is the best and surest sign that she may, with his slight further assistance, still someday find that "pearl without price," her human self.

Some serious questions remain. In the story of Van Dorn's recovery of his powers of speech under the loving tutelage of Eve the gorilla, Percy is again poking fun at the animal language researchers whom he has attacked in *Lost in the Cosmos* and elsewhere, and a kind of fun that grows ever more wearisome. Certainly such researchers are vulnerable on a number of issues, not the least important of them the question of the hurt that is done to experimental animals who are returned to the wild after having become accustomed to human society, and who find themselves then totally isolated, unable to communicate satisfactorily with members of their own species. But the brief suggestion of More's solicitude for the forsaken Eve (pp. 344–45) is, at best, a sentimental afterthought. There is a tragic dimension in all this, the situation of our alienation from our fellow creatures, non-human as well as human, that Percy has not begun to plumb, in any of his writings either fictional or non-fictional. Surely for the needs of our now post-post-post-Darwinian, desperate situation on this crowded planet, that is no adequate theory of language, no adequate theology, which is not vitally and centrally concerned with the terrible, in every sense the unspeakable, suffering of our fellow animals.

Further, apart from the question of his culpability in his abandonment of Eve—his culpability, and More's, since it was More who had the idea of getting them together in the first place—is such a man as Van Dorn really *redeemable*? Redeemable, that is to say, in any sense of the term that should be theoretically acceptable to either Smith or More.

It is not that Van Dorn might be considered beyond the pale on account of his pedophilia. Very early in the novel, the subject of incestuous abuse is introduced in the case history of Donna, the first woman in whose sexual behavior, after Tom's return from prison, he observes the disturbingly apelike maneuver of "presenting rearward" (p. 20). At one point in the course of analysis, Donna sees in More himself, not surprisingly, a "son of a bitch" like her father/lover, "a seedy but kindly gentle wise Atticus Finch who messed with Scout." [27] Besides wantonly killing her horses, and in some way connectedly, Mickey LaFaye is accused of "coming on" sexually to an underaged groom (pp. 8, 100). The novel reaches its climax in the raid on Belle Ame. The average citizen, *l'homme moyen sensuel*, might at least offhand agree with Uncle Hugh Bob or with Elmo the amiable guard at Angola that "I mean, when it comes to messing with chirren—" (p. 268) we are approaching the unspeakable. But that view is not reflected in the usual practice of the criminal courts. And it is clear that neither More nor Smith regards sexual abuse of children as absolutely the worst crime of which adult human beings are capable. Both, from long years of experience in the consulting room and the confessional if nothing else, know how shadowy the line is between loving and abusing in the care of children as in all other situations of human attraction and responsibility. As early as in the first account of Donna's case, and several times thereafter, More refers to the especially troubling fact (distant and somber shades of *Auntie Mame?*) that sexually exploited children often themselves *like* what is happening to them: "(yes, that's the worst of it, the part you don't read about)" (p. 14). [28]

In short, pedophilia is but one of the total complex of symptoms that make up the thanatos syndrome, and even the worst of the child-molesters is not anathema.

The other offending members of the staff at Belle Ame, having gotten off on a plea bargain with five-year "community service" sentences, willingly accept assignments to various useful jobs at the hospice. Even the Brunettes work "in good heart" and are described by Father Smith as "a caring couple." And Van Dorn himself—once he has recovered from the effects of the sodium additive and, with Eve's help, learned to speak again—gets a comparatively light sentence of ten years at Angola, and is pardoned by the governor even before he has served much of that (p. 344).

The main question, rather, is again that of whether either Comeaux or Van Dorn, in spite of being so richly endowed with that singularly human faculty of language—i.e., in the broadest sense, the faculty of abstract thought and expression, but in their case only as it relates to the experience of external reality—have not somehow completely lost contact with themselves, and therefore with the selves of others. One appreciates Percy's little joke about Van Dorn's desire to "rejoin his own kind," which means at its ultimate finest the likes of Phil Donahue, or Dr. Ruth, and others on the "talk-show circuit" (p. 344). But the implicit question is whether the kind of talk that goes on there is not a still worse travesty of truly human communication than the "signing" with which Van Dorn and Eve got on together.

In any event, it is hard to say which is the more nearly unimaginable, that Van Dorn and Comeaux should ever find themselves at St. Margaret's or in Tom More's little tin-roofed office, seeking at one or the other place either care for themselves or a request for their assistance as staff members. And that is a most disturbing reflection. For no matter how few or how many it is in our society of whom Van Dorn and Comeaux, these walking dead, are meant to be representative—and I am afraid it is the many rather than the few—it is hard to reconcile their apparent *incapacity* to respond with the universal charity of Father Smith's appeal.

On the subject of homosexuality, never one on which he has wasted much compassion or intelligence either, Percy has made in this novel even less satisfactory progress than on questions concerning women and blacks. Beyond statistical references, blacks are confined as in all Percy's novels to supporting and walk-on roles of greater or lesser significance. And it tends to undercut our appreciation of the satiric humor at Comeaux's expense in the account of the blissful cottonpickers at Angola when we observe that More's black associates too, not just Hudeen but for all their liberated modernity Vergil and Chandra as well, are still pretty good old darkies at heart. There is not a really *bad* black in sight. Homosexuals of the non-pedophilic variety are hardly mentioned except in connection with the doings of the ex-priest and ex-nun couple Kev Kevin and Debbie Boudreaux (p. 350), and with the AIDS problem (pp. 191–92). Van Dorn reports (p. 218) that cases of AIDS infection in the country have risen to some five million—many times the figure in 1987, I believe. But one must look sharp for such references as that to "AIDS infants" (p. 333) in order to be sure that the five million includes significant numbers of people other than adult males. Otherwise, it might seem that the "haggard young men" whom More visits at the hospice (p. 363) are the only kind of AIDS patients around. And it is still harder to avoid the implication that their having AIDS—i.e., being at death's door and having, presumably, learned the error of their former ways, being now given over to "depression and terrors"—is the only thing that makes the company of the sometime "gays" and bisexuals at all tolerable to More.

I am also reluctant to accept at face value Father Smith's judgment that the "dear physicians . . . dear Qualitarians, abortionists, euthanasists" in his audience at the reopening ceremonies wish "for the best of reasons to put out of [their] misery" the kind of patients whom they regularly certify as expendable (p. 361). I doubt that they act for the best of *reasons*, or even with the best of *intentions*. They probably act, as often as not, for "reasons" of something like case-inventory control, and not so much with the intention of putting the patient out of his/her misery as of relieving their own stress symptoms. Of course, Father Smith is deliberately trying to butter the doctors up on this occasion. He wants their cooperation, and it would hardly work to rail at them as knowing criminals. Perhaps his statements are hardheaded practical rhetoric, not an expression of misguided charity. But I am afraid they smack of the latter.

The outline of medieval romance, particularly of the grail quest story, again with modifications attributable to various modern authors (Eliot, Hemingway, Fitzgerald, et al.), is evident here as it has been, in one way or another, in all Percy's novels. A mysterious blight has settled upon the land. There is the obligatory fishing trip—with Tom's participating only as observer of the actual angling (p. 58), in a way oddly reminiscent, and at the same time notably different in that here the observer is an *expert*, of the scene with Binx Bolling and his mother in *The Moviegoer* (pp. 149–59). The hero's adventures include visits to two, variously spooky castles, Pantherburn and Belle Ame. In one, he is sorely tempted by the beauteous and lustful mistress, who wants to keep him there forever. At the other, he delivers the inhabitants from the evil enchantment cast upon them by their dread master. For spiritual counsel, so to speak, and a kind of reverse confession with no certain absolution either way, he repairs to the forest hermitage of an aged priest, who is himself suspect at times of devilish disguise. (The conventions of the modern "thriller" story, which so obviously influence the design of this novel, are themselves derived in considerable part from the medieval tradition.) Yet, for all this, the theme of the hero's individual and deliberate quest for spiritual awakening, "the search," is somehow less prominent here than it was in Percy's earlier novels.

However consciously on his part, More's continuing to toy with the idea of taking on the hospice directorship is a sign that he has not entirely abandoned the search for faith. He has not despaired. But when he explains why he refused to serve Mass for Father Smith "routinely," on the grounds simply that "since [he] no longer was sure what [he] believe[d], [and] didn't think much about religion, participation in Mass would seem to be deceitful" (p. 363), the statement seems entirely candid, and not out of keeping with the evidence of his general behavior either before or after the occasion of that interview with the priest. I have no quarrel with any of this. But Tom's tolerance for his wife's religious caprices is another matter, as suspect in its way as Father Smith's overtures to the Qualitarians.

Ellen has, to be sure, had a rough time of it with Van Dorn and his experiments. Perhaps she remains to the end "too stoned on sodium ions to talk right" (p. 337), or think right, about anything, and Tom only wants to wait until she is thoroughly in her right mind before trying to engage her in a serious discussion about religion. But somehow one doubts it. In faith or unfaith, he is simply too proud of his Catholicism—and the smaller the band of loyalists becomes, the "remnant of a remnant" (p. 354), the more superior he feels—too proud a "Roman" to bother feeling anything but an indulgent contempt for the succession of heretical affiliations, with everything from Presbyterians to Episcopalians to Pentecostals, that Ellen has tried. Too proud a Catholic, no matter how uncertain of his beliefs, and too indolent a male supremacist to argue with his wife. Male chauvinism that masks as uxorious docility is nothing at all new under the sun, of course. But whatever his motives, it is surely no proper model of either husbandly or fatherly conduct, not to speak of any lingering responsibility he might feel to the Catholic church, for him to sit by without once raising his voice or a hand, even in warning, while Ellen is ripped off by "the Baton Rouge evangelist" (p. 367) and the children are enrolled in yet another phony school. This one, a Pentecostal institution called "Feliciana Christian Academy," teaches creationism "and won't have *Huckleberry Finn* or *The Catcher in the Rye* in the library." While acknowledging that he does "worry about [the children] growing up as Louisiana dumbbells," Tom consoles himself with the thought that "at least it's better than Belle Ame" (p. 354), meaning presumably that at least the staff don't sexually abuse the children. But one must wonder how he can be so sure even of that. The practice of such abuse, if seldom on so regular and systematic a basis as at Belle Ame, is by no means confined to secular progressivist schools. There is also a long, sad history of it among church-school teachers, everybody from sadistic priests and nuns to oily-tongued or whooping and hollering fundamentalists.

Everything is, after all, a bit too genially latitudinarian in this novel. The prevailing attitude of moral sloth can only be encouraged by such cheerful apocalyptics as Father Smith's notion that the hundred-year tenure of "Great Prince Satan" (pp. 364–65) is about at an end. As the author is at considerable and hardly necessary pains to persuade us, the crime for which Tom was sent to prison, selling amphetamines and hypnotic drugs to interstate truckdrivers, was really no very serious offense. Tom himself does not waste any time brooding upon it, once he is out of jail. And he is hardly more outraged by anything that anyone else has done. Cool, resourceful, very much in command of the practical situation most of the time, when he can be shaken out of his indolence. But in the moral and metaphysical spheres, even the aesthetic on occasion, a trifle namby-pamby, truth to tell. He has his cherished aversions, and his low-voltage, gentlemanly prejudices, but "savage indignation" is not his style.[29] I liked the old bumbling, hapless, but always combative Tom of *Love in the Ruins* a good deal better. Not just the lovable drunken reprobate and self-frustrating rake, nor the proud, absurdly ambitious man of ideas, but the truly and deeply conscience-stricken man too, man pursued by furies of remorse and unextinguishable regret. Except by contrast to those incapable of guilt, such as Comeaux

265

and Van Dorn, the new, older Tom is neither, on the one hand, consciously *guilty* enough as the anti-hero of this novel, nor on the other hand capable of despair.

The thanatos syndrome—embracing everything, from pedophilia to euthanasia, that in seeking a life of pleasure without biological or other responsibility, life free of the ugliness and pain of disease and aging, of the consciousness of dying, a society wholly "purified" of racial conflict by any means up to and including genocide, seeks the impossible, seeks not life but death-in-life—is surely but a new name for the great sickness of despair that has been Percy's more or less constant and central theological theme from the beginning of his career as novelist. The same disease, with a very interesting new set of symptoms, certainly. But in this novel anything resembling the purest form of the malady, the despair that is "unaware of being despair," is notably suffered only by Tom's adversaries, Van Dorn and Comeaux, who if to some extent pitiable are still too decidedly low-comic to arouse in the reader the peculiar terror that is the appropriate response to despair.[30] In all Percy's other novels the hero is represented, more or less convincingly and for a longer or shorter period of time, as existing in a state of despair. Here, Tom often seems very, very *tired*, so tired that he is almost if not entirely past caring about the question of his personal safety, not to speak of the state of his feelings, in such matters as Lucy's report that Ellen is infected with a new and especially dangerous strain of herpes (p. 157). But fatigue, although it may sometimes occur simultaneously, is not despair. Perhaps Percy meant us to remember Tom's ordeal in *Love in the Ruins*, and felt there was no point in repeating it here. But, again, the writer of a sequel cannot count on his readers' knowing the earlier work, or, if they should know it, on their willingness to accept the notion of a tandem design.

Still, I do not mean to suggest that the final effect of this novel is one either of disabling weariness and confusion or of total moral fatuity. It is certainly all to the good that Percy at least did not try to force a "happy ending" on this novel. Whether such an ending is satisfactorily accomplished even in *The Second Coming* is open to serious question.[31] Here, it obviously could not work. If Tom More is not, as I have argued, at any point in *The Thanatos Syndrome* in despair, he is most assuredly in *trouble* from the beginning, and the prospect is notably clouded at the end.

That is quite as it should be. There remains here, as one of the novel's greatest strengths, a rather somber sense of the uncertainties of existence, deepening at last into mystery.

First, there is the question simply of "how things are going to turn out." Are Tom and Ellen capable of permanently rebuilding their marriage? They appear to have made some small progress. But the sexual/medical situation, for one thing, is not very clear.

Again, what about that "Herpes IV" infection (p. 157ff.)? A thing like that could certainly make it awkward for them in the bedroom. But, besides its being uncertain *precisely* what part-to-part bodily contact is involved in his first intercourse with Ellen after his return from prison (pp. 52–53), we are not told whether Tom ever took the two capsules of "Alanone" (whatever *that* is) Lucy kept pressing upon him (pp. 156–58).[32] And the entire subject is never mentioned again in Tom's narrative. Barring the possibility that Percy simply forgot about it in writing the later chapters, are we to assume that Lucy was mistaken in her report, maybe even deliberately lying? If, indeed, Ellen had contracted the disease, or Tom was convinced that she had, that could well have been involved in the motivation for his subtly vindictive later dealings with Van Dorn, who would naturally be suspect as the one who had infected her. But, beyond taking his revenge on Van Dorn, has Tom simply repressed his concern with Ellen's possibly diseased condition, possibly his own by now? If not that, is he taking any practical measures to deal with it? Or could he be using it, or the threat of it, consciously or unconsciously, as an *excuse* for a sexless marriage, and, as part of the same psychological maneuver, resuming his heavy drinking?

There is an interesting evasiveness, toward the close, in all of Tom's references to his marriage. For any number of reasons not difficult to guess, it is not at all inconceivable that he should be off soon after another woman, even one of his patients.

In Mickey LaFaye's case, aside from questions about her personal relationship with Tom, what does her recurrent dream signify? The architectural and landscape symbols, the apples, the unseen *stranger*, all are tempting in fairly obvious ways, Freudian, Kierkegaardian, and what have you. But even Dr. More has only an inkling here, and the reader is well advised not to try getting ahead of him. There is also the whole mystery, again, of the human personality, *any* human personality, and the ultimate unpredictability of human actions, of which I spoke at the end of chapter 2 in praising the supreme realism of Percy's characterizations.

But finally, I mean theological mystery; specifically, the mystery of Agape. William Allen (*Walker Percy*, p. 51) rightly argues, although he remains doubtful whether the effort succeeds, that "*The Second Coming* represents not only the victory of Eros over Thanatos, but an attempt to resolve Eros and Agape." The same is unquestionably true of *The Thanatos Syndrome*. Unquestionably, and necessarily, for in any possibly effective Christian revision of Freud's thinking on the "death instinct" the contrary power of Eros alone is obviously incapable of assuring victory. Not, I hasten to add, that Percy formally attempts in *The Thanatos Syndrome* any such "Christian revision of Freud's thinking." Had he done so, it would certainly have been a very bad novel. Ernest Jones (*The Life and Work of Sigmund Freud*, Vol. 3, p. 273; see Bibliography) remarks that "it is a little odd that Freud himself never, except in conversation, used for the death instinct the term *Thanatos*." Perhaps I have overlooked it, but I do not recall having come across in this novel, at the other end of the spectrum, the term *Agape*. Aside from the scene of the reopening ceremonies at the hospice, we have to infer the presence of that power here on the strength of even less solid internal evidence than was available in *The Second Coming*. Overtly, there is little here to suggest that Percy takes any sign of vitality, explicitly sexual or otherwise, as indicative of a power greater than that which serves the individual human being only, in Freud's phrase, "to make ever more complicated *détours* before reaching its aim of death." [33]

Consider the inmates of St. Margaret's hospice, which I have seen as model of the New Church to come. The problem is not only that Tom's getting patients transferred there from the Qualitarian Center is only a local, and probably temporary, success. It is all very well to talk, as Tom said Harry Stack Sullivan did, of adult patients of normal intelligence, "even psychotics," who have the power to cure their psychic ills with "a little help" from the doctors. It is all very well to talk of humankind as *homo loquens*, and of the Word of Christ which is brought to sinners by the priest. But what of those among Smith's charges who, by accident of birth or genetic defect or any other cause totally beyond their control, have no power of speech at all, no power even to lift up their heads to receive the wafer and wine, or if they have that strength no proper mouths to open, who if they make any sounds at all they are sounds not only not "like anything in the world that is human" but nothing resembling the sounds of beasts either? What of these creatures' dreadful *innocence*? Here is the question that haunts the novel from beginning to end, but cannot be spoken anywhere by anyone on either side of the More/Smith–Comeaux/Van Dorn conflict. For the only conceivable "answer" is too preposterous, too *absurd* if you will, for anyone to consider uttering either in persuasion or mockery. Like all Percy's novels in their "Catholic" aspect, this one seems designed mainly to *test* faith and the strength of those who pretend to seek it, not directly to sustain it.

"Well well well." Those, echoing Mickey's near the beginning (p. 7), are the last words. And "all's well that ends well" is one obvious way to construe them. But I said that Tom's getting Mickey talking again is "the best and surest sign that she *may* . . . someday find that 'pearl without price,' her human self." I did not say, positively will find it.

The final words of the novel are characteristically enigmatic: a kind of ritually repetitive formula perhaps, a benediction it may be, "and all shall be well, and all manner of thing shall be well," [34] or only a guardedly hopeful murmur of half surprise, half-suppressed and not yet gratified expectation, a "well, well, well, and what have we here" sort of thing? It is hard to say, and there is no more. But, if for no other reason than that it leaves us not quite satisfied, it is a beginning, not wholly ending.

Like Mickey's recurrent dream in Tom's first assessment, the whole novel is well "worth working on" (p. 6). And the work has only begun.

269

Notes

1. Introduction

1. For information about Walker Percy's life, I have relied upon the following published sources (see Bibliography): Lewis Baker, *The Percys of Mississippi* (hereafter referred to as Baker, *The Percys*); Robert Coles, *Walker Percy: An American Search* (hereafter referred to as Coles, *Walker Percy*); Ellen Douglas, *Walker Percy's "The Last Gentleman": Introduction and Commentary* (hereafter referred to as Douglas, *Percy's "The Last Gentleman"*); Linda Whitney Hobson, "Man vs. Malaise, In the Eyes of Louisiana's Walker Percy" (hereafter referred to as Hobson, "Man vs. Malaise"); Lewis A. Lawson and Victor A. Kramer, eds., *Conversations with Walker Percy* (hereafter referred to as Lawson and Kramer, *Conversations*; Martin Luschei, *The Sovereign Wayfarer: Walker Percy's Diagnosis of the Malaise* (hereafter referred to as Luschei, *Wayfarer*); William Alexander Percy, *Lanterns on the Levee: Recollections of a Planter's Son* (hereafter referred to as William Alexander Percy, *Lanterns*).

2. Cf. the family history of "Percival," in *Lancelot*. Charles had the title of "Alcalde" in the Spanish territory, and was called "Don Carlos." William Alexander Percy (*Lanterns*, p. 39) reflects with a show of amusement upon the romantic obscurity of his ancestor's origins. "Was he a pirate? Or the lost heir of the earls of Northumberland? Or a hero of the Spanish wars? Silence. Mystery." Bradley Dewey (in Lawson and Kramer, *Conversations*, p. 101) says Charles Percy was "a British naval lieutenant." William Delaney (in Lawson and Kramer, *Conversations*, p. 156), refers to "English-loyalist Americans like Charles Percy" who came to the Spanish territory "fleeing the Revolution."

3. William Alexander Percy (*Lanterns*, p. 39) says that the American wife was "an intelligent French lady from the other side of the river."

Baker (*The Percys*, p. 3) identifies her as "Susanna Collins." French on her mother's side, perhaps? William Alexander suggests that the suicide was an escape from the "commotion" created by the English wife. Baker's account mentions unspecified troubles with neighbors, and anxieties stemming from the French declaration of war against Spain in 1793.

4. Percy told John Griffin Jones (Lawson and Kramer, *Conversations*, p. 254) that after his father's suicide his mother first took the children to the maternal grandmother's home in Athens, Georgia, for a year, before moving with them in the summer of 1930 to Greenville, Mississippi.

5. "Ithaca"—the fictional hometown of Will Barrett, hero of *The Last Gentleman* and *The Second Coming*—has many features in common with Greenville. Percy's friend and fellow novelist Shelby Foote, also a Greenvillean, invented "Ithaca."

6. Coles (*Walker Percy*, p. 67) mentions D. H. Lawrence as one of the authors in whom Percy took an especially avid interest during the trip to the Southwest. See Coles also on Percy's earlier readings during his illness.

7. Coles, *Walker Percy*, p. 68.

8. Lawson and Kramer, *Conversations*, p. 268. In the interview with John Griffin Jones (1981), Percy and his wife had difficulty in agreeing on when it was they first met. Percy said 1941; Mrs. Percy thought it was about four years earlier, *before* he went to medical school.

9. In the interview with Jones (Lawson and Kramer, *Conversations*, p. 269), Percy explained that Mary was working for a doctor in New Orleans when they were married. After marriage, they went for about a year to the place in Sewanee, Tennessee, that had belonged to William Alexander Percy, were converted to Catholicism there, and then returned to New Orleans to live. The chronology page of Jac Tharpe's book on Percy in the Twayne series indicates that the Percys moved to Covington in 1950. (This book by Tharpe, see Bibliography, is referred to hereafter as Tharpe, *Walker Percy*, and is not to be confused with the edited volume *Walker Percy: Art and Ethics*, which is referred to hereafter as Tharpe, ed., *Percy: Art and Ethics*.)

10. Hobson, "Man vs. Malaise," p. 54.

11. LeRoy represented Mississippi for a short time in the U.S. Senate, filling out the unexpired term of Anselm McLaurin, who died in December, 1909. Baker, *The Percys*, chap. 3.

12. But see Lawson and Kramer, *Conversations*, the interview with John Griffin Jones, pp. 260–62. Walker Percy has little patience with latter-day "comfortable academic liberals" who would "denigrate what Will Percy did in the 1920s and '30s" as a champion of oppressed blacks in Mississippi. About the Percys as "aristocrats," see Lawson and Kramer,

Conversations, p. 91, and 251–52. When Barbara King referred in 1974 to someone who had used the term, Walker Percy responded: "Good God, I didn't know we *had* any aristocrats in this country." Talking to Jones in 1983, Percy himself suggested that "maybe [Senator LeRoy Percy] was too much of an aristocrat," but went on a moment later to comment on what a "tricky term" it is.

13. William Alexander Percy, *Lanterns*, pp. 304–5 and elsewhere.

14. See Lawson and Kramer, *Conversations*, pp. 179–81. In a mock interview with himself (1977) Percy refers to a portrait of him which hangs over the fireplace in a sitting room of his home. In the background of the painting is the representation of another framed painting, which we may gather from the context is another portrait of Percy. Percy the Answerer remarks: "I can only say what I see. The artist may very well disagree, but after all the subject and viewer is entitled to his own ideas— like a book reviewer. I identify the subject of the portraits as a kind of composite of the protagonists of my novels, but most especially Lancelot." But Percy the Questioner seems unable to keep his mind on what Percy the Answerer is saying, and the wise reader will remain wary of both.

15. Especially interesting, in connection with Percy's language studies, is his experience with a daughter who was born deaf. See Coles, *Walker Percy*, pp. 72–73.

16. See, for example, Percy's remarks to Barbara King, in Lawson and Kramer, *Conversations*, p. 91.

17. Coles, *Walker Percy*, pp. 62–63.

18. It appears that Percy was never sure just what his "uncle" expected of him. See Luschei, *Wayfarer*, p. 5, note; Baker, *The Percys*, pp. 178–79; Lawson and Kramer, *Conversations*, pp. 92, 152. Of related interest are Percy's remarks to Carlton Cremeens in their 1968 interview (Lawson and Kramer, *Conversations*, p. 26) on "the importance of a knowledge of science to any serious writer."

19. The terms "implied author" and "unreliable narrator" are borrowed, of course, from Wayne C. Booth's *The Rhetoric of Fiction* (see Bibliography), but in my frequent use of them throughout this book I have made no effort to adhere very rigorously to Booth's definitions. About authors, it seems to me the most important thing—by no means easy—is to try keeping clear the distinctions among 1) the implied author in each novel, whom ideally we can identify only on the basis of internal evidence, 2) the narrator or narrators, whether first-person or third-person, in the same novel, and 3) any or all of those Walker Percys who engage in such extra-novelistic activities as marrying and having children, writing philosophical essays and letters to newspaper editors (about fractious nuns and their

views on abortion, etc.), collecting royalties, and granting interviews. (The Walker Percy of the interviews, talking about his work, I have attempted to identify in various ways—e.g., as a "reader/discussant," or the "ex-author," of the novels bearing his name—that might help to distinguish him from the implied authors. But all this is, at best, tricky business; and the burden of proof is always on the critical rigorist.)

20. Coles, *Walker Percy*, pp. 65–66.

21. No very clear chronology can be established from the various accounts of Percy's readings in the philosophers and novelists. See Lawson and Kramer, *Conversations*, pp. 10–11, 12, 106–7, 136–37. In his 1967 interview with Ashley Brown, Percy referred to the "couple of enforced years in the Adirondacks," i.e., the years of his first hospitalization with tuberculosis, as the time "when [he] became interested in existentialism. [He] read Dostoevsky's *Notes from Underground* and then went on to Kierkegaard, some of whose books were being translated at the time." Percy said to Brown: "In somewhat this order I have read Kierkegaard, Heidegger, Gabriel Marcel, then Sartre and Camus." But in 1974 he told Bradley R. Dewey that it was the other way around, that he got interested in Kierkegaard through references to him in the writings of "the modern existentialists . . . [such as] Jaspers . . . Heidegger . . . Sartre . . . Marcel." In answer to Dewey's direct question—"Did you read any Kierkegaard in the sanatorium?"—Percy replied: "No. I was reading novels mostly, and linguistic philosophy. . . . The existentialism came later. Before that, I was much interested in Russian—European—novels, for example, Dostoevsky and Camus." Dewey, in his annotations, asserts that "after working through some philosophers of language, European novelists, and existentialists, Percy came to Kierkegaard in the early 1950s." The word "almost" in Dewey's next sentence—"It was almost their first *and last* meeting" (emphasis Dewey's)—is somewhat equivocal, but does not quite prepare the reader for the Marcus Smith interview in 1976, when Percy again said that he had worked his way "through two years of Dostoevsky, through Kierkegaard, into the French existentialist novelists and philosophers, Sartre and Marcel." The order here is much like that stated in the Brown interview nine years earlier.

22. Gabriel Marcel, in "Truth as a Value: The Intelligible Background," chapter 4 of *The Mystery of Being*, suggests that "the role of the drama, at a certain level, seems to be to place us at a point of vantage at which truth is made concrete to us, far above any level of abstract definitions." (See also my remarks, pursuant to Marcel's argument, on the novel as "a form both dramatic and reflective," in *Man and the Modern Novel*, p. 15. See Bibliography.) Patricia Lewis Poteat, in *Walker Percy and the Old Modern*

Age (see Bibliography), cogently argues that the presentation of Percy's philosophical ideas is often, in fact, clearer and more convincingly consistent in the novels than in the essays.

23. See, for example, Percy's remarks to Bradley R. Dewey (Lawson and Kramer, *Conversations*, pp. 125–26) on Sartre.

24. William Alexander Percy, *Lanterns*, p. 95.

25. Douglas, Percy's *"The Last Gentleman,"* p. 7.

26. See Percy's remarks to John Carr, in Lawson and Kramer, *Conversations*, pp. 70–71. Percy made it plain to Carr that he was none too happy about Ellen Douglas's attitude toward his and the earlier Percys' Catholicism.

27. Douglas, Percy's *"The Last Gentleman,"* p. 7.

28. Luschei (*Wayfarer*, p. 9) and Coles (*Walker Percy*, p. 69 and elsewhere) stress the Percy family tradition of hard work in honorable professions, a tradition which Walker might seem to have flouted when he abandoned his medical career.

29. Luschei, *Wayfarer*, p. 14.

30. See Tharpe, ed., *Percy: Art and Ethics*, for a bibliography of Percy's publications in periodicals up to 1979.

31. The previously published essays in the collected volume are not arranged in the chronological order of their appearances in periodicals. "Symbol as Need" is next to last in the table of contents. (The collection entitled *The Message in the Bottle*, see Bibliography, is hereafter referred to as Percy, *Message*.)

32. *Lost in the Cosmos: The Last Self-Help Book* (see Bibliography) is hereafter referred to as Percy, *Lost in the Cosmos*.

33. Coles (*Walker Percy*, p. 69ff.) tells of the happy "coincidence" of Percy's renting a house in New Orleans, in 1947, owned by the philosopher Julius Friend, who was co-author with James Feibleman of two books published in the thirties—*Science and the Spirit of Man* and *The Unlimited Community*—which showed the combined intellectual influences, both at the time equally unfashionable, of Peirce and Thomism.

34. See Lawson and Kramer, *Conversations*, p. 231, for an interesting exchange between Percy and Ben Forkner on language, religion, and the novel as a literary form that can "incorporate everything." Percy remarked that if Flannery O'Connor had been there to talk about the matter she would probably have taken the view "that the great virtue of the novel is that it describes man in transit, what Marcel called *homo viator*. She would look on the novel as the Judeo-Christian form par excellence."

35. Percy, *Message*, p. 167, note.

36. Percy, *Message*, p. 158.

37. Percy, *Lost in the Cosmos*, p. 168, p. 94 (in that order).

38. Percy, *Lost in the Cosmos*, p. 240. As Percy acknowledges in a footnote, p. 225, he is indebted, in "A Space Odyssey, II," to Walter M. Miller's novel *A Canticle for Liebowitz*.

39. William H. Poteat, "Reflections on Walker Percy's Theory of Language," in Panthea Reid Broughton, ed., *The Art of Walker Percy* (see Bibliography), hereafter referred to as Broughton, *Art of Walker Percy*.

40. See the exchange between Percy and Marcus Smith, in Lawson and Kramer, *Conversations*, p. 134. There the only specific example of a "responding organism" mentioned is "an anenome [*sic*] on a tidal flat"; but the context makes it clear that Percy believes the behavior of all "non-speaking" animals can be accounted for on "fairly adequate mechanistic models."

41. See note 22, above, on Patricia Poteat. She too, on another and much more sophisticated line of philosophical argument than mine, convicts Percy of covert behaviorism in his essays.

42. Jo Gulledge, "The Reentry Option: An Interview with Walker Percy" (Lawson and Kramer, *Conversations*, p. 285).

43. See Lawson and Kramer, *Conversations*, p. 235. Percy told J. Gerald Kennedy how in *The Second Coming* he moved Lost Cove Cave from Tennessee to North Carolina.

44. Walker Percy, "The Diagnostic Novel," *Harper's Magazine* (June 1986): 39–45.

45. Interview with John Carr, in Lawson and Kramer, *Conversations*, p. 64.

46. See Lawson and Kramer, *Conversations*, pp. 88–89, 124, 125, 242–43, and 279, for a variety of Percy's statements on religious, political, and social thinking and the art of fiction. Especially interesting is his acknowledgment (p. 124) of his indebtedness to Gerard Manley Hopkins for the poet's Catholic view of "nature . . . as a sacramental kind of existence." To J. Gerald Kennedy (pp. 242–43) he spoke of the "seductive" powers of narrative, and of how "you can do all kinds of subversive and polemical and satirical things" in the novel. To John Griffin Jones in 1983 (p. 279) he admitted that there was, after all, some truth to the view (which he attributed to John Gardner) that "art should be edifying . . . edifying in the best sense."

47. See my discussion of Binx's "unreliability," in chapter 2, part 3, and notes 11 and 12 for that chapter.

48. Lawson and Kramer, *Conversations*, p. 17.

49. Lawson and Kramer, *Conversations*, pp. 23, 157.

50. Lawson and Kramer, *Conversations*, p. 279.

51. Lawson and Kramer, *Conversations*, p. 286.

52. Lawson and Kramer, *Conversations*, p. 141.

53. Lawson and Kramer, *Conversations*, p. 212.

54. Lawson and Kramer, *Conversations*, p. 69.

55. In his interviews with John Carr and Barbara King (Lawson and Kramer, *Conversations*, pp. 69, 99) Percy denied any significant connection between his work and the older popular tradition of storytelling in the South. According to Cleanth Brooks in *The Language of the American South*, pp. 48–49 (see Bibliography), Percy is a master of Southern speech and the "manners and . . . maneuvers that regulate Southern conversation." Brooks remarks: "In [Percy's] work I find the Southern language—always fitted and adjusted to his own fictional purposes—alive, well, and vigorous."

56. The three writers discussed in Brinkmeyer's book (see Bibliography) are Allen Tate, Caroline Gordon, and Percy.

57. In 1972, Martin Luschei concluded his chapter on *Love in the Ruins* with a heartfelt "Hurrah for Walker Percy!" (Luschei, *Wayfarer*, p. 232). There is none of that tone in Brinkmeyer's study, or Patricia Poteat's, or Peter Hawkins's, or William Allen's, or in most of the other commentaries that have appeared in the eighties.

58. William Rodney Allen, *Walker Percy: A Southern Wayfarer* (see Bibliography), hereafter referred to as Allen, *Walker Percy*. See especially the index entries in Allen's book under the names of various American writers, and under "Father/son theme" and "Suicide." On autobiographical elements of the fiction and on Percy and Kierkegaard, recent studies by Ted Spivey and Jerome Taylor are of interest. (See Bibliography.)

2. *The Moviegoer*

1. Percy said to Jo Gulledge (Lawson and Kramer, *Conversations*, p. 300): "In a way, Binx Bolling is Quentin Compson who didn't commit suicide." Mary Thale (see Bibliography) sees the heroes of *The Moviegoer* and Nathanael West's *Miss Lonelyhearts* as two "20th century Rasselases [who have] faced the problem of 'the choice of life' and found that there is no happy way of life." On Binx and Jack Burden, see Allen, *Walker Percy*, pp. 35–36 and notes.

2. See my essay, "Percy and Place: Some Beginnings and Endings," Tharpe, ed., *Percy: Art and Ethics*, pp. 5–25.

3. See Luschei, *Wayfarer*, p. 76 and note. Luschei asserts cautiously that the landlady's name "could suggest the nadir of [Binx's] existence." In the footnote, he quotes Brainard Cheney's remark (*Sewanee Review* 69:693)

that the name means "she's nadir," and "obviously . . . is manufactured for ends of symbolism." Improbable as it may look at first glance, the name "Schexnaydre," a Frenchified rendering of a German name, is well known in south Louisiana. A recent Baton Rouge telephone directory contains—with slight variations in spelling, including the one Percy chose —some fifty listings of the surname. I once knew a priest of that name who would have been severely nettled by the suggestion that anyone had "manufactured" him for any purpose, but perhaps most especially for ends symbolic. See also Allen, *Walker Percy*, p. 25.

4. See Lewis Lawson, "Moviegoing in *The Moviegoer*" (in Tharpe, ed., *Percy: Art and Ethics*, pp. 26–42). Lawson provides in an endnote a well-annotated list of other articles on the subject.

5. See Percy's epigraph quotation from Kierkegaard, ". . . the specific character of despair is precisely this: it is unaware of being despair." Luschei and others have discussed at length the relevance of the quotation to Binx's experiences and observations, and the multiple ironies of his choice of a place of residence.

6. Luschei, *Wayfarer*, p. 65.

7. I use the word "snob" advisedly. Deriving from a dialectal word for "cobbler," shoemaker or shoemaker's apprentice, it was frequently used in the nineteenth century to designate, first, any ignorant fellow, member of the lower or working class—as opposed to a gentleman, or university man—and then, more precisely, any such fellow who *affected* manners, taste, or knowledge above his station. Many dictionaries gave this last as the primary or only definition of "snob" until fairly recently. My impression is that something close to definition two provided in *The American Heritage Dictionary* edition of 1969—"one who despises his inferiors and whose condescension arises from class or intellectual pretension," not pretension in the sense that there is no basis for a claim of superiority, but only that the claim is arrogantly asserted—had in common usage long since all but completely replaced definition one, "an arrogant or affected person who strives to flatter, imitate, or associate with people of higher station or prestige." It is gratifying to note that the Second College Edition of *American Heritage Dictionary* (1985) has caught up with the times, giving two definitions in both of which there is little trace of definition one in the 1969 edition. In 1985, "person of the lower classes" is designated as an obsolete definition. Binx, perhaps, is a super-snob, one who is a gentleman by right of paternal heritage and a "fellow" on his mother's side, and so ineffably conscious of his superiority that he can show it only by an affectation of self-effacement.

8. See chapter 1, note 19, above.

9. I should think that the make of the black man's automobile is meant to suggest, with a touch of indulgent skepticism on the implied author's part, something of the role of mysterious messenger in which Binx is tempted to cast the Negro. Percy's fascination in his fiction with all manner of vehicles—cars, buses, trains, boats, merry-go-rounds—is complex and pervasive. Cf. here, in the way of automobiles which are somehow mythic "attributes" of their owners, Binx's MG, Kate Cutrer's Plymouth, Sutter Vaught's Edsel, Forney Aiken's bottle-green Chevrolet, Uncle Fannin's De Soto, the middle-aged Will Barrett's Mercedes 450 SEL, and Tom More's old Chevrolet Caprice in *The Thanatos Syndrome*. The Trav-L-Aire, in *The Last Gentleman*, does not in quite the same way "belong" to any one person.

10. After emerging from the church, the black man sits behind the wheel of the Mercury looking down for a moment at something beside him on the front seat. "A sample case? An insurance manual?" Binx wonders (p. 235).

11. Binx tells us (p. 25) that his father "was commissioned in the RCAF in 1940 and got himself killed before his country entered the war." Let us assume that the year of the father's death was 1941. Binx continues (p. 26): "When my father was killed, my mother, who had been a trained nurse, went back to her hospital in Biloxi. My aunt offered to provide my education. As a consequence much of the past fifteen years has been spent in her house." If we count ahead fifteen years from 1941, we arrive at 1956 as the year of the novel's present-tense action. (Binx, who is thirty years old on the last day of the present-tense action, would have been fourteen or fifteen when his father was killed.) If, then, we count back four years for Binx's stay in Gentilly, plus two for the French Quarter (p. 6), we come up with 1950—which leaves us with a discrepancy of only one year in accounting for Binx's waking up (p. 10) with "the queasy-quince taste of 1951 and the Orient" in his mouth. But if we have to count back *eight* Gentilly years (pp. 41–42) from 1956, plus the two years for the French Quarter, we arrive at 1946 as the year of Binx's return from the war in Korea. In actuality, of course, following the North Korean army's invasion of South Korea, the first American combat troops joined forces with R.O.K. units near Osan in July of 1950; and, as we have noted, Binx himself recalls that he was wounded in 1951.

12. My guess is that Percy revised the novel, and Binx's life story, several times, combining and recombining various episodes in succeeding versions without due care to see that the narrative calendar was properly adjusted from stage to stage. Cf. Percy's comments to J. G. Kennedy (Lawson and Kramer, *Conversations*, pp. 229–30) on his problems with chronology in

The Second Coming, relative to events in *The Last Gentleman*. Percy admitted to Kennedy that he "hate[s] to go back and reread."

13. See Lawson and Kramer, *Conversations*, p. 64–65 (the interview with John Carr) and Luschei, *Wayfarer*, p. 102 and note. Emily is toying with a sword-shaped letter opener while she talks to Binx. "Years ago," Binx had "bent the tip trying to open a drawer" (*The Moviegoer*, p. 224). He notices that Emily too is looking at the damaged implement, and wonders whether she suspects anything. Luschei decides, on what grounds I cannot make out, that she "lacks the awareness even to observe" that the sword is bent.

14. Binx has told Kate (p. 57) that he is going to Magazine Street. That, presumably, is where the oyster bar is in which she finds him later (p. 60), after first having said that she would not join him.

15. *Kite-Flying and Other Irrational Acts*, edited by John Carr (hereafter referred to in the notes as Carr, ed., *Kite-Flying*), p. 65. (See Bibliography.) The version of the 1971 interview with Carr printed in Lawson and Kramer's *Conversations* does not contain the passage cited here.

16. Luschei, *Wayfarer*, pp. 105–6.

17. Luschei, *Wayfarer*, p. 106, quoting Kierkegaard, *Fear and Trembling*.

18. T. S. Eliot, *The Waste Land*, line 404.

19. Luschei, *Wayfarer*, p. 110.

20. Luschei, *Wayfarer*, p. 109. The phrase "the infinite passion" is Kierkegaard's.

21. Lawson and Kramer, *Conversations*, p. 66. In 1973, talking to Zoltan Abadi-Nagy, Percy said that "the ending [of *The Moviegoer*] is ambiguous. It is not made clear whether he [Binx] returns to his mother's religion or takes on his aunt's stoic values. But he does manage to make another life by going into medicine, helping Kate by marrying her. I suppose Sartre and Camus would look on this as a bourgeois retreat he had made." This statement, if not itself a "retreat" from the strong position he took with Carr, does show Percy in a rather surprisingly conciliatory frame of mind. But a few pages later, still with Abadi-Nagy, he is back to talking of what happened "when [Binx] regained his mother's religion," as if the basic fact of the reconversion were beyond dispute. Lawson and Kramer, *Conversations*, pp. 75, 83.

22. Carr, ed., *Kite-Flying*, p. 46. Again, part of the passage of the interview cited here does not appear in the version used by Lawson and Kramer in *Conversations*. See Bibliography, and note 15, above.

23. Wolfgang Iser, "Indeterminacy and the Reader's Response in Prose Fiction," in J. Hillis Miller, ed., *Aspects of Narrative*. Wolfgang Iser, *The Implied Reader*. (See Bibliography.)

24. See the discussions of "Senses," "Nature," and "Language" in Tharpe, *Walker Percy*, chapter 4.

25. Luschei, *Wayfarer*, pp. 15–16, quotes in a footnote the opening passages of *The Moviegoer* and *The Stranger* in support of his statement that "the voice in *The Moviegoer* owes a good deal to Albert Camus, as Percy has acknowledged, but it is impossible to miss the distinctive Percyan tone." Both novels begin with the narrator's receiving a message.

26. Lawson and Kramer, *Conversations*, p. 64, the interview with John Carr.

3. The Last Gentleman

1. It is somewhat more difficult, but not impossible, to distinguish between the narrator and the implied author. See chapter 1, note 19, above.

2. Cf. Gerard Manley Hopkins, "God's Grandeur," lines 4-8.

3. In 1986, a project for raising peregrine falcons was started on the campus of the University of Illinois at Chicago, ostensibly in the hope of reducing the city's pigeon population. On bird-and-people-watching in New York, see also Donald Knowler's *The Falconer of Central Park*. (See Bibliography.)

4. Ominous birds, a-wing and otherwise situated, figure prominently in all Percy's novels, attracting the more and less acute and knowledgeable attention of the heroes. Lance Lamar is not much of a bird-watcher, but his doings in the pigeonnier also belong to the larger pattern of prophetic significance in which all Percy's references to birds are involved. The pattern is often closely related to that of Percy's preoccupation with language, and is, of course, ultimately derived from classical mythology and the biblical writings, especially the prophetic books of the Old Testament, and the medieval and Renaissance literary traditions which draw upon the ancient sources. In earlier twentieth-century literature, the falcon most readers will think of in connection with Will Barrett's is probably William Butler Yeats's in "The Second Coming." Hopkins's "The Windhover," among nineteenth-century sources, also comes quickly to mind.

5. See my discussion of movies and moviegoing in chapter 2, part 2.

6. Luschei, *Wayfarer*, p. 167, gives Will an "outside chance" of making a go of marriage with Kitty. Percy, in various interviews dated both before and after publication of *The Second Coming*—in which it develops that Will did not marry Kitty—continues to maintain fairly consistently that the "probabilities" of the situation in *The Last Gentleman* were in favor of the marriage. See Lawson and Kramer, *Conversations*, pp. 48, 80, 205.

In 1971, talking to Charles Bunting, Percy said: "Of course [Will] married Kitty . . . and I think maybe he lived tolerably." In 1973 (?), to Zoltan Abadi-Nagy: "He probably went back to the South, married Kitty, and worked in the Chevrolet agency." In 1981(?), after *The Second Coming*, to Jan Nordby Gretlund: "The implication was that Will Barrett was going to go back to the South, probably marry Kitty, and probably go into business with the Vaughts. . . . That was the implication. —But he didn't." Jac Tharpe (*Walker Percy*, pp. 77, 105), although he finds the prospect somehow "either incomprehensible or impossible," and duly notes the revelations in *The Second Coming*, nonetheless continues to think that "the end of *The Last Gentleman* appeared to suggest" Will and Kitty would marry. It is, obviously, about the "probabilities"—or "implications," "suggestions"—in the earlier novel that I disagree with Luschei, Percy, and Tharpe. What we are told about Kitty and Will in *The Second Coming* does not prove me right and the others wrong on what is going on in *The Last Gentleman*. The two novels are two separate texts, each demanding a separate analysis of its internal order. In this connection, it is interesting to note Percy's remarks to J. G. Kennedy and John Griffin Jones (Lawson and Kramer, *Conversations*, pp. 229, 281) about the writing of *The Second Coming*: that he was a hundred pages or so into that novel before he decided (or "knew," or "realized") that the principal male character was Will Barrett. At first, Percy had given him another name.

7. Percy said to Ashley Brown in 1967 (?): "Barrett . . . has a passionate pilgrimage that he must follow, and he is looking for a father-figure" (Lawson and Kramer, *Conversations*, p. 13).

8. See chapter 2, note 9, above.

9. See my discussion, in chapter 1, of LeRoy Percy's and William Alexander Percy's attitudes toward blacks. Ed Barrett's attitude seems closer to LeRoy's than to William Alexander's. But it is in a number of important ways different from both.

10. Walker Percy, of course, was still a boy when his father committed suicide. It is possible, I suppose, that that memory affected his thinking about the father-son relationship at this point in *The Last Gentleman*.

11. Although it is difficult to make out from other evidence in the rambling reconstructive narrative just how old Will is supposed to be, the explicit statement at the end of chapter 1 (p. 41) can hardly be overlooked. Will has just paid his last visit to Dr. Gamow: "So it was that Williston Bibb Barrett once again set forth in the wide world at the age of twenty-five, Keats's age at his death, in possession of $8.35, a Tetzlar

telescope, an old frame house, and a defunct plantation." (It is less than a year later that he leaves the Vaughts' home and stops off at Ithaca on his way to Santa Fe.) Yet, in his re-reading of *The Last Gentleman* for purposes of trying to establish a plausible chronology in *The Second Coming*, Percy himself apparently managed somehow to miss this crucial passage in the earlier novel, for he told J. G. Kennedy: "[Will Barrett] was thirty years old when he went back to the South with the Vaughts" (Lawson and Kramer, *Conversations*, p. 229).

12. It should be noted (p. 393) that Val, impatient with Will's "solemn" protest that he is "not of [her] faith," challenges him then to "call a minister for God's sake"—i.e., instead of a priest—to baptize Jamie. But it seems to me that the challenge, followed immediately as it is by the peremptory alternative "or do it yourself," is meant only to clear the air of irrelevancies, not seriously to suggest that "a minister," of just any denominational persuasion, would serve as well "for God's sake" as either a Roman Catholic priest or Will himself could in the situation.

13. See Panthea Reid Broughton, "Gentlemen and Fornicators: *The Last Gentleman* and a Bisected Reality," in Broughton, *Art of Walker Percy*, pp. 96–114. This essay is especially noteworthy for its treatment of the role of Sutter Vaught as father figure, and of the significance of the word "wait" in that connection. See also Allen, *Walker Percy*, on father figures.

14. See note 8, above, and chapter 2, note 9, above.

15. Robert Penn Warren, "Pondy Woods," line 33. (See Bibliography.)

16. Luschei, *Wayfarer*, p. 165.

17. Broughton, "Gentlemen and Fornicators," p. 109.

18. Lawson and Kramer, *Conversations*, pp. 67–68. Although no doubt unintentional, the syntactical ambiguity in the final phrases of Percy's remarks—"becomes a believer, in his own rather laconic style"— is interesting as a clue to what may be the real nature of Binx's faith.

19. Lawson and Kramer, *Conversations*, p. 67.

20. Sutter tries to explain (p. 223) how "Jamie's baptism got lost in the shuffle" of his parents' denominational affiliations, and Will finds himself "scandalized by Sutter's perky, almost gossipy interest in such matters." The psychological basis of Will's sense of "scandal" is highly complex.

21. Lawson and Kramer, *Conversations*, pp. 67–68.

22. Luschei, *Wayfarer*, p. 163, notes that the phrase "contribution, however small" echoes Nell Lovell in *The Moviegoer* (p. 101). It may be worthwhile also to observe that when Will Barrett does speak to Sutter Vaught about the contribution that Sutter could make (*The Last Gentle-*

man, p. 387), the phrase is "an enormous contribution." Finally, there is the confusion worse confounded of Percy's exchange with John Griffin Jones (Lawson and Kramer, *Conversations*, p. 253). Author and interviewer have been talking about Senator LeRoy Percy's letter "to a fellow in Winona" in which LeRoy said something to the effect that "shooting for the stars has always been pretty poor marksmanship, it seemed to him, and he came later in his life to decide that a man had to be as good a man as he could be in his own little postage stamp corner of the world." Says Jones, ever so confidently, "I know Will Barrett in *The Last Gentleman* tells Sutter after Jamie dies that he ought to come back to the South and make a contribution, however small. Did you draw that parallel consciously? Did you have that in mind?" Says Percy, promptly and with remarkable generosity: "Yes, I had it in mind. That's pretty close reading. Nobody, I think, has ever picked up on that before." Whatever else either Percy or Jones might have subjected to "close reading," it was not the ending of *The Last Gentleman*.

4. *Love in the Ruins*

1. Northrop Frye, *Anatomy of Criticism* (see Bibliography), Fourth Essay, "Rhetorical Criticism: Theory of Genres."

2. Luschei, *Wayfarer*, p. 199 and note, on the strength of rather doubtful internal evidence and a letter from Percy, suggests a time "in the early nineties." But the case for 1983 is fairly firmly grounded in the series of dates provided in Tom More's reflections (*Love in the Ruins*, p. 57) on the sad history of race relations in the United States: "God, was it always the nigger business, now [1983?] just as in 1883, 1783, 1683. . . ."

3. John Huntington offers a valuable discussion of the terms *utopia*, *dystopia*, and *anti-utopia* in chapter 7 of *The Logic of Fantasy*. (See Bibliography.)

4. Luschei, *Wayfarer*, p. 189, note, mentions "Percy's [unpublished] apprentice novel *The Charterhouse*, where the golf course and country club had taken the place of the cathedral." Golf and golf courses figure prominently in both of the Will Barrett novels as well as in this one. It is not surprising to learn from Hobson, "Man vs. Malaise," p. 57, that Walker Percy, like Will Barrett, is a golfer as well as a bird-watcher.

5. See my discussion, in chapter 1, of Percy's essays on language.

6. William Butler Yeats, "The Second Coming," lines 21–22.

7. See chapter 3, notes 8 and 14, chapter 2, note 9, above.

8. Is there, in the complex allusional orchestration of the garden scene, a muted strain also of Virginia Woolf: Mr. Ramsay and Lily Briscoe on

"the blessed island of good boots?" (Virginia Woolf, "The Lighthouse," *To the Lighthouse*, Part 3, p. 230 [see Bibliography]).

9. See the earlier description of Father Smith's establishment (*Love in the Ruins*, p. 188). Luschei, *Wayfarer*, p. 115 and note, cites the influence of Joel Chandler Harris in Will Barrett's (*The Last Gentleman*) thoughts about his outcast state. Unquestionably, an allusion to the story of Br'er Rabbit and the Tar Baby is also implicit, and to much the same ironic effect, in Tom More's reflections on his situation as a member of Father Smith's little flock. In this novel, the allusion is also subtly relevant to More's involvement with the blacks.

10. See my essay "Percy and Place: Some Beginnings and Endings" (in Tharpe, ed., *Percy: Art and Ethics*, pp. 5–25) for a comment on the allusion to Clement Moore's "A Visit from St. Nicholas" in Tom More's anticipation of the "long winter's nap" he will have with Ellen.

5. *Lancelot*

1. See pp. 9–10, *Lancelot*, on the various names by which the present priest/psychiatrist has been known. With reference to the name of the family home—"Northumberland," which was also the name of Charles Percy's place (see my sketch of the family history in chapter 1)—some critics have seen the name "Percival" as involving a play on Walker Percy's own family name as well as the more obvious historical and literary allusions.

2. Robert Browning, "My Last Duchess."

3. Shakespeare, *Hamlet*, 2. 2. 405.

4. Jessie L. Weston, *From Ritual to Romance*. (See Bibliography.)

5. In her essay "*Lancelot* and the Medieval Quests of Sir Lancelot and Dante" (Tharpe, ed., *Percy: Art and Ethics*, p. 101), Corinne Dale notes in passing that "Lance is sometimes confused about the details of the quest for the Holy Grail: for example, he states that only two knights achieve the Grail, forgetting that Galahad, Sir Lancelot's son, is also successful," before she proceeds with her central argument that "the structural similarities in the two stories [of Lancelot Lamar and Sir Lancelot du Lac] are extensive." (See note 11, below.)

6. Sir Thomas Malory, "The Tale of the Sankgreal," book 13. (See Bibliography, and note 11, below.)

7. See Lance (p. 239) on the way Margot's "toes curled up and out . . . as a sign of her common Irish or country-Texas origins or both."

8. See Lewis A. Lawson's essay "The Fall of the House of Lamar" (in Broughton, *Art of Walker Percy*, pp. 234–35) for an interesting comment

on the Bowie knife and an ironic allusion to Malory in the incident
(*Lancelot*, p. 65) of Lance's unsuccessful effort to draw the knife out of
the wall with his left hand after he has driven it in with his right.

9. A "Creole" can be anything from an upperclass Peruvian of pure
Spanish ancestry, to a descendant of the original French settlers of Louisiana (as distinguishable from a "Cajun"), to a person of mixed white-
European and Negro ancestry whose forebears for a generation or more
have lived in the West Indies or adjacent territories, to a "native" Negro
of that area (including parts of the U.S. Gulf Coast) as distinguishable
from a Negro of direct African descent. The etymological evidence is
extremely complex. And usage is almost as wildly inconsistent with respect to cookery as it is with respect to people. Various companies of
purist experts will argue endlessly over the precise blend of bloodlines or
spices that may be properly called "Creole." (See *OED*, *American Heritage Dictionary*, *Encyclopedia Britannica*, etc., and talk to literary people,
professional and amateur chefs and cultural historians black and white,
and assorted other friends from Pascagoula, Mobile, Baton Rouge, St.
Gabriel, Paincourtville, New Orleans, Scarsdale, Belize, Chicago, Dear-
born, and Reeves.)

10. See chapter 1, note 12, above, on Walker Percy's varied reactions to
questions about his own family and the definition of an "aristocrat."

11. Tennyson's "The Holy Grail" (see Bibliography) resembles Malory's
narrative in very few particulars. But the two substantially agree in identifying Galahad as the only one who achieves the final vision, and, in so
doing, or as an immediate consequence, ascends into heaven. In Malory's
rather low-keyed account of the affair (book 17)—"And so suddeynly
departed hys soule to Jesu Cryste, and a grete multitude of angels bare hit
up to hevyn evyn in the syght of hys two felowis." The "two fellows" are
Bors and Percival. In Malory, they and Galahad are the only three who
are permitted to enter the "cite of Sarras," where at length Galahad is
invited by "Joseph of Aramathy" to see what he has sought so long to see,
and accepting, "began to tremble ryght harde whan the dedly fleysh began
to beholde the spirituall thynges." The point that Lancelot is *not* among
the finalists in the quest is abundantly clear from the commission given to
Bors by Galahad just before his ascent into heaven: "'My fayre lorde
salew me unto my lorde sir Launcelot, my fadir, and as sone as ye se hym
bydde hym remembir of this worlde unstable.'" In Tennyson's poem,
Percivale tells of how he "yearn'd to follow"—but, weakened we may
assume by the effects of pride, was unable to keep pace—as he saw Galahad pursue the vision of the Grail out across the mystical burning bridges,
while "thrice above him all the heavens / Open'd and blazed with thunder

such as seem'd / Shoutings of all the sons of God," and at last soar aloft in a kind of ethereal boat, "if boat it were." In any event, Lancelot is not present even to witness his son's glorification. It is interesting, at least incidentally, to reflect upon what might be made of Lance Lamar's much-experienced bisexual son as a parody of Galahad, that "clene mayde."

12. Cf. Binx Bolling's reference (*The Moviegoer*, p. 13) to the kind of movie in which "a fellow come[s] to himself in a strange place . . . [and] takes up with the local librarian." The manner of the "taking up" in the Merlin/Jacoby movie marks it distinctly as belonging to a later era of film history.

13. After witnessing Galahad's death, the ascent of his soul into heaven, and the burial of the body, the legendary Percival entered the religious life: as Malory has it (book 17) "yelded hym to an ermytayge oute of the cite, and toke religious clothyng."

14. In talking to Jan Nordby Gretlund (Lawson and Kramer, *Conversations*, p. 208) about what went into the making of Lancelot's image of the young revolutionary, Percy mentioned a Confederate soldier, Robert Jordan of *For Whom the Bell Tolls*, and "a young Nazi storm-trooper," revealing that he (Percy) had "spent a summer in Germany in 1934," and "lived with a family in Bonn [of which] the father was a member of the S.A., *Schutz Abwehr* [*sic*], and the son was a member of *Hitlerjugend*." Percy went on to Gretlund: "I remember this young *Hitlerjugend* was very excited about the possibilities of the future. There was nothing about the Jews at the beginning. I had all this in mind when I thought of a young man standing in a pass of Massanutten mountain. Lancelot is a conscious combination of something quite positive and quite evil." And further: "Maybe I was also thinking of Gabriel Marcel, he is French, a Jew, a Catholic convert, who had the nerve to say: we tend to overlook something positive about the mass movements. It is easy to say how wrong they were. It is easy to overlook the positive things: the great sense of verve and vitality." It is hard, on the other hand, to tell where the ostensible paraphrase of Marcel leaves off in this disturbing speech, and hard to overlook the historical facts: e.g., that in 1933, the year before Percy's visit, Jews were officially barred from government service, the universities, and many professions, and Hitler's uniformed thugs were already in the streets proclaiming a boycott of Jewish businesses. Of course, it is easy to understand how an idealistic, eighteen-year-old visitor from the United States, charmed by the "verve and vitality" of his forward-looking Aryan hosts, might not have noticed all these unpleasant goings-on. Still, Gretlund's taking the earliest opportunity to retreat to questions about Lance Lamar and "the values of the old South" comes as a welcome relief.

15. See Jerome C. Christensen, "*Lancelot*: Sign for the Times," in Tharpe, ed., *Percy: Art and Ethics*, pp. 107–20.

16. Ibid.

17. Margot put people to work (*Lancelot*, p. 18) "scraping off 150 years of pigeon shit" from the floor of the pigeonnier to convert the place into a study for Lance, an undertaking in which she supervises as a kind of Lady Hercules. It is never quite clear just how or where Lance hopes to enlist qualified help for his heroic project. In the final paragraph of his article "The Omega Factor: Apocalyptic Visions in Walker Percy's *Lancelot*" (see Bibliography), Gary M. Ciuba follows up the ironic implications of Lancelot Lamar's middle name, "Andrewes," to remind the reader of the seventeenth-century Anglican divine's "Sermon on the Nativity, 1611," in which he preached on the mystery of the Incarnation, the "good news" that "the word is now become flesh"—news, Ciuba argues, which Lance Lamar is unprepared to proclaim because "for [him] flesh has become filthy." On the other hand, according to Ciuba, the reader should recognize Lance's visitor—"Percival," or "Father John"—as fully qualified bearer of the glad tidings.

6. The Second Coming

1. See also the use of the word "come" as summons, in the title essay of *The Message in the Bottle*, p. 133ff.

2. Percy has expressed to a number of interviewers his own satisfaction with the representation of a joyous and redemptive love in this novel. See, for example, his talk with Marc Kirkeby (Lawson and Kramer, *Conversations*, p. 91): "Maybe for the first time I saw the possibility of a clear resolution, a classical, novelistic resolution, a victory of eros over thanatos and life over death. . . . I like to think, half seriously, that this may be the first unalienated novel written since Tolstoy."

3. The question of who fathered Allison is not overtly dealt with in Percy's comments to J. G. Kennedy (Lawson and Kramer, *Conversations*, pp. 229–30) about the problems with the fictional chronology that came up when Percy "realized," well into work on *The Second Coming*, that the hero was Will Barrett, who had appeared in *The Last Gentleman* as a much younger man. (See chapter 3, note 11, above.)

4. Will's attraction to Allie is in some respects—the age differential and the fascination with suffering and abnormality, in association with a rare problem of communication—disquietingly like that of Lance Lamar to Anna. We must trust that Percy was only kidding when he remarked to James Atlas (Lawson and Kramer, *Conversations*, p. 183) that the story in

The Second Coming is "a very ordinary, conventional story that could even be seen in Hollywood terms: Boy meets girl, boy loses girl, and boy gets girl." Perhaps he had in mind the new conventions, of "Hollywood" since the mid-seventies. In that case, the remark is indeed witty.

5. Percy said to Marc Kirkeby (Lawson and Kramer, *Conversations*, pp. 190–91): "I don't know where [Allison] came from . . . but I feel happier with her than with any other female in my books. I receive complaints about my books from women, who say to me I don't know anything about women, which I'm the first person to admit. But Allison pleases me very much." No doubt. But talk of such pleasure has not appeased, and almost surely was not meant to appease, both the men *and* women who have found fault with his other portraits of females.

6. Percy said to Ben Forkner (Lawson and Kramer, *Conversations*, pp. 228–29): "I wanted Allie to start off afresh with language. . . . I was trying to get her to use schizophrenic speech in the same discovering way of metaphor as a two-year-old child, so that she actually rediscovers language all over again." In answer to a question from Forkner about schizophrenia and Allison's habit of rhyming, Percy answered: "Yes, they (schizophrenics) do rhyme words."

7. Percy's repeatedly expressed confidence (e.g., Lawson and Kramer, *Conversations*, pp. 190, 204, the interviews with Kirkeby and Gretlund) that the ending of *The Second Coming*, unlike the endings of his earlier novels, is "not ambiguous," that "it is absolutely clear what Will Barrett is going to do" (i.e., about himself and Allie), showed signs of weakening as early as the talk with J. G. Kennedy (Lawson and Kramer, *Conversations*, p. 235). Percy said: "I think at the end . . . [Will Barrett in *The Second Coming*] actually sees a way to live and to work, and [Allie] does too. I mean, I do believe that I actually came on a happy ending." In fact, final doubts are warranted on a number of questions, only the first of them that of whether Will and Allie will be married.

8. After his inconclusive adventures in Lost Cove Cave (see chapter 1, note 43, above), Will may be seen as exploring, more successfully, the mysterious cave of Allison herself, rejoicing with her in the exquisite difficulty, the ecstatic "fit," of achieving a "fit" of his body into hers (p. 327) —as emblematic of the perilous union of flesh and spirit that is the human state. Both Lost Cove Cave and the cave of Allison's body, like Lancelot's cell, may also be regarded as metaphors of the book itself.

9. T. S. Eliot, "East Coker," II.

10. T. S. Eliot, "Choruses from *The Rock*," III.

11. Gerard Manley Hopkins, "Pied Beauty."

12. See chapter 2, note 9, chapter 3, notes 8, 14, and chapter 4, note 6,

above. In connection with Will's and his father's attitudes toward the Germans and Nazism, see chapter 5, note 14, on Percy's recollections of his visit to Germany in 1934.

13. Little is revealed in *The Second Coming* to account for the fact that Sutter did not commit suicide after Jamie's death (in *The Last Gentleman*).

14. Among earlier modern novels of which Percy must have been to some extent conscious in writing of the cave in *The Second Coming* are E. M. Forster's *A Passage to India* and Robert Penn Warren's *The Cave*.

15. Cf. the mordant and morbid humor of Tom More's self-mocking vision of "the new Christ" in the bar mirror at The Little Napoleon, *Love in the Ruins*, p. 153.

16. In St. John's gospel, Jesus does not explicitly instruct Mary either to say or not to say that she has seen him, but only to tell his disciples that the Ascension is imminent. In any event, Mary does tell the disciples that she has seen him. In *The Second Coming*, Will instructs Allison to summon Dr. Battle to the greenhouse (p. 245).

17. Gerard Manley Hopkins, "Spring," lines 10–11.

18. Percy told Ben Forkner (Lawson and Kramer, *Conversations*, p. 236) that he "made up" not only the syndrome and its name, but "a treatment for it [which] might work—with hydrogen ions." It turned out, according to Percy, that there actually is such a syndrome—called "temporal-lobe epilepsy"—about which a "doctor friend" sent him an article. (The "doctor friend" is presumably the neurologist referred to in the interview with Henry Kisor, Lawson and Kramer, *Conversations*, p. 195. The neurologist, Percy said, had "read the manuscript" of the novel.)

19. Arnold Stein, *Answerable Style: Essays on "Paradise Lost"*. (See Bibliography.)

20. Allison herself is a "sign." She is also, on several occasions, attended by signs. Although Will himself (p. 51) thinks that in middle age he has outgrown that "time when he believed there were fabulous birds," the reader who is mindful both of the preceding events of chapter 2 in this novel and of the opening scenes of *The Last Gentleman* will recognize in the diving hawk (*The Second Coming*, pp. 40, 51, 70) a sign, portent, of the hero's imminent meeting with Allison. Presumably, the important difference between the situations in the two novels is that the pursuit of Kitty in the earlier story turns out to be mostly a distraction from the spiritual search portended by the fabulous bird, while in the case of Allison "girl search" and "God search" seem finally to coincide.

21. Paul Gray, *Time*, July 14, 1980, pp. 53–54.

22. See Lawson and Kramer, *Conversations*, p. 236. Percy complained

to Ben Forkner and J. G. Kennedy that "some of the reviewers [of *The Second Coming*] were unfair" in saying that "all [his] characters are loafers, [that] they don't do anything." Will Barrett, Percy protested, "had worked very hard and had done exactly what he was supposed to do: he'd gone to college, to law school, he worked for a firm, made a lot of money, married a rich girl. I mean, it's the American success story." Nothing could better express Percy's failure to understand the difference between *choosing* to work hard—for "success," and "a lot of money"—and *having* to work, for a living.

23. Will Barrett is extraordinarily sensitive, often with excruciatingly ambivalent feelings of attraction and repulsion, to physical contact, or the near prospect of such contact, with virtually everyone he encounters. And Allison exhibits much the same tendencies. In immediate connection with the references to the Apostolic Succession and the ritual "laying on of hands," it is especially important to note that Will himself, in his final conversation with Father Weatherbee, almost violently lays hands on the old man, "gripp[ing] . . . [his] wrists as if he were a child." The perilous balance of emotions involved here is somewhat reminiscent of that I have observed in a crucial episode of Eudora Welty's *The Optimist's Daughter*, where the ambiguous expression "laid hands on him" is used. See my essay, "Marrying Down in Eudora Welty's Novels," in *Eudora Welty: Critical Essays*, edited by Peggy Whitman Prenshaw. (See Bibliography.)

24. Lawson and Kramer, *Conversations*, p. 64. By "preacher," I assume from the context that Percy means an ordained minister, Protestant clergyman. But the distinction he tries to draw between "preacher" and "apostle"—since the original apostles, "messengers," were commissioned precisely to go and preach the gospel—is by no means clear to me.

25. When Will tells Father Weatherbee that he is not a member of St. John's congregation or of the Episcopal Church (p. 357), and then goes on to explain that Allison is "not a member of this or any church," we might be tempted to infer that he, on the other hand, already *is* a member of some church. But there is no evidence elsewhere in the novel to support the suggestion. (See also chapter 3, note 12, above.)

26. On a number of issues, the English and the American Episcopal churches have long had better relations with the Eastern churches than with Rome. The See of Constantinople formally recognized the validity of Anglican orders in 1922. Since Maronite Catholics are subject to Rome, Curl's choice of conferees for the Hilton Head meeting might be seen as a canny maneuver to involve the Latin-rite authorities without directly notifying them at the outset—a specific example, no doubt, of "the sort of damn fool thing God might favor."

27. Will Barrett is obsessed with the notion that the Jews are leaving North Carolina. One might wonder if an exodus of Roman Catholics is not also in progress. In *Love in the Ruins*, (see chapter 4, note 9, above), even after the Bantu takeover, Father Smith's little band of South Louisiana Roman loyalists retain at least shared rights (with Jews and various Protestants) to use of the tinroofed chapel in the briarpatch. In the North Carolina of *The Second Coming*, it is hard to tell where if anywhere the "ordinary" Catholics might be meeting. Maybe they have all taken up with the Maronites.

28. See above, chapter 3, notes 6 and 11, and note 3 for this chapter, on Percy's somewhat belated "realization" that the hero of *The Second Coming* was Will Barrett, whom he had introduced as a young man in *The Last Gentleman*.

29. Lawson and Kramer, *Conversations*, p. 67.

30. In other contexts, "authoritative" may be virtually synonymous with "unequivocal." But equivocation is the fictional norm. (See my remarks on authors in chapter 1, note 19, above.)

31. It is interesting that Percy, in talking to John Griffin Jones (Lawson and Kramer, *Conversations*, p. 280) did not make the exception for *The Second Coming* that he had tried with more and less confidence to establish in his comments to Kirkeby, Gretlund, and Kennedy (see note 7, above), but acknowledged his critics' complaint that his novels "all end indecisively," asserted that the effect "is very deliberate," and concluded: "They'd be in big trouble if they ended decisively." Of course, Percy's point here is not precisely identical with mine. Robert H. Brinkmeyer, Jr. (*Three Catholic Writers*, p. 168) finds the conclusion of *The Second Coming* "flawed by sentimentality," especially in the episode of Will's rescue of the old men from St. Mark's—"all is rosy, as the deserving elderly help the new lovers with their idealistic projects"—but still asserts that the "happy ending resolves many of the disturbing issues Percy has raised here and in his other works about man's existential dilemmas."

7. The Thanatos Syndrome

1. The region includes fictionalized versions of the now-existing Louisiana parishes (counties) of East Feliciana and West Feliciana, but is much larger than their combined territories. "Here's Feliciana, from the Mississippi to the Pearl, from the thirty-first parallel to . . . Lake Pontchartrain" (p. 153). See also, in the italicized headnote to *The Moviegoer*, Percy's remarks concerning the "Feliciana Parish" of which Binx Bolling is a native.

2. William Allen (*Walker Percy*, p. 80) simply asserts, without explanation, that the year of the principal action of *Love in the Ruins* is 1983.

3. It is, however, extremely difficult to calculate the children's ages as well. Tommy with the soccer ball (p. 38) acts like a junior high schooler, it seems to me. But his responses to his father's and Lucy Lipscomb's questions about the "treat-a-treat" and "sardines" games at Belle Ame (pp. 224–25) are hardly worthy of a bright seven-year-old.

4. For references to Walker Percy's early thoughts of becoming a psychiatrist, his acquaintance with Sullivan, and Sullivan's recommendation that he consult Dr. Janet Rioch, see Baker, *The Percys of Mississippi*, p. 178, and Allen, *Walker Percy*, p. 14. On the life (including the "many troubles" that Tom More mentions, p. 17), the work and ideas, and the influence of Sullivan, see A. H. Chapman, *Harry Stack Sullivan: His Life and His Work*; Gerard Chrzanowski, *Interpersonal Approach to Psychoanalysis: Contemporary View of Harry Stack Sullivan*; and Helen Swick Perry, *Psychiatrist of America: The Life of Harry Stack Sullivan*. Chrzanowski's book is especially useful for discussion of the importance of Sullivan's idea of the Self. (See Bibliography.) The passage in *Love in the Ruins* concerning Ellen's celebration of Tom More's forty-fifth birthday (pp. 155–57) is of further interest, in a retrospective view from *The Thanatos Syndrome*, for its concern with the problems of child and adult sexuality, and with the persistence of individual human identity—the unique self—throughout the process of physical aging. See also my remarks earlier in this chapter on More's age and his claim to having served a residency under Sullivan.

5. See Hobson, "Man vs. Malaise," p. 54. The Bogue Falaya, I believe, empties into the Tchefuncte River, somewhere down in those obscure parts, and thence into Lake Pontchartrain.

6. See p. 133, "Take to the blue highways, skirting Baton Rouge. . . ." The allusion is to William Least Heat Moon's *Blue Highways: A Journey into America* (see Bibliography). Lesser highways are marked in blue on many older roadmaps.

7. T. S. Eliot, "The Dry Salvages," line 2.

8. See note 9 for chapter 1, Introduction, and later references to Percy's characters and their automobiles.

9. See *The Moviegoer*, pp. 3–5, and my discussion of the passage in chapter 2, above.

10. Percy makes frequent references in his novels, including this one, to detective stories. I have mentioned in the Introduction the essay on S. S. Van Dine he wrote during his college years. Recently ("There's a Contra in My Gumbo," *New York Times Book Review*, January 4, 1987, p. 7)

he reviewed Elmore Leonard's *Bandits*, a detective story with a New Orleans setting. Beginning with a reference to Raymond Chandler, one of his all-time favorites, Percy discusses the liberties Leonard has taken with the genre. For information on fiction with psychiatrist/detective heroes, consult Steinbrunner, *Detectionary*. (See Bibliography.)

11. Edward and Lavinia Chamberlain and Dr. Harcourt-Reilly are characters in T. S. Eliot's *The Cocktail Party* (see Bibliography). The play is based to some extent on the *Alcestis* of Euripides. Besides those of priest and psychiatrist, Harcourt-Reilly has also some of the characteristics of a "private eye." There are, of course, many priests as well as medical doctors of one sort and another among the well-known characters of detective literature.

12. See *Love in the Ruins*, p. 155, and *The Thanatos Syndrome*, p. 161.

13. The militantly anti-religious Comeaux is so overcome with gratitude at the news of Ricky's deliverance (p. 331) that he twice inadvertently uses the name of Jesus, and first exclaims "Thank God" before acknowledging, almost as an afterthought, Tom's part in the matter.

14. Van Dorn's reference to "Hadacol juice" (p. 216) is a somewhat anachronistic "in-joke" calculated to verify his familiarity with Louisiana folklore. Hadacol (I don't know whether a product of the same name is still being marketed) was a patent medicine, at the height of its popularity in the early 1950s, manufactured and promoted by a well-known Louisiana business man and state legislator. The elixir was generally credited with the power, if not to cure all ills, at any rate to make you feel a lot better no matter what ailed you. There were hundreds of "Hadacol" jokes and stories going about at the time.

15. Mark Twain, *The Adventures of Huckleberry Finn*, chapter 33, p. 222 in the Bantam Books edition (see Bibliography).

16. See Leviticus 16:7–26, in the King James Bible, where the word "scapegoat" appears, carried over from the earlier English translation by William Tindale, who, as the *Oxford English Dictionary* explains, apparently "invented" the word as an effort at literal translation of the Hebrew. *American Heritage Dictionary*, while failing to mention Tindale, provides a somewhat clearer statement of the etymological tactic as follows: "[(E)SCAPE + GOAT, as transl. of Heb. *azāzēl*, goat of Azazel, construed as *ēz-ōzēl*, goat that *escapes*]." As *OED* puts it, Tindale's construction has been deemed "untenable" by modern scholars, and the word *scapegoat* does not appear in the so-called Revised Version of the English Bible of 1884 and succeeding editions of that work. Instead, *Azazel* is used as a proper name, in such passages as that of Leviticus 16:6, where we read of the live goat that is to be "sent away into the wilderness to

Azazel." Apparently, Percy/More used either some edition of the Revised Version or other modern English translation for his note, rather than the King James Bible, since the proper name *Azazel* does not appear in the latter.

17. Richmond Y. Hathorn's *Greek Mythology*, XI.3, p. 162 (see Bibliography) offers a concise commentary on ancient ritual involving human "scapegoats," and an explanation of how they got their Greek name of *pharmakoi*. It is curious that Percy, in the set-off passage on Azazel at the end of part 1 (p. 64), does not mention the crucial ceremonial described in verses 21–22 of Leviticus 16: "And Aaron shall lay both his hands upon the head of the live goat [the scapegoat], and confess over him all the iniquities of the children of Israel, and all their transgressions in all their sins, putting them upon the head of the goat, and shall send *him* away by the hand of a fit man into the wilderness: And the goat shall bear upon him all their iniquities unto a land not inhabited: and he shall let go the goat in the wilderness." (I am quoting here from the King James Bible; differences between this and the Revised Standard Version text of these verses are negligible.) Without knowing that the goat first has the sins of the people put upon his head before he makes his "escape" into the wilderness, the reader of Percy's novel might identify Comeaux, rather than Van Dorn, as the scapegoat. But Comeaux, it is important to note, gets away not only without being prosecuted, but with virtually no reproaches, from More or anyone else. As More explains the strategy he has decided upon (p. 332): "Don't shoot Bob Comeaux. Use him." And, he adds a moment later, "blame Van Dorn for now."

18. The one brief document on which the whole false theory is chiefly based—an informal memorandum from Hitler addressed to his chief of chancellery, Philipp Bouhler, and his personal physician and Reich Commissioner for Health, Dr. Karl Brandt—was, it appears, written long after meetings of psychiatrists had already been held to work out the "euthanasia" programs, and clearly does not, Wertham argues, "give the order to kill, but the *power* to kill . . . something very different." (*A Sign for Cain: An Exploration of Human Violence*, by Frederic Wertham, M.D. —hereafter referred to as Wertham, *A Sign for Cain*—pp. 164, 166. See Bibliography.) Wertham's distinction between "the order to kill" and "the power to kill" is roughly analogous to the one Tom More makes in pointing out to Max Gottlieb and Bob Comeaux that "the law of the land [in the fictional United States of their time] does not require gereuthanasia of the old [sic] or pedeuthanasia of pre-personhood infants [but] only permits it under certain circumstances." For more recent discussion of the Nazi mass-murderers, and of the problem of "understanding" them, con-

sult Robert Jay Lifton's *The Nazi Doctors* (see Bibliography) and Bruno Bettelheim's somber review of that book in *The New York Times Book Review*, October 5, 1986, pp. 1, 61–62.

19. The real-life model for Tom's and Lucy's common ancestor (pp. 136, 348), down to the detail of his drowning himself with a sugar kettle tied to his neck, is obviously Charles Percy, the eighteenth-century founder of Walker Percy's family whom I have mentioned here in the Introduction and in the notes for subsequent chapters. On Percy's 1934 trip to Germany, see my remarks in note 14 for chapter 5, above.

20. Ludovic Kennedy's *The Airman and the Carpenter* (1985, see Bibliography) is one of the recent studies of the Lindbergh kidnapping case that might have attracted Percy's attention while he was working on *The Thanatos Syndrome*. Kennedy's book contains a good bibliography, including Anthony Scaduto's *Scapegoat: The Lonesome Death of Bruno Richard Hauptmann*, a title suggesting still another central theme of *The Thanatos Syndrome*. It is further worth noting: 1) that the surrealist mirror in Leroy Ledbetter's bar, in which Tom More now catches a glimpse of himself in the "Bruno Hauptmann suit" (p. 55), is the same glass that once showed him (*Love in the Ruins*, pp. 151–53) as a "dim hollow-eyed Spanish Christ . . . the new Christ, the spotted Christ, the maculate Christ, the sinful Christ" (Christ Himself being, of course, the supreme "scapegoat" figure of all time); 2) that More was once a business partner of the racist Ledbetter (see my discussion of the matter in chapter 4, above); 3) that the reference (*The Thanatos Syndrome*, p. 55) to Hauptmann's execution "fifty years ago" further obscures the question of dating the action in this novel. Perhaps "fifty" is either a "round number" or a misprint for "sixty." Otherwise, since Bruno Hauptmann was executed in 1936, the arithmetic yields 1986 as the year of *The Thanatos Syndrome*, a solution that makes no sense at all with reference to *Love in the Ruins*.

21. St. Simeon (the usual spelling) was a Syrian ascetic born about 390. He died in 459, and was buried in Antioch. He is reputed to have stayed most of the time for the last twenty years of his life on an open-topped tower some fifty feet high. (Father Smith, p. 360, says it was forty feet. Other authorities put it at fifty and still others at as much as sixty. Apparently, he kept building it higher and higher over the years.) On his frightful perch, he stood all the while, night and day, exposed to all weathers, eating virtually nothing and praying constantly except when he preached to the crowds of penitents gathered below, or gave them advice for settling their disputes and consoled the sick and the sorrowful. It is little wonder that Father Smith, what with his relatively cozy situation in the fire tower lookout room, should feel in every sense mortified in all his

efforts to follow such an example. The very fact that Smith's watchtower is forty to sixty feet higher than St. Simeon's retreat is somehow a put-down, a reminder to Smith, shall we say, of the *vanity* of his ascetic wishes. Father Smith's apocalyptic leanings, together with his choice of living quarters, is obviously meant to remind the reader of the title of the well-known journal published by Jehovah's Witnesses.

22. Matthew 16:15–19.

23. In *Lancelot*, the man called "Percival" is both ordained priest and licensed psychiatrist, and, so it would seem at the beginning, a failure in both roles.

24. Asceticism is also commonly regarded by psychologists as a form of what Karl Menninger (in *Man Against Himself*, see Bibliography) called "chronic suicide," and in a case like that of St. Simeon might well involve self-punishment, and a kind of elaborately dramatized "justification," for exhibitionist tendencies. In any event, the fact that Father Smith has re-vealed a suicidal bent in a number of different ways—including, of course, the alcoholism that is so important in his friendship with Tom More—lends a peculiar poignancy to the answer he gives (p. 257) to Tom's question about why he became a priest: "In the end, one must choose—given the chance—. . . life or death. What else?"

25. Oliver Sacks's fascinating article "Tics," in *The New York Review of Books* for January 29, 1987, pp. 37–41, while centrally and specifically concerned with a history of the study of "Tourette's syndrome," argues first and last, on the basis of that history, that "neuropsychiatry is an old term which needs a new meaning . . . [a] meaning [that] has to do with the dynamics, the activities, of brain-mind—unlike biological psychiatry and behavioral neurology, which are static, diagrammatic—phrenology in new clothes." (Sacks's punctuation here, p. 41, with the use of the long dashes, unfortunately creates an impression of syntactical ambiguity. But, in the total context of the article, the meaning is clear: that it is "biological psychiatry and behavioral neurology" which he is calling "phrenology in new clothes.") Moreover, Sacks asserts with characteristic optimism that "the time is ripe" for emergence of the "new neuropsychiatry." The idea of our need for such a science is certainly one with which Tom More would be generally sympathetic. The "Tics" article appeared, of course, after *The Thanatos Syndrome* was written. But the main point of that essay is implicit in earlier writings by Sacks with which Percy may or may not be familiar. As most "common readers" these days probably would, I think of Sacks also in connection with such matters as the repeated refer-ences in *The Thanatos Syndrome* to the mentality of the *idiot savant*: see chapter 23, "The Twins," of Sacks's collection *The Man Who Mistook*

His Wife for a Hat. (See Bibliography.) Some of Sacks's observations on the remarkable twins and their prime-numbers game, etc., as well as other pieces in the collected volume, were published earlier in periodicals.

26. Percy speaks only of "Christina in Wyeth's painting" (p. 6). Andrew Wyeth did several paintings of Christina Olson, but I take it from the context that the one Percy has in mind in this first reference is the much-reproduced *Christina's World*. The real-life Christina was a polio victim, the skeletal condition of her limbs presumably an effect of that disease, not an anorexia such as Mickey LaFaye falls into from time to time. In connection with the identity theme in Tom More's report of Mickey's case, it is interesting to note that Wanda M. Corn, *The Art of Andrew Wyeth* (p. 38), quotes Wyeth as saying that in his work on *Christina's World* he got Christina to sit briefly for a drawing of her "crippled arms and hands," but that "finally, [he] was so shy about posing her, [he] got [his] wife Betsy to pose for her figure." In his repeated references to Mickey as a "Duchess of Alba," I assume from the general context that Percy has at least chiefly in mind Goya's famous pair of paintings (for which it is popularly supposed the Duchess was the model) *The Maja Clothed* and *The Maja Nude*, although in neither of these is the woman posed as Mickey is, back turned to the viewer and "full round arm lying along sumptuous curve of hip," when Tom More walks into the room (p. 9). But again, if I am right about which painting(s) Percy has reference to, there is an interesting question about the total identity of the model. José Gudiol, *Goya* (p. 108), remarks that in *The Maja Clothed* the woman's "turgid, well-modeled form . . . follows as closely as possible the structure of *The Maja Nude* . . . intimately outlined by her closely fitted dress." On the other hand, Kenneth Clark argues in *The Romantic Rebellion* (p. 75) that the Duchess of Alba "was not . . . the model" for *The Maja Nude*, and that the principal evidence for his assertion is in the painting itself. Clark continues: "We do not know who was [the model] but one thing is certain, the fortunate owner of that neat little body was not the owner of the head. They do not fit and Goya would never have made such an awkward relationship between the head and the body if they had been painted from the same model. About ten years later he did a clothed figure in the same pose . . . , much more freely painted, and I think a better picture." (Gudiol dates both paintings simply as "c. 1800.") Finally, on Mickey LaFaye and Wyeth's Christina, the critical situation is further complicated by the fact that when More walks into his office for the concluding session with Mickey (p. 370), she is lying facing the window, her back turned to him, and yet he begins immediately to observe in close detail the beauty of her face—*before* he asks her to get up and come

over where they can "see each other." In others of Wyeth's paintings of Christina, the face is partly visible, but in *Christina's World* it is totally hidden. That is, of course, in every sense a central source of the painting's unique and terrible power. (See Bibliography.) It should also be noted (p. 6) that Mickey herself is an amateur painter.

27. Atticus Finch and his daughter Scout are characters in Harper Lee's novel *To Kill a Mockingbird* (see Bibliography). Donna's notion of an incestuous relationship between the father and daughter is unquestionably one that most readers of this still very popular novel would find offensive. The book was considerably "controversial" at one time, at the level of disputes about reading lists for high school English classes, but not on the grounds that Donna's interpretation suggests.

28. In the chapter of *Auntie Mame* entitled "Auntie Mame and the Children's Hour," the narrator is taken to Ralph Devine's "progressive" school, where the little girls and boys use communal toilets, go about naked all day long, crawl in and out of a "big white structure that looked like a cow's pelvis" (while Ralph looks on encouragingly and whacks his lusty female assistant's broad bottom, chuckling " 'Back to the womb, eh Nat!' "), and play various fascinating, educational games like Laundry (washing Ralph's underwear) and, "one of the favorite[s] . . . of the smaller fry," something called Fish Families. In this exercise "Natalie [the assistant] and all the girls would crouch on the floor and pretend to lay fish eggs and then Ralph, followed by the boys, would skip among them, arms thrust sideways and fingers wiggling—'in a swimming motion, a swimming motion'—and fertilize the eggs. It always brought down the house." Little Patrick finds the whole experience not too disquieting. "I always felt a little like a picked chicken at Ralph's school, but it was pleasant. . . ." Fortunately or unfortunately, he does not stay there very long, only six weeks, before he is rescued by his irate trustee, Mr. Babcock, and the school is raided by the police the next day and closed down. The tabloid newspapers are the chief beneficiaries in the case, with lurid head-lines, "delicately retouched" photographs of Ralph and Natalie and their charges, and "articles by civic leaders and an outraged clergy." (*Auntie Mame*, by Patrick Dennis, a pseudonym of E. E. Tanner, pp. 34–38. See Bibliography.) Tom More's remark that children's enjoyment of sexual encounters with adults is "the part you don't read about" is, of course, not entirely accurate even with respect to the popular press. But it is true that many serious researchers and research-publicists in the field, for a variety of reasons both theoretical and practical, tend to discredit or de-emphasize the idea. It is, for example, obviously advisable from the point of view of concerned parents, educators, social workers, and legislators to

avoid saying anything that might encourage legal recognition of the adult perpetrator's commonplace plea that he/she was in fact purposefully "seduced" by a prepubescent child. For psychological researchers, from Freud's day to our own, a major and perhaps insurmountable difficulty is the lack of reliable clinical evidence concerning children's emotional attitudes in such encounters. In any event, whether most people have the opportunity to "read about it" or not, the notion that children may to some extent encourage adults' sexual advances is by no means alien to the public imagination. As David Finkelhor and Dennis Redfield report on the basis of a "vignette experiment" survey they conducted: "In spite of laws that presume the contrary, the public apparently does feel that children bear substantial responsibility in matters of sexual contact with older persons. . . . The judge from Wisconsin who put some of the blame on the 5-year-old girl for her own victimization was reflecting an attitude that has some general support." (David Finkelhor, *Child Sexual Abuse: New Theory and Research*, p. 119. See Bibliography.)

29. "Swift has sailed into his rest; / Savage indignation there / Cannot lacerate his breast" (W. B. Yeats, "Swift's Epitaph," lines 1–3). The phrase "savage indignation" is translated from the Latin inscription on Jonathan Swift's grave at St. Patrick's, Dublin: *Ubi saeva indignatio ulterius cor lacerare nequit.*

30. See *The Moviegoer*, the epigraph quotation from Kierkegaard: ". . . the specific character of despair is precisely this: it is unaware of being despair." An association of Van Dorn with despair is established fairly early in *The Thanatos Syndrome*, in the notes on Azazel which follow (p. 64) the account of the fishing trip and Van Dorn's explanation of the "Azazel convention" in bridge. Percy/More tells of how the fallen angel's name "was changed from Azazel to Eblis, which means despair." (I can find no external authority for this interpretation of the name of *Eblis*, the chief devil in Islamic mythology. Milton's depiction of Azazel as standard bearer for the rebel angels is in *Paradise Lost*, Book 1, line 531ff. See Bibliography.)

31. Percy told Marc Kirkeby (Lawson and Kramer, *Conversations*, p. 190; and see my remarks in note 7 for chapter 6, above) that the situation in *The Second Coming* "may be the first time [in his fiction] where the ending is not ambiguous. . . . the first time [he] saw the possibility of a clear resolution, a classic, novelistic resolution, a victory of eros over thanatos and life over death."

32. The fact that Tom drinks heavily before going to bed at Pantherburn the night Lucy tells him about Ellen and the "Herpes IV" may help to explain the name of the drug "Alanone," which I assume is a fictional

substance. (It is not listed in the 1987 *PDR*, and my friends in medicine and pharmacology cannot enlighten me.) To precisely what final purpose it is hard to say, but the name may involve a cryptic play on "Al-Anon," a family support-group program sponsored by Alcoholics Anonymous.

33. *Beyond the Pleasure Principle*, in the translated *Complete Psychological Works of Sigmund Freud*, edited by James Strachey et al., Vol. 18, p. 39. (See Bibliography.)

34. T. S. Eliot, *Little Gidding*, part 3, lines 18–19. (See Bibliography.)

Bibliography

Allen, William Rodney. *Walker Percy: A Southern Wayfarer*. Jackson: University Press of Mississippi, 1986.

Baker, Lewis. *The Percys of Mississippi*. Baton Rouge: Louisiana State University Press, 1983.

Booth, Wayne C. *The Rhetoric of Fiction*. Chicago: University of Chicago Press, 1961.

Brinkmeyer, Robert H., Jr. *Three Catholic Writers of the Modern South*. Jackson: University Press of Mississippi, 1985.

Brooks, Cleanth. *The Language of the American South*. Mercer University Lamar Memorial Lectures No. 28. Athens, Ga.: University of Georgia Press, 1985.

Broughton, Panthea Reid, ed. *The Art of Walker Percy: Strategems for Being*. Baton Rouge: Louisiana State University Press, 1979.

Carr, John, ed. *Kite-Flying and Other Irrational Acts: Conversations with Twelve Southern Writers*. Baton Rouge: Louisiana State University Press, 1972. (The version of Carr's January, 1970, interview with Percy printed in *Kite-Flying* differs in some significant details both from the version in *The Georgia Review* 25, Fall, 1971, and from that provided by Lawson and Kramer, see below.)

Chapman, A. H. *Harry Stack Sullivan: His Life and His Work*. New York: G. P. Putnam's Sons, 1976.

Chrzanowski, Gerard. *Interpersonal Approach to Psychoanalysis: Contemporary View of Harry Stack Sullivan*. New York: Gardner Press, 1977.

Ciuba, Gary M. "The Omega Factor: Apocalyptic Visions in Walker Percy's *Lancelot*." *American Literature* 57, no. 1 (March 1985): 98–112.

Clark, Kenneth. *The Romantic Rebellion: Romantic Versus Classic Art*. New York: Harper & Row, 1973.

Coles, Robert. *Walker Percy: An American Search*. Boston: Little, Brown and Company, 1978.

Corn, Wanda M. *The Art of Andrew Wyeth*. Boston: Published for the Fine Arts Museums of San Francisco by the New York Graphics Society, 1973.

Dennis, Patrick [E. E. Tanner]. *Auntie Mame: An Irreverent Escapade*. New York: Vanguard Press, 1955.

Douglas, Ellen. *Walker Percy's "The Last Gentleman": Introduction and Commentary*. Pamphlet. New York: Seabury Press, 1969.

Eliot, T. S. *The Complete Poems and Plays*. New York: Harcourt, Brace & World, 1952.

Finkelhor, David. *Child Sexual Abuse: New Theory and Research*. New York: Free Press, 1984.

Freud, Sigmund. *The Standard Edition of the Complete Psychological Works of Sigmund Freud*. Translated from the German under the general editorship of James Strachey, in collaboration with Anna Freud, assisted by Alix Strachey and Alan Tyson. London: The Hogarth Press and the Institute of Psycho-Analysis, 1961.

Frye, Northrop. *Anatomy of Criticism*. Princeton: Princeton University Press, 1957.

Gudiol, José. *Goya*. Text by José Gudiol. The Library of Great Painters. New York: Harry N. Abrams, 1965.

Hardy, John Edward. *Man in the Modern Novel*. Seattle and London: University of Washington Press, 1964.

Hathorn, Richmond Y. *Greek Mythology*. Beirut: The American University of Beirut, 1977; distributed in U.S. by Syracuse University Press.

Hawkins, Peter S. *The Language of Grace: Flannery O'Connor, Walker Percy, & Iris Murdoch*. Cambridge, Mass.: Cowley Publications, 1983.

Heat Moon, William Least [William Trogdon]. *Blue Highways: A Journey Into America*. Boston: Little, Brown and Company, 1982.

Hobson, Linda Whitney. "Man vs. Malaise, In the Eyes of Louisiana's Walker Percy." *Louisiana Life* 3, no. 3 (July/August 1983): 54–61.

Hopkins, Gerard Manley. *Poems*. Edited by W. H. Gardner. London: Oxford University Press, 1948.

Huntington, John. *The Logic of Fantasy: H. G. Wells and Science Fiction*. New York: Columbia University Press, 1982.

Iser, Wolfgang. *The Implied Reader*. Baltimore: Johns Hopkins University Press, 1974.

Jones, Ernest. *The Life and Work of Sigmund Freud.* New York: Basic Books, 1957.

Kennedy, Ludovic. *The Airman and the Carpenter.* New York: Viking, 1985.

Kramer, Victor A., Patricia A. Bailey, Carol G. Dana, and Carl H. Griffin. *Andrew Lytle, Walker Percy, Peter Taylor: A Reference Guide.* Boston: G. K. Hall & Co., 1983.

Knowler, Donald. *The Falconer of Central Park.* New York/Princeton: Karz-Cohl, 1984.

Lawson, Lewis A., and Victor A. Kramer, eds. *Conversations with Walker Percy.* Literary Conversations Series, Peggy Whitman Prenshaw, general editor. Jackson: University Press of Mississippi, 1985. The interviews reprinted in this volume are arranged in the chronological order of their first publication. In some instances, the date of first publication is considerably later than that of the actual interview. Only in the case of John Carr's interview with Percy, which I first read in *Kite-Flying* (see above), have I seen fit to refer to a variant text of a conversation included in the Lawson/Kramer collection.

Lee, Harper. *To Kill a Mockingbird.* Philadelphia and New York: J. B. Lippincott, 1960.

Lifton, Robert Jay. *The Nazi Doctors: Medical Killing and the Psychology of Genocide.* New York: Basic Books, 1986.

Luschei, Martin. *The Sovereign Wayfarer: Walker Percy's Diagnosis of the Malaise.* Baton Rouge: Louisiana State University Press, 1972.

Malory, Sir Thomas. *The Works of Sir Thomas Malory.* Edited by Eugene Vinaver. London: Oxford University Press, 1954.

Marcel, Gabriel. *The Mystery of Being.* Chicago: Henry Regnery Co., Gateway Edition, 1960.

Masson, Jeffry M. *The Assault on Truth: Freud's Suppression of the Seduction Theory.* New York: Farrar, Straus and Giroux, 1984.

Menninger, Karl. *Man Against Himself.* New York: Harcourt, Brace & World, 1938.

Miller, J. Hillis, ed. *Aspects of Narrative.* New York: Columbia University Press, 1971.

Milton, John. *Paradise Lost.* Edited by Merritt Y. Hughes. New York: Odyssey Press, 1935.

Percy, Walker. *Lancelot.* New York: Farrar, Straus and Giroux, 1977.

————. *The Last Gentleman.* New York: Farrar, Straus and Giroux, 1966. New York: Noonday Press edition, Farrar, Straus and Giroux, 1971.

————. *Lost in the Cosmos: The Last Self-Help Book.* New York: Farrar, Straus and Giroux, 1983.

————. *Love in the Ruins: The Adventures of a Bad Catholic at a Time Near the End of the World.* New York: Farrar, Straus and Giroux, 1971.

————. *The Message in the Bottle: How Queer Man Is, How Queer Language Is, and What One Has to Do with the Other.* New York: Farrar, Straus and Giroux, 1975.

————. *The Moviegoer.* New York: Alfred A. Knopf, 1961. New York: Noonday Press edition, Farrar, Straus and Giroux, 1967.

————. *The Second Coming.* New York: Farrar, Straus and Giroux, 1980.

————. *The Thanatos Syndrome.* New York: Farrar, Straus and Giroux, 1987.

Percy, William Alexander. *Lanterns on the Levee: Recollections of a Planter's Son.* New York: Alfred A. Knopf, 1966. (First published by Knopf in 1941.)

Perry, Helen Swick. *Psychiatrist of America: The Life of Harry Stack Sullivan.* Cambridge, Mass.: The Belknap Press of Harvard University Press, 1982.

Poteat, Patricia Lewis. *Walker Percy and the Old Modern Age: Reflections on Language, Argument, and the Telling of Stories.* Baton Rouge: Louisiana State University Press, 1985.

Prenshaw, Peggy Whitman, ed. *Eudora Welty: Critical Essays.* Jackson: University Press of Mississippi, 1979.

Sacks, Oliver. *The Man Who Mistook His Wife for a Hat.* N.Y.: Summit Books, 1985.

Spivey, Ted Ray. *The Writer as Shaman: The Pilgrimages of Conrad Aiken and Walker Percy.* Macon, Ga.: Mercer University Press, 1986.

Stein, Arnold. *Answerable Style: Essays on Paradise Lost.* Minneapolis: University of Minnesota Press, 1953.

Steinbrunner, Chris, et al., eds. *Detectionary: A Biographical Dictionary of Leading Characters in Detective and Mystery Fiction.* Lock Haven, Pa.: Published privately by Hammermill Paper Company, Lock Haven Division, 1972.

Taylor, L. Jerome. *In Search of Self: Life, Death, and Walker Percy.* Cambridge, Mass.: Cowley Publications, 1986.

Tennyson, Alfred, Lord. *The Idylls of the King.* Edited by Charles Tennyson. London and Glasgow: Collins, 1956.

Thale, Mary. "The Moviegoer in the 1950's." *Twentieth Century Litera-ture* 14 (1968): 84–89.

Tharpe, Jac. *Walker Percy.* Twayne's United States Authors Series, Warren French, general editor. Boston: Twayne, 1983.

———, ed. *Walker Percy: Art and Ethics.* Jackson: University Press of Mississippi, 1980.

Twain, Mark. *The Adventures of Huckleberry Finn.* New York: Bantam Books, 1965.

Warren, Robert Penn. *Selected Poems.* New York: Harcourt, Brace, 1944.

Wertham, Frederic. *A Sign for Cain: An Exploration of Human Violence.* New York: Macmillan, 1966.

Weston, Jessie L. *From Ritual to Romance.* Doubleday Anchor Books Edition. Garden City: Doubleday (by arrangement with Cambridge University Press), 1957.

Woolf, Virginia. *To the Lighthouse.* New York: Harcourt, Brace, 1927.

Yeats, William Butler. *The Collected Poems.* New York: Macmillan, 1956.

Index

Scaduto, Anthony, 296n.20
Scapegoat, 243–44, 294–95n.16,
 295n.17
Schadenfreude, 137
Schexnaydre, 277–78n.3
Schizophrenia, and rhyming, 289n.6
Science: and scientific method, limits of,
 9; and scientism, 119, 131; and super-
 stition, 62; and writing, 273n.18. *See
 also* Medicine
Second Coming, the, 125–26, 187,
 215–17, 219
Seduction, spiritual, 107
Self: and aging, 293n.4; appreciation
 and deprecation, 107; deception, 168;
 examination, 255; identification, 97;
 interest, "enlightened," 199;
 knowledge, 40, 75; loathing, 169;
 love, 61; preservation, 234; and
 psychoanalysis, 256–60; recognition,
 and guilt, 255–56; reliance, and
 charity, 197–99; and selflessness, 70;
 and soul, 255–57; surrender, 188–89
Semiotics, 14, 16
Sentimentality, 39, 260, 292n.31
Sequel: *The Second Coming* as, 187–91,
 193, 196, 199–205, 217, 219, 223;
 The Thanatos Syndrome as, 225–30,
 232, 234–42, 245, 248, 253–54,
 258, 265–67, 296n.20
Sermon, in fiction, 245
Sewanee, 4, 272n.9
Sex, 119–20, 134, 136; abuse, 145,
 166–67, 169; abuse of children, 238,
 249, 254–56; abuse of children, and
 the law, 261–62, 299–300n.28; abuse
 of children, public attitude toward,
 299–300n.28; abuse of children, in
 religious schools, 265; aging and, 226;
 Binx Bolling and, 30–31; death and
 violence and, 188; freedom and, 176;
 gentleman and, 73–74, 122, 174; the
 Grail legend and, 146–47; humor of,
 39, 188; incest and, 189; love and,

189; madness and horror of, 187;
 mental illness and, 189, 288–89n.4;
 money and, 152; morality and psychology of, 189; personal identity
 and, 238; positions in sexual intercourse and, 166–67, 174–76, 180,
 238–39; professional associations and,
 238; religion of, 76, 174; sexology
 and, 37, 112–13, 215; "sexual revolution" and, 187; Sutter Vaught and,
 92–93; Van Dorn and Ellen and, 243;
 virginity and, 69, 73–74
Shakespeare, William, 11, 37, 201–2
Shibboleth, 76
Signs: of destiny, 62–65; Allison as,
 290n.20; "Free & Ma B," 176–84;
 portents and, 139, 178–79, 216; sign,
 signal, and symbol, 14
Simon Peter, 249
Simeon Stylites, Saint, 248, 254,
 296n.21, 297n.24
Sin, 134–35, 147, 243–44; conception
 of, 253; modern theology and, 146;
 original, 147, 210; original, and
 labor, 218; social, 86
Skinner, B. F., 16, 117, 122, 138, 144
Sloth, moral, 265–66
Smith, Marcus, 22, 274n.21, 276n.40
Snob, 37; definition of, 278n.7
Social issues, and art of the novel,
 20–22, 218–19
Sodom, 156
South: "new South" and, 80–82;
 Southern novelist, Percy as, 22–23,
 277n.55; Southerners and story
 telling, 81; Southerners in New York,
 65–66; Southernism, affected, 241,
 294n.14
Space travel, 16–17
Speech: freedom of, 176; powers of,
 251, 260; quality of Allison's, 191,
 195, 289n.6; speaker and listener in,
 15
Spengler, Oswald, 47

A Note on the Author

John Edward Hardy is Professor of English and head of the department at the University of Illinois at Chicago. His books of literary criticism include *The Curious Frame, Man in the Modern Novel*, and *Katherine Anne Porter*. He was co-author and editor, with Cleanth Brooks, of *Poems of Mr. John Milton: The 1645 Edition with Essays in Analysis*; co-editor, with Seymour L. Gross, of *Images of the Negro in American Literature: A Critical Anthology*; and editor of *The Modern Talent: An Anthology of Short Stories*. In addition to numerous articles and reviews, Hardy has published a volume of verse, *Certain Poems*; his poems also have appeared in *Hopkins Review, Kenyon Review, Poetry*, and *Sewanee Review*.